A WORLD BANK COUNTRY STUDY

Chile's High Growth Economy

Poverty and Income Distribution, 1987–1998

The World Bank
Washington, D.C.

ISBN: 0-8213-5108-7
ISSN: 0253-2123

Library of Congress Cataloging-in-Publication Data

Chile's high growth economy : poverty and income distribution, 1987-1998.
    p. cm. — (A World Bank country study)
  Includes bibliographical references.
  ISBN 0-8213-5108-7
  1. Chile—Economic conditions—1988- 2. Chile—Economic policy. I. World Bank. II.
Series.

HC192. C5217 2002

330.983'065—dc21

2002024540

TABLE OF CONTENTS

ABSTRACT

This volume provides two recent analyses, spurred by the recent East Asian Crisis, of government responses to financial distress. It also presents a comprehensive database on systemic and borderline banking crises.

In the first chapter Stijn Claessens, Daniela Klingebiel, and Luc Laeven review the tradeoffs involved in public policies for systemic financial and corporate sector restructuring. The authors find that consistent policies are crucial for success, though such consistency is often missing. This consistency covers many dimensions and entails, among other things, ensuring that there are sufficient resources for absorbing losses and that private agents face appropriate incentives for restructuring. The authors also find that sustainable restructuring requires deep structural reforms, which typically require that political economy factors be addressed upfront.

In the second chapter Patrick Honohan and Daniela Klingebiel use cross-country evidence to determine whether specific crisis containment and resolution policies systematically influence the fiscal costs of resolving a crisis. The authors find that accommodating policies—such as blanket deposit guarantees, open-ended liquidity support, repeated (and so partial) recapitalizations debtor bailouts, and regulatory forbearance – significantly increase fiscal costs.

The third chapter, by Gerard Caprio and Daniela Klingebiel, is a comprehensive database on 113 systemic banking crises that have occurred in 93 countries since the late 1970s. The database (nonsystemic) banking crises in 44 countries during the same period.

ACKNOWLEDGMENTS

This report was prepared by a team led by Alberto Valdes and Norman Hicks (Task Manager), and consisting of Julie Litchfield (University of Sussex, U.K.), Osvaldo Larrañaga, Dante Contreras, Isabel Millan and David Bravo (all from Universidad de Chile, Santiago), and Rodrigo Castro-Fernandez, Carine Clert, Estanislao Gacitúa-Marió, and Quentin Wodon (all from the World Bank). The valuable comments of Aristides Torche, Marcelo Tokman and Paul Levy are gratefully acknowledged. A preliminary version of the report was discussed at a seminar in Santiago, Chile in June, 2000 as part of the Bank's work on preparing its report "Policy Notes", and the report incorporates some of the comments made at that seminar.

CURRENCY EQUIVALENTS

US$1.0 = 672.6 Chilean Pesos
(August 2001)

FISCAL YEAR
January 1 – December 31

ABBREVIATIONS AND ACRONYMS

ADI	Indigenous Development Areas
CASEN	*Caracterización Socioeconómica Nacional*
CENABAST	*Central de Abastecimientos*
CEPAL	UN Economic Commission for Latin America
CONADI	National Corporation for Indigenous Development
GDP	Gross Domestic Product
FGT	Foster-Greer-Thorbecke
FONASA	*Fondo Nacional de Salud*
JUNAEB	*Junta Nacional de Auxilio Escolar y Becas*
INTEGRA	*Fundación Nacional para el Desarrollo Integral del Menor*
JUNJI	*Junta Nacional de Jardines Infantiles*
MIDEPLAN	Ministry of Planning
MINEDUCT	Ministry of Education
MINSAL	Ministry of Health
MINVU	Ministry of Housing
PMJH	*Capacitación para Mujeres Jefas de Hogar*

EXECUTIVE SUMMARY

The Fall of Poverty

Chile remains one of the outstanding countries in Latin America in terms of its record in reducing poverty. A combination of strong growth and well directed social programs have combined to reduce the poverty rate in half during a period of just eleven years. This study shows that previously noted trends in falling poverty, in terms of incidence, depth and severity, continued into 1998. As a result, only 17% of the population now lives in poverty (compared to 40% in 1987), while those living in extreme poverty are barely 4% of the population.

This report focuses on updating the situation between 1994 (the previous Bank report) and 1998. The analysis shows that there was unambiguously less poverty between 1994 and 1998 than in all earlier years, whether poverty is measured by the headcount, the poverty deficit or by any of the most sensitive poverty indices. The reductions in poverty observed between 1994 and 1998 are observed at all levels of income including those in the very extreme tail of the distribution.

Income poverty is clearly related to a number of important factors. Some of these correlates relate to the demographic make-up of the family. In general, large families tend to be poorer, as do families headed by women. Households whose head or spouse of head has substantial education, will have less poverty. Completing secondary school brings a 70% gain in income, over a household whose head has no education at all. Primary education produces a 30 to 40 percent income gain. Returns to education at all levels are higher for people living in urban, as opposed to rural, areas. Employment patterns are also important. In urban areas, being unemployed reduces household per capita income on average by about 20%; in rural areas by as much as 70%. Lower income is also associated with self employment and unpaid family work.

Social Indicators and Access to Social Services

Poverty is a multi-dimensional concept, including both income and access to social services, as well as such intangibles as empowerment and social capital. As a compliment to the income poverty measures, social indicators can provide other direct measures of welfare for the poorest segments of society, focusing on such aspects as health, nutrition and educational status. The evidence shows that Chile has achieved considerable improvements in key social indicators such as infant mortality, life expectancy, coverage of primary and secondary education, and in housing during the past decade. Mean labor income and labor force participation has increased, particularly for women. However, the rate of unemployment has also increased reaching 10% in 1998 after having been at half that rate for several years, a situation that is associated with the economic slowdown related to the Asian crisis and events in Brazil and other countries.

Progress in poverty reduction can also be measured in terms of access to social services. Using monetary income only to measure poverty can give an incomplete assessment of the extent of the deprivation of the poor. This study presents a quantitative assessment of the "deficit" in education, health and housing status during the years 1990 and 1998, by comparing the access to these services with various thresholds based on widely accepted standards in each area.

In education, the percentage of households with two or more members experiencing educational deficit declined from 13% in 1990 to 8% in 1998. The analysis reports a significant reduction in the percentage of the population which dropped out from primary school (from 5% to 1.4%) and secondary school (from 15% to 10%). The percentage of students behind the expected level of grade attainment fell by significantly less (only three percentage points). Overall, the reduction in the educational deficit appears to be a direct result of the substantial increase in government spending during this period (an increase of 125% in real terms between 1990 and 1998).

In contrast, the reduction in housing deficits is considerably higher than that in education. The percentage of households that exhibit at least one dimension below standards declined from 43% in 1990 to 27% in 1998. Those with deficits in four or more dimensions declined from 10.5% to 4.4%. The largest gains occurred in access to electricity, where households without access represented less than 4% of the total in 1998. The lowest gains occurred in access to sanitation facilities. Overall, the incidence of the housing deficit declined by almost one half during this 8 year period.

Combining the three social sector deficit measures of poverty (education, health, and housing), with our income poverty measure, reveals that 51% of all households have neither a social sector deficit nor an income deficit. By contrast,. only 1.5% of all households have a deficit in all four dimensions. Thus, while there are few households demonstrating chronic or severe poverty in a multidimensional sense, about one-half of all households have some sort of social or income deficit.

Income Inequality:1987-98

Income inequality in Chile remains high by international standards. Income inequality appears to have substantially worsened between 1994 and 1998, with most of the deterioration happening during 1994-96. Within these four years there has been an increase in the dispersion within both the top and the bottom of the income distribution; while the bottom decile increased its real income by 15%, the real income of the top decile grew by 31%. However, the level of the Gini or other measures of income distribution in 1998 is broadly similar to that of 1987, so that the overall picture on inequality is one of a fairly stable distribution for the period as a whole. Furthermore, if one adjusts the income distribution statistics for the distributive impact of social spending, one sees an improvement in distribution during the period (see below).

 Chile continues to become more urbanized over time; the rural population fell as a share of the total from 20% in 1987 to just under 15% by 1998.. The study shows that both urban and rural areas experienced strong increases in mean incomes during the period 1987 to 1998, although incomes in urban areas rose proportionally slightly more, thus widening the income gap between urban and rural areas. Continued rural-urban migration should be a factor reducing income inequalities in the future.

Adjusting Income Inequality for Social Spending

Most analyses of income distribution do not take into account the impact of government social spending. To the extent that social programs are having a major influence in transferring resources from richer to poorer parts of the population, this can be an important misestimation, particularly when social programs are growing.

This study develops and applies a methodology for the estimate of the imputed income transfers from government subsidies in health, education, and housing, for the years 1990, 1994, 1996 and 1998. The analysis has confirmed that adjustments for in-kind income transfers substantially reduce the Gini coefficient on income inequality. For 1998, this coefficient falls from 0.56 (unadjusted) to 0.50 (adjusted) and the ratio of the highest (richest) to the lowest (poorest) quintile falls from 20 to 11.

These results suggest that social policies in Chile have had a significant impact in reducing income inequality, in spite of the fact that such policies are oriented towards poverty reduction rather than reduction in inequality per se. Moreover, the analysis concludes that the impact of social policies was more significant in 1998 than in 1990. This resulted primarily from the significant increases in the budget allocation to such programs between 1990 and 1998, rather than from better targeting or lower delivery costs. Expressed in 1998 pesos, the subsidy component of social programs increased from $4,486 per capita in 1990 to $10,225 per capita in 1998.

Of the various social programs considered, subsidies to education were the main contributors to the reduction in inequality (60% of the total transfer), followed by health (26%), monetary transfers (11%), and housing (6.5%). From a regional perspective, the analysis shows that social programs have had a more significant impact in Metropolitan Santiago and several other regions, but had no significant effect in reducing income inequality in regions VIII and XI.[1]

Chile's success in reducing income disparities through social spending is linked to its system for targeting social programs, the *ficha* CAS. This system for proxy means testing provides a cheap and relatively easy mechanism for determining eligibility, which is consistent across programs. It appears that targeted programs such as family allowances, pensions, water and housing subsidies and child care programs help reduce the overall Gini concentration of household incomes. Nevertheless, the coverage of these programs among the poor is far from universal, and substantial amounts go to non-poor households. Part of the problem appears to be that poor families are often unaware of their eligibility for certain programs, although the level of awareness vary between programs.

The Problem of Unemployment

Unemployment is a severe problem for younger and poorer workers. Overall, unemployment rates have generally averaged about 6-8% of the labor force, although in recent years there has been some acceleration in this rate. Unemployment among the poorest has been much higher. Men from the lowest quintile had an unemployment rate (in 1998) of 24%, and those aged 18-24 an unemployment rate of 28%, compared to a general unemployment rate of 7% overall for men. In general, women tend to have lower unemployment rates at all income quintiles.

What causes such high rates of unemployment for the young? One factor is the high costs imposed by the labor codes in terms of job security requirements. These seem to work against

---

[1] These two regions are both south of Santiago.

job creation for the young, unskilled and female workers. A key element in job security costs is the expensive system of mandated severance payments. While a new system of unemployment insurance supplemented by individual unemployment accounts has been introduced, there has been no change in the mandated severance payment system. Another factor is the relatively high minimum wage, which in recent years has been increased faster than the average wage, and also has more negative impacts for the younger and less skilled worker. However, the impact of minimum wages is not entirely clear, and there are other factors at play in the labor market: increased labor force participation by females over the decade has increased labor supply, and rigid nominal wages combined with low inflation has meant that labor market adjustments have occurred by employment, not wage, reductions.

Chile has an extensive system of job training. While job training programs have a spotty record in many countries, including those in the OECD, an evaluation of Chile's programs seems to show they are relatively effective in providing secure employment. The success of these programs seems to be derived from the close links they have with prospective employers. Nevertheless, these programs may not be reaching the poorest groups, who often lack information on their availability.

Indigenous People

Chileans of indigenous origin represent a special group of concern, because of their chronic high rates of poverty. Evidence shows that indigenous people are 56% more likely to be in poverty, and receive half the income of non-indigenous people, and have 2.2 years less schooling. Overtime, indigenous people have become increasingly urban, with 80% now living in urban areas. A number of Government programs have been put in place to assist indigenous people, and greater protection now exists for the land and water rights of the rural indigenous. However, tensions between indigenous groups and the Government continue. Part of the problem has been the weakness of indigenous organizations, and a lack of coordination between groups.

Recommendations

Chile has make remarkable progress in reducing poverty, both through macro policies which have produced a sustained rate of rapid growth, and well directed social programs. Few countries can match Chile's record of cutting its poverty rate in half over a period of 20 years. However, problems do remain. Unemployment is high, particularly among the young, and many of the poorest groups suffer from conditions of social exclusion. This report is intended to be largely an update of the poverty and income distribution situation in Chile, and related social issues, and was not designed to map out an anti-poverty strategy. However, a number of important points emerge that might be considered by the Government for further study and consideration. These include:

- Further labor code reforms that would reduce the very high costs of hiring new workers, particularly younger workers.
- Further reform of the unemployment insurance system, eliminating severance payments and putting more reliance on the newly established system that combines public insurance with private accounts.
- Reducing minimum wages, or at least modifying the rate of increase in minimum wages, so as not to discourage employment of younger and more inexperienced workers.

- More investment in basic infrastructure and housing in poor communities, particularly to address water and sanitation shortfalls.
- Improving the targeting of social programs so as to be more focused on the poor, and thus reducing benefits that go to the non-poor.
- More attention to evening the regional disparities in the allocation of social spending.
- More attention to the poverty problems of indigenous communities.

PART I: MAIN REPORT—AN OVERVIEW

INTRODUCTION

Chile is one of the earliest of countries in Latin America to undertake a structural reform program. Starting as early as 1974, the country introduced policy reforms that included trade liberalization, monetary and fiscal controls, realistic exchange rates, and privatization of banks and infrastructure. While the process started in the mid 1970s, economic growth became strong starting from the mid-1980s, particularly after the financial crisis of 1982-83.[2] Between 1985 and 2000, GDP growth has averaged about 6.6 percent per year. At the same time, Chile became known as a pioneer in social reform, including the implementation of targeted employment programs and reforms in education and health. This was especially the case after the return to democratic government in 1990. Indeed, Chile is now seen by other countries in the region as a model of successful reform.

The initial reform efforts in the 1970s and 1980s were associated with substantially higher unemployment, sluggish growth and many social and economic hardships. At the worst moments during the 1982-83 banking crisis, unemployment rose to over 20 percent. However, the longer term impact of the reforms has produced a major improvement of welfare at all levels, and a substantial decline in the numbers living in poverty. An analysis undertaken by the World Bank in 1997,[3] which examined the situation from 1987 to 1994, concluded that the high GDP growth rates had unambiguously contributed to a considerable reduction in poverty, in terms of incidence, depth and severity. The incidence of indigence fell from 13 percent in 1987 to 5 percent by 1994, and the headcount estimate showed that the population that lived in poverty fell from 40 percent in 1987 to 23 percent by 1994. This reduction in poverty during 1987-94 benefited almost all groups classified as vulnerable at the beginning of the period. Furthermore, the broad picture of income distribution that arises from the 1997 report was that of stable distribution during the period.

The present study has four main objectives: *First*, to present an update of the poverty and income distribution measures reported in the 1997 World Bank study for the period 1990-1998 using the same sampling methodology and survey questions as in the 1997 report; *Second*, to look at deficiencies in social services, and to see how well social services are targeted to the poor; *Third*, to consider how trends in income distribution would be modified if one took into account the transfer effect of social programs; and, *Fourth*, to look at some special issues that impact on poverty, namely unemployment and the problems of indigenous people. The major analytic background work for this report is contained in a series of background papers, found in Part II. This overview provides a general summary of their findings.

---

[2] The only exception was 1999 when GDP fell by 1.1 percent (source: Central Bank of Chile).

[3] "Chile: Poverty and Income Distribution in a High-Growth Economy: 1987-1985" (Report No. 16377-CH, 1997).

The Empirical Foundations of the Analysis

This update uses information comprising six household survey micro-data sets—the *Caracterizacion Socioeconomica Nacional* (CASEN) for the years 1987, 1992, 1994, 1994 and 1996 and 1998.[4] CASEN is a nationally and regionally representative household survey with a sample size of 48,588 households (in 1998). The original Bank study published in 1997 used the CASEN survey from 1987 to 1994. This update follows the same methodology of the earlier study.

The CASEN survey is carried out on a biannual basis by the Ministry of Planning, (MIDEPLAN) through the Department of Economics of the *Universidad de Chile* in Santiago. The sampling methodology can be described as multi-stage random sampling with geographical stratification and clustering. Once each survey is completed, the data are entrusted to CEPAL (UN Economic Commission for Latin America and the Caribbean) in Santiago to make adjustments for non-response, missing income values, and the under (or over) reporting of different income categories, with the National Accounts System being used as a reference.

Several additional adjustments, which differ from other poverty research based on the CASEN, were made to the Bank's 1997 report and these same adjustments have also been applied to the update. Some of these adjustments lead to higher poverty estimates while others to lower as compared to the results of other research. For example, the Bank's analysis relies on household income per equivalent adult (rather than simple per capita income) as the chosen income indicator, and reports the proportion of individuals (rather than households) below the poverty line. Also, differences in average price levels across regions of Chile as well as for live-in employees were adjusted. Unlike other research, no adjustment has been made to lower the poverty line in rural areas due to lower prices in these areas, since there is no rural consumer price index. (See Background Paper No. 1 for a detailed description of the database and methodology.)

---

[4] The resulting panel data set is unbalanced in the sense that one does not observe the same sample in each year, but each of the samples is representative for that year.

POVERTY TRENDS AND DETERMINANTS: 1987–98

The Evolution of Poverty

Three poverty lines are used in computing poverty measures, all of them expressed in 1998 Chilean pesos. These are the indigence line, a lower-bound poverty line, and an upper-bound poverty line.[5] The first two lines are widely used in Chile (see Appendix I, Background Paper No. 1). For each poverty line, three poverty measures are reported. The simplest and most common measure is the headcount index (the proportion of individuals with income below the poverty line). It does not indicate the depth of poverty of the poor, nor does it capture whether a person below the poverty line becomes relatively poorer. The second measure is the poverty deficit index (an aggregate of the income shortfalls of the poor relative to the poverty line, divided by the population size). This measure essentially reflects the depth of poverty. A family that it is barely below the poverty line adds only a little to the poverty gap index, but a family that is destitute adds a great deal. The third indicator is the Foster-Greer-Thorbecke (FGT) index, which provides a distribution-sensitive measure that gives a greater weight to larger shortfalls, and thus is more sensitive to extreme poverty.

Table 1: Poverty Measures: Household Incomes per Equivalent Adult

	1987	1990	1992	1994	1996	1998
Indigence Line:	P\$ 18,944					
Headcount	12.7	9.0	4.7	5.1	4.2	3.9
Poverty Deficit	4.1	3.1	1.7	2.0	1.5	1.5
FGT (2)	2.1	1.8	1.1	1.2	0.9	0.9
Poverty Line L:	P\$ 37,889					
Headcount	40.0	33.1	24.2	23.1	19.9	17.0
Poverty Deficit	15.7	12.0	7.8	7.6	6.5	5.7
FGT (2)	8.2	6.1	3.8	3.8	3.2	2.9
Poverty Line H:	P\$ 43,004					
Headcount	47.3	38.9	30.0	29.0	24.6	21.2
Poverty Deficit	19.1	14.8	10.1	9.8	8.4	7.3
FGT (2)	10.3	7.8	4.9	5.0	4.1	3.7

Note: Litchfield's own calculations from CASEN 1987-1998. Incomes are monthly incomes and are expressed in 1998 pesos. There were 460.3 Chilean pesos per US dollar in 1998.

Source: Background Paper No.1 by J. Litchfield in Part II.

What does this indicate for the period 1994-98? The study shows that the trends in falling poverty, in terms of incidence, depth and severity, continued through to 1998 (see Table 1). The proportion of people in poverty, as measured by the headcount poverty measure, continued to fall. The two other indices of poverty also decrease substantially, regardless of the poverty line used. In contrast to the fluctuating trends in inequality (discussed below), poverty has followed a downward trend for almost the entire period of 1987-98. Nevertheless, after 1994, poverty levels fell at slower rates than during the years of rapid growth (1987-92).

---

[5] The upper and lower poverty lines are P\$43,004 and P\$37,889 per month per adult equivalent. At an average exchange rate of P\$460.3 per US\$ in 1998, this is equivalent to \$93 and \$82 per adult equivalent per month in 1998 US \$, or about US\$3 per adult person per day.

Based on the standard poverty line used in Chile, the headcount measure shows that poverty fell from 23.1 percent in 1994 to 17.0 percent in 1998. Extreme poverty (indigence) fell from 5.1 percent in 1994 to 3.9 percent in 1998. The analysis shows that there was unambiguously less poverty between 1996 and 1998 than in all earlier years, whether poverty is measured by the headcount, the poverty deficit or by any of the most sensible poverty indices. This sort of unambiguous poverty reduction, across such a large range of different poverty measures, is not commonly observed in Latin America or other regions.

Table 2: Mean Incomes per Decile: Household Incomes per Equivalent Adult
(monthly income in 1998 Pesos)

Decile	1987	1990	1992	1994	1996	1998
1	11374	13098	17385	16954	18629	19450
2	20398	24225	29726	30369	32560	35474
3	26793	31432	38627	39735	43327	47502
4	33610	39552	47506	49426	54321	60021
5	41308	48543	57607	60798	66817	73831
6	51105	59261	70402	74919	82341	91301
7	64809	74742	88322	93805	104067	116281
8	86628	98129	116097	124842	138543	154115
9	132936	146468	169423	186436	206154	231405
10	377276	408647	507791	506125	587924	663359
Top 1%	1017577	1166108	1563013	1486160	1695712	1973692

Note: There were 460.3 Chilean pesos per US dollar in 1998.

Source: Background Paper No. 1 by J. Litchfield in Part II., based on Litchfield's own calculations from CASEN 1987-1998.

The observed reductions in poverty between 1994 and 1998 are also valid at the decile level (see Table 2). Mean incomes per decile (in terms of household income per equivalent adult) increased for all decile levels. For the lowest decile, the increase between these years was 15 percent in real terms. However, the increase for the upper deciles is far greater. The tenth decile had a real increase in the same period of 31 percent. In addition, although the headcount indicates a reduction in the number of poor people, the real income of the very poorest 2 to 3 percent of the population actually fell between 1996 and 1998.[6]

The significant decline in poverty during this period is a function of the rapid growth in per capita income. Between 1987 and 1998, real per capita income increased at an annual rate of 5.7 percent. As a result, the poverty rate fell by 58 percent (see Figure 1). The relationship between poverty reduction and growth seems clear from the graph. A regression of the poverty rate on per capita income and the Gini coefficient finds an elasticity between per capita income and the poverty rate of -1.26. By comparison, a recent study of poverty trends in the Latin America and Caribbean Region (Wodon, *et. al.*, 2000), found a regional elasticity of -.94. This suggests that the impact of growth on poverty has been slightly above average in Chile in recent years, but these estimates are based on only six poverty observations, and may not be robust.[7]

---

[6] However, this result is somewhat hard to interpret because these small changes occur in the very extreme tail of the distribution where income data are likely to be more unreliable.

[7] The estimated equation is: $\ln PR = 13.83 - 1.256 \ln YPC + .586 \ln GINI$ $R^2 = .987$, n = 6, df = 3
         t statistics: (15.272)   (.377)
where PR is the poverty rate, YPC is GNP per capita in 1995 prices, and GINI is the Gini coefficient, and ln indicates natural logarithms. Only the lnYPC variable is significant at 5%.

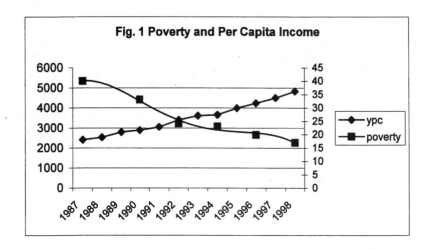

Fig. 1 Poverty and Per Capita Income

Determinants of Income and Poverty: Education, Demographics, and Employment[8]

An updated poverty profile has not been prepared, nor are there new estimates of regional poverty since the 1997 study, as the expectation is that there have not been dramatic changes in this short period. Nevertheless, this section takes a fresh look at some of the factors that determine income poverty, focusing on three key ones: household composition/demographics, education, and employment. The earlier 1997 report found that regional disparities were not very large, and there was some evidence of a convergence of per capita income across regions. It is also true, however, that between 1987 and 1994, the most dramatic reductions in poverty occurred in Greater Santiago. The earlier study had further indicated that poverty rates had been the highest among young workers with low education, female heads of households with low education, a large proportion of workers in the agricultural sector, non-labor force participants with low education, and elderly living in rural and urban areas with low education, and unemployed heads of households with low education. The highest concentration of poverty, nevertheless, was among young workers (even those with high education) and adults with low education working in the non-tradeable sector. This picture of the poor and vulnerable groups continues to ring true today in Chile and is consistent with the current preoccupations in the country on education and unemployment.

Table 3: Marginal Percentage Increase in per capita Income due to Demographic Variables

	Urban	Rural		Urban	Rural
Number of infants	-0.105	-0.143	Number of adult squared	0.005	0.009
Number of infants squared	-0.002	0.036	Female head	-0.108	-0.112
Number of children	-0.186	-0.204	Age of the head	0.005	0.034
Number of child squared	0.018	0.017	Age of the head squared	-0.001	-0.001
Number of adults	-0.047	-0.038	No spouse for the head	0.018	0.004

Note: The excluded reference categories are a household with a male head and a spouse.

Source: World Bank staff using: CASEN 1998 (see Background Paper No 6 by Castro-Fernandez and Wodon). Coefficients underlined are significant at the 10% level. Coefficients not underlined are significant at the 5% level.

---

[8] This section draws on R. Castro-Fernandez and Quentin Wodon, "Protecting the Unemployed in Chile: From State Assistance to Individual Insurance?", Background Paper No. 6, Part II.

Demographics. Estimates given in Table 3 show that per capita income decreases, and thereby poverty increases, with the number of infants and children in the household. For the first child, an infant lowers per capita income by about 11 percent in urban areas, and 14 percent in rural areas. For additional children, the figure is closer to 20 percent. These numbers reflect the fact that larger families are dividing a fixed income over more members in the household, resulting in lower per capita income.[9] Larger families seem to perpetuate poverty since, among other things, school attendance is negatively related to family size (Aldaz-Carroll and Moran, 2000). Per capita income tends to rise with a larger number of adults in the household, and with older adults. However, female headed households have a level of per capita income about 10 percent below that of male headed households.

Education. The gains from education are substantial. A household with a head having gone to the university (see Table 4) has almost twice the expected level of income of an otherwise similar household whose head has no education at all. Completing secondary schooling brings in an 70 percent gain versus no schooling. Completing primary school brings in a 30 to 40 percent gain. In all cases, the returns to education are higher in urban areas compared to rural areas. The returns to the education of a spouse, however, are somewhat lower. These lower figures may reflect, in part, the fact that at any given age, spouses are less likely to work.

Table 4: Marginal Percentage increase in Per Capita Income Due to Education

	Urban	Rural		Urban	Rural
Household head			Household spouse		
Primary partial	0.398	0.256	Primary partial	0.205	0.325
Primary total	0.365	0.302	Primary total	0.198	0.187
Secondary partial	0.701	0.513	Secondary partial	0.351	0.523
Secondary total	0.651	0.612	Secondary total	0.413	0.506
Superior (university)	0.901	0.814	Superior (university)	0.687	0.789

Note: The excluded reference categories are a household head and a spouse with no education at all.

Source: World Bank staff using CASEN 1998 (see Background Paper No.6). Coefficients underlined are significant at the 10% level. Coefficients not underlined are significant at the 5% level.

Employment. A key determinant of poverty is the quality of labor force participation. Employment patterns for the household head and the spouse also have a large impact on per capita income and therefore on poverty. Not surprisingly, having a household head or a spouse available for work or searching for employment has a large negative impact on per capita income in both urban and rural areas. In rural areas, the household suffers from a drop in income of 20 percent as compared to the case when the household head or the spouse is fully employed.[10] In rural areas, having an unemployed household head implies a 70 percent drop in per capita household income. While these results probably overstate the impact of unemployment on poverty as measured by consumption, since consumption levels tend to be more stable over time, it is clear that unemployment can lead to serious consequences. Moreover, households with a

---

[9] Per capita income calculations do not allow for the possibilities of scale economies in the household. Thus, a household with eight members would have half the per capita income of a household with four, assuming total household income were the same. However, even adjusting for scale economies would not change the basic conclusion that large families are associated with poverty (see Background Paper No. 6).

[10] While a figure of 20% may seem low, it must be remembered that average household income includes income from other household members, severance payments, transfers, etc.

head or spouse not working also tend to have lower levels of income (for details, see Background Paper No. 6). Household heads who are self-employed or unpaid family workers have lower incomes (compared to salaried household heads). However, those working in the public sector have incomes that are substantially higher compared to the private sector (see Table 5).[11]

Table 5: Marginal Percentage Increase in Per Capita Income Due to Employment Variables of Household Head
(increment in income compared to employed HH head, working as a wage earner in the private sector)

	Urban	Rural
Employment Status of head		
Available (unemployed)	-0.198	-0.029
Searching (unemployed)	-0.225	-0.725
Not working	0.058	-0.517
Type of employment of head		
Self-employed	-0.105	-0.540
Employer	0.515	-0.054
Unpaid family work	-0.403	-0.274
Public sector	1.105	2.154
Size of firm > 10 people	0.104	0.054
Underemployment of head		
Hours of work per week < 20	0.125	0.154
20≤ hours per week ≤39	-0.155	-0.256

Source: World Bank staff using CASEN 1998 (see Background Paper No. 6) All coefficients are significant at 5% level.

Key Social Indicators

Poverty is a multi-dimensional concept, including both income and access to social services, as well as such intangibles as empowerment and social capital. As a complement to income poverty measures, there are a variety of social indicators, some of which are shown in Table 6, which provide other measures of welfare. A more detailed analysis of social indicators for Chile is available in publications by MIDEPLAN, and a comprehensive analysis is found in UNDP's Human Development Report.

This sample of social indicators for Chile shows that it has achieved considerable improvements in key areas such as infant mortality, life expectancy, coverage of primary and secondary education, and housing. Labor income and labor force participation have increased, particularly for women. However, the rate of unemployment has also increased, reaching 10 percent in 1998 after having been at half that rate for several years, a situation that is attributed to the economic slowdown related to the Asian crisis and events in Brazil and other countries. By mid-2000, this relatively high unemployment rate persists at about 10 percent, and has led to a major concern around current labor reform proposals and other measures to encourage employment, especially of youths and other vulnerable groups.

---

[11] The reason for this is not clear, but may be related to the fact that the public sector includes public sector financial institutions.

Table 6: Key Social Indicators

	1990	1998
Population (millions)	12.85	14.56
Education		
Primary education coverage (%)	96.8	98.3
Secondary education coverage (%)	80.5	86.9
Illiteracy (%, older than 15)	3.7	4.6
Housing		
% of dwellings without deficit (building materials, crowding or infrastructure)	57.2	72.7
Health		
Results indicators:		
Life Expectancy, total (yrs.)	73.7	75.4
Life Expectancy, female (yrs.)	76.8	78.4
Infant mortality rate (per '000)	16.0	10.3
Under 5 mortality (per '000)	20.0	12.5
Input Indicators:		
Physicians (per '000)	11.0	9.5
Hospital Beds (per '000)	3.2	2.7*
Health Expenditures per capita (1998 $)	182	289
Labor Market Statistics		
Unemployment rate (%)	8.4	10.0
Participation in labor force: men (%)	73.6	74.6
Participation in labor force: women (%)	31.3	38.1
Average years schooling for workers (yrs.)	9.8	10.5
Employment index	100.0	115.5
Mean labor income index	100.0	155.0
% wage earners in labor force	75.8	77.7

* refers to 1996.

Source: Calculations based on 1990 and 1998 Casen survey. Health statistics
from World Bank WDI data base. The unemployment rate from CASEN is
slightly higher than the official INE figures of 7.8% in 1990 and 9.8% in 1998.

Deficits in Social Services[12]

An important dimension of Chile's social progress can be measured by the expanded access of the poor to social services, reflecting the large investment having been made since 1990 to rectify inequities. Presently, Now, as described below, middle and low income families have access to a broad spectrum of social services at costs considerably below their market prices as judged by similar services provided by the private sector. This begs the question of the comparable quality of services between the public and private sector, but attests to the wide spread availability. This is important from two perspectives: *First,* due to the omission of these publicly provided social services, the typical measure of income in Chile underestimates the real

---

[12] The analysis in this section focuses on education, housing and health because these areas are covered by the CASEN surveys. Other factors which could also be important in determining the quality of life, such as violence and security, are not covered in this discussion, but are nevertheless quite important.

income of the poor; and, *second,* to the extent that the poor in Chile do not receive such services or if standards are not being met, then a social "deficit" can be considered to exist. Filling these deficits in access and standards can therefore be seen as a core element of Chile's social policy agenda.

A look at social sector progress in recent years, using appropriate standards, reveals the following[13]:

Educational Achievements

- Based on 1998 data, 16.5 percent of the 8 to 24 year old population had dropped out from school before receiving 12 years of education. Although the difference between the poor and the non-poor is significant, the gap is much lower than the difference in incomes.
- Demand rather than supply factors dominate school non-attendance. Reasons include looking for a job (42%), helping with household activities (13%), pregnancy or already having a child (9.5%) and others.
- 19.5 percent of the student population (primary and secondary) is behind the norm (relative to expected grade by age). The corresponding value for the very poor was 30 percent, compared to 24.4 percent for the poor and 16.9 percent for the non-poor.
- An analysis of education deficits at the household level--defined as household members who are illiterate, members aged 8-23 who have not completed primary education and are not attending school, or are two years behind normal school level-- shows that 49 percent of the very poor households have one or more deficits, compared to only 24 percent of the non-poor households (see Table 7).

Table 7: Educational Deficit at the Household Level
(% of households)

% of households	Very poor	Poor	Non-poor	Total
Without deficit	51.5	54.7	76.4	73.1
With deficit	48.5	45.3	23.6	26.9
Total	100.0	100.0	100.0	100.0

Source: Background Paper No. 3 O. Larrañaga . Calculations based on 1998 Casen survey. See background paper for definitions of deficits.

Housing

- Approximately 70 percent of houses are owned by the families who live in them; 16.5 percent of households rent their dwellings; the remainder of dwellings being lent by relatives and/or provided by the employer.
- 77.7 percent of owners have fully paid for their property.
- 34.5 percent of the current owners had access to a public subsidy for the purchase of the property.
- An analysis of housing deficits based on minimum standards of the quality of the housing[14] reveals that 72.7 percent of households have no deficit in housing, and 11.9 percent have only one deficit (see Table 8).

---

[13] Based on O. Larrañaga, "Incorporating Social Services in the Measurement of Poverty", Background Paper No.3 , Vol II. Please note that the standards being used in this section range from widely accepted definitions such as those to measure the quality of housing, to less commonly used and evolving definitions such as those used for health. Developing such service standards to measure social deficits is an area for further discussion and research.

- Additional details, nevertheless, show that the housing deficit is considerably more pronounced in rural areas than in urban areas. Only 20 percent of families in the rural areas have no deficit, as compared to over 80 percent in the urban areas, and 19 percent of rural families have four or more deficiencies, as compared to 2.4 percent of urban families.

- Among the poor, moreover, 57 percent live in housing with one or more deficits, and 36 percent in housing with two or more deficits. There is a substantial gap between the poor and non-poor in terms of sewerage—with more than 38 percent of the poor having no access, as compared to only 12 percent for the non-poor--and in terms of piped water--20 percent of the poor are without such service as compared to 5 percent for the non-poor.

Table 8: Housing deficits
(% households)

No.	Very poor	Poor	Non-poor	Total
0	37.7	42.9	78.7	72.7
1	17.7	21.0	10.3	11.9
2	14.2	13.3	5.2	6.5
3	14.7	11.2	3.4	4.8
4	8.2	6.2	1.4	2.2
5	4.5	3.2	0.6	1.1
6	2.2	1.4	0.4	0.6
7	0.7	0.5	0.0	0.1
Total	100.0	100.0	100.0	100.0

Source: Calculations based on 1998 Casen survey.

- Housing acquired with public subsidies is slightly more likely to meet standards in terms of materials, infrastructure and occupancy but the fact that 22 percent of families having received subsidies still have some housing deficit indicates that housing quality is not fully addressed by the subsidy program. Moreover, one would expect that difference in the occurrence of deficits for those not receiving public subsidies would be significantly higher than it is, showing that housing policy may not be adequately addressing housing deficits. This is most likely to be the case with respect to the lack of sewerage connections.

Table 9: The Proportion of the Population Affiliated to a Health Insurance System, Chile 1998

	very poor	poor	non poor	Total
Public Non-Contributory	67.9	44.6	17.3	24.5
Public Contributory	19.6	39.8	38.0	37.2
Private	2.6	5.3	28.3	23.1
Other	0.5	0.9	4.0	3.3
Not Affiliated	9.2	8.8	11.5	10.9
Unknown	0.3	0.7	1.0	0.9
Total	100.00	100.00	100.00	100.00

Note: Calculations based on 1998 Casen survey.

Source: Background Paper No. 3

Health Care

- About 90 percent of the population is covered by either a public (61.7%) or a private (28.3%) health system affiliation. The rest is either not affiliated or "does not know" (see Table 9).

- Approximately 40 percent of those affiliated to the public health system do not pay any contribution.

---

[14] Housing deficits consist of below standard floors, ceiling or walls, overcrowding, and lack of access to electricity, drinking water and sanitation facilities. See Background Paper No. 3, Table 10, for a complete definition.

- About 17 percent of the population report not having attended a medical facility when in need which, in part, may be explained by self treatment and use of alternative medicines. Considering that everybody has access to the Chilean public health facilities, which acts as a provider of last resort, supply constraints are unlikely to represent a reason why Chileans did not get medical attention when needed.

- Other factors such as timeliness can be important: about 15 percent of the population reports not getting timely access to health care.

- Dental attention shows clear deficiencies. Thirty eight percent of the population who required some kind of treatment did not have access. This is explained by the fact that dental treatment is not usually covered by either public or private health insurance.

- Regarding health prevention, the frequency of health checkups, Pap smears for older women, and smoking show very little difference between the poor and non-poor (see Background Paper No. 3).

- Overall, some 19 percent of families are evaluated as having some health deficit. Looking at access to medical services, timeliness of those services, and dental services, there are significant differences by poor and non-poor: the richest population is twice as likely to receive attention when in need as compared to the poorest population.

Trends in Social Sector Deficits between 1990 and 1998

Education. Throughout the 1990s, Chile's educational system has seen rapid changes, especially in terms of enrollment of 4 and 5 year olds, reduction in repetition rates and average years to graduate from primary school, and elimination of incomplete rural schools. This has been accompanied by improvements in cognitive achievements, more pronounced among students in municipal schools as compared to those private schools, even though attainment differences between the two systems remain large.[15] Nevertheless, there is widespread concern that attainment levels are not yet where they should be: this is particularly true for the 'stock" of human capital which by a recent international test was far below expectations. While it would be most desirable to measure the educational deficit in terms of differences in educational attainment internationally and by income levels, available statistics cannot provide this.

Looking at the available indicators, there are signs of improvement. The percentage of households with at least one deficit in education declined from 30.6 percent to 26.9 percent during the 1990-98 period. In terms of severity of the deficit, the gains are even larger. Households with two or more members experiencing educational deficit declined from 12.8 percent in 1990 to 7.8 percent in 1998. The analysis reports a significant reduction in the percentage of the population who have dropped out from primary school (from 5.1% to 1.4%), and those who dropped out from secondary school (4 or more years before graduation) fell from 15.1 percent to 9.9 percent. The percentage of students behind the expected level of grade attainment fell less (only three percentages points). Despite these improvements, more might have been anticipated in reducing the educational deficit given the substantial increases in government spending on education during the period.

---

[15] See the Implementation Completion Report for the Primary Education Improvement Project (Loan 3410-CH), report number 19184-CL, dated May 17, 1999.

Housing. Gains in reducing the housing deficit are considerable. The percentage of house-holds that had one or more dimension below standard declined from 42.8 percent in 1990 to 27.3 percent in 1998 (see Table 10). Those with deficits in four or more dimensions declined from 10.5 percent to 4.4 percent. The largest gains occurred in access to electricity, where households without access represented no more than 3.8 percent in 1998. The lowest gains occurred in access to sewerage. Overall, the incidence of the housing deficit declined by almost one half during the eight years.

Table 10: Comparison of the Housing Deficit Index (Households) between 1990-98

	1990	1998
No deficit	57.2	72.7
One	14.7	11.9
Two	9.5	6.5
Three	8.1	4.8
Four or more	10.5	4.9
Total	100.0	100.0

Source: Background Paper No.3 by Larrañaga
Notes: Calculations based on 1998 Casen survey.

Health. The findings for health services are less conclusive, in terms of changes over time. This is largely due to the inadequate information provided in the CASEN survey regarding access and quality of health care services and inadequate definition of the most appropriate way to measure deficiencies in health services. What data are available are not conclusive: they show a decline in the need of medical and dental services, a decline in receiving medical attention when in need, and no change in receiving dental services when in need between 1990 and 1998. Time series on the timeliness of medical services are not available. However, this analysis is limited by the questions in the CASEN survey. Aggregate data (Table 6) show that infant and child mortality have declined between 1990 and 1998. Life expectancy, at 75 years overall, is only two years below the level the United States. Health expenditures per person have risen 59% in real terms. However, doctors per 1,000 people and hospital beds per 1,000 have both decreased.

When looking at the intersection of the social deficit encountered by Chileans in all four dimensions --income, education, housing and health care-- it turns out that about half the families—48.9 percent of households—exhibit at least one form of social deficit, the most common deficits being housing or education. However, only 1.5 percent of households show deficits in all four dimensions. These numbers suggest a rather heterogeneous profile of households and a very small population which faces multiple challenges in improving their well-being. Thus, on the positive side, it can be said that poverty is no longer an overwhelming condition in Chile. On the negative side, over half of households demonstrate some deprivation according to these four indicators, the most frequent of which continue to be education and housing.

TRENDS IN INEQUALITY AND THE IMPACT OF SOCIAL EXPENDITURES

Reducing Income Inequality

Income distribution in Chile has been relatively stable. If the relative gains (and losses) over the period (see Table 11) are examined, the overall impression is one of little movement for the period as a whole, with changes being relatively small. Yet, there has been a significant rise in inequality since 1994: the Gini coefficient fell slightly between 1987 and 1994 but rose thereafter and again reached the 1987 level by 1998 (from 0.5468 in 1987 to 0.5298 in 1994 and back to 0.5465 in 1998). Between 1994 and 1998, the four measures of inequality showed that there was lower inequality in 1994 than in 1998, with most of the change occurring between 1994 and 1996. Between 1996 and 1998, the differences between coefficients were extremely small.

Table 11: Income Shares per Decile - Household Incomes per Equivalent Adult

Decile	1987	1990	1992	1994	1996	1998
1	1.34	1.39	1.52	1.43	1.40	1.30
2	2.41	2.57	2.6	2.57	2.44	2.37
3	3.17	3.33	3.38	3.36	3.25	3.18
4	3.97	4.19	4.16	4.18	4.07	4.02
5	4.88	5.14	5.04	5.14	5.01	4.95
6	6.04	6.28	6.16	6.33	6.17	6.12
7	7.66	7.92	7.73	7.93	7.80	7.79
8	10.24	10.39	10.16	10.55	10.38	10.32
9	15.71	15.51	14.82	15.76	15.45	15.50
10	44.58	43.28	44.43	42.73	44.05	44.43
Top 1%	12.02	12.35	13.68	12.41	12.70	13.22
Mean	84,628	94,414	114,290	118,298	133,476	149,289
Median	45,648	53,440	63,204	66,960	74,043	81,809
Gini	0.5468	0.5322	0.5362	0.5298	0.5409	0.5465
$E(0)$	0.5266	0.4945	0.4891	0.4846	0.5139	0.5265
$E(1)$	0.6053	0.5842	0.6151	0.5858	0.6058	0.6264
$E(2)$	1.3007	1.3992	1.505	1.5634	1.4123	1.6172

Source: Background Paper No. 1 by J. Litchfield, CASEN 1987-1998. Note: $E(0)$ equals the log deviation, $E(1)$ is the Thiel index, and $E(2)$ equals half of the squared coefficient of variation.

Changes between years and between the beginning and the end years are not statistically significant, with the exception of the increase in inequality observed between 1994 and 1998. Between these two years, there has been an increase in dispersion within both the top and the bottom of the income distribution (e.g. rise in both $E(0)$ and $E(2)$ measures) (see Table 11). It is too early to determine whether this is a temporary diversion from a previously stable path or whether this is the beginning of an upward trend.[16] Furthermore, the worsening of income distribution was offset by expanded social sector spending (see below), and it occurred in the context of rising living standards and falling poverty up to 1998, the latest year for which statistics are available.

---

[16] Ferreira and Litchfield(1999) note that inequality in Chile appears to have worsened during the 1960s, improved during the early 1970s, and then worsened again from the mid-seventies to the mid-eighties. However, the overall trend is one of gradual worsening over the whole period. See also Londoño and Székely (1997).

The poverty and inequality analysis was also extended to allow for a comparison between rural and urban areas. The total rural population represented approximately 20 percent in 1987 but fell to just under 15 percent by 1998. An examination of rural and urban differences indicates that both urban and rural populations experienced strong increases in mean incomes during the period 1987 to 1998, although incomes in urban areas rose proportionally by slightly more than in rural areas. This faster rate of growth in urban areas led to a very slight widening of the income gap between urban and rural areas.

Chile's stability in income distribution is no cause for complacency, even though globally many countries are experiencing a deterioration of income equality. Chile remains a country with relative poor performance on income distribution when compared to other countries in the region and elsewhere. According to the data shown in Table 12, only Brazil, Colombia and Honduras in the region have worse income distribution, although it should be noted that many of these comparator countries report statistics for urban populations only. Furthermore, the Latin America region itself is one of the worst in terms of income distribution, when compared to other regions, such as Asia. Clearly OECD countries are ahead in terms of income distribution and serve as a model for Chile to emulate.

Table 12: Gini Coefficients for Various Countries 1998

Country	Gini
Latin America:	
Brazil	.61
Colombia*	.58
Honduras	.57
Chile	**.56**
México	.56
Ecuador*	.53
Argentina**	.53
Paraguay*	.51
Venezuela	.49
Dom. Republic	.50
Bolivia*	.49
Uruguay*	.45
Other Countries:	
France(1995)	.33
Russian Fed.	.49
Japan (1993)	.25
United States(1997)	.41

* urban only **only Buenos Aires
Source: For LAC: household surveys from World Bank data bank, based on per capita income, which differs slightly from the results on the basis of adult equivalence used elsewhere in this report. For Other Countries from World Development Report 2000/2001, Table 5 (World Bank, Washington DC).

Impact of Social Expenditures on Income Distribution, 1990-98

The income data used to measure income poverty so far in this study were defined to include all primary incomes, cash transfers from government programs (family allowance, pensions, family subsidies, and unemployment insurance) as well as imputed rents, gifts and remittances. These income data did not include, however, the value of in-kind transfers made to households by the government through programs in education, health, and housing. By excluding the value of these in-kind services, the data underestimate total income. This is especially important in Chile since many of these programs are intended for the poor and reduce the constraints on household budgets, freeing income for the consumption of other goods and services. Hence, the omission of such in-kind transfers overstates the level of both poverty and income inequality in Chile.

The issue of what is the implicit income transfer equivalence of social programs has drawn the attention of Chilean economists. The key questions addressed in previous research are: (i) what has been the impact of social programs in alleviating poverty; (ii) how well targeted are social programs; and (iii) what has been the impact of such programs in reducing income inequality, as measured for example by the Gini coefficient? Studies by MIDEPLAN (1996), de Gregorio and Cowan (1996), Scholnick (1996), Beyer (1997), and Contreras, Bravo and Millan (2000) presented preliminary estimates of imputed income transfers for some social programs based on a specific year of the CASEN survey. These studies reported comparisons of the income situation of the higher and lower quintiles with and without adjustments for the in-kind transfers.

These studies were extremely useful in: (a) indicating that this particular adjustment could result in substantially lower Gini coefficients; and (b) raising a number of conceptual and measurement issues. However, they have been limited to the analysis of the income distribution by quintiles (and not at the percentile level) and in most cases for only one year, thus, not providing an overview on the evolution of the indicators (with/without adjustments) required to test the impact of such policies through time. Furthermore, these previous studies did not present the impact of social programs by region.

This report develops and applies a methodology for estimating the imputed income transfers from government subsidies in health, education, and housing based on the information collected by the CASEN survey for the years 1990, 1994, 1996 and 1998.[17] Because of lack of data it was not possible to extend the analysis back to 1987. In contrast to the previous studies, the imputed values in this study are assigned to each individual household based on the services actually received by the members of that household.

Measuring the implicit income transfer from social programs raises several complex conceptual and empirical issues. For instance, should a one-to-one relationship between monetary cost of the service and the implicit income transfer be assumed? Or do the recipients of such transfers value them less than their monetary cost to the government? Are there substantial leakages in social expenditures towards the non-poor groups and/or are there high delivery costs so that the actual transfer received by poor households is less than the cost of the programs? This study tests the effect of applying alternative assumed values of the programs to households.

Which subsidies were included? The individual's own monetary income was adjusted for the imputed value (income transfer) of the following government programs: monetary transfers, imputed rental value of his owned house, implicit transfer (net of co-payments) for health, education, and housing. The same criteria for the valuation of these transfers was applied through the period. The health, education and housing programs include many different types of benefits. To estimate the imputed values, a detailed analysis of the various sub-components of each program was undertaken and developed into valuation criteria. The corresponding monthly benefit received by each member of the household was then calculated according to the frequency and type of service used. For example, 17 health categories were identified, such as surgery, dental services, laboratory tests, preventive check-ups, X-rays, emergency services, and other hospital expenses net of the above. For each of these categories, average monthly values were estimated. In education, more than 25 sub-components were identified with their corresponding valuation criteria. For housing, six sub-components were defined and valued.

---

[17] D. Bravo, D. Contreras, and Isabel Millán, "The Distributional Impact of Social Expenditure: Chile 1990-98" Background Paper No. 2.

The valuation criteria, discussed in detail in Background Paper No.2, are based on the assumption that the benefit from any program equals its cost of production, and that the quality of services does not vary by income group.[18] In education, the basic funding sources considered were the school meals program, pre-school programs under JUNJI and INTEGRA, contributions from MINEDUC, the budget transfers to municipal and private subsidized schools in primary, secondary and especial education, government budget allocations for school books and equipment, special teacher post-graduate training programs, JUNAEB, scholarships, and some others. In health, the public health insurance program, the 2 percent contribution to ISAPRES, maternity leave, the PNAC program, and others, net of co-payments, were included.

Table 13: Income Distribution Indicators Adjusted for Cash and In-Kind Transfers, Chile 1998

Indicator	A Monetary Income	B A + Health	C A + Education	D A + Cash Transfers	E A + Housing	F A + Fiscal Credit	G Total
income shares:							
Q1	3.06	3.76	4.18	3.36	3.13	3.06	5.16
Q2	6.68	7.14	7.55	6.88	6.75	6.69	8.20
Q3	10.81	10.99	11.31	10.89	10.87	10.81	11.60
Q4	18.31	18.12	18.24	18.25	18.35	18.36	18.02
Q5	61.14	59.99	58.71	60.62	60.90	61.08	57.02
Q5/Q1	20	16	14	18	19.5	20	11.1
distribution coefficients:							
Atkinson Coefficient	0.689	0.570	0.551	0.631	0.664	0.689	0.451
Theil	0.655	0.621	0.586	0.639	0.649	0.654	0.540
Log(P90/P10)	2.55	2.34	2.21	2.46	2.52	2.55	1.99
Log Variance	1.104	0.898	0.823	1.001	1.032	1.106	0.663
Gini	0.5644	0.5460	0.5259	0.5563	0.5616	0.5641	0.5028

Source: Background Paper No. 2 by Contreras et. al. Column A shows the distribution of monetary income, without cash transfers from the government. Columns B to F show the impact of a specific type of transfer; column G shows the total effect of all transfers together. Note that this table uses a Gini based on income per capita, without adjusting for adult equivalents.

What Has Been Confirmed? The analysis, presented in Table 13, has confirmed that adjustments for cash and in-kind transfers from the public sector substantially reduce income inequality, regardless of which measure is used. To interpret the table, the columns B to F represent the contribution of each of the public social programs, in succession, combined with the original own measure of per capita household income, presented in Column A. The results in Column G represent the aggregate contribution of own monetary income plus the combined impact on equivalent income of all the programs.

For 1998, the Gini coefficient falls from 0.56 when only own monetary income is considered to measure income distribution to 0.50 when the value of cash and in-kind transfers from social programs is included. The ratio of the highest to the lowest income quintile falls from 20 to 11. A substantial reduction in inequality is also observed when applying alternative poverty measures, namely the Theil Index, a transformation of the coefficient of variation, and the mean log variation coefficient. This reduction in inequality is robust to reducing the imputed value of the program benefits received by households by 30 percent.

---

[18] It could be argued that the true benefits are actually greater or lesser than the costs of production, depending on how recipients value the service. It is possible that the quality of services received by lower income groups is below average. The authors of Background Paper No. 2 show that even if benefits were reduced to 30% of their costs, there still would be a statistically significant change in the Gini.

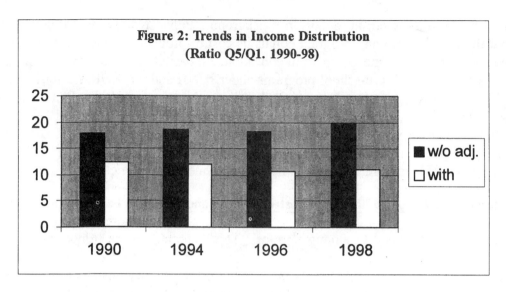

Source: Backround Paper No. 2 by Contreras et.al.

These results suggests that social policies and programs in Chile have had a significant impact in reducing income inequality, in spite of the fact such policies are intended to be oriented towards poverty reduction rather than reduction of inequality *per se*. Moreover, the analysis concludes that the impact of social programs was more significant in 1998 and 1990. This resulted primarily from the significant increase in the budget allocation to such programs between 1990 and 1998 rather than from better targeting or lower delivery costs. Moreover, the overall trend in the adjusted income distribution shows a slight improvement over the period, the reverse of the conclusion that would be had with the unadjusted series (Fig 2).[19] Thus, expanded social programs have effectively *improved* income distribution, and reversed the tendency for income distribution to deteriorate.

Table 14: Average Value in 1998 Pesos of Social Programs by Quintile
(P$000's/month)

Indicator	Monetary Income	Cash Transfers	Health	Education	Housing	Total Social Transfers
Q1	19.0	2.3	4.9	9.2	0.6	17.0
Q2	41.5	1.5	3.8	7.5	0.6	13.4
Q3	67.2	1.0	2.5	6.3	0.8	10.6
Q4	113.9	0.6	0.7	4.9	0.8	6.9
Q5	380.1	0.2	-0.3	2.8	0.6	3.3
Average	124.3	1.1	2.3	6.1	0.6	10.2
Dist.(%)		11.1	25.5	59.9	6.5	100.0

Source: Background Paper No. 2 by Contreras et. al.

Of the various social programs considered, Table 14 shows that subsidies to education were the main contributors to the reduction in inequality (59.9% of the total transfers), followed by health (25.5%), monetary transfers (11.1%) and housing (6.5%). Relative to various income classes, social sector subsidies are almost equal to the total of monetary income of the lowest quintile. The value of education services received alone equals 48 percent of monetary income. For the richest quintile, however, social subsidies barely constitute 1 percent of total income. Thus, for

---

[19] Table 1a measures income distribution by the ratio of incomes in the fifth quintile and the first (Q5/Q1).

the poorest, social programs make a material difference in their welfare, almost as much as earned income.

In terms of the impact of social programs on the reduction of inequality at the regional level, the picture that emerges suggests that the results are sensitive to the particular year, varying in their relative effect through the period 1990-98. In addition, there are variations by regions. The analysis concludes that social programs did have a more significant impact in Metropolitan Santiago and some other regions on distribution, but had no significant effect in Regions VIII and XI (see map). These are still among the poorest regions of the country even though there has been significant reductions in poverty since the 1980s. It is also important to note that the VIIIth region is the next most populated region after Metropolitan Santiago. This could indicate that there is an issue of the regional distribution of social programs and more aggressive targeting might be needed to ensure access among regions. This is perhaps more important for public spending in areas such as housing and related public works, as compared to education. It may also reflect variations in local municipal institutional capacity to administer programs and to manage the *ficha* CAS which is used to identify program beneficiaries and determine their eligibility as discussed below.

Targeting of Social Programs[20]

The impact of social programs depends not only on their overall size, but also on how well they are targeted to the poor. Social programs in Chile are generally targeted using the *ficha* CAS system (see box). The object of the CAS is to avoid using a measure of income, where proof of income is difficult to determine and respondents have an incentive to understate their true income in order to be eligible. The scoring of the CAS ensures that households in upper deciles of the income distribution are excluded from social programs designed for the poor. However, the scoring system is not keyed directly to the poverty line so that some CAS eligible households may, in fact, be above the poverty line. Moreover, based on a qualitative, albeit limited assessment of the *ficha* CAS, it appears that questions themselves may not be sensitive to household vulnerability such as illness or job loss.

---

[20] This section is based on Carine Clert and Quentin Wodon, "The Targeting of Government Programs in Chile: A Quantitative and Qualitative Assessment", Background Paper No. 4, Vol. II.

Box 1: The *Ficha* CAS

Introduced during the military regime (1973-1989) and modified by the post-1990 democratic governments, the *ficha* CAS (*Ficha de Estratificación Social, Comite Accion Social*) is two-page form which is used for determining the eligibility of households to a number of government programs including not only monetary transfers (*Subsidios Monetarios*), but also access to low income housing, childcare centres and other programs. At present the official name of the form is the *ficha* CAS-II. The first page of the form provides detailed information on the housing conditions of the household (e.g., material used for the construction of the housing unit, number and type of rooms, access to water, latrine and sanitary services, etc.) The second page of the form provides a list of the household members, with information on their occupation, educational level, date of birth, and income. At the bottom of the second page, additional information is provided on the assets held by the household (e.g. housing status, heating equipment, and refrigerator). Points are allocated to households on the basis of the information provided, with the number of points fluctuating between 380 and 770 points. Households with a total of inferior to 500 points are considered as extremely poor and those with a total number of between 500 and 540 points are considered as poor.

The Ministry of Planning (MIDEPLAN) is responsible for the design of the *ficha* CAS, with implementation at the municipality level. Municipalities usually separate the activities of data collection and data entry from those of needs assessment. Data collection and entry tend to be done by a department of social information within the municipality, while the control of the needs assessment is usually done by social workers and *técnico-sociales* (welfare assistants).

The national income transfer programs which are targeted using the CAS scoring system apply the formula in a strict manner in order for determining eligibility. The score obtained by a household automatically and exclusively prevails, so that eligibility depends only on the number of points obtained. The *ficha* is also used for targeting locally financed safety nets, but in this case social workers and other professionals can often give some weight to other eligibility criteria such as the presence of a chronic illness, the civil status of household members, and their actual financial resources at the time of request as the ficha is completed every three years, and there may be differences between the status of households when they apply for benefits, as compared to their status when they filled the form.

Using the data from the 1998 CASEN survey, it is possible to analyze the coverage and targeting of several important programs, including pensions, family allowances, water subsidies, child care, and housing. Data in Table 15 show both the coverage of the overall population, the participation in the program of the poorest quintile and the Gini income elasticity (GIE, see Background Paper No. 4 for details).

The first major observation is that these social programs cover a relatively small percentage of the population in poverty. The most extensive program, SUF or family allowances, only reaches about 32 percent of the poor (here defined as the poorest 20% of households). Programs such as subsidized child care reach about 5 percent of the poor (although all of the poor may not be eligible for the program, which supplies child care to low income working women).

The second major observation is that these programs do not focus exclusively on the poor and there are substantial leakage. For example, of the beneficiaries of SUF, about 56 percent are poor, and about 36 percent of the beneficiaries of PASIS are in the lowest quintile. On average, the targeted programs listed here have a targeting efficiency of only about 38 percent [21]. That is, about 62 percent of the beneficiaries of targeted programs are not poor. One of the reasons for

---

[21] This is the average of the figures shown in Table 16 for "targeting", excluding the non-PASIS pensions.

this might be that the CAS system does not focus on income poverty, but uses proxies which are heavily dominated by housing and education measures.

The rather low levels of targeting and coverage to the poor contrast with the previous finding that social spending programs have had a material effect on income distribution, as measured by the Gini coefficient. However, these two findings are not inconsistent since it appears that many social programs have been important for redistribution from the upper levels of the income distribution to the middle and lower levels, smoothing the Lorenz curve but not necessarily benefiting the poor as defined by the poverty line. From Table 14, it is possible to calculate that the poorest 20 percent of the population receive 33 percent of total social programs, and 41 percent of cash transfers (the type most likely to be targeted with the *ficha* CAS). However, the next two quintiles which are above the poverty line receive about 60 percent of total social programs and 55 percent of cash grants. These figures are consistent with the estimated targeting efficiency shown for selected programs in Table 15, where roughly 30-40 percent of the benefits of these programs go to the poor.

Table 15: Targeting and Coverage of Selected Social Programs-1998

Program	Participation rate (% of total population)	Coverage: (participation rate of poorest 20%)	Targeting: (% of beneficiaries in poorest 20%)	Gini Elasticity
Pension Assistance (PASIS)	6.1	10.9	35.7%	-0.56
Non-PASIS (not targeted)	15.7	6.1	7.8%	0.91
Family Allowances (SUF)	11.5	32.1	55.8%	-1.03
Water Subsidies	6.4	10.6	33.1%	-0.35
Housing:				
Vivienda Basica	5.8	8.2	28.3%	-0.41
Vivienda Programa I	1.1	2.2	40.0%	-0.68
Vivenda Programa II	0.2	0.4	40.0%	-0.59
Child Care:				
JUNJI	1.7	2.7	31.8%	-0.50
INTEGRA	1.3	2.6	40.0%	-0.71

Source: Based on CASEN, 1998 data, as in Clert and Wodon, Background Paper No. 4. GIEs for housing and child care are estimated assuming that allocation elasticities are equal to 1.0; i.e. there are no differences in benefits received by socio-economic level.

The impact of programs on income distribution, rather than on just the poor, can be measured by the concept of the Gini income elasticity (GIE). This elasticity shows the impact of an expansion of the program on the Gini coefficient. An index of one indicates that a program raises incomes equally across all deciles, and there is no effect on income distribution. Elasticities below one indicate that expanding the program improves income distribution; negative coefficients indicate strong redistribution of income from the wealthy to the poor. As shown in Table 15, all programs appear to help improve income distribution. However, the impacts vary by program. Family allowances are strongly redistributive, with a GIE of -1.03, whereas water subsidies have less impact with a GIE of -.35. The PASIS pension program has a favorable GIE of -.56; in comparison, the regular, non-targeted, pensions programs of the Government are virtually neutral, with a GIE of .91.

Improving the Ficha CAS

There are numerous advantages in using the *ficha* CAS, and it is central for the administration of social programs in Chile. One of the main advantages of using the *ficha* for many different programs is that this reduces the cost of means-testing. The cost of a CAS interview is about US$8.65 per household but because these costs are spread across several programs, the system is very cost effective. In 1996, administrative costs represented only 1.2 percent of the benefits being distributed using the CAS system. If the administrative costs of the CAS system were to be borne by water subsidies alone, for example, they would represent 17.8 percent of the value of the subsidies. The *ficha* CAS also offers a systematic and consistent way to manage diverse social programs, which brings advantages in terms of targeting, monitoring and evaluation.

However, there are some problems with relying on the *ficha* CAS. A study of the effectiveness of government programs and social exclusion by Clert (2000a, 2000b) using more qualitative methods revealed some important insights.[22] First, there seems to be poor transmission of information, which may explain, in part, the relatively poor coverage rates of targeted programs in Chile. Based on a study of the *Comuna de Huechuraba*, the proportion of respondents who had not heard of the government social entitlement programs under review was relatively high, at 51 percent of the sample. The awareness rates were higher for certain programs than for others. For instance, 74 percent were aware of municipal programs in health and education, such as the free provision of medicines or school uniforms. However, 70 percent had not heard of the main national program to combat poverty in female-headed households. Even when they were aware of programs, many did not know how to apply for benefits. Part of the problem is that the poor are not in contact with municipal welfare offices where they can obtain information, and social workers are not given the necessary resources (time arrangements, vehicles) to be sufficiently mobile to make home visits. In general, social workers tend to serve those who come looking for assistance, but they rarely can go out into the community attempting to identify eligible people who have not applied for assistance.[23]

Another problem raised by the poor is that the point system in the *ficha* CAS may be too rigid. The emphasis of the CAS on the material aspects of the household tends to overlook cases where unemployment or health crises have led to a loss of income. In the case of locally financed safety nets, social workers are given some leeway to take account of income, health and employment problems. However, there is little or no discretion in the use of the CAS for nationally financed programs. Some rules also work against the poorest. For housing programs, besides being eligible under the CAS, applicants have to have a level of required savings. This is particularly a problem among the low-income elderly who lack the ability to generate savings, while rules work against them in qualifying for housing support if they combine efforts with children or other family relatives. In the case of child care, applicants have to show proof of employment and associated working hours. This works against teenage mothers wishing to complete schooling, women working irregular hours, such as cleaners and domestic workers, and the unemployed who want to search for work. In addition, in the case of housing, it may be the

---

[22] This qualitative evaluation of the *ficha* CAS is based on the perceptions of the interviewees and could be at variance with reality. However, to the extent that these perceptions exist itself may reflect a failure at the level of information management.

[23] However, these findings are based on a survey of only one community, so one needs to be careful in generalizing to the entire country.

case that housing conditions improve--not because of greater income but because of self-help efforts. This too can put a family at disadvantage for qualifying for income programs.

Several other problems have been detected. One concern is how to convert private in-kind transfers—support from the family or from neighbors—into monetary equivalents, especially when these transfers may be erratic. Another is how to recognize intra-household allocations, an important issue from a gender perspective. This affects pregnant teenagers, for example, as they do not receive maternity benefits as dependents.

In September, 1999, the Government introduced changes to the CAS weighting system in an attempt to correct some of these problems. Among other changes, the revised CAS drops two questions on electricity access and television, and it introduces new weights for the various indicators. In addition, different systems for rural and urban areas have been eliminated. Simulations suggest that the new system is more effective in identifying the poor and the non-poor, thereby reducing the errors of inclusion and exclusion in the targeting of social programs. However, the system still places a high weight on housing and other material assets as proxies for income without including key indicators of vulnerability. Qualitative evidence suggests that finding ways to better take vulnerability into account would improve the system further.

EMPLOYMENT, UNEMPLOYMENT, AND SPECIAL PROGRAMS OF ASSISTANCE

The Problem of Unemployment

Unemployment rates in Chile have been at about 6-8 percent of the labor force during the past decade. More recently, unemployment has risen, from 6.3 percent in 1998 to a peak of 9.9 percent in September 2000. As Chile emerged from the 1999 recession, the rate has been declining somewhat, ending the year 2000 at 8.9 percent. As shown in Figure 3 (below), fluctuations in unemployment over the period 1997-2000 appear to have little or no correlation with changes in real wages.[24] The rise in unemployment in 1999 and again in 2000 was not associated with any decline in real wages; in fact, real wages increased slightly.

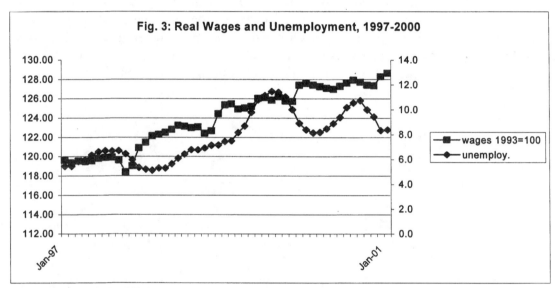

Source: Central Bank of Chile.

Continuing high unemployment is of increasing concern and there are doubts if and when the rate of unemployment will fall to the pre-1999 levels.[25] Part of the problem is that nominal wages are relatively rigid, and labor force adjustments take place through the creation of unemployment rather than through a decline in nominal or real wages. This is a common problem in low inflation economies which cannot use inflation to reduce real wages (see Gonzalez, 1999). Moreover, unemployment has a clearly greater impact on more vulnerable groups--the poorly educated and less experienced, younger workers. As shown in Table 16, male workers in the lowest quintile had an unemployment rate of about 24 percent overall, when the total unemployment rate was only 6 percent in 1998.[26] Younger workers have twice the rate

---

[24] Data on unemployment and wages from Central Bank of Chile (2001).

[25] Based on INE data for the whole country. University of Chile data for Greater Santiago give somewhat higher unemployment rates, at about 14% for 1999, and 15% in September, 2000.

[26] Since unemployment automatically eliminates a major source of income, this finding is a bit tautological. It would be better to measure unemployment according to consumption poverty, since consumption levels tend to be more stable over time.

of unemployment of older workers. Male workers aged 18-24 had an unemployment rate in 1998 of 11.7 percent, while those aged 55-64 had an unemployment rate of only 5.5 percent.[27]

Table 16: Unemployment by Quintiles, Age, and Sex
(% of labor force)

Quintiles:	1	2	3	4	5	total
Male	24.4	7.6	5.3	3.4	1.8	7.1
age: 18-24	27.9	13.6	10.0	5.9	3.6	11.7
25-34	25.2	7.7	6.8	4.3	2.8	8.2
35-54	23.6	5.8	2.6	2.0	0.4	5.9
55-64	20.4	7.4	3.8	2.4	0.7	5.5
Female	10.1	5.1	4.6	3.2	2.2	4.9
age: 18-24	16.0	10.7	8.8	7.6	3.5	9.2
25-34	10.7	6.8	6.1	4.2	2.6	6.0
35-54	9.5	3.3	3.1	2.2	1.4	3.7
55-64	3.1	1.9	1.1	0.8	0.7	1.4
total	17.3	6.4	4.9	3.3	1.8	6.0

Source: CASEN, 1998; see Background Paper No.5, Appendix Table 1 and 2.

Unemployment rates for women show a similar pattern, with higher rates for the younger and poorer women even though unemployment rates of women are generally lower than those of men. For those in the first quintile, for instance, the unemployment rate among women is 10 percent, compared to 24 percent among men. As pointed out in Background Paper 5, there are also much lower levels of activity or labor force participation among the poor groups, particularly women. While 58 percent of women aged 15-64 in the highest decile were in the labor force in 1998, the ratio is only 19 percent for women in the lowest decile (see Table 17). This suggests that poorer women are perhaps unable to participate in the labor force because of child care responsibilities, 'which is also related to the fact that poor households tend to have more children. In addition, women are more likely to be employed part time, and young workers and women are more likely to be involved in more precarious employment situations (working without contract).

Table 17: Labor Force Participation Rates, Females Aged 14-65
(percent of total in age group)

Decile Group	1987	1990	1994	1998
1	12.3	14.7	15.3	19.3
2	13.1	16.3	18.7	27.0
3	14.4	16.2	21.9	32.3
4	17.1	20.7	25.1	38.1
5	20.1	24.5	29.4	39.6
6	24.1	30.0	33.8	43.5
7	28.9	33.1	39.6	50.3
8	31.9	35.1	41.8	52.4
9	37.2	41.5	46.6	53.4
10	54.0	53.1	57.0	58.0
Average	26.4	29.3	33.7	40.6
Ratio 10:1	4.4	3.6	3.7	3.0

Note: Decile groups are calculated using Household Per Capita Income.
Source: CASEN surveys, as quoted in Ferreira and Litchfield (1999), updated by Bank staff.

---

[27] This finding is not unique to Chile. The ILO reports unemployment rates (1998) for all youths (male and female) of 20.4% for Argentina (age: 15-24), 14.3% for Brazil (18-24), and 21.9% for Venezuela (15-24). See ILO(1999).

On the other hand, there has been a continuous increase in the labor force participation rate of women in Chile, as in other countries, over the last twenty years, and this also has put pressure on labor markets to absorb these additional workers. Female labor force participation rates rose from 26 percent in 1987, to 41 percent in 1998. Between 1994 and 1998, a major growth in labor force participation seems to have occurred among women in deciles 2 to 9, and much smaller growth rates among the richest and poorest women.

Why unemployment remains so high for the poor and the young after such a long period of prosperity has not been fully explained. One possible explanation is the rigidities that remain in the Chilean labor market. Heckman and Pages (2000) examined the relationship between job security regulations and employment and unemployment in Latin America, including Chile. Job security regulations are the labor code regulations that increase the cost of dismissing a worker, including prior notification, severance payment, and foregone wages during any legal proceeding made by the worker against a firm.

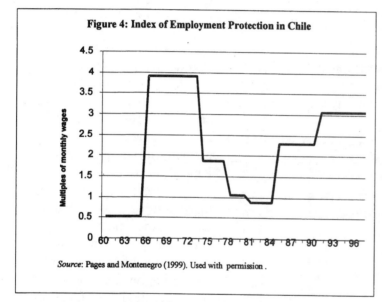

Figure 4: Index of Employment Protection in Chile

Source: Pages and Montenegro (1999). Used with permission.

While these costs have been reduced in some countries, job security costs rose in Chile after 1991 (Figure 4). The overall finding is that job security regulations are inefficient and increase inequality and reduce employment opportunities for young, female and unskilled workers. However, they do not appear to be related to rates of unemployment *per se*. Rather, they tend to result in a larger informal sector of workers who are outside the provisions of the labor codes. Furthermore, their empirical results demonstrate that job security costs are higher in Latin American countries, compared to OECD countries, and are among the highest in Chile. In terms of a percentage of the average annual wage, job security regulations add an estimated 28.1 percent to the annual wage in Chile, compared to only 12.1 percent in the U.K., 4.6 percent in Canada, and zero in the U.S.A.

Minimum Wages. Another possible factor that can influence unemployment is the relatively high level of the minimum wage in Chile. In the short run, increases in minimum wages could reduce poverty and reduce the gap between rich and poor. In the longer term, however, high minimum wages tend to make the use of low-skilled workers less attractive, leading to higher levels of unemployment among these groups, which are typically among the poorest and youngest workers. The minimum wage structure in Chile is complicated, with three different minimum wages, and a system of indexation based on inflation, productivity and a redistribution element. As a result, during the 1990s, minimum wages increased faster than the average wage level (5.6% vs. 3.8%). In 2000, the agreed minimum wage will increase a further 6.5 percent, while the expected increase in average wages is only 1.4 percent. As a result, the minimum wage has become closer to the median wage, rising from 46 percent of the median in 1998, to 56 percent in 2000.

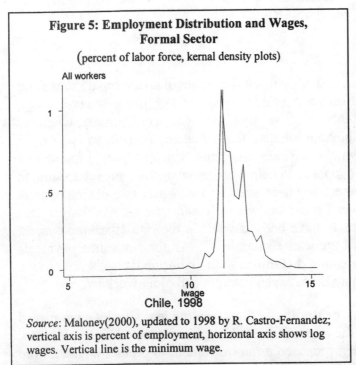

Figure 5: Employment Distribution and Wages, Formal Sector

(percent of labor force, kernal density plots)

Source: Maloney(2000), updated to 1998 by R. Castro-Fernandez; vertical axis is percent of employment, horizontal axis shows log wages. Vertical line is the minimum wage.

In many countries, minimum wages are not binding because they are not enforced. This is particularly true of countries with large informal sectors where employees are not registered as part of the social security/unemployment insurance systems, and are not subject to labor regulations. In contrast to Argentina, for example, Chile has a relatively small informal sector—about 15 percent of the labor force--so minimum wages do not seem to have an impact on the decision by firms and/or workers to drop out of formal systems. Yet, as shown by Maloney (2000), there is some evidence that minimum wages do affect wages in certain countries, including Chile. The kernal density plots (essentially smoothed histograms) of wage rates and employment for Chile does indicate a "piling up" of people at the minimum wage rate (the vertical line in Figure 5 above) rather than a smoother distribution. Surprisingly, the effect of minimum wages seems even stronger in the informal sector. The majority of workers in the informal sector seem to be clustered the minimum wage, even though it is not legally binding (Figure 6).

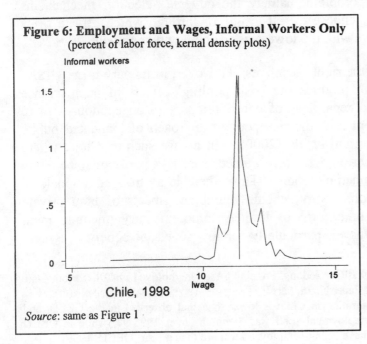

Figure 6: Employment and Wages, Informal Workers Only
(percent of labor force, kernal density plots)

Source: same as Figure 1

However, the relationship between minimum wages and employment and poverty is not entirely clear. Research by Bravo and Contreras (1998) shows that, at least prior to 1998) there appears to be no relationship between the minimum wage and unemployment. In addition, Lopez (1997) shows that, using regional data over four years (1987,'90,'92 and '94), the level of minimum wage is significant but has a negative sign in explaining poverty increases. That is, an increase in minimum wages appears to reduce poverty, in this case with an estimated elasticity of -.7. This finding is consistent with a binding minimum wage and an inelastic labor demand. Raising minimum wages pushes people near the poverty line up into non-poverty, but at the same time causes additional unemployment which is detrimental to other poor people and other entrants to the labor market. While the poverty rate might decline, the poverty gap could be increasing.

Providing Support for the Unemployed[28]

Overview. Workers are typically at risk of losing their job due to involuntary separations from firms, and such risks have greater impact on poor families who typically have fewer savings, assets to sell, or access to credit to offset income losses than the rich. Traditionally, countries have dealt with those risks through a combination of state-funded unemployment assistance (or insurance) and firm-funded severance payments. These programs typically have a number of weaknesses. Unemployment assistance is supposed to help workers who lose their job to smooth their consumption spending during an unemployment spell. Yet when the unemployment benefits are large, they may create incentives for the workers to remain unemployed longer than necessary. This "moral hazard" problem may have been at work in the rise of unemployment rates and the length of unemployment in European economies.[29] As for severance payments programs, they also have the potential of creating distortions in the labor market, not only in the relationships between firms and workers, but also between younger and older workers.

The weaknesses of these typical programs for dealing with unemployment shocks have placed the reform of social insurance programs at the center of the public policy debate. Unemployment insurance saving accounts (UISA) have been proposed as an instrument to protect workers from the loss in earnings associated with unemployment. The idea is to have all workers (and possibly their employers as well) deposit a share of their monthly incomes into their UISA, with the balance in the account accruing market interest rates. During an unemployment spell, workers withdraw funds from their individual account. The fact that the accounts are individualized helps to solve the moral hazard problem. Moreover, the fact that the contribution system is mandatory also helps to solve another problem, namely the adverse selection mechanisms through which only some workers might choose to self-insure, or through which private firms insuring workers would hand-pick workers with the lowest risk of being unemployed.

Overall, the objective of UISAs is to set the right incentives. However, in its pure form, UISAs have a disadvantage in that they do not produce the "risk pooling' effects of an insurance scheme, wherein benefits are predefined regardless of contributions. In an economy where unemployment is a rare event and is kept low, the risk pooling approach of mandated public insurance makes more sense (see De Ferranti *et. al.* (2000)). In a case such as Chile, where unemployment is a more likely event, there is less to be gained from risk pooling, since many more people are subject to the risk of unemployment. Thus, there is a stronger rationale to support individual accounts. Furthermore, many schemes combine aspects of both private accounts and risk pooling, providing some form of limited complementary unemployment assistance once private funds were exhausted, particularly for low levels of benefits. Recent

---

[28] This section is based on R. Castro-Fernandez and Q. Wodon, "Protecting the Unemployed in Chile: From State Assistance to Individual Insurance?", Background Paper No. 6, Part II.

[29] Beyer (2000) shows that the unemployment duration in Chile is lower than that observed in the OECD, and especially in Europe. In Chile, the average unemployment spell was 3 months over 1995-97, while in OECD countries, more than half of unemployed workers have been unemployed for more than a year (OECD, 1999).

proposals for replacing standard forms of unemployment assistance by UISAs are being implemented in several Latin American countries (e.g., Brazil and Colombia).

The Current System. Chile currently has both of the typical programs found in many countries to provide support for the unemployed. A key finding from Section II is that unemployment for a household head or his/her spouse generates a loss of up to 20 percent or more in the household's per capita income. The unemployment assistance and severance payments systems that have been in existence for many years in Chile are supposed to offset such losses, but in practice, they do not succeed in adequately protecting the unemployed.

Unemployment assistance (UA) provides a minimum payment to unemployed workers in the formal sector, financed from general tax revenues, but with a payment that is much lower than the minimum wage. Even though the program is highly progressive in terms of income distribution, its main problem is that it has very limited impact (see Table 19). In 1998, the average unemployed worker received US$300 for the full length of the unemployment spell, which had a median duration of about four months (or about $40 per month). By comparison, in June 1998, the minimum wage was worth US$178 per month and since has been increased. In the 1998 CASEN survey, unemployment assistance benefits represent only 0.3 percent of total income. In terms of coverage, only 8 percent of all unemployed workers were receiving benefits in 1998.

Table 18: Unemployment Rate and Unemployment Assistance Outlays

	Unemp. rate (%)	Number receiving assistance	Assistance outlays (US$M)	Outlays as share of GDP (%)		Unemp. Rate (%)	Number receiving assistance	Assistance outlays (US$M)	Outlays as share of GDP (%)
1980	10.40	74,000	56,000	0.23	1990	7.79	33,845	6,000	0.02
1981	11.30	75,000	65,000	0.25	1991	8.16	30,246	6,000	0.02
1982	19.60	131,000	103,000	0.46	1992	6.71	23,432	6,000	0.01
1983	14.60	142,000	95,000	0.43	1993	6.56	19,147	4,000	0.01
1984	13.90	98,000	52,000	0.22	1994	7.83	20,572	6,000	0.01
1985	12.10	97,000	47,000	0.19	1995	7.38	21,282	6,756	0.01
1986	8.80	85,000	31,000	0.12	1996	6.44	21,343	7,234	0.01
1987	10.93	66,051	18,000	0.07	1997	6.09	22,586	7,610	0.01
1988	9.76	51,750	14,000	0.06	1998	6.29	27,290	8,014	0.01
1989	7.91	39,245	9,000	0.03	1999	9.65			

Source: Compendios Estadisticos, INE (Instituto Nacional de Estadisticas) and Boletines Mensuales, SSS (Superintendencia de Seguridad Social), see Background Paper No. 6.

Severance payments are an acquired right of workers in the formal sector to receive, upon dismissal, one month's salary for every full year worked, up to a maximum of eleven months. While severance payments form a positive incentive against firms laying off workers in a recession, they also form a perverse incentive against hiring more workers in a recovery. A major study of job security costs in Chile, of which severance payments is a major factor, shows that over time, job security costs have discouraged employment among younger workers (see Pages and Montenegro, 1999). Since these payments are linked to tenure, they tend to favor older workers and men. As a result, Pages and Montenegro find there has been a substantial decline in the ratio of wage-employment to population among younger workers, while there has been no such decline for older workers. Although there seems to be no direct link between job security costs and unemployment, an index of these costs constructed by Pages and Montenegro shows that they have risen substantially since 1987, suggesting that this factor may be pushing younger workers into informal employment.

Proposals for Unemployment Insurance Savings Accounts

Recently (April, 2001) the Congress approved a new system of unemployment insurance which will replace the present system, while keeping in place the system of severance payments. This proposal introduces a system of USIAs, while retaining unemployment insurance for those who have exhausted their USIA benefits.. Under the new *Seguro de Desempleo* (SD) , the UISAs would be financed with contributions from workers (0.6% of the gross wage) and employers (2.4%) during the first 11 years of the labor relationship. Workers who would be eligible for the new system are basically those eligible for unemployment assistance today. Out of the 2.4 percent contributed by the employer, 1.6 percentage points will go to the UISA and 0.8 percentage points pooled into an unemployment assistance fund which would provide benefits under certain defined circumstances, but basically when the individual's USIA is unable to finance a predefined minimum benefit. This fund would be complemented by a government transfer of $10.5 million per year from tax revenues.

The system would work in the following way. When unemployed, the workers would withdraw funds from their UISAs. The maximum number of monthly withdrawals is equal to the number of years during which the worker contributed. For example, a worker who contributed for three years could withdraw funds from his/her account for three months. However, there is a maximum limit of five for the total number of withdrawals, which corresponds to the average length of unemployment in 1998. The amount of the each withdrawal is computed on a sliding scale, reflecting the total number of withdrawals allowed, the amount in the account, and a factor that makes the first withdrawals somewhat larger than later withdrawals. A last withdrawal is also made once the worker finds a new job, although the worker can elect to leave this in the USIA. . The total amount of the account becomes available when the worker retires, or upon death, to his/her heirs.

An analysis of the distribution impact of the proposed program reveals that, while it is highly redistributive, it is somewhat less redistributive than the present system. In other words, replacing the present system with SC, or a program similar to it, would lead to slight worsening of income distribution among current recipients. However, since the reach of the present program is so small and the proposed program would likely include more participants, its net effect could be to improve income distribution.

Job Training[30]

To improve the employment prospects of two particular groups which face higher than average difficulty in the labor market--young workers and women from disadvantaged social backgrounds--the government has created two vocational training programs: *Chile Joven*, a program for low-income youth between ages of 15-24 years, and PMJH (*Capacitacion para Mujeres Jefas de Hogar),* a program for low-income women. Both programs have been

---

[30] This section is based on R. Castro-Fernandez, Carine Clert, and Quentin Wodon," Government Programs for the Insertion of Youths and Women in Chile's Labor Market: A Discussion", Background Paper No. 5, Part II.

modified in recent years in an attempt to place stronger emphasis on labor market participation by trainees after completion of the program.

A recent evaluation of these programs found them to be quite effective.[31] For *Chile Joven*, unemployment for the beneficiaries fell between 21 to 36 percent (depending on the type of training given), while there was no change in a similarly constructed control group over the same period. Likewise, an evaluation of PMJH found a decline in unemployment of about 15 percent, and improvements in job quality. These findings are encouraging, since most training programs in OECD countries have been found to have limited impact, and any positive impact tends to vanish after a few years (Dar and Gill, 1998).

The success of Chile's programs may be linked to certain key attributes, such as providing a direct contact with prospective employers. Poor and younger workers often lack the informal contact networks necessary to find employment. In the case of *Chile Joven*, a system of internships in firms provides a key entry to potential employers. In addition, the training programs put emphasis on building social and relational skills, and help reduce the costs of job search.

Nevertheless, there is some evidence that these programs may not be reaching the poorest. PMJH is restricted to women who are literate, thus leaving out one of the poorest groups. Success of the programs in helping beneficiaries find employment seems to be limited to the older, male workers and those with education. And some training centers appear to select trainees on the basis of the ability to be employed in the future, rather than on the basis of their needs, thus pre-selecting those beneficiaries who are most likely to find employment. Survey data show that the poor are slightly more likely to participate in government training programs than the non-poor, but this is offset by the fact that the non-poor pay for private training, or receive it free from their employers. A lack of knowledge of government training programs is also a reason why the poor do not participate to a greater extent. In addition, there are other segments of the population which are particularly subject to labor market exclusion and who should receive more attention from policy programs. Clert (2000a) study suggested that individuals in their forties, who are excluded from the labor market due to age stigmatization, cannot participate in state vocational training programmes restricted to the young. Other factors than age affect the access of the poor to employment, including discrimination based on appearance or the area where they live. Dealing with these kinds of exclusionary mechanisms is difficult, but can be addressed in some cases by well designed assistance (see box).

---

[31] Santiago Consultores, "Principales Aspectos de Estudio "Evaluación Ex Post Porgrama Chile Joven Fase II", Santiago, Chile. These results should be treated with some caution, however, because of biases arising from differences between the treatment and control groups.

Box 2: Social Exclusion in the Labor Market

Discrimination by age and/or physical appearance: In Clert's study, some of the more subtle perceptions of exclusion from labor markets relate to elements of the respondents' identity such as age, physical appearance, place of residence and disability. Margarita, a women aged 52, had worked as a domestic worker all her life but was fired by her employer two years before and has remained unemployed since then. She explains: *"One goes to a place and the offer says 'Needs domestic worker more than 25 until, let's say, 40'. So what's the matter? Those of us who are over 50, we don't have the right to work?* The social construction of physical appearance also affects women and young men. A key informant from the municipal job bureau explained that qualifications were not the only factor at a job interview: *"The employer weighs certain criteria: good appearance (buena presencia), experience, knowledge. [A good appearance relates to] the look, there are things about details. For instance, you have people who come here with their pony tail, their earring... Presentation counts for 25 percent. But it is true that they will tell them 'I already hired someone else'. They won't say I don't take you because you look ugly."* The training programs show an awareness of the subtle mechanisms of discrimination which tend to be used by employers in their hiring practices. Non-written rules of selection have been addressed in the contents of vocational training courses. Program participants value the acquisition of presentation skills, writing skills for resumes, and communication skills. Interestingly, the program *Mujeres Jefas de Hogar* gives participants free access to dental health, in part because early consultations with participants for the program design showed that women faced discrimination due to the importance given to physical appearance and personal presentation by firms. However, similar initiatives are still lacking for other segments of the population who may also need assistance, such as low qualified, middle age men.

Area Stigma. The residents of the *Pincoya* Sector of the *comuna* of Huechuraba have felt discriminated against because of the reputation of the area as a rough and dangerous area peopled by dishonest inhabitants. For example, Jose who lived in the Pincoya sector, reported the following: *"They ask me from which comuna I come from. I say 'Huechuraba'. And where is that? Nothing more but they look at me in a certain way with a gesture as if it meant... ah, there you have to come in with your back turned to make people believe that you are getting out."* This and similar type of discrimination are especially difficult to fight, but the government has promoted awareness and sensitization campaigns to combat the stigma attached to low-income youth, which often tends to be associated with delinquency, violence and threat.

Valuing diversity. Similarly, the program *Mujeres Jefas de Hogar* has promoted a recognition of social diversity within Chilean society by disseminating a positive image of various types of families. Within the government, the program contributed to a better recognition of the heterogeneity of poverty by public policy. As a senior official put it: *"Women heads of households used to suffer from a triple discrimination: being poor, being a woman and being a single mother... With regard to women heads of household for instance, there's now greater cultural acceptance of the diversity of family types ... Years ago they appeared in statistics but there wasn't a social recognition that they existed."*

Source: Background Paper No.5. See also Clert (2000a).

INDIGENOUS PEOPLES, SOCIAL EXCLUSION, AND POVERTY[32]

Poverty Among Indigenous People

Chile has a significant indigenous population, even though not at the level of neighboring countries such as Peru and Bolivia. Chilean law recognizes eight different groups and, according to the 1992 population census, these groups represented about 7.5 percent of the total population. (An estimate based on the CASEN 1996 survey suggests a much lower figure of 4.5 percent. However, most analysts agree that the census figure is a better estimate.) The census shows that the Mapuche form the largest indigenous group, followed by the Aymaras and the Rapanui, with the remaining indigenous groups consisting of only a few hundred people each.

Indigenous populations of Chile remain among the poorest and most vulnerable groups. The CASEN survey indicates that incidence of poverty is 36 percent among the indigenous, compared to 23 percent among the non-indigenous population (1996). Thus, the chance of being poor is 56 percent greater if one is indigenous. On average, indigenous families receive almost half the income of non-indigenous families, and 65 percent of the indigenous families are within the lowest two quintiles of income distribution. Most economically active indigenous people are in unskilled jobs (31%) and in agriculture and fisheries (25%). In terms of education, schooling among indigenous peoples is about 2.2 years below the average of non-indigenous.

Contrary to popular perceptions, almost 80 percent of the indigenous population lives in urban areas, and most of them in Santiago (40%), a over the last 15 years there has been a steady trend toward urbanization. Nevertheless, with population growth, the numbers living in rural areas has remained roughly constant and it is in these rural areas, as a subset of rural poverty, that one finds the worst poverty and the most contentious issues over land and water. On the other hand, those in the urban areas, particularly Santiago, may have better living conditions and income opportunities but report discrimination in labor markets, credit and schools, and some may hide their indigenous backgrounds.

The lack of a coherent national understanding of the status and recognition of indigenous peoples among Chileans at large, despite official recognition in 1993, seems to be one of the largest barriers of these groups to secure their place in society. Starting in 1990, the government has taken several steps to improve the situation. It created the Special Commission for Indigenous Peoples (CEPI), which in turn drafted an indigenous bill that was widely discussed throughout the country. This law recognizes indigenous peoples, gives them legal standing, protects their lands, and recognizes their culture. After the law's approval in 1993, a government agency, the National Corporation for Indigenous Development (CONADI) was established under the Minister of Planning and Cooperation. CONADI launched several special programs for indigenous peoples, and began coordinating with other government programs to facilitate indigenous peoples access to them. CONADI's operations are governed by a council, which includes indigenous representatives, but the government maintains majority control.

Among the special programs for indigenous people, CONADI operates a Land and Water Fund, designed to finance land and water right acquisition, irrigation sub-projects, and the resolution of

---

[32] This section is based on E. Gacitúa-Mario, "Indigenous People in Chile", Background Paper No. 7, Part II.

land tenure conflicts. In addition, the Development Fund provides credit, technical assistance, seed money and subsidies to indigenous micro-enterprises. Other government ministries have special programs targeted at indigenous people in such areas as health, education, and agriculture. CONADI is also setting up Indigenous Development Areas (ADI), which are local planning unit designed to coordinate different government programs to indigenous peoples. Nevertheless, there has been continued unhappiness among the indigenous groups over the level of public support being channeled to them through CONADI, and increased demands for a larger flow of resources.

Major Challenges and Issues

Indigenous people in Chile face major challenges in gaining access to economic resources and overcoming social exclusion. In the case of the *urban* indigenous population, the key issues are related to: (i) human capital; (ii) labor market discrimination; and (iii) access to financial capital. These issues are compounded by social exclusion based on location, as most indigenous live in poor areas in the periphery, depressed downtown areas, or in specific neighborhoods. Location as an explanatory variable for poverty has already been shown to be important in the case of Chile in the 1997 Bank study, as well as in other countries, such as Uruguay, indicating a clustering of the poor accompanied by poor services. Moreover, urban indigenous peoples report difficulties to express and carry out their religious beliefs and ceremonies. Regarding human capital, most of the indigenous peoples living in urban centers or migrating to them do not have the technical skills required to have access to better employment opportunities. Most of the urban migrants work as unskilled construction workers (males), domestic services (females) or food industry/service employees (males and females). In the case of Mapuches living in small towns and secondary cities, there is also a significant number of both males and females who combine seasonal agricultural work and informal sector activities.

A further problem is that even when a indigenous worker has technical skills he or she faces a strong labor market discrimination. There are multiple examples of this discrimination from professionals to middle level technical staff, but more importantly among skilled and non-skilled workers who are subject to discrimination in hiring and dismissal practices, affecting typical female categories of occupation such as secretarial work, as well as male-dominated categories, such as construction.

Finally, small/micro entrepreneurs or self employed workers face significant constraints accessing (seed or operational) capital for starting and/or expanding their activities. First, the issue of discrimination plays a significant role in limiting their access to credit. Second, lack of collateral and poor knowledge of the system restrict their access. In this regard, the Development Fund established by CONADI is filling a gap. Nevertheless, the budgetary constraints of CONADI have imposed a severe constraint to the program.

Of the rural indigenous people, 95 percent are Mapuche with most rural Mapuche being small scale subsistence farmers who combine on-farm activities with off-farm employment. Over time, the survival of the rural Mapuche have become increasingly difficult due to the decreasing amount of land available for family farming, the lack of local employment opportunities, and the poor quality of available services. Overtime, average farm size has declined as a result of population growth, land division, and the colonialization of indigenous lands.

For the *rural* indigenous population, there are two main issues, both conflictive ones-- land and water rights. The land problem primarily affects the Mapuche rural population, while the water issue is relevant for Aymara and Quechua as well as Mapuche communities. For Mapuches, land is a central feature of their view of the world, not only as a mean of subsistence but also as an integral part of their identity. In addition, the economic horizon for many indigenous peoples must take into account the gradual decline of the importance of the primary sectors in Chile's economy combined with the changes in agricultural production. As well, indigenous peoples confront the same or even worse living conditions, especially in terms of housing, as the rural population in general.

Land. Since their forced confinement to reservations, the Mapuche have demanded compensation for what they consider a debt by Chilean society for depriving them of vast areas of land. Estimates suggest that, by the late 1970s, Mapuche communities had lost some 250,000 hectares from the original *Títulos de Merced.*[33] Today, Mapuche leaders are demanding land compensation ranging from 150,000 hectares by those seeking restoration of land granted in the *Títulos de Merced,* to more ambitious claims for the territories occupied before the settlement in reservations, or about 1 million hectares. Other claims do not set a specific target but leave it open to the establishment of territorial autonomy.[34]

Addressing the legal and civil dimensions of the land question is a necessary step to resolve the current impasse. However, it is essential to keep in mind that the restoration of land does not guarantee--in and of itself--socially and environmentally sustainable development for the Mapuche, nor does it resolve the long term problem of rural indigenous poverty and increasing land pressure due to demographic growth. The fact is that most rural indigenous families have little land, located in rapidly deteriorating environments, with few productive alternatives. Even if the land available to these families would be doubled from 5 hectares per family to 10 hectares, or tripled to 15 hectares per family, most of would still not be able to get enough income to move out of poverty based on farm-production alone: small land holdings with the production of crops such as potatoes and wheat have become increasingly less economics and efforts at diversification are costly and out of reach of most small-holders. Sustainable natural resources management and agricultural production strategies are necessary to generate a subsistence base in combination with off-farm productive activities. Further, generating off-farm employment opportunities and providing training to the young rural indigenous population is essential to facilitate their out-migration and insertion in the labor market.

Water. Water is another critical area for rural indigenous people. According to the water legislation (*Código de Aguas*) passed in 1981 and the Constitution of Chile, individuals or enterprises can obtain private water rights by receiving a grant from the state for new water sources, by prescription or by purchasing water rights which are fully tradable and transferable. The law establishes two types of water rights: (i) those for consumption which entitles the owner to consume water without any obligation to replenish it, or (ii) those for production which means

---

[33] See Gacitúa-Mario (1992) "Fundamentos Socio-Económicos, Culturales y Jurídicos para el Establecimiento de un Banco de Tierras para Pequeños Productores Mapuches en Tres Microregiones de la IX Región" Informe de Consultoría Instituto Nacional de Desarrollo Agropecuario (INDAP).

[34] See Ancan, Jose and Margarita Calfio (1999), "*El retorno al País Mapuche. Preliminares para una utopia por construir*" en Liwen # 5 Pp 43-78.

that the holder must restore water used at a stipulated quality and quantity. The law also distinguishes among categories of these rights.[35]

Indigenous rights to water have not acknowledged or accommodated in official water policies. In 1975, the government froze the use of water at 1975 levels locking in established use. After that, when the new water law was passed in 1981, assumed water rights of indigenous groups were either transferred directly to the private sector (through prescription) or were acquired through non-contested application or bidding and subsequent registration (*Registro de Propiedad de Aguas del Conservador de Bienes Raices*). As a result of the above, water rights of indigenous communities have not been regularized, or are being contested, particularly by productive users (power-hydroelectric companies).

During the 1990s, several conflicts occurred among different users of water resources, particularly between consumers and producers. Indigenous groups have been involved in conflicts over water rights with power companies, as well as with water and sewerage companies, the mining industry, and the forest industry. To a lesser degree, there have also been conflicts with other private users. Currently there is no estimate of how many families or communities are part of these conflicts, or how much resources are involved. But it is important to note that CONADI has assisted more than 4,500 families claiming water rights over the past five years.

Institutional Development. The situation facing indigenous peoples in Chile, as in many other countries including OECD members, is complex and taxes the best, well intentioned efforts by the parties to find lasting solutions. The path to resolution depends to a considerable extent on the institutional capacities of those representing the parties—indigenous, government, societal and private sector alike—to be imaginative, open to differences and constructive.

At present, the legal framework and institutional arrangements for dealing with indigenous issues need to be improved in Chile. The current legislation has significant limitations that make it difficult to resolve the impasse. First, the law does not provide for constitutional recognition of indigenous peoples as distinct groups with special rights. Similarly, there is no ratification of ILO's 1989 Indigenous and Tribal Populations Convention.[36] Indigenous leaders have already proposed a new indigenous bill addressing these two issues, as well as the right of indigenous peoples to elect their own representatives to the congress and local governments.[37]

Second, at the operational level, the institutional arrangements have proven insufficient to deal with the problems. The mixed composition of CONADI's governing board (indigenous representatives elected by universal vote and government representatives appointed by the executive) is not working as intended. Indigenous interests have frequently been subordinated to

---

[35] See Rios, Monica and Jorge Quiroz, 1995, *The Market for Water Rights in Chile*, World Bank Technical Paper 285.

[36] The signatories of the ILO's Indigenous and Tribal Populations Convention (1989) agree to protect the human rights of indigenous peoples, eliminate discrimination, recognize and safeguard social, cultural, religious and spiritual values and practices, and insure that indigenous groups are able to participate in decision making processes and institutions which concern them, and exercise control over their own economic, social and cultural development.

[37] See Proyecto de Reforma Constitucional que Reconoce la Existencia de los Pueblos Indígenas y les Otorga Participación Política en el Estado. An indigenous bill proposed by Congressman Francisco Huenchumilla, submitted for consideration to the National Congress on June 24, 1999.

"national interests" when conflict has arisen. CONADI has not been able to provide or develop the mechanisms for allowing independent indigenous participation and, at the same time, it is unable to advance a clear an unequivocal government policy towards the indigenous peoples. As a result, decisions over sensitive issues in which there is no agreement among the Board members are delayed or carried out without the support of the indigenous representatives who are a minority (8 to 9) in the board. This situation has generated frustration among indigenous peoples and increasing mistrust on CONADI and the government in general.

From an operational standpoint, CONADI, as the institution in charge of implementing the indigenous policy, lacks the resources and staff required to carry out its responsibilities.[38] The responsibilities are considerable. Despite the budget increases in 1999 (17.7%) and 2000 (22.5%), CONADI still does not have enough funds to respond to the demands coming to the Land and Water Fund or the Development Fund.

At the same time, it must be recognized that CONADI cannot in and of itself find a solution to all of the problems faced by indigenous communities. This will take the concerted effort of the relevant authorities: for example, Ministry of Education to promote opportunity, the Ministry of Interior to ensure equitable distribution of services, and the Ministry of Health to overcome any deficiencies in access and quality. A particular commitment needs to be made by those local governments with a significant indigenous population to encourage participation and access to services. At the same, there needs to be a societal effort to bring down barriers to indigenous people–and others–who are discriminated against in society. Chile has some successive programs addressing these problems which could be brought to bear specifically to indigenous groups.

Indigenous peoples too must be full partner of this process with the equal responsibility for constructive dialogue and building internal conflict resolution capacity. At present, most indigenous organizations are weak, numerous and lack strong coordination among themselves. There are over 200 local and regional Amayra organizations, and several hundred Mapuche organizations, both rural and urban. Further, the existing organizations have been unable to generate grassroots support. Each organization has a small group of supporters (or clientele) and most indigenous peoples (particularly among the Mapuche) do not feel represented by the existing national level organizations. There is a problem of representativeness which poses a serious challenge for indigenous organizations. While the existence of multiple organizations will continue to be a reality, and it could be argued is a strength of the indigenous movement in Chile, the need for coordination and common strategies aimed at increasing representativeness and participation at all levels is crucial.

Unfortunately, the current impasse on indigenous land and water claims, like in many other countries, polarizes communities and saps the energy of those most directly concerned, while progress lags on solving the myriad of other development problems facing what probably is the most disadvantaged group in Chilean society. While not ignoring these claims, there should be a concerted effort made to work on the problems faced by urban and rural indigenous populations and on creating within Chilean society overall a sense of commitment, national pride and identity with indigenous groups as a distinctive and unique characteristic of the country, what makes Chile, Chile.

---

[38] A recent IDB loan ($35 million) will help strengthen CONADI, as web as provide funds for education , health and rural development activities in several indigenous areas.

CONCLUSIONS

From 1987 to 1998, Chile has made impressive progress reducing the incidence, severity and depth of poverty and improving overall social conditions. This is credit to the economic and social policies followed by the government during the past decade which have brought both sustained growth and expansion of social services. The overall rate of poverty has continued to fall, reaching a level of 17 percent in 1998, as compared to a rate of 40 percent in 1987. While a note of caution must be raised in terms of the experience of the last two years, considering the rise in unemployment in 1999 and 2000, there is very reason to believe that Chile cannot continue this performance: halving of the poverty rate in twelve years is a record matched by few other countries in the world. Much of this reduction in poverty is directly related to a high and sustained rate of economic growth. At the same time, the Government has devoted extensive resources to social programs, including health, education, job training and basic infrastructure.

Starting from a relatively high level of income inequality, greater equality in Chile remains an aspiration. Compared both to other Latin American countries and to OECD members, trends in income distribution show much stability over the period, albeit with noticeable deterioration in 1996-98. This has been off-set, however, by the implicit value of expanding social programs which has been redistributive, so that an adjusted measure of income distribution shows improvement over the period. The overall effect of in-kind transfers reduces the Gini coefficient by about 8 percent. Thus, the worrisome trend of a growing gap between rich and poor has been mitigated by positive actions by the government, and social programs that are generally well directed to the lower half of the income distribution. However, on a regional basis, the impact of social programs appears somewhat uneven, being more concentrated in Metropolitan Santiago and having lower impact in some of the poorest regions. Thus, more aggressive efforts might be required to ensure equal access among regions.

The approach taken in this study—focusing on social deficits—provides an interesting framework for establishing a social policy agenda and priorities in Chile. Measuring poverty in terms of access to social services and standards provides an important non-monetary metric of poverty. On this score, there have been impressive gains and the results show that Chile has almost eliminated extreme poverty. Over 90 percent of the poor are affiliated with health care insurance; schooling at the primary and secondary levels is widespread and accessible; during the past decade, there have been significant gains in such areas as housing quality and access to water. Nevertheless, the analysis shows that about one-half of the population is still in deficit with regards to at least one of the dimensions included in the study. Education and housing stand out.

The study further points the following concerns:
• *Unemployment* remains very high, especially among the poorest workers and among the youngest; this may be related to the costs associated with hiring new workers, severance payments and other obligations as well as relatively high minimum wages. Programs to counteract these problems appear to be effective but more might be done to ease the participation of poor women with children in the labor force. Other important factors influencing unemployment include the rising participation rates of women, and the general rigidity of nominal and real wages in a low inflation environment. The apparent binding

effect of the minimum wage on both the informal sector and formal sector indicated that changes in this variable need to be thought through carefully to balance the impact on job creation versus poverty reduction. These are important policy choices which deserve further attention and study by the government. This is especially relevant to the present conditions in Chile, where the job creation does not appear to be responding to renewed economic growth as it did in the past.

- Given the relatively high and persistent levels of unemployment, greater attention needs to be paid to the support provided to the unemployed. Existing unemployment insurance programs provide very little support, both in coverage and amount, and the severance payments system serves to discourage formal sector employment and younger workers. Moving toward a system of public unemployment insurance combined with private accounts would help make labor markets more flexible and improve employment opportunities for younger and poorer workers. The current proposal by the Government provides a good balance between private accounts and public insurance mechanisms and would provide a more adequate safety net.

In light of the importance of education in overcoming poverty and the persistence of educational deficits, there is no doubt that the government's priority to improving the quality and relevance of education in Chile ought to continue and be fortified. Gains in primary and secondary education need to be consolidated, and the on-going efforts to improve quality and equality in tertiary education, intensified. And finally, the new initiatives for adult education and life-long-learning will be a very good move to deal with the "stock" of Chile's human capital, the quality of which recent international surveys have shown to be disappointing.

Combined with the significant reduction in income poverty during the 1990s, Chile has done a good job in developing social programs that have provided support to people in the middle and lower deciles of the income distribution, and a mechanism for determining eligibility on a low cost basis. Nevertheless, an analysis of the *ficha* CAS shows that it can be improved, especially to take into account vulnerability to income loss and illness, as well as other special circumstances. The CASEN could also be improved in some the area of areas, such as health, for example. It may be that, in light of progress on housing in particular, that the *ficha* CAS system now gives too much weight to that dimension. Importantly, any revision to the *ficha* CAS should involve those at the local level who use it and are most intimately knowledgeable of how it works.

Surprisingly, social programs in Chile have low coverage amongst the poor, and they are not as well targeted as they could be. This points to revising the *ficha* CAS and using it to better target the poor and to limiting access by the middle class. In particular, special attention should be paid to expanding access of the poor to family allowances and child care, and pension assistance for the elderly poor. More effort might be made to redirect water subsidies and some housing programs. While there is undoubtedly benefit in terms income distribution for having less restrictive access, this does present a contradiction if at the same time the poor do not have access.

This also points to addressing some of the other problems of access, notably, the lack of information on programs, especially those administered by the central level, and the administrative capacities at the municipal level, especially for these agencies to take a more pro-active stance to seek out eligible beneficiaries. It may also entail a more careful analysis of demand driven programs which do not adequately taken into account regional and poverty differences and points to distribution of central funding with greater redistribution in mind.

Indigenous people represent a unique challenge for Chile and the pronounced lags in social and economic progress should not be overshadowed by the present conflicts. These groups exhibit high rates of poverty, and have not benefited as much from conditions of general prosperity. While most indigenous people have become urban dwellers, serious conflicts exist over questions of access to land, land titling and access to water in rural areas. Moreover, the possibilities of pursuing subsistence agriculture are more limited day by day. At the same time, social exclusion, discrimination in the labor force and in schools, and area stigma are likely to be even more pronounced for indigenous groups than others. The lack of a coherent national understanding of the status and recognition of indigenous people among Chileans at large seems to be one of the largest barriers for these groups to secure their place in society.

REFERENCES

Aldaz-Carroll, Enrique and Ricardo Moran. (Forthcoming). "Family Factors in the Intergenerational Transmission of Poverty: Empirical Results and Policy Implications for Latin America." *Cuadernos de Economía.*

Beyer, Harald. 1997. "Distribucion de Ingreso: Antecedentes para la Discusión." *Estudios Publicos* 65. Centro de Estudios Publicos (CEP), Santiago.

Bravo, David, and Dante Contreras. 1998. "Is There Any Relationship Between Minimum Wage and Employment? Empirical Evidence Using Natural Experiments in a Developing Country." University of Chile, Economics Dept.

Central Bank of Chile. 2001. *Indicadores Economicos.* www.bcentral.cl.

Clert, C. 2000a. "Social Exclusion, Gender and the Chilean Government's Anti-Poverty Strategy: Priorities and Methods in Question." In E. Gacitua Mario and C. Sojo, Editors, *Social Exclusion and Poverty Reduction in Latin America.* Washington, DC: World Bank and FLACSO.

Clert, C., (2000b), *Policy Implications of a Social Exclusion Perspective in Chile: Priorities, Discourse and Methods in Question,* Ph.D. thesis, London School of Economics, London

Dar, A., and I. S. Gill, 1998, "On Evaluating Retraining Programs in OECD Countries", *World Bank Research Observer,* 13:79–101

De Gregorio Jose and K. Cowan (1996), "Distrubución de Ingreso en Chile: Estamos Mal? Ha Habido Progreso? Hemos Retrocedido?", *Estudios Publicos* No 64 (CEP), Santiago

De Ferranti, D., G. Perry , I. Gill and L. Servén (2000), *Securing Our Future in a Global Economy.* Viewpoints: World Bank Latin American and Caribbean Studies. Washington, DC: World Bank

Ferreira, Francisco H. G. and Julie A. Litchfield (1999), "Calm After Storms: Income Distribution in Chile, 1987–1994", *World Bank Economic Review*

Gonzalez, Jose Antonio (1999), *Labor Market Flexibility in 13 Latin American Countries and the U.S.,* World Bank Latin American Viewpoints Series, Washington DC: World Bank.

Heckman, James and Carmen Pages (Forthcoming), "The Cost of Job Security Regulation: Evidence from Latin American Labor Markets". *Economía.*

International Labour Office (1999). *Decent Work and Protection for All: Priority of the Americas,* Report of the Director-General, Fourteenth Regional Meeting of ILO American Member States, Lima, Peru, Geneva: ILO.

Feldstein, M. and D. Altman (1998). "Unemployment Insurance Savings Accounts." *NBER Working Paper* 6860. Cambridge, Mass: NBER

Londoño, Juan Luis and Miguel Székely. 1997 "Persistent Poverty and Excess Inequality: Latin America, 1970-1995." Washington, DC: Inter-American Development Bank, Working Paper Series, No. 357.

Lopex, Ramon. 1997 "The Regional Dimension of Poverty." Annex 3 in World Bank, *Chile: Poverty and Income Distribution in a High-Growth Economy, 1987-95,* Vol. II. Washington, DC., Report No. 16377-CH.

Maloney, William (2000), "A Note on Minimum Wages in Latin America." World Bank, Wash. D.C., (unpublished).

MIDEPLAN (1996), "Pobreza y Distribución de Ingreso en Chile – Resultados de la Encuesta de Caracterizacion Socioeconómica Nacional (CASEN)." Julio, Santiago.

MIDEPLAN (1996), "Realidad Economica-Social de los Hogares de Chile: Algunos Indicadores Relevantes de las Encuestas CASEN 1992 y 1994", Julio, Santiago.

Orszag, J. and D. Snower.(1997) "From Unemployment Benefits to Unemployment Accounts". Birkbech College, London. (unpublished).

Pages, Carmen and C. Montenegro (1999)."Job Security and the Age-Composition of Employment: The Evidence from Chile" (unpublished).

Scholnick, Mariana (1996), "Estudio de la Incidencia Presupuestaria: el Caso de Chile", Serie Regional de Política Fiscal No 83, CEPAL-PNUD, Santiago.

Wodon, Q. et. al.(2000) *Poverty and Policy in Latin America and the Caribbean,* World Bank Technical Paper No. 467, World Bank, Wash. D.C.

World Bank (1997), *Chile: Poverty and Income Distribution in a High- Growth Economy – 1987-1995,* Report No 16377-CH, November 25, Washington DC.

World Bank (2000), *World Development Report 2000/2001: Attacking Poverty.* New York: Oxford University Press.

PART II: BACKGROUND PAPERS

Background Paper 1

UPDATED INCOME DISTRIBUTION AND POVERTY
MEASURES FOR CHILE: 1987-98[39]
Julie Litchfield

Introduction

The aim of this chapter of the report is to provide a comprehensive picture of the levels and trends in income inequality and poverty in Chile during the period 1987 to 1998. It uses six household survey micro-data sets – the Caracterización Socioeconómica Nacional (CASEN) for the years 1987, 1990, 1992, 1994, 1996 and 1998 – and applies a range of statistical techniques to estimate levels of and changes in income, income inequality and poverty over this period.

Concepts

As in the original report, three key concepts are used here: welfare, poverty and inequality. Although these concepts are frequently used interchangeably to describe well-being and living standards, we are interested in three very precise definitions that avoid the possibility of misunderstanding and misinterpretation. Welfare is perhaps the broadest of the three concepts, capturing the level of well-being of an individual, household or society, and is often proxied for by the level of income or consumption. Broader interpretations are possible, and desirable,[40] but data availability and data reliability usually constrains the choice to simply income or consumption. In the absence of a frequent or regular survey on household expenditures, this study, and its predecessor, uses income as the indicator of welfare. To be more precise, this study uses two definitions of income, firstly total household income per equivalent adult and secondly total household income per capita, both of which are defined in section 3 below.[41]

Most other studies of inequality and poverty in Chile, and elsewhere in Latin America, adopt total household income per household as the welfare indicator: this may be less demanding of data, as it does not require any information on the household size and composition but it does create at least two limitations to interpretation of the results. Firstly, poorer households tend to be larger than richer households, comprised of more children and/or more dependent adults (the

---

[39] This report is an update of an earlier report on income distribution and poverty in Chile covering the period 1987-1994 and written by Francisco Ferreira and Julie Litchfield for the World Bank (World Bank, 1997). This update relies heavily on the methodology and results of the earlier study and owes much to the original co-author.
[40] The ideal concept is some measure of an individuals life-time purchasing power, or permanent income, which may also include an imputed value for leisure (Becker, 1965) and/or an imputed value for the benefit of public goods (Sen, 1981).
[41] The estimates of income inequality, welfare and poverty using total household income per equivalent adult are presented in the body of the report, while those for the second, per capita concept, are presented in the appendix to this report.

elderly or infirm) than richer households, so that poorer decile groups have larger shares of the total population than richer decile groups and that poverty headcounts, for example, give no clear indication of the proportion of the *population* that are poor. Secondly, using an distribution of income among individuals (equivalised adults or per capita) allows us to compare results from household surveys, such as the CASEN, with those of national accounts data where income estimates are computed for the distribution of individuals rather than households.

The second concept used in this study is poverty and is related to the welfare concept, although in a negative sense. That is, a rise in welfare will, all other things being equal, be associated with a fall in poverty. Poverty measures are defined over a censored distribution and hence measure the welfare of individuals below a certain threshold or poverty line.[42] The poverty lines used in this study are described in section 4 below. We restrict our poverty measures to members of the Foster, Greer and Thorbecke class, P_a, which contains the three commonest poverty measures, defined in general terms as:

$$(1) \qquad P_\alpha = \frac{1}{N} \sum_{i=1}^{k} \left[\frac{z - y_i}{z} \right]^\alpha$$

where Y_i is the income of the ith poor individual (of which there are k), z is the poverty line and N is the total number of individuals in the population (Foster et al., 1984). The interpretation of these measures is as follows. When *a=0*, the expression simplifies to *k/N*, i.e. the headcount index, which gives the proportion of the population that is poor, i.e. the *incidence* of poverty. When *a=1*, we have the poverty gap, the average gap of the poor from the poverty line, expressed as a proportion of the poverty line, which indicates the depth or *intensity* of poverty. When *a=2*, we have the FGT(2) or P_2 measure, which is the average *squared* poverty gap, and so incorporates to some extent the *inequality* of incomes below the poverty line. Different poverty lines may suggest different rankings of distributions, so rather than relying solely on aggregate poverty estimates we also use poverty dominance techniques to test the robustness of our aggregate trends to the level of the poverty line.[43]

Inequality, the third concept, is similar to the welfare concept in that it is defined over complete distributions, rather than censored distributions, but it is independent of the mean (location) of the distribution, being defined in terms of the second moment of distributions. Two distributions may represent two different levels of welfare if one distribution represents a country say with much higher incomes, but they may have identical levels of inequality if the incomes are distributed among the population of each country in the same way.[44] The level of inequality will clearly depend on the distribution of incomes but also on the particular measure of inequality used. Different measures display different levels of sensitivity to gaps between incomes at different parts of the distribution. We will present inequality estimates using the Gini coefficient

---

[42] One desirable property of poverty measures is that they satisfy the focus axiom, that is they are invariant to any change in incomes above the poverty line (Atkinson, 1987). All the measures used in this study have this property.

[43] See section 5 for further details of this technique.

[44] Our choice of inequality measures, like our poverty measures, are restricted to those that have a number of desirable properties, notably the Pigou-Dalton transfer principle, which demands that the measure rise (or at least not fall) in response to a mean preserving spread, i.e. an income transfer from a poorer to a richer person.

(the most widely used inequality measure, and most sensitive to incomes in the middle of the distribution) and three members of the Generalized Entropy class, defined as:

$$(2) \qquad E(\alpha) = \frac{1}{\alpha^2 - \alpha}\left[\frac{1}{N}\sum_{i=1}^{N}\left(\frac{y_i}{\bar{y}}\right)^{\alpha} - 1\right]$$

where y_i is the income of individual i, $\bar{y}$ is mean income and N is the total number of individuals in the population. If a=0, we can apply l'Hopital's rule to obtain E(0) the mean log deviation:

$$(3) \qquad E(0) = \frac{1}{N}\sum_{i=1}^{N}\log\left[\frac{\bar{y}}{y_i}\right]$$

which is most sensitive to distances between incomes at the bottom of the distribution, Setting produces E(1), the Theil index:

$$(4) \qquad E(1) = \frac{1}{N}\sum_{i=1}^{N}\frac{y_i}{\bar{y}}\log\left[\frac{y_i}{\bar{y}}\right]$$

which has constant sensitivity across the income distribution. Finally, if a=2, we derive the E(2), equal to half the squared coefficient of variation:

$$(5) \qquad E(2) = \frac{1}{2N\bar{y}^2}\sum_{i=1}^{N}(y_i - \bar{y})^2$$

which is most sensitive to distances between incomes at the top of the distribution. Different inequality measures may therefore rank distributions in different ways depending on their sensitivity to distances between incomes at different parts of the distribution: we will therefore supplement the aggregate measures with tests of stochastic dominance, described below in section 4.

We can conceptualize social welfare as a separable function of the mean of the distribution (the average income level) and of inequality: $W=W[\bar{y}, I(y)]$, where W is increasing in the first argument, $\bar{y}$, and decreasing in the second, I(y). This leads to three relationships: 1) if inequality is constant, increases in mean income (i.e. economic growth) will lead to increases in social welfare; 2) if mean income is constant and inequality rises (falls), then welfare will fall (rise) and poverty rise (fall), and 3) increases (decreases) in inequality may be compatible with increases (decreases) in welfare if there is sufficient growth (contraction) in mean income. These are the patterns that will be examined in this study.

This report is structured as follows. Section 3 provides a brief description of the data sets used in the analysis, and describes the methodology used in our derivation of the two welfare indicators, income per equivalised adult and income per capita. Section 4 presents and discusses the results on inequality and social welfare, using scalar measures of inequality, decile means and shares and stochastic dominance. Section 5 presents and discusses the set of poverty lines and poverty estimates, as well as testing for robustness of conclusions to the choice of poverty line. Section 6 presents and discusses the evolution of inequality and poverty at a slightly less aggregate level by examining urban and rural inequality and poverty estimates. Section 6 concludes.

Data and Methodology

The analysis reported in this chapter is based on the micro-data sets of the CASEN household surveys for 1987, 1990, 1992, 1994, 1996 and 1998. The CASEN is a nationally and regionally representative household survey carried out by MIDEPLAN through the Department of Economics at the Universidad de Chile, with the dual objectives of generating a reliable portrait of socio-economic conditions across the country and of monitoring the incidence and effectiveness of the government's social programs and expenditures. Questions are asked pertaining to both the household and the individuals within the household, on topics ranging from demographics, characteristics of the dwelling, access to utilities and public services, educational attainment (and if currently enrolled, on the type of school, fee payments, benefits received etc), health conditions, insurance, receipt of health benefits and use of health services, occupations and employment, to incomes from a wide range of sources. The income questions are designed to permit the distinction between labor incomes in cash and in kind (agricultural and non-agricultural), income from capital, rental income, imputed rent, employment related transfers (occupational, invalidity and widow's pensions) and entitlement transfers (such as the basic pension PASIS and the family allowance SUF).

The sampling methodology can be described as multi-stage random sampling with geographical stratification and clustering. The country was first divided into strata comprising the rural and urban sectors of each of the 13 regions.[45] The rural sectors were final level strata. The urban sectors were further divided into three categories of towns, according to population: 2,000 to 9,999 inhabitants, 10,000 to 39,999 inhabitants and those with 40,000 or more. All of the latter were sampled (i.e. they were final level strata). For the other towns there was a level of clustering in the selection of towns sampling. At this level, selected smaller towns, all the larger towns and all the rural areas, a first stage samples primary units (*zonas de empadronamiento*), with probabilities proportional to population. A second stage samples households within these primary units[46]. The sample sizes for our analysis are shown in Table 1 below.[47]

Table 1: Sample Sizes: Households and Individuals

	1987	1990	1992	1994	1996	1998
Households	23,034	26,248	36,587	45,993	33,964	48,588
Individuals	97,044	105,189	143,459	178,057	134,262	188,360

Source: Author's calculations from CASEN 1987-1998.

Once each survey was completed, the data was then handed on to CEPAL (The United Nations Economic Commission for Latin America and the Caribbean), which conducted two types of

---

[45] In the CASEN surveys for 1987 through to 1994, an urban area was any grouping of dwellings with a population in excess of 2000. For 1996 and 1998, urban areas were redefined slightly as any grouping of dwellings with a population in excess of 2000 OR with a population of between 1001 and 2000 where at least 50% of the economically active population were employed in secondary or tertiary activities (MIDEPLAN, 1999). This break in methodology means that the results from 1987-1994 may not be strictly comparable with those of 1996 and 1998.
[46] See MIDEPLAN, 1992, for full details.
[47] These sample sizes are slightly larger than those reported in the official MIDEPLAN records, reflecting our treatment of live-in domestic servants as separate households.

adjustments to the raw figures. The first type comprises corrections for non-response, which are made in three instances: when people who declare themselves employed report no income from their main occupation; when people who state that they receive an occupational or widow's pension do not report a value for this benefit; or when owner-occupiers of their dwellings do not report a value for imputed rent. In all three cases, missing income values are replaced by the average value of the specific income variable in the household group to which the household belongs, where the group is defined by a partition according to a number of variables, including region, gender of head, educational attainment of head, occupational sector and category.[48]

The second type of adjustment seeks to correct for under- (or over-) reporting of different income categories, a common problem with household income surveys everywhere. For this purpose CEPAL uses as the reference point for aggregate income flows the Household Incomes and Expenditures Account of the National Accounts System (SCN) of the Central Bank of Chile. First, a careful process is undertaken to convert the information in the original Central Bank accounts to the income concepts survey by CASEN. Once that is achieved, totals by specific income category are compared for CASEN (with recourse to the appropriate expansion weights) and the National Accounts.

Finally, the proportional differences for each income category between the two sources are imputed uniformly to each income recipient in CASEN, with two notable exceptions: the adjustment in capital incomes is applied only to the top quintile (of households), proportionately to the primary incomes (*ingresos autonomous*) of all recipients there; and incomes from entitlement transfers and gifts are not adjusted.[49] The underlying assumption justifying this procedure is that mis-reporting differs fundamentally across income categories, rather than income levels[50]. In fact, the imputation would be strictly correct only if the income-elasticity of reporting within each income category was unitary. The only exception to this assumption, as noted, was in the treatment of capital incomes, which were imputed proportionately, but exclusively within the richest 20% of households.[51]

We have also made some adjustments to the data set, after it was processed by CEPAL. The income variable from the CASEN records on which our analysis is primarily based is total adjusted household income per month (labeled YTOTHAJ in the CASEN micro-datasets), which includes all primary incomes, monetary transfers[52] and gifts, as well as imputed rent, after the CEPAL adjustments. It was from this variable that we constructed our income concept—household income per equivalent adult—by appropriate choice of denominator. Our first adjustment was in the treatment of live-in domestic servants. It is unclear how previous studies treated them, since YTOTHAJ is defined to exclude their incomes. Household-based studies are

---

[48] See Appendix 1 to CEPAL, 1995, for full details.

[49] It is suggested that the main reason for not adjusting these is that under-reporting of transfers consists mostly of complete omissions of benefits by some households rather than proportional under-reporting of values by all recipients. There being no way to identify the omiters, no adjustment was found which would have improved the picture obtained from the survey.

[50] It may be interesting to note that the proportional adjustments did vary substantially across income categories. In fact, imputed rents were consistently found to be over-reported, and were adjusted downward in every survey.

[51] See CEPAL (1995) for full details.

[52] We believe that the questionnaire coverage of monetary transfers from the State, whether at the federal or municipal level, is exhaustive. Questions are asked and amounts are registered for the following benefits: *Asignaciones Familiares*, PASIS, SUF, *Subsidio al Consumo de Agua Potable* and *Subsidio de Cesantia*. See MIDEPLAN (1996) for a description of each of these benefits. Others associated with formal employment, such as *jubilaciones, pensiones de invalidez* and *montepios* are also included, although they are aggregated as part of primary, rather than secondary incomes.

likely to have unwittingly excluded them from the sample altogether, by simply imputing YTOTHAJ to the household. For this report, like the earlier report, in households with live-in domestic servants, all other members received YTOTHAJ divided by the equivalence scale defined over them, while the servants were treated as a separate household, whose income was the sum of total adjusted individual incomes (YTOTAJ) over them.

The second adjustment was to exclude from the analysis the three richest households in the 1994 sample only. This decision was carefully considered, and was based on the impression that these households reported sufficiently disproportionate incomes to be regarded as genuine outliers.[53] This impression was reinforced by the fact that two of these households were identical in every respect, having clearly been double-sampled,[54] and by the position of the three households as outliers in a plot of the Pareto distribution of the top 1% of the sample.

The third adjustment was to deflate all household incomes by a regional price index, with Santiago as the base location. Traditionally, nominal incomes have only been deflated by a common national consumer price index, taking no account of regional variations in price levels, which, as Table 2 indicates, can in some cases be considerable. This is reinforced by Chile's geography, with extreme southern and northern regions having substantially higher average prices than those closer to Santiago. Our regional price deflation is based on the only source of prices outside Santiago, the National Statistical Institute's (INE) *Anuario de Precios* survey of 16 cities.[55]

Given the variation in price levels from year to year, we used an average of the index from 1985 to 1994; the values are given in Table 2. Regionally adjusted incomes were then deflated over time by the national consumer price index for November (the survey month) of the relevant years. All income values reported in this paper are expressed in 1998 Santiago pesos.

Table 2: Regional Prices

Region	I	II	III	IV	V	VI	VII	VIII	IX	X	XI	XII	RM
Price Index	1.22	1.17	1.11	1.09	1.04	1.03	1.01	1.04	1.05	1.04	1.09	1.22	1.00

The final adjustment was to introduce the concept of household income per equivalent adult, through the adoption of an equivalence scale. This was done to capture the changes in measured inequality and poverty which arise out of taking into account the differences in needs between households with different compositions (e.g. four adults as opposed to a couple with two small children), as well as economies of scale which arise from sharing fixed housing or other costs. There are a number of different approaches to deriving an equivalence scale, and there is no accepted dominant method. Rather than attaching excessive importance to the specific values of our chosen coefficients, we sought to provide a reasonably reliable alternative to the per capita

---

[53] The value of E(2) - see below - when the outliers are included, is 6.58 in 1994. Its range over the other years is from 1.39 to 1.74.

[54] The practice of imputing all values from one household (randomly selected within the cluster) to another, when the latter has failed to respond, is often adopted as a way of maintaining representativeness within a small cluster. When the 'doubled' household are the Rockefellers, the practice requires revision.

[55] There are no systematic surveys of prices in rural areas anywhere in Chile. Though in the past rural prices have been assumed to be lower than in urban areas, we have found no justification for this arbitrary mark-down, and generalized urban prices to the whole region.

income concept, which is well known to constitute an extreme assumption in terms of differences in needs, as well as in terms of economies of scale.

Our chosen scale is a revised version of the equivalence scale for Chile, calculated by Contreras (1995), using the Rothbarth adult goods method. Contreras' scale was estimated excluding all households with a single adult from the sample, and taking two-adult households as the reference type. Since we must also cover those households made up by a single individual, and in order to take into account some economies of scale within the household, we assume the cost of a single person to be 60% of that of a couple (roughly equivalent to saying that the second adult costs 70% of the cost of the first adult).[56] Our equivalence scale is therefore:

$$Y_i = X_i / M_i, \text{ with } M_i = 1.2 + 0.8 \, (N_{aa} + N_{11\text{-}15}) + 0.4 \, N_{5\text{-}10} + 0.3 \, N_{0\text{-}4}$$

where: N_{aa} is the number of additional adults in the household; $N_{11\text{-}15}$ is the number of children aged 11-15 (inc.) in the household; $N_{5\text{-}10}$ is the number of children aged 5-10 (inc.) in the household; $N_{0\text{-}4}$ is the number of children aged 0-4 (inc.) in the household.

Note that this maintains households with two adults as the reference group. Their household income will be divided by two. An additional child in the 11-15 age category 'costs' an extra 40%. An additional child in the 5-10 category costs an extra 20%. An additional child in the 0-4 age category costs an extra 15%. The second adult costs 70% of the first (or 40% of the couple's total cost).

By introducing the equivalence scale and the regional price adjustments directly on to the income concepts to be analyzed, consistency is ensured in the assumptions applying to the inequality and the poverty analyses. Also, since all incomes are effectively expressed in 1998 Santiago pesos, there will be no need for regional poverty lines. Lines expressed in 1998 Santiago pesos will be the appropriate comparators for all incomes. Similarly, there will be no need for poverty lines for different household types; it will suffice to compare the household incomes per equivalent adult with an individual adult poverty line.[57] The advantage of this approach over introducing those concepts through different poverty lines, in addition to simplicity, is that the inequality analysis would not then - as it does now - incorporate regional price and equivalence scale adjustments.

Welfare and Income Distribution, 1987-98

This section presents and discusses the analysis of the evolution of income inequality and welfare during the decade or so between 1987 and 1998. It is useful to summarize here the broad findings of this section and then proceed to discuss each in turn.

- Firstly, the entire income distribution shifts to the right over time. This was established in the earlier report for the years 1987 through 1994, and continues beyond that through 1996 and 1998, as a result of economic growth. This means that individuals at each part of the income distribution generally receive more incomes each year. There are some exceptions to this general finding, to which we return below.

---

[56] This is a common assumption, adopted for instance in the construction of the OECD equivalence scale (see OECD, 1982).
[57] Though the absolute values of the poverty measures will, of course, depend on the household reference type chosen in defining the scale.

- The second key finding is that while the dispersion of the distribution appears to have been broadly stable over the period as a whole, the year-on-year changes are different, with some improvements during the first years, 1987-1992 but an upward trend in inequality in the latter part of the series, 1994 to 1998. This suggests that the benefits of economic growth over the period as a whole have been distributed in a pattern similar to that of the original 1987 income distribution, i.e. that economic growth for 1987-1998 has been roughly distributionally neutral, neither reducing nor increasing inequality. While we can at least conclude that economic growth over the period as a whole has done nothing to exacerbate inequality (vis-à-vis the level in 1987), it is perhaps disappointing that the benefits accrued by the relatively poor in terms of increasing shares in income of high growth in the period leading up to 1992 have been subsequently eroded.
- Thirdly, the shape of the distribution has changed. Again, in contrast to the trend emerging for the period 1987 to 1994, when the small changes in the shape of the distribution appear to consist of a slight compression in the lower tail and a slight increase in dispersion in the upper tail,[58] the trend for 1994 to 1998 appears to suggest an increase in dispersion in both the lower and upper tails of the distribution. This is cause for some concern: these latest results suggest that inequality is increasing not only among the rich, but also among poorer segments of the population. However, these increases in inequality must be interpreted within the context of improving living standards across the distribution.

This picture of the evolution of inequality and welfare is robust to the income concept used. We present the results for household income per equivalised adult here, and include those for per capita household income in the appendix. Table 3 below shows the evolution of mean and median incomes, as well as four scalar measures of inequality, defined above in section 2.

Table 3: Descriptive Statistics: Household Incomes per Equivalent Adult

	1987	1990	1992	1994	1996	1998
Mean	84,628	94,414	114,290	118,298	133,476	149,289
Median	45,648	53,440	63,204	66,960	74,043	81,809
Gini	0.5468	0.5322	0.5362	0.5298	0.5409	0.5465
E(0)	0.5266	0.4945	0.4891	0.4846	0.5139	0.5265
E(1)	0.6053	0.5842	0.6151	0.5858	0.6058	0.6264
E(2)	1.3007	1.3992	1.505	1.5634	1.4123	1.6172

Note: Incomes are monthly incomes and are expressed in 1998 pesos.
Source: author's own calculations from CASEN 1987-1998.

The sustained large rise in mean income over the period clearly reflects the impact of economic growth throughout the period, while the persistent differential between mean and median income indicates the extent of skew ness in the distribution. Mean incomes are approximately twice the level of median incomes in each year: fifty percent of the population receives incomes that are around only half or less of mean income.

---

[58] Between 1987 and 1994 inequality among the poor fell while among the very rich, and between them and those just poorer than them, appears to have increased.

The four measures of inequality confirm this highly unequal distribution[59] but also show that little is happening to the level of inequality for the period as a whole. The Gini coefficient changes very little over the period, with the 1987 and 1998 levels being very similar. However the Gini fell slightly between 1987 and 1994 but rose again to the 1987 level by 1998. These small changes between years and between the beginning and end years are unlikely to be statistically significant, a view borne out by the lack of Lorenz dominance between any pair of years (see below), with the exception of the increase in inequality between 1996 and 1998. E(0), the measure most sensitive to income gaps in the lower tail of the distribution, also falls between 1987 and 1994, but rises between 1994 and 1998, reaching the 1987 level. This is indicative of increasing dispersion in the lower tail of the distribution, a feature mentioned above and to which we return below.

E(1) behaved fairly erratically between 1987 and 1994, with no clear direction of change being discernible, but a clear increase between 1994 and 1998. Finally E(2) presents a picture of rising inequality throughout the period, with the exception of between 1994 and 1996 when it fell, before rising again in 1998. E(2) gives greater weight to gaps between incomes at the top of the distribution, so we can concluded that the upper tail was becoming more dispersed over time. Between 1994 and 1996, there appears to have been a slight compression at the very top: as we will see below, the very rich (the richest 1%) did not do quite so well in relative terms as the rich (the richest 10%).

Table 4 below presents mean equivalized incomes per decile group for each year and demonstrates the gains from growth that accrued between 1987 and 1998 (see the appendix for per capita income results). Average income of the whole distribution rose by almost 80% between 1987 and 1998, and each part of the distribution gained by broadly similar proportions, with slightly larger than average proportionate gains (around 80%) by the rich and slightly lower gains by the poor (around 70%). However all groups did experience increases in mean incomes over the period as a whole and for most of the year-on-year comparisons. This sustained rise in living standards was highlighted in the earlier report and is further confirmed by this update. There are two exceptions to this sustained increase in incomes for all decile.

Firstly, mean incomes for the lowest decile, the poorest 10% of the population, falls between 1992 and 1994 for both equivalized income and per capita income. This was in part due to the decline in the overall rate of GDP growth, which was 11.8% in the second semester of 1992, and 4.3% in the same period in 1994. This cyclical deceleration caused a rise in the overall unemployment rate from 4.8% to 6.26%, and unemployment among the poorest quintile (which includes the poorest decile) from 18% to 22% (Cowan and De Gregorio, 1996). Given the importance of labor incomes to poor households, the reduction in labor demand, especially for unskilled labor, is likely to have had a role in declining household incomes.

The second exception to the pattern of a sustained rise in mean incomes occurs, again between 1992 and 1994 and for both income concepts, for the very top of the income distribution. We observe a fall in average incomes for the richest one percent of the population, although the

---

[59] Inequality in Chile is high by international standards. The original report shows how Chile compared internationally: not only was Chilean inequality in the period 1987-1994 high relative to other regions (including sub-Saharan Africa) but was also higher than the Latin American and Caribbean average (see World Bank, 1997).

average of the top ten percent rises. This may be related, at least in part, to the economic slowdown, affecting not wages in this instance but income from capital.

Table 4: Mean Incomes per Decile: Household Incomes per Equivalent Adult

Decile	1987	1990	1992	1994	1996	1998
1	11374	13098	17385	16954	18629	19450
2	20398	24225	29726	30369	32560	35474
3	26793	31432	38627	39735	43327	47502
4	33610	39552	47506	49426	54321	60021
5	41308	48543	57607	60798	66817	73831
6	51105	59261	70402	74919	82341	91301
7	64809	74742	88322	93805	104067	116281
8	86628	98129	116097	124842	138543	154115
9	132936	146468	169423	186436	206154	231405
10	377276	408647	507791	506125	587924	663359
Top 1%	1017577	1166108	1563013	1486160	1695712	1973692

Note: Incomes are monthly incomes and are expressed in 1998 pesos.

Source: author's own calculations from CASEN 1987-1998.

If we focus entirely on income inequality, and abstract from the absolute gains made by each decile, we can examine the relative gains (and losses) over the period. Table 6 below shows income shares per decile group for equivalised household income (figures for per capita income appear in the appendix). The overall impression is once again of a fairly stable (mean-normalized) distribution for the period as a whole, with changes in shares being generally small in proportion to the shares themselves. The lowest two deciles (bottom twenty percent) appear to be relatively worse off in 1998 than they were in 1987, with slightly lower shares of total income, but the differences are small and not significant. Nevertheless, there is some evidence of the trend for a compression at the bottom and increased dispersion at the top, between 1987 and 1992.

Table 5: Income Shares per Decile: Household Incomes per Equivalent Adult

Decile	1987	1990	1992	1994	1996	1998
1	1.34	1.39	1.52	1.43	1.40	1.30
2	2.41	2.57	2.6	2.57	2.44	2.37
3	3.17	3.33	3.38	3.36	3.25	3.18
4	3.97	4.19	4.16	4.18	4.07	4.02
5	4.88	5.14	5.04	5.14	5.01	4.95
6	6.04	6.28	6.16	6.33	6.17	6.12
7	7.66	7.92	7.73	7.93	7.80	7.79
8	10.24	10.39	10.16	10.55	10.38	10.32
9	15.71	15.51	14.82	15.76	15.45	15.50
10	44.58	43.28	44.43	42.73	44.05	44.43
Top 1%	12.02	12.35	13.68	12.41	12.70	13.22

Source: Author's own calculations from CASEN 1987-1998.

For the first three years in the sample, decile shares for the bottom four deciles rise, while those for decile 9 fall. The top decile is trend less, but there is some indication that incomes at the very top are climbing faster than others, with the share of the richest 1% of the population rising over the period. Evidence for the later turnaround in the trend for the bottom of the distribution towards increased dispersion is found in the fall in the shares of the poorest four deciles between 1992 and 1998, and of those in the lowest eight deciles between 1994 and 1998.

Before developing this analysis to test whether any of these apparent changes are either unambiguous or significant, it is useful to summarize the key points. Table 7 below summarizes the winners and losers in absolute (i.e. real income) terms and relative (i.e. income share) terms. The first panel shows the positive impact of economic growth on all parts of the distribution, with the two exceptions noted above. The second panel presents a much less clear picture: some deciles gained in relative terms sometimes, but lost during others. The period of rapid growth between 1990 and 1992 had clear benefits for the poorest three deciles, through increased employment, but these were eroded somewhat during the slowdown after 1992.

Table 6: Winners and Losers: Decile Groups

		1987-90	1990-92	1992-94	1994-96	1996-98	1987-98
Absolute	Winners	1-10	1-10	2-9	1-10	1-10	1-10
	Losers			1,10			
Relative	Winners	1-9	1-3,10	5-9	10	9-10	3-9
	Losers	10	4-9	1-4,10	1-9	1-8	1-2,10

We now turn to assessing whether any of these changes in incomes and income shares are unambiguous (i.e. would be ranked consistently by a wide range of inequality measures) and/or statistically significant. We apply stochastic dominance to test the former, and a simple test for significance to test the latter. There are three types of dominance that can be applied to test for welfare changes, each embodying a different concept of social welfare function.

- First-order dominance requires examination of the cumulative distribution functions (c.d.f.) of each year. If the c.d.f. of year t lies nowhere above and at least somewhere below that of year t+i, then we can conclude that any social welfare function that is increasing in income (i.e. more income confers higher levels of social welfare) will rank year t above year t+i, i.e. year t first-order dominates year t+i (Saposnik, 1981). The intuition is simple: if first-order dominance of t over t+i holds, then there will be fewer individuals with incomes less than a given level of income in year t for any level of income. See Figure 1 in the Appendix.

- Second order dominance requires examination of the integral of the c.d.f., the deficit function for each year. If the deficit function for year t lies nowhere above and at least somewhere below that of year t+i, then we can conclude that any social welfare function that is increasing but concave in income so that there are diminishing returns to income, will rank year t above year t+i, i.e. year t second-order dominates year t+i (Shorrocks, 1983). See Figure 2 in the Appendix.

- Mean-normalized second order dominance requires examination of the Lorenz curves. If the Lorenz curve for year t lies nowhere below and at least somewhere above that of year t+i, then any inequality measure that satisfies the Pigou-Dalton transfer axiom will rank year t above year t+i (Atkinson, 1970). See Figure 3 in the Appendix.

Table 7 presents the results of this dominance analysis for each pair-wise comparison of years for both income concepts. The comparisons were carried out first at the percentile level of aggregation, and then checked for the completely disaggregated sample, with its statistical significance tested according to the endogenous bounds method of Howes (1993). A letter F, S, or L in cell (i, j) in Table 7 indicates that year i respectively first-order, second-order or Lorenz dominates year j. The letter was inserted when dominance was found at the percentile level. An asterisk indicates that the dominance was statistically significant at the 95% confidence level over a range greater than or equal to 99% in Howes's endogenous bounds test for the complete sample, and hence that the hypothesis of no population dominance can be rejected at that level.[60] An empty cell indicates that the curves crossed and so no dominance result could be established.

Table 7: Welfare and Inequality Dominance Comparisons

	1987	1990	1992	1994	1996	1998
1987						
1990						
1992	F*,S*	S*				
1994	F*,S*	F*,S* (L)				
1996	F*,S*	F*,S*	F*,S*	F*,S*		L*
1998	F*,S*	F*,S*	F*,S*	F*,S*		

Source: Author's own calculations from CASEN 1987-1998.

Two observations can immediately be made: first, there are a number of significant welfare dominance results below the diagonal, indicating that welfare rose unambiguously from some earlier to some later years. Second there are very few cases of Lorenz dominance, except first when comparing the per capita household income distribution between 1994 and 1990, which suggests a decline, but not a statistically significant one, in inequality[61] and second when comparing 1996 and 1998, when there was a statistically significant increase in inequality. The overall lack of significant Lorenz dominance suggests that inequality comparisons between the years in this period are not unambiguous, and will depend on the specific measure used. This confirms the results presented in Table 3.

The exception to this general absence of Lorenz dominance occurs between 1996 and 1998 when not only did the Lorenz curve for 1996 lie above that of 1998 but that the differences between the two curves were statistically significant. This means that inequality unambiguously rose between 1996 and 1998 and that most sensible measures of inequality would rank inequality in 1998 as being higher than in 1996. Note that that all four measures of inequality reported in Table 3 do indeed rank 1996 as having lower inequality than 1998, although the difference in the value of the Gini coefficient in particular is very small, rising from 0.5409 in 1996 to 0.5465 in 1998, that is, a rise of just over one percent.

Much more can be said in terms of the evolution of social welfare. Since our measure of welfare depends entirely on income, as discussed in the introduction, one would expect rapid economic growth to have a powerful impact. Nevertheless, the dominance results are interesting because they tell us something about the distribution of the gains from growth across households. Rapid growth between 1987 and 1990, for instance, was not sufficient to lead to unambiguous welfare gains, because the poorest one or two percent of the population were worse off in 1990. Gains above the second or third percentile meant that there was still a rise in the mean income of the first decile, as reported earlier in this section. The very disaggregated nature of dominance

---

[60] Statistical significance does not imply anything about the magnitude of the change in welfare between two years, only that we can conclude that the difference between two levels of welfare was not zero. Statistical significance depends not only on the estimates of the population parameter, but on the standard error of the estimate.
[61] The L in brackets for Lorenz dominance of 1994 over 1992 occurs only for the per capita income distribution, but is not statistically significant.

analysis allows us to capture finer changes. This loss to the very poorest people in Chile at the end of the last decade meant that welfare functions very sensitive to their circumstances would not have shown an increase in social welfare since 1987, despite the substantial increase in incomes elsewhere in the distribution.

Growth from 1990 to 1992 did not seem to have this perverse effect at the bottom of the distribution. Income rises across every percentile ensured that 1992 and 1994 both first-order dominate 1987. Both years also second-order dominate 1990.[62] 1994 and 1992, however, can not be ranked, whether by the first or second order criterion. This is due to a decline in incomes for those below the eighth or ninth percentile (which, on this occasion, was sufficient to lower the mean income of the first decile, as seen in Table 4 above), which co-existed with gains for all other social groups. This welfare loss to the very poor means that social welfare can not unambiguously be said to have risen over the last two years in our sample. The loss was not sufficient, however, to outweigh gains to those at the bottom of the distribution since 1990: 1994 does display first-order dominance over both 1987 and 1990.

The years 1996 and 1998 both dominate 1994 and all earlier years, illustrating the large increase in incomes during the period, but the two years themselves cannot be ranked, by either first or second order criteria, despite the apparent increases in incomes for all decile groups between 1996 and 1998 in Table 4. The c.d.f.s and the deficit functions both cross within the first decile: some very poor individuals (the poorest 2-3%) became worse off in real terms and this combined with their falling share in total income to create overall losses in welfare for these groups, although all other groups were better off in 1998 than in 1996.

These changes between 1996 and 1998 may appear rather alarming. We have found that inequality rose by all measures of inequality used in this paper, and that from the dominance analysis, all sensible measures of inequality would record a rise in inequality between the two years. We also find that real incomes of the very poorest 2-3% of the population fell between 1996 and 1998. However, we must remember that these small, subtle changes are happening at the very extreme tail of the distribution where income data is likely to be at its most unreliable. These specific results should therefore be treated with extreme caution.

To sum up, these dominance results add rigor to our earlier analysis, while broadly supporting its findings. The first fundamental feature of the period is economic growth, which led to welfare dominance of the later years over earlier years. On three occasions, however, economic growth failed to improve measured living standards for the most vulnerable people in society: from 1987 to 1990, from 1992 to 1994 and from 1996 to 1998. For those pairs of years, no such unambiguous welfare comparison is possible.

The second fundamental feature (the relative stability in the dispersion of the distribution, but with a slight compression at the bottom and a stretching at the top for the early years but increased dispersion in both tails during the last two years) is also compatible with the results on Lorenz dominance. The absence of significant Lorenz dominance results for the early part confirms the early trend and the statistically significant Lorenz dominance of 1996 over 1998 confirms the latest trend. The reduction of distances in one part of the distribution with

---

[62] 1992 does not first-order dominate 1990 because of a crossing above the 99th percentile. Except for the very rich, everyone (in an 'anonymous' sense) was better off in 1992 than in 1990.

simultaneous increases elsewhere is exactly what causes different inequality indices to rank distributions in opposite ways, as occurred for the period up to 1994, and hence the lack of any statistically significant Lorenz dominance. However the increased dispersion in both tails after 1994 lies behind the clear ranking of 1996 over 1998 on both scalar measures of inequality and the Lorenz dominance analysis.

The Evolution of Poverty, 1987-98

The high GDP growth rates achieved by Chile over much of the period have undeniably contributed to a considerable reduction in poverty from the relatively high levels of the mid-1980s. This section presents detailed results on the changes between 1987 and 1998, relying on our adjusted data set. Again we present results for household income per equivalent adult here, and include in the appendix those of per capita income. Though the general downward trend confirms previous findings (see, e.g. Larrañaga, 1994, Contreras, 1995, Mideplan, 1999), the numbers do reflect our adjustments, such as the incorporation of regional price differences, the new equivalence scale adopted and the improved treatment of domestic servants. Before presenting the specific results, we briefly discuss the derivation of the poverty lines, with respect to which all of the measures must be understood.

We use three poverty lines in this study, all of them expressed in 1998 Santiago pesos: an indigence line set at P$18,944 a lower-bound poverty line set at P$37,889, and an upper-bound poverty line equal to P$43,004[63]. All three lines are absolute poverty lines, and derive from a standard food basket specified by CEPAL. The basket is chosen so as to provide 2,187 Kcal per person per day, the national average caloric requirement, which is obtained from the demographic characteristics of the population and from the FAO/WHO recommended caloric intakes for different age and gender groups. The specific commodity composition of the basket is based on the actual consumption patterns of a reference group chosen by CEPAL, which is the third quintile by expenditures in the Household Expenditure Survey of 1987/88.[64]

The monthly cost of this standard CEPAL food basket has traditionally been used in Chile as an 'indigence' (or extreme poverty) line, separating the hard core of the poor - those whose current monthly incomes are insufficient even for the purchase of a minimum diet - from the rest of society. In 1998, this amount was P$18,944, which is therefore reported below as the indigence line. In accordance with international practice, however, that is deemed too strict a criterion to identify the poor. There are, after all, other basic expenditures in addition to food that everyone must make, such as shelter, clothing and public transport. A standard methodology is then applied to arrive at a sensible poverty line: the cost of the food basket is multiplied by the inverse of the food share in total expenditure (the Engel coefficient) for some suitable reference group. Based on the estimates of the Engel coefficient for the lower quintiles in the Chilean expenditure distribution, we decided to adopt the standard value of 0.5, which implies a doubling of the indigence line to arrive at the poverty line, P$37,889. As a final poverty line, we adopted a third

---

[63] The former two poverty lines are those used by MIDEPLAN, although they make (arbitrary) adjustments to the poverty lines to account for differences in urban and rural prices, while we adjust incomes to account for regional differences in prices.

[64] A 1997 expenditure survey data set is now available. Research is in progress to test whether the food share in total expenditure has remained stable, but for the purpose of comparison of the later CASEN surveys for 1996 and 1998 with results in the earlier report we have continued to use the Engel coefficients as reported above.

Engel coefficient of 0.44, based on the food expenditure share of the lowest two quintiles of the distribution of per capita income including imputed rent. Applying its inverse (2.27) to the cost of the food basket yields our upper-bound poverty line of P$43,004.

A general formula for the class of poverty measures used and a basic description of each index were provided in the introduction. Table 8 below lists the values of the headcount index, the poverty deficit and the FGT(2) index (P_a, a = 0,1,2) for the whole country, in each relevant year, for the distribution of household per equivalent adult incomes. Each index is listed for each of the three poverty lines discussed above. According to all three measures, there was undoubtedly a remarkable reduction in both poverty and extreme poverty from 1987 to 1998, in terms of incidence, depth and severity. Poverty in Chile was quite high in the mid-1980s in the aftermath of the serious recession of 1982-84. 41-47% of the population lived in poverty in 1987 (as measured by the lower and upper poverty lines, L and H) if one relies on the income per equivalent adult concept, which takes better account of household needs and economies of scale. By 1998, the figures were 17-21%. The incidence of indigence fell from 13% to just 4%. The reduction of the numbers of those in poverty from just under half of the population to around a fifth, as well as the substantial fall in the share of those in extreme poverty, are considerable achievements.

Table 8: Poverty Measures: Household Incomes per Equivalent Adult

	1987	1990	1992	1994	1996	1998
Indigence Line:	P$ 18,944					
Headcount	12.7	9.0	4.7	5.1	4.2	3.9
Poverty Deficit	4.1	3.1	1.7	2.0	1.5	1.5
FGT (2)	2.1	1.8	1.1	1.2	0.9	0.9
Poverty Line L:	P$ 37,889					
Headcount	40.0	33.1	24.2	23.1	19.9	17.0
Poverty Deficit	15.7	12.0	7.8	7.6	6.5	5.7
FGT (2)	8.2	6.1	3.8	3.8	3.2	2.9
Poverty Line H:	P$ 43,004					
Headcount	47.3	38.9	30.0	29.0	24.6	21.2
Poverty Deficit	19.1	14.8	10.1	9.8	8.4	7.3
FGT (2)	10.3	7.8	4.9	5.0	4.1	3.7

Source: Author's own calculations from CASEN 1987-1998.

Note: Incomes are monthly incomes and are expressed in 1998 pesos.

The uniform picture presented by all three poverty measures is reassuring. Not only did the proportion of people in poverty fall over the period, as shown by the dramatic reduction in the headcount, but the other two measures also fall substantially, regardless of the poverty line used. The poverty deficit and FGT(2) capture the distance below the poverty line of each poor individual: the fall in their values for all poverty lines indicates that the poor were on average closer to the poverty line, and there were fewer individuals very far below the poverty line, i.e. there were fewer poor in later years than in earlier years and those that were poor were less poor. The poverty deficit fell by two-thirds over the period as a whole, which ever poverty line is used: in 1987 the poor received an income of on average eighty percent of the poverty line H, but by 1998 this had risen to over ninety percent.

The value of FGT(2) is slightly harder to interpret in an intuitive sense as it measures the squared distance below the poverty line, so is in effect a weighted average where the weights are the squared gap: a value of 10.7 in 1987 for poverty line H (P$43004) suggests that the poor received an income of, on average (and weighted), seventy percent of the poverty line H, rising to eighty percent in 1998.[65]

In contrast to the fluctuating trend in inequality, demonstrated by the ambiguous movements in the scalar inequality measures in Table 3 and by the almost complete lack of Lorenz dominance between any pair of years, poverty has followed a downward trend for almost the entire period, with the exception of an increase between 1992 and 1994. One must recall that inequality and poverty are two distinct concepts: poverty is measured across a censored distribution, and therefore is insensitive to changes in incomes above the poverty line[66] while estimates of inequality will capture changes in incomes at all points of the distribution. The increases in dispersion in the upper tail throughout the period will have had no effect on poverty estimates but clearly will drive the inequality estimates, particularly $E(2)$, the measure most sensitive to the upper tail. The decrease in dispersion in the lower tail during the early years will however affect those estimates of poverty which take into account distances below the poverty line, i.e. the poverty gap and FGT(2), as demonstrated by the substantial fall in both these measures for all poverty lines between 1987 and 1992. The increase in dispersion in the lower tail picked up by the rise in inequality between 1996 and 1998 is reflected in the poverty measures, but is not enough to cause poverty to rise: in fact all measures for all lines continue to fall despite the rise in inequality.[67]

As others have pointed out before, the reductions were largest in the years of faster growth, from 1987 to 1992, and smallest in the relatively more sluggish years after 1992. However, the picture is more severe for the indigent poor between 1992 and 1994: in addition to increases in the Poverty Deficit and FGT(2), the indigence headcount also rises, suggesting that the number of those living in extreme poverty increased from 1992 to 1994, despite continued economic growth. Furthermore, FGT(2) also rises (marginally) for the other two poverty lines as well. After 1994 the poverty estimates all fall again, but at much slower rates than during the years of rapid growth.

The rise in poverty between 1992 and 1994 is a result of the decline in real incomes within the first decile of the income distribution, which was discussed in the previous section.

Clearly, the closer a poverty line is to that decile, the likelier it is to record an increase, whereas more generous lines still record declines as a result of income gains to people in the second and third deciles. But even for those lines, poverty measures which are more sensitive to large distances between incomes and the poverty line (i.e. that place greater weight on greater destitution) - such as FGT(2) - are liable to pick up the losses at the very bottom and have them outweigh gains closer to the upper poverty lines.

This picture of considerable reductions in poverty throughout the period, albeit with some ambiguity between 1992 and 1994, is confirmed by stochastic dominance analysis. It has been

---

[65] To see this simply manipulate the expression for the FGT class in section 2 above, insert the values z=43004, FGT(2) in 1987=0.103 and FGT(2) in 1998=0.037.

[66] The use of a set of absolute poverty lines prevents changes in incomes above the poverty line affecting the level of poverty for any of the measures used here.

[67] The figures in Table 8 are presented to 1 decimal place. In fact, the poverty gap for extreme poverty fell from 0.52 to 1.47 and the FGT(2) fell from 0.90 to 0.88 between 1996 and 1998.

shown that if a distribution A displays poverty mixed dominance ($PMD(z^-, z^+)$) over a distribution B, then any poverty measure which is decreasing in income, satisfies the focus axiom and the transfer axiom (in situations where a crossing of the poverty line does not occur), will indicate that poverty is lower in A than in B, for any poverty line between z^- and z^{+}.[68] This class of poverty measures includes all members of the Foster-Greer-Thorbecke P_α class, and is therefore particularly appropriate for this study. Poverty mixed dominance essentially requires that distribution A display second-order dominance over B from zero to the lower bound poverty line (z^-), and first-order dominance from z^- to z^+. Table 9 below, which is analogous to Table 7, presents the results for Chile, with z^- set at the indigence line and z^+ set at the upper-bound poverty line. The letter P in cell (i, j) indicates that year i dominates year j. As before, dominance was checked for both per capita income and income per equivalent adult; on this occasion both concepts yield the same results.

Table 9: Poverty (Mixed) Stochastic Dominance Comparisons

	1987	1990	1992	1994	1996	1998
1987						
1990						
1992	P	P				
1994	P	P				
1996	P	P	P	P		
1998	P	P	P	P		

Source: Author's own calculations from CASEN 1987-1998.

These results reveal that there was unambiguously less poverty in 1996 and 1998 than in all earlier years and less poverty in 1992 and in 1994 than in either 1987 or 1990, whether poverty is measured by the headcount, the poverty deficit or indeed any of a host of other sensible poverty measures, and for any poverty line set anywhere between the indigence line and upper bound poverty line. This sort of unambiguous poverty reduction, quite independent of the specific measure used and valid for such a large range of poverty lines, is not common. Its achievement confirms the widely held view that Chile has made substantial strides in the fight against poverty during the last decade.[69]

Yet, there is also confirmation of three sub-periods in which growth did not lead to unambiguous poverty reductions: from 1987 to 1990, from 1992 to 1994 and from 1996 to 1998. On each occasions, although the headcount for the headline poverty line indicates a reduction in the number of poor people, there were income losses in the lowest percentiles of the distribution. These losses imply that some poverty measures in the wide class defined above would have indicated increases in poverty for at least some of the poverty lines in the covered range. Indeed, in the second sub-period this was the case for all three indigence measures reported in Table 8. Still, the dominance of 1994, 1996 and 1998 over both 1987 and 1990 indicates that the losses to some of the poor in the later years were at least not sufficient to outweigh the gains made by them in the middle of the period.

---

[68] See Howes (1993) for a discussion, and Ferreira and Litchfield (1996) for an application to Brazil.

[69] All but one of the positive dominance results reported in the above table follow directly from the first order-dominances reported in Table 7. The table contains new information only for the cases where there was no dominance, as well as for the dominance of 1992 over 1990, the distribution functions of which clearly do not cross between z^- and z^+.

Overall, there is no question that Chile's growth and social policies[70] were tremendously successful in reducing the incidence, intensity and inequality of poverty between 1987 and 1998, with the proportion of those in poverty falling by between a half and two-thirds, the average poverty gap being cut by around two-thirds across all three poverty lines, and the severity of poverty falling by between one half and two-thirds, depending on the poverty line chosen.

Urban and Rural Inequalities, 1987-1998

Our analysis of poverty and inequality levels and trends now turns to a slightly more disaggregated examination of rural and urban differences. The original report did not include data at this level (although did at the regional level) so our analysis here is a new contribution. The same methodology as before is applied, i.e. we use the same two concepts of income, with the same adjustments made for regional price differences, live-in domestic servants etc. Note that unlike other studies of inequality and poverty, we have not applied any adjustments for urban and rural price differences. Our price adjustments are only at the regional level on the basis of clear differences being found in price data, shown in Table 2 above. Hence our estimates of rural poverty will appear higher than those from other studies where the rural poverty line is shifted down.

The usefulness of this slightly more disaggregated picture of urban and rural poverty and inequality is to provide some insight into the underlying changes in the income distribution vis-à-vis changes in urban and rural. We will focus on whether changes in overall poverty and inequality are accompanied by similar changes in urban and rural poverty and inequality. Several scenarios are possible: an increase in aggregate inequality (poverty) may be due to increases in both urban and rural inequality (poverty) or to offsetting changes in each sector. This last scenario is unlikely: given the small rural population share changes in rural poverty and inequality would have to be very large in order to offset changes in the opposite direction of urban poverty and inequality.

Table 10 presents four summary measures of inequality along with mean and median incomes and population shares. The final row of the table shows Rb: this is the proportion of total inequality that can be accounted for by differences between urban and rural areas. As expected the rural population forms a small and declining share of total population, from just under twenty percent in 1987 to just under fifteen percent in 1998, so rural changes in inequality will have to be very large in order to dominate urban changes. Both rural and urban areas experienced strong increases in mean incomes during the period 1987 to 1998, although incomes in urban areas rose proportionately by slightly more than rural incomes. This faster rate of growth of incomes in urban areas than in rural areas led a slight widening of the gap between urban and rural areas. Urban inequality levels follow much the same path as the overall trend, while rural inequality often moves in different directions. Only between 1996 and 1998 does rural inequality follow the same upward path as urban and overall inequality.

---

[70] Larrañaga (1994) has decomposed the changes in poverty in Chile between 1987 and 1992 into a growth and a redistribution component, using a methodology due to Datt and Ravallion (1992). While he found that some 80% of the reduction could be explained by the effects of growth, some of the changes were also due to a redistribution effect, which may very well have followed - at least in part - from the government's social policies and expenditures.

Finally, we can examine how much of total inequality is due to differences between the two sectors. The decomposition of E(0) yields a "within" inequality component equal to the population-share weighted sum of the levels of inequality within each sector, and a "between" inequality component equal to the population-share weighted sum of mean income differences. Since inequality is fairly high within each sector (rural and urban inequality levels are very similar to the overall level of inequality in each year), the within inequality component dominates: in fact differences in mean incomes between the urban and rural sectors account for less than 8 percent of overall inequality.[71]

Table 10: Urban and Rural Inequality: Household Income per Equivalent Adult

	1987	1990	1992	1994	1996	1998
			Urban			
Share	80.53%	81.45%	81.96%	83.46%	83.88%	85.43%
Mean	74,763	79,959	98,614	102,004	146,694	153,258
Median	41,065	46,317	55,237	59,225	82,404	83,153
Gini	0.5436	0.5207	0.5328	0.5229	0.5319	0.5507
E(0)	0.5241	0.4723	0.4816	0.4714	0.4939	0.5332
E(1)	0.5856	0.5477	0.5975	0.5647	0.5818	0.6323
E(2)	1.1771	1.2368	1.3926	1.4586	1.3215	1.5858
			Rural			
Share	19.47%	18.55%	18.04%	16.54%	16.12%	14.57%
Mean	36,086	53,257	55,275	53,508	64,694	69,815
Median	24,284	29,700	35,104	34,194	42,991	44,869
Gini	0.4521	0.5464	0.4837	0.4816	0.4692	0.4895
E(0)	0.3534	0.5303	0.4019	0.4006	0.3849	0.4237
E(1)	0.4868	0.7459	0.5847	0.5650	0.4986	0.6018
E(2)	1.8291	2.6180	2.1205	2.0709	1.2661	3.4177
R_b	6.78%	2.32%	4.47%	5.15%	7.32%	1.76%

Note: Incomes are monthly incomes in 1998 pesos.

Surce: Author's calculations from CASEN 1987-1998.

Table 11 below shows the evolution of urban and rural poverty between 1987 and 1998. As noted above, we use the same set of poverty lines for both urban and rural areas. Our estimates of rural poverty are therefore higher than those provided by Mideplan, where the poverty line L is deflated by a factor of between 0.60 and 0.67, depending on the survey year, and the extreme poverty line is deflated by a factor of 0.77 for rural areas (MIDEPLAN, 1999). We find this practice somewhat arbitrary as there is no systematic survey of rural prices in Chile and hence prefer to generalize urban prices to rural areas.

Rural poverty is much higher than urban poverty: estimates of the incidence of rural poverty are typically around twice the incidence of urban poverty, and the depth and severity of poverty is much greater in rural areas, with the rural poor being further below the poverty line than the urban poor in any given year. The gap between the urban and rural sectors appears to be widening too: in 1987 the incidence of extreme poverty in urban areas was half that of rural areas, while in 1998 it was only a third, and similar differentials exist for the other poverty lines.

---

[71] Other measures of inequality can be decomposed. The original report show the decomposition of total inequality by sector, region and a range of household characteristics.

Table 11: Urban and Rural Poverty: Household Incomes per Equivalent Adult

	1987	1990	1992	1994	1996	1998
Urban						
Indigence line : P$18,944 per month						
Headcount	10.6	7.3	4.0	4.1	3.0	3.1
Poverty Deficit	3.6	2.5	1.5	1.7	1.1	1.3
FGT(2)	1.9	1.4	1.0	1.1	0.7	0.8
Poverty Line L: P$37,889 per month						
Headcount	35.2	29.1	20.7	19.3	15.6	13.5
Poverty Deficit	13.4	10.2	6.5	6.3	4.8	4.5
FGT(2)	7.0	5.1	3.2	3.2	2.4	2.3
Poverty Line H: P$43,004 per month						
Headcount	41.6	34.8	26.0	24.3	19.7	17.3
Poverty Deficit	16.3	12.8	8.5	8.2	6.4	5.8
FGT(2)	8.8	6.6	4.2	4.1	3.1	2.9
Rural						
Indigence line: P$18,944 per month						
Headcount	21.2	16.1	8.3	10.2	10.3	9.1
Poverty Deficit	6.2	5.6	2.7	3.1	3.4	2.7
FGT(2)	2.9	3.1	1.4	1.6	1.7	1.3
Poverty Line L: P$37,889 per month						
Headcount	63.5	50.6	40.1	42.1	42.5	37.26
Poverty Deficit	25.3	19.7	13.4	14.2	15.0	12.6
FGT(2)	13.1	10.5	6.4	6.9	7.4	6.1
Poverty Line H: P$43,004 per month						
Headcount	70.5	56.9	48.2	50.0	50.0	44.0
Poverty Deficit	30.3	23.8	17.1	18.0	18.7	15.9
FGT(2)	16.4	13.0	8.4	9.0	9.6	7.9

Source: Author's own calculations from CASEN 1987-1998.

However the pattern of generally falling poverty at the national level is shared by both urban and rural areas, with each sector experiencing a dramatic reduction in poverty every year, by all measures and all poverty lines, with only two exceptions. Firstly, and not surprisingly given the small rise in national extreme poverty between 1992 and 1994, urban extreme poverty and rural poverty by all poverty lines rose, reflecting the overall slowdown in growth and rise in unemployment, particularly among the lower tail of the distribution. Secondly, between 1996 and 1998, extreme poverty among the urban population (but not rural) rose very slightly, which ties in with the fall in real incomes of those in the bottom 2-3% of the distribution. This suggests that the very bottom of the distribution in Chile in 1998 is not comprised of predominantly rural households, but in fact contains urban households, although as stressed earlier, caution must be exercised when drawing conclusions based on evidence from the very extreme upper or lower tails of the distribution.

As with the national level results, poverty reductions were greatest in the early years of higher growth, for both sectors, with both the rural and urban sectors experiencing substantial falls in the earlier years of the period covered.

Conclusions

This statistical analysis of poverty, inequality and welfare in Chile during the period 1987 through to 1998 has highlighted a number of interesting results. Some of these are confirmation of trends established in the earlier report covering the period 1987 to 1994, while other show that new patterns are emerging:

- The level of inequality appears to have been broadly stable over the period as a whole, with little change in some measures and slight increases in others, this picture masks a worrying trend of rising inequality since 1996. All scalar measures of inequality report increases between 1996 and 1998 and Lorenz dominance analysis shows that inequality is unambiguously higher (i.e. the Lorenz curves do not cross) in 1998 than in 1996. Between these two years there has been an increase in dispersion within both the top and bottom of the income distribution, as demonstrated by the rise in both $E(0)$ and $E(2)$, measures particularly sensitive to incomes in the lower and upper tails of the distribution respectively. It remains to be seen whether this is the beginning of an upward trend in inequality or a temporary diversion from a previously stable path.

- Economic growth has had a substantial beneficial effect on social welfare: our analysis shows that welfare was unambiguously higher in almost every later year compared to earlier years. However most of the gains accrued in the early years of very high growth: the slowdown in growth after 1992 were associated with initial real losses among the poorest eight or nine percent of the distribution in 1994, with gradual recovery and improvement by 1998.

- Over the period as a whole, economic growth has made a substantial contribution to reducing poverty. The trend of falling poverty, in terms of incidence, depth and severity, almost throughout the entire period 1987 to 1994 is continued through to 1998. The increase in extreme poverty between 1992 and 1994, which led to speculation about a trend to rising poverty, did not continue past the initial slowdown in economic growth, although the resumption of a downward trend in poverty occurred at a much slower rate than in earlier, high-growth years.

- Our adjustments to the CASEN data have caused our estimates of poverty and inequality to differ from those calculated in other studies. Some of our adjustments lead to higher estimates, namely our practice of not lowering rural poverty lines produces higher estimates of rural poverty than in other studies. Other adjustments lead our estimates to be lower: in particular, we find that adjusting household income by the size and composition of the household, rather than just household size, leads to lower estimates of national poverty and inequality. Household economies of scale are clearly an important factor that must be taken into account when analyzing poverty and inequality.

- Our examination of urban and rural poverty and inequality trends shows that the gap between the two sectors has widened very slightly over the period, although both sectors experienced substantial increases in real incomes and dramatic reductions in poverty.

REFERENCES

Atkinson, A.B. 1970. "On the Measurement of Inequality." *Journal of Economic Theory* 2: 244-263.

Atkinson, A.B. 1987: "On the Measurement of Poverty." *Econometrica* 55: 749-64.

Becker, G.S. 1965. "A Theory of the Allocation of Time." *Economic Journal.* 75: 493-517.

CEPAL 1995. "La Medición de los Ingresos en la Perspectiva de los Estudios de Pobreza: El caso de la Encuesta CASEN de Chile: 1987-1994." CEPAL Working Paper LC/R.1604.

Contreras, D. 1995. "Poverty, Inequality and Welfare in Chile: 1987-1992." Universidad de California, Los Angeles.

Cowan, K. and J. De Gregorio 1996. "Distribución y Pobreza en Chile: Estamos mal? Ha habido progresos? Hemos retrocedido?." Ministerio de Hacienda de Chile.

Datt, G. and M. Ravallion 1992. "Growth and Redistribution Components of Changes in Poverty Measures." *Journal of Development Economics.* 38: 275-295.

Ferreira, F.H.G. and J.A. Litchfield. 1996. "Growing Apart: Inequality and poverty trends in Brazil in the 1980s." LSE STICERD DARP Discussion Paper 23.

Foster, J.E., J. Greer and E. Thorbecke 1984. "A Class of Decomposable Poverty Indices." *Econometrica.* 52: 761-766.

Howes, S.R. 1993. *Income Distribution: Measurement, transition and analysis of urban China, 1981-1990*, Ph.D. dissertation, London School of Economics.

Larrañaga, O. 1994. "Pobreza, Crecimiento y Desigualdad: Chile, 1987-1992." *Revista de Análisis Económico*, 9 (2): 69-92.

MIDEPLAN 1992. *Población, Educación, Vivienda, Salud, Empleo y Pobreza: CASEN 1990.* Santiago: Ministerio de Planificación y Cooperación.

MIDEPLAN 1998. *Manual para el Trabajo de Campo: Encuesta de Caracterización Socioeconómica Nacional.* Santiago: Ministerio de Planificación y Cooperación.

MIDEPLAN 1999. *Resultados Encuesta CASEN 1998: Pobreza y distribución del ingreso en Chile, 1990-1998.* ((Santiago: Ministerio de Planificación y Cooperación).

OECD 1982. *The OECD List of Social Indicators.* Paris: OECD.

Saposnik, R. 1981. "Rank-Dominance in Income Distribution". *Public Choice*, 36: 147-151.

Sen, A.K. 1981. *Poverty and Famines: An Essay on Entitlement and Deprivation.* Oxford: Clarendon Press.

Shorrocks, A.F. 1983. "Ranking Income Distributions," *Economica.* 50:.3-17.

World Bank (1997): *Chile. Poverty and Income Distribution in a High-Growth Economy: 1987-1995.* World Bank Country Report No. 16377-CH.

APPENDIX 1

Results for Household Incomes Per Capita

This appendix contains the results on inequality and poverty using household income per capita, rather than household income per equivalised adult. The results are broadly the same as those for the equivalised income distribution, presented in the body of the report. One important difference is in the change in poverty between 1992 and 1994. The equivalised income distribution records an increase in poverty, while the per capita distribution records a fall in poverty. Giving less weight to children shifts these households with children up the distribution, leaving a greater concentration of adult only households: equivalised income-poverty rising between 1992 and 1994 suggests that these adult only households became poorer (or more of them were below the poverty line) between 1992 and 1994. If these poor, adult only households are younger, less skilled, less experienced, than say poor households with children, then this is consistent with the large rise in unemployment between during this time. The fact that per capita income shows a fall in poverty suggests that households with children were less affected by unemployment during this time.

Table A1: Descriptive Statistics: Household Incomes Per Capita

	1987	1990	1992	1994	1996	1998
Mean	69693	79669	94872	98535	110643	124658
Median	36690	42990	50825	54474	59257	66347
Gini	0.5603	0.5563	0.5534	0.5454	0.5548	0.5611
E(0)	0.5611	0.5495	0.5287	0.5212	0.5476	0.5623
E(1)	0.6349	0.6509	0.6551	0.6194	0.6365	0.6594
E(2)	1.3903	1.7447	1.668	1.7121	1.5727	1.7308

Note: Incomes are monthly incomes and are expressed in 1998 pesos.

Source: Author's own calculations from CASEN 1987-1998.

Table A2: Mean incomes per Decile: Household Incomes Per Capita

Decile	1987	1990	1992	1994	1996	1998
1	8404	9644	12799	12575	13860	14668
2	15271	18031	22287	22988	24735	27074
3	20540	24127	29687	30636	33552	37047
4	26281	30843	37054	39001	42756	47646
5	32886	38560	45808	48900	53498	59352
6	41385	48386	57408	61336	66829	74464
7	53372	61463	73057	77563	85985	95559
8	72266	81622	96562	104417	115524	129100
9	110766	123433	142036	157168	173257	196047
10	315736	360566	431963	430779	496409	565605
Top 1%	874015	1083691	1357173	1291700	1439766	1720497

Note: Incomes are monthly incomes and are expressed in 1998 pesos.

Source: Author's own calculations from CASEN 1987-1998.

Table A3: Income Shares per Decile: Household Incomes per Capita

Decile	1987	1990	1992	1994	1996	1998
1	1.21	1.21	1.35	1.28	1.25	1.18
2	2.19	2.26	2.35	2.33	2.24	2.17
3	2.95	3.03	3.13	3.11	3.03	2.97
4	3.77	3.87	3.91	3.96	3.86	3.82
5	4.72	4.84	4.83	4.96	4.84	4.76
6	5.94	6.07	6.05	6.22	6.04	5.97
7	7.66	7.71	7.70	7.91	7.77	7.67
8	10.37	10.25	10.18	10.60	10.44	10.36
9	15.89	15.49	14.97	15.95	15.66	15.73
10	45.30	45.26	45.63	43.66	44.87	45.37
Top 1%	12.54	13.60	14.31	12.94	13.01	13.80

Source: Author's own calculations from CASEN 1987-1998.

Table A4: Poverty Measures: Household Incomes Per Capita

	1987	1990	1992	1994	1996	1998
Indigence Line:	P$ 18,944					
Headcount	22.1	16.5	14.0	10.0	8.6	7.2
Poverty Deficit	7.6	5.6	3.3	3.4	2.7	2.5
FGT (2)	3.8	3.0	1.7	1.8	1.4	1.4
Poverty Line L:	P$ 37,889					
Headcount	51.4	44.3	36.0	33.9	29.9	25.9
Poverty Deficit	22.7	18.3	13.3	12.7	11.0	9.4
FGT (2)	13.0	10.2	6.8	6.6	5.6	4.9
Poverty Line H:	P$ 43,004					
Headcount	56.8	50.0	42.1	39.4	35.3	30.7
Poverty Deficit	26.5	21.8	16.4	15.5	13.5	11.7
FGT (2)	15.6	12.4	8.6	8.3	7.1	6.2

Note: Incomes are monthly incomes and are expressed in 1998 pesos.

Source: Author's own calculations from CASEN 1987-1998.

APPENDIX 2

Dominance illustrations

Figure 1 below illustrates first order dominance, by plotting the cumulative distribution functions for two hypothetical distributions. Distribution A displays 1st order dominance over distribution B if $F_A(y)$ smaller than or equal $F_B(y)$ for all y.

Figure 1: First Order Dominance

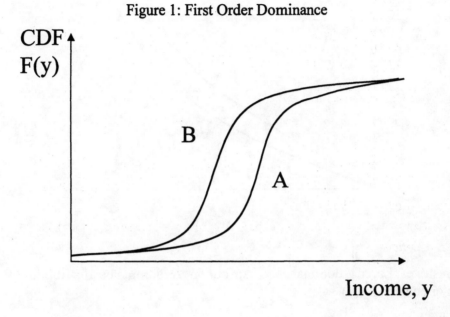

Figure 2 below shows second order dominance. Distribution A displays 2nd order dominance over distribution B if $D_A(y)$ smaller than or equal to $D_B(y)$ for all y.

Figure 2: Second Order Dominance

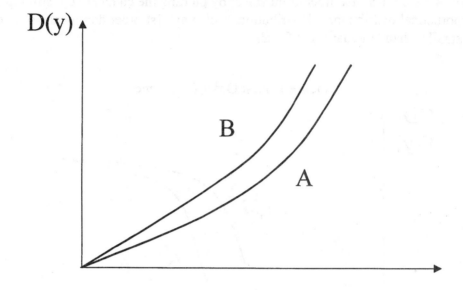

Figure 3 illustrates Lorenz dominance. Distribution A dominates distribution B if $L_B(y)$ is smaller than or equal to $L_A(y)$.

Figure 3: Second Order Mean-Normalized (Lorenz) Dominance

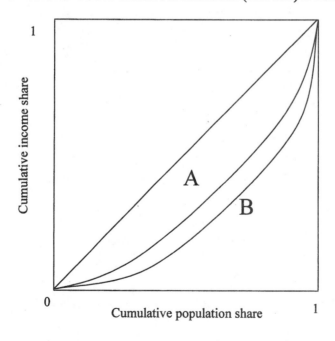

BACKGROUND PAPER 2

THE DISTRIBUTIONAL IMPACT
OF SOCIAL EXPENDITURE: CHILE 1990-98[†]

David Bravo, Dante Contreras, and Isabel Millán

Abstract

Chile has been characterized in recent years as an economy of rapid growth and unequal distribution of income. However, this diagnosis does not consider the effort of the public sector in terms of social policy. This study shows that these types of policies constitute an effective tool towards improving inequality in a context of rapid growth.

A methodology of valuation is set forth for subsidies in health, education and housing- as received by the members of Chilean households included in the National Socio-Economic Characterization Surveys (CASEN) carried out in November of 1990, 1994, 1996 and 1998. As opposed to prior studies, this methodology attributes to each household exclusively the subsidies in kind really received by its members during the period of analysis, as based on self-reporting. In this way, it is possible to derive conclusions regarding the short-run impact of health, education and housing policies on household income: the transfers received by each member permit the household to free up income for the consumption of other goods, or simply to access services that otherwise they would not have consumed. From this viewpoint, diverse measurements of inequality are performed based on income net of subsidies vs. corrected income (increased by monetary, health, education and housing subsidies, either sequentially and simultaneously) revealing the short term impact of the subsidies mentioned. The statistical significance of the change is estimated by means of the bootstrapping technique.

Application of this methodology makes it evident that social policy, implemented in the form of subsidies for health, housing and, especially, in education are key to improving distribution of income. The results show that the reduction in inequality at the national level is robust for the various indicators chosen, which is reflected in the fall of the Gini coefficient in 1998 from 0.56 to 0.50; and the ratio between the income of the richest quintile and the poorest changed from 20 to 11 times. However, the impact of social policy differs among regions of the country and its significance is sensitive to the indicator of distribution chosen.

[†] This paper has significantly benefited from comments and contributions made by Osvaldo Larrañaga. We are also grateful to Alberto Arenas, Edmundo Beteta, Harald Beyer, Pablo González, José De Gregorio, Patricio Mujica, Ricardo Paredes, Jaime Ruiz-Tagle V., Ricardo Sanhueza and Humberto Vega for comments. We would like to thank Ricardo Consiglio and Carlos Noton for research assistance and to the Fondo para el Estudio de las Políticas Públicas for financial support.

Introduction

In recent years, several studies have described the behavior of distribution of income in Chile based on differing methodologies. Accordingly, Chile has been characterized as an economy of rapid growth and unequal distribution of income.

Official figures presented by MIDEPLAN[72] (1999) reveal, based on the National Socio-Economic Characterization Surveys (CASEN), that the incidence of poverty was reduced practically in half for the period 1987-1998, dropping from 45.1% of the population to 21.7%. For the same period, income distribution remained highly concentrated: in 1998 the richest quintile of households earned 56.9% of monetary income, while the poorest quintile received only 4.1%.

Some studies have emphasized that the significant inequality in the distribution of income in Chile has been relatively stable over time (see Beyer (1997), De Gregorio and Cowan (1996) and MIDEPLAN (1999)). However, there is considerable variation across time as it is shown in the evidence on wage inequality. Robbins (1994) and Bravo and Marinovic (1997) report a significant increase in wage inequality within wage earners between 1974 and 1987 in Santiago (see also Meller and Tokman(1996)) followed by a decrease in the 90s. Apparent stability could come from comparing data from 1970 (or before) with 1990 (or later) without considering the fluctuations in the middle. Contreras (1999) and Ruiz-Tagle (1999) present evidence supporting this point using a measure of total household income. Finally Bravo, Contreras and Rau (1999) show that stability in per-capita total household income between 1990 and 1996 is the result from opposite trends.

Likewise, Contreras and Ruiz-Tagle (1997) reveal significant disparities in the behavior of income distribution at a regional level, attributing them to the varying evolution of job-market demand for qualified and unqualified labor in distinct geographical zones. In addition, they present a series of methodological aspects that should be considered in the measurement of inequality, among them, the advantages and disadvantages of supposing that the income of the members of a family form a common fund, and the importance of incorporating into the estimations the economies of scale that could be produced within the families.

As this review implies, the majority of the previous studies provide inequality indicators based on measurements of monetary income. This could distort the real picture because monetary income from household services does not include the benefits received from the Government's Social Expenditure, in the form of subsidies in kind. Two arguments are relevant to this point of view. First, Chile has almost doubled its Fiscal Social Expenditure in the 90s in areas like Education and Health (see MIDEPLAN(1996)). Second, and more conceptually, subsidies in kind enlarge people's consumption opportunities, allowing them to free up income flows and consume other goods; therefore, including in-kind subsidies will allow us to work with an indicator which is closer to household consumption and welfare.

The point made before has been recognized by some authors. MIDEPLAN (1997 and 1999) conducted various studies incorporating into the estimations, in addition to monetary income,

---

[72] Department of Planning and Cooperation.

expenditures by the public sector in education and health. To do this they value the monetary and non-monetary subsidies contained in the CASEN Survey, and then assign them to the households classified by quintiles of income. In this way, an estimation of income distribution in Chile is obtained for quintiles of households, adding to the monetary income of each household the rent implied by home ownership and the expenditures by the public sector in programs of education and health (see Appendix N°1 for more details on this methodology).

On the other hand, Cowan and De Gregorio (1996), based on the statistics of Public Finance of the Ministry of Finance, achieved a preliminary estimation of income distribution by quintiles of households for the year 1994, based on the assumption of an unvarying focusing of social expenditures between 1992 and 1994. It has to be mentioned the study by Larrañaga (1994), who distributes among the quintiles of households the expenditures budgeted for various social programs in the period 1990-1993. Besides, each program considered has its own assignment criterion associated with it. Furthermore, not only are the social programs mentioned in the CASEN Survey included, but also others of smaller relative importance to total social expenditures are added, since these are also determinants of the final income distribution (a greater detail of this methodology is given in Appendix N°1).

In addition, it is worth mentioning that Schkolnik (1996) analyzed, for the year 1990, the net effect of fiscal action on income concentration. On one hand, this analysis indicated that the progressivity of the income tax was compensated for by the regressivity of the Value Added Tax, thus annulling a tax effect on income inequality. On the other hand, the contribution of social expenditure on the autonomous income of households did show a progressive impact, therefore the importance of social programs on the total household income was reduced to the extent that it raised the level of income. In any case, problems in the assignment of benefits to their intended beneficiaries were discovered. Schkolnik emphasized the need to consider what type of program is being valuated in order to analyze its distributive impact, because the character of each program -subsistence, selective, universal or non-redistributable- reflects its objectives.

Finally, Shorrocks (1997) in the context of a World Bank study estimates the impact of taxes and social expenditures on income distribution. This study basically discusses the degree of focusing and incidence of the tax structure and social expenditures in Chile. From its results a number of simulation exercises are carried out. This study confirms the progressivity of the income tax and the regressivity of the value added tax. As a result, the aggregate impact of the tax structure on the distribution of income is null. Additionally, it is shown that social expenditure, especially on education, has a significant impact on inequality. All this analysis was carried out by means of the use of income quintiles. Shorrocks, outlines the need for an analysis at an individual level in such a way as to obtain more reliable results.

Consequently, the conclusions of the studies carried out in the past in Chile refer, basically, to the distribution of monetary incomes. And when social policies are considered, the studies: 1) distribute the social expenditures among income quintiles; and 2) do not perform measurements of poverty and inequality that consider the impact of such subsidies,[73] or that correct for economies of scale and/or permit a regional analysis of inequality.

The present investigation hopes to fill part of the aforementioned gaps. Based on information collected by the CASEN surveys, conducted in November of 1990, 1994, 1996 and 1998, the income for each household is adjusted, adding to the autonomous income of each one of its members, the rent attributed to the home, monetary subsidies, and those health, education and housing subsidies that they report having received from the Government. Towards this end a specific form is introduced appraising health insurance and the various education and housing subsidies that the Government may have awarded.

Behind this addition of health, education and housing subsidies to the income of households lies the assumption that in-kind subsidies enlarge people's consumption opportunities, permitting them to free up income flows and consume other goods. In our analysis, this is translated, first into a gradual increase in available household income, and then into consequent changes in distribution.

Subsequently, several measurements of income distribution are obtained, with and without imputation of monetary, health, education and housing subsidies to household members. The analysis and statistical comparison of such measurements allows us to derive clearer conclusions regarding the behavior of income inequality at both a national and regional level.[74]

Methodological Issues

In this section we report the data used to pursue the analysis, mentioning some differences that there will be in contrast with the analysis developed in chapter 2. In addition we present a description of the methodology followed.

Data

The basic source of information for this investigation are the National Socio-Economic Characterization Surveys (CASEN), conducted in 1990, 1994, 1996 and 1998.

These surveys collect information on demographics, employment, income, housing, health, and the educational aspects of households and for each member. In addition, the survey is a representative sample at both the national and regional level, and for the rural and urban zones of Chile. In particular, for the year 1998, the Survey covered 48,107 households in the country and 188,360 people.[75]

---

[73] Only Schkolnik (1996) obtains measurements of inequality with and without a redistributive effect of fiscal action, through the Gini Coefficient. However, this refers to an analysis by household for the year 1990, and does not carry out an impact analysis of social programs at a regional level, nor does it verify the statistical significance of the changes found.

[74] Certainly, the proposed methodology will be able to be applied in the future to diverse levels of breakdowns (by geographical zones and/or type of programs).

[75] On the basis of the 1992 Census and the population projections done by the National Institute of Statistics and the Latin-American Demographics Center, the sample of this Survey itself was expanded to the total population for each one of the strata.

On the other hand, it is worth mentioning that the concepts of income and subsidies utilized are the following: Autonomous Income (IA), Monetary subsidies (SM), Monetary Income (IM), Rent Attributed to Home Ownership (AICP) and Total Income (IT), all of them commonly used in the CASEN Survey;[76] in addition we define: Net Income from Social Policies (IN), Housing subsidies (SV), Health subsidies valued on the basis of Public Insurance (SSS), Education subsidies (SE), Income Corrected for Housing (IV), Income Corrected for Health based on Public Insurance (ISS), Income Corrected for Education (IE), Income Corrected for Monetary subsidies (ISM), Income Corrected for Social Policy considering Public Health Insurance (IPSS), Financial Credit for Higher Education (CF) and Income Corrected for Social Policy including Financial Credit (ICF).

Where,

$$
\begin{array}{ll}
(1) & IA + SM = IM \\
(2) & IM + AICP = IT \\
(3) & IN = IA + AICP - SV = IT - SM - SV \\
(4) & IV = IN + SV \\
(5) & ISS = IN + SSS \\
(6) & IE = IN + SE \\
(7) & ISM = IN + SM \\
(8) & IPSS = IN + SM + SV + SSS + SE \\
(9) & ICF = IPSS + CF
\end{array}
$$

Each one of the previous definitions is utilized in computing the corresponding per capita household income, which will serve as a basis for alternative measurements of inequality.[77]

The estimation of the value of the subsidies of various types is carried out on the basis of information provided by the following institutions: Ministerio de Salud (MINSAL), Fondo Nacional de Salud (FONASA), Central de Abastecimientos (CENABAST), Superintendencia de Seguridad Social, Superintendencia de Instituciones de Salud Previsional, Ministerio de Vivienda (MINVU), Subsecretaría de Desarrollo Regional del Ministerio del Interior, Ministerio de Educación (MINEDUC), Junta Nacional de Auxilio Escolar y Becas (JUNAEB), Junta Nacional de Jardines Infantiles (JUNJI), Fundación Nacional para el Desarrollo Integral del Menor (INTEGRA) and Contraloría General de la República.

Prior to reviewing the study methodology of the impact of social expenditures on income distribution, it is necessary to mention some differences that there will be in the treatment given the data with respect to chapter 2. This will allow a greater clarity as to the true comparability and consistency of the estimations presented earlier and the ones that result from this chapter.

---

[76] For an exact definition, refer to MIDEPLAN (1996), pp. 50-51.

[77] The income figures used in this paper are those adjusted by CEPAL, on the basis of National Accounts information, in order to handle under reporting or partial omission of income data.

As a measurement of income distribution, Table 1 presents the Gini coefficients and the ratio between quintiles calculated for various levels of household income included in the CASEN Survey of 1998.

Table 1
Indicators of the Distribution of Per-Capita Income
Chile, 1998 (Total Country)

Indicator	Total Income Adjusted by EEE and Regional Prices	Total Income Adjusted by EEE	Total Household Income	Income Net of Social Policies	Income with Social Policies
	(1)	(2)	(3)	(4)	(5)
Q1	3,67	3,70	3,43	3,06	5,16
Q2	7,20	7,23	6,94	6,68	8,20
Q3	11,07	11,10	10,95	10,81	11,60
Q4	18,11	18,17	18,29	18,31	18,02
Q5	59,93	59,80	60,39	61,14	57,02
Q5/Q1	16,3	16,2	17,6	20,0	11,1
Gini	0,5465	0,5449	0,5535	0,5644	0,5028

Notes:

(1) Total household income per equivalent adult, adjusted for scale economies and regional prices, and treating live-in domestic household. EEE = scale economies and adult equivalents.

(2) Total income of the household per equivalent adult, with scale economies, without considering regional prices and excluding live-in service

(3) Per-Capita income of the household, without regional prices and excluding live-in domestic service. Includes autonomous income, monetary subsidies and rent attributed to the house.

(4) Net income per capita: per capita income of the household minus monetary subsidies and housing.

(5) Per-Capita income with social policies: net income per-capita plus monetary and in-kind subsidies (housing, health and education).

Source: Calculated by the authors, based on 1998 CASEN Survey . For more complete description see text.

Column (1) corresponds to the indicators obtained (in the previous chapter) for household income per equivalent adult, that is, for the measurement of income that corrects for the equivalences and economies of scale (EEE) within the household; in addition, in order to carry out such an estimation, the incomes of each household have been deflated by a regional price index, and live-in domestic service is considered as another household.

Column (2) refers to the household income adjusted only by EEE, without considering regional prices and excluding from the sample live-in domestic service.

Column (3) estimates the inequality in per capita household income, that is to say, the most traditional measurement is utilized that includes autonomous income, monetary subsidies and the rent attributed to households that own the housing that they occupy, without considering EEE or regional prices, and excluding live-in domestic service.

Finally, the last two columns give a preview of the findings of this chapter. On one hand, column (4) estimates the net per capita income of each household from social policies or, in other words, the total income (3) minus the monetary and housing subsidies. On the other hand, in column (5) to the net income per capita of each household (4) are added all those benefits that its members declare having received, whether they are monetary subsidies or subsidies in kind (health, education and housing). None of these cases is corrected for EEE or regional prices, and live-in domestic service is excluded.

Methodology

- The methodology proposed in this investigation in order to measure the impact of social expenditures on income inequality in Chile, rests in the following assumptions:
- The estimated impact of social expenditure on income distribution is the immediate, no considering possible medium or long term effects on the personal or household incomes. Therefore, aspects such as the future return of investments in human capital (greater employment opportunities and income in the future) coming from wider access to education, health services and nutritional programs for the population, are not considered (See Velez (1994) for an analogous approach).
- At first, it is assumed that $1 in in-kind subsidies equals $\alpha=$ $1 in available income for its beneficiary, with which it is possible to add the value of these subsidies in health, education and housing directly to the income of each household member. Then, from a second perspective, $\alpha \neq 1$ is allowed, because:
- if in-kind subsidies represent greater consumption opportunities offered to the beneficiaries, $\alpha=1$ would assume that these people value 100% of the social expenditure, which does not necessarily occur.
- on the other hand, part of the social expenditure in in-kind subsidies could deviate from its potential beneficiaries at the moment of distribution, in which case, $(1-\alpha)$ would represent the potential inefficiency of social expenditure;
- lastly, it would also be possible to argue that $\alpha > 1$, if the difference in quality between the goods provided by the public and private sectors is smaller than the price differential governing them.

For these reasons, at the end of this paper we run some sensitivity analysis of the impact of social expenditure on income inequality, and we obtain the level of α for which this impact is not zero.

Only those subsidies that its members have declared receiving are attributed to each household, which, particularly in the case of health, means assigning value to the public insurance given by FONASA to its beneficiaries.

In this context, the present study is developed in three steps:

Step 1: Valuation of the subsidies in education, health, and housing that benefit a group of Chilean households

The scheme of valuation of the multiple subsidies considering Health, Education and Housing is detailed in Appendixes N° 2, 3 and 4, where in addition, the distinct modalities of each type of subsidy and their average estimated values are mentioned for each year of interest.

It is worth mentioning that to the extent possible the same valuation criteria have been utilized in every year under consideration. However, there have been certain difficulties in homogenizing the criteria in some cases: some social programs in effect prior to 1994 did not exist in 1990 (among these, the School Nutrition Program for secondary students); there are differences among the questionnaires of CASEN Surveys, which complicates their strict comparability (for example, in 1990 the educational establishment that household members attended was not identified unequivocally in the study). All this imposed the need to seek diverse forms of approximation among the criteria of valuation and assignment of the subsidies as obtained by the members of each household, for each year of analysis.

Subsidies in Education

In the area of the education, the basic source of subsidies are: the School Nutrition Program (Programa de Alimentación Escolar, PAE); Pre-school education in JUNJI and INTEGRA establishments; the transfer of MINEDUC to corporations of delegated administration (institutions who are in charge of managing some public vocational schools); the per-pupil subsidies to municipal and private-subsidized establishments (for primary, secondary and special education); the additional resources to establishments on a per-pupil basis; some special programs of school supplies (JUNAEB), school texts (MINEDUC), oral health and school health (JUNAEB), and scholarships.

Once assigned monetary value these subsidies are assigned to those declared to be studying, according to the level and type of education received, the educational establishment attended (that determines the amount of the per-pupil subsidy) and self-reporting (statement of having received the benefit, in the case of school nutrition and special programs).

Subsidies in Health

Among the subsidies in health, were included the public health insurance; the additional 2% contribution that certain beneficiaries receive if affiliated in the private-insurance sector (ISAPREs); maternity leave; leaves in case of serious illness of a child less than a year old, and the National Program of Complementary Nutrition.

With respect to public health insurance, this has been estimated as the difference between the valuation that each individual affiliated to FONASA[78] has on his/her her individual health insurance and the payments made for it (contributions and co-payments). The expected value of public health insurance is approximated from the information collected by the CASEN Survey. That is, demographic cells are defined in which the population affiliated with FONASA is classified according to gender and age, the average expenditure of an individual of each cell is observed (an expenditure that depends on the frequency of medical attention received by an average individual of each cell) and then the average total expenditure of cells is adjusted for each period according to the total expenditure on medical services registered by the Public sector at a country level. This approximation must be carried out due to the fact that the true data of average individual expenditure for different ages and genders are not available. Likewise, the prices for health services utilized were those that showed the greatest believability and comparability, knowing the tariffs and average gross values in place in November of 1996 (expressed in money of each period).

In order to estimate the social security contributions to health of workers or retired workers, the legal discounts in place in October of each year of interest were considered, which is the same month that household income is registered. Starting from this point, and using the income of the primary occupation reported, base income for social security and its respective contributions for health (7% of base income) were calculated. Of course, to do this only non-indigent cases with

---

[78] It corresponds to the national Fund of health. Public system of attention.

affiliation to FONASA were considered and classified in 3 groups according to income (B, C and D). Such a classification was also utilized to calculate the co-payments made by the household members affiliated with the public system, when they declared that they had received medical attention. The discount of the co-payments was controlled in addition to self-reporting, that is to say, by the statement of payments made in the same surveys.

Subsidies in Housing

To assign value to housing subsidies we estimated what proportion of the flow of services that each owned-house reported, be it totally or partially paid, originated from access to a government subsidy. Such a flow, corresponding to the alternative cost of housing, has been approximated through the monthly amount of rent that its owner thinks that he would have to pay if, instead of being the owner of the house, he leased it (rent attributed to the household, estimated by the owner of the house in the CASEN Survey).

At the same time, for each year composing the period 1990-1998 we estimated what fraction of the total value of the housing, as included in various MINVU and Ministerio del Interior programs, was subsidized. Then, according to the year in which the individuals declared to have received the certificate of subsidy or subsidized housing, the respective percentage of subsidy was identified and, thus, that part of the monthly lease that would have been subsidized[79]. The housing subsidy programs considered here are: Progressive and Basic Housing, Special Program for Workers, Unified Subsidy and Rural Subsidy, all by the Ministry of Housing; and the Neighborhood Improvement Program (lots with services) by the Ministry of the Interior.

This focus of valuation of the subsidies in housing might be considered conservative, because it does not take into account an implicit series of subsidies that have characterized Chilean housing policy since its beginnings, to wit: government compensation for eventual losses in the sale of mortgages of subsidized housing, other guarantees such as insurance against legal auction of some housing, and other subsidies of the past, such as access to credit with rates of interest not adjusted by inflation.

Nevertheless, there are also certain private costs associated with housing programs that have not been included in the analysis due to problems of information, among these: the increase in monetary costs and time commuting to work, characteristic of programs of eradication, in which the beneficiaries of a subsidy would be transferred to another neighborhood, possibly farther away from their work.

---

[79] Due to the fact that the CASEN Survey of 1990 does not provide information regarding the year in which the beneficiaries of the housing programs received the benefit, we opted for valuating the monthly flow of services for various types of housing according to the percentage of subsidy for programs existing in 1990. On the other hand, it not being possible to unequivocally identify certain types of housing (Traditional, Unified Subsidy, Special Program for Workers and the Rural Subsidy), it was assumed that in rural zones the households had only benefited from Rural Subsidies and in urban zones the average percentage was utilized (weighted) for subsidies in housing financed by the Unified Subsidy and the Special Workers Program.

Step 2:   Adjustment of the per capita income of each household, according to the subsidies received by its members

The net income of social policy for a household, in per capita terms, is equivalent to their total income (as typically utilized in other studies regarding the analysis of poverty and distribution) minus Monetary and Housing subsidies that their members have received.

Once the per capita net income of each household is obtained, each type of subsidy was added separately, to be able to identify its individual contribution to the changes in inequality. Then, available per capita income was computed, including all subsidies that the members of each household have received. That is, the Income Corrected by Social Policies, based on the valuation of public health insurance (IPSS).

Finally, the crédito fiscal (loans to university students) received by some household members is added to the Income Corrected by Social Policies. In this way, it is possible to get first look at the immediate impact of the program on income distribution upon computing the Income Corrected for social policy, including the Fiscal Credit (ICF). However, the analysis of this variable will not be deepened further, for although the fiscal credit is a government program, it does not wholly correspond to a government subsidy.

Step 3:   Measurement of income inequality in Chile and its regions, with and without correction for social policies

The comparison of alternative inequality measurements, with and without correction for social policies, allows gauging the impact of the various subsidy programs on the distribution of per capita income for each year of interest. Simultaneously, this framework of analysis allows us to characterize the evolution of inequality for the period 1990-1998 with and without considering the impact of social policies.

Among the measurements of distribution chosen, those that stand out are: the Gini coefficient, the Variance of Log Incomes, the per- capita income quintiles and the ratio of income (Q5/Q1), that indicates the relation between the income received by the richest 20% of the population and the poorest 20%. Besides observing how these indicators change as we incorporate the different types of subsidies into the per capita household income, a statistical analysis of the significance of the impact of each is provided. Therefore, it is possible to determine the real significance of social policy in affecting inequality, at both a country and regional level. The statistical technique utilized is non-parametric (bootstrapping).

RESULTS

Within the framework of the assumptions and limitations of this methodology, as indicated in section II, it will be clear from the results presented in this section that valuation and allocation of social expenditure to the income of each beneficiary household reduces inequality at a country level. This is true even when only the immediate impact of social policy is being computed.

National Impact

In Figures 1 and 2, it can be seen that in 1990 and 1998 the policy of subsidies reduced inequality in all regions of the country, whether this is measured by the Gini coefficient or by the ratio of incomes. Although disparities in concentration of income remain among the regions, there seems to be no doubt regarding the contribution of the monetary subsidies in housing, health and, especially education, to a drop in inequality.

A summary of the preceding is provided by Tables N°2, 3, 4 and 5. In these Tables, the first column shows the inequality indicators. The second column shows these indicators after being applied in the per capita income without considering any transfer on the part of the public sector. Columns 3-7 present the inequality indicators after individually adding the health, education, monetary, and housing subsidies, and then crédito fiscal, respectively. Finally, the last column shows the inequality indicators after adding all subsidies received by the households (not including crédito fiscal).

In the Tables the drop in inequality is evident as much in the Metropolitan Region, as in the remainder of the country. While in 1990 the Gini coefficient at a country level decreases from 0.56 to 0.52, in 1998 the same indicator falls from 0.56 to 0.50. Analogously, the ratio of income descends, in 1990, from 17.8 times to 12.4 times, while in 1998 it is reduced from 20.0 times to 11.1 times. From this perspective, it can be inferred that social policies reduced the inequality in each year of interest, but they showed a relatively greater impact in 1998 than in 1990, which could be explained by a greater assignment of resources to the subsidy programs, a greater efficacy of the Government in the focusing of resources, and/or self-selection of the beneficiaries of subsidies (to the extent that households have greater per capita income at their disposal, it is more probable that they buy education, health and housing services in the private market, and that they lose the possibility of accessing specific monetary subsidies).

In contrast, consideration of the fiscal credit does not seem to contribute to reduced inequality, even giving indications of regressivity. The last column does not include this component because correspond to loans and only a fraction of them are subsidized.

Figure N° 1
Impact of Social Policies in Chile (National and Regions)
Gini Coefficients, Years 1990 and 1998

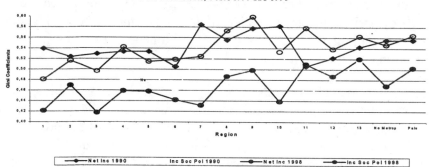

Figure N° 2
Impact of Social Policies in Chile (National and Regions)
Ratio of Incomes, Years 1990 and 1998

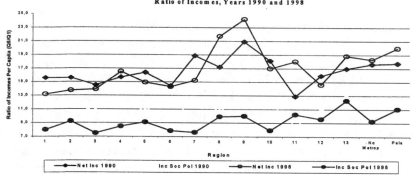

Table 2
Indicators of the Per-Capita Income Distribution
Chile, 1990

Metropolitan Region

Indicator	Income Net of Social Policies	Income with Health Subs.	Income with Education Subs.	Income with Monetary Subs.	Income with Housing Subs.	Income with Credito Fiscal	Income with Social Policies
Q1	3,51	3,86	3,99	3,65	3,55	3,51	4,50
Q2	6,99	7,19	7,35	7,10	7,04	6,99	7,69
Q3	11,12	11,20	11,28	11,18	11,17	11,12	11,43
Q4	18,75	18,63	18,65	18,68	18,73	18,75	18,54
Q5	59,64	59,12	58,74	59,38	59,52	59,63	57,84
Q5/Q1	17,0	15,3	14,7	16,3	16,8	17,0	12,9
Atkinson Coeff.	0,6865	0,6225	0,5783	0,6637	0,6777	0,6865	0,5268
Theil Coeff.	0,5668	0,5514	0,5407	0,5585	0,5630	0,5667	0,5159
Log(P90/P10)	2,4900	2,4050	2,3780	2,4510	2,4910	2,4900	2,2540
Variance Log.	0,9746	0,9059	0,8584	0,9442	0,9633	0,9746	0,7790
Gini	0,5426	0,5340	0,5288	0,5383	0,5407	0,5425	0,5147

Rest of the Country

Indicator	Income Net of Social Policies	Income with Health Subs.	Income with Education Subs.	Income with Monetary Subs.	Income with Housing Subs.	Income with Credito Fiscal	Income with Social Policies
Q1	3,42	3,93	4,21	3,63	3,46	3,42	4,95
Q2	7,04	7,41	7,62	7,20	7,08	7,04	8,14
Q3	11,06	11,23	11,36	11,16	11,10	11,07	11,64
Q4	18,11	18,04	18,06	18,11	18,14	18,13	18,01
Q5	60,37	59,38	58,75	59,91	60,22	60,35	57,26
Q5/Q1	17,7	15,1	14,0	16,5	17,4	17,6	11,6
Atkinson Coeff.	0,6719	0,5702	0,5745	0,6464	0,6633	0,6719	0,5148
Theil Coeff.	0,6793	0,6495	0,6299	0,6648	0,6750	0,6785	0,5883
Log(P90/P10)	2,3470	2,2210	2,1330	2,2890	2,3390	2,3460	1,9700
Variance Log.	0,9746	0,8586	0,7919	0,9362	0,9559	0,9746	0,6838
Gini	0,5556	0,5406	0,5316	0,5489	0,5538	0,5554	0,5097

Total Country

Indicator	Income Net of Social Policies	Income with Health Subs.	Income with Education Subs.	Income with Monetary Subs.	Income with Housing Subs.	Income with Credito Fiscal	Income with Social Policies
Q1	3,41	3,81	4,03	3,55	3,41	3,40	4,67
Q2	6,85	7,18	7,37	7,02	6,92	6,84	7,82
Q3	10,94	11,08	11,19	11,03	11,00	10,97	11,41
Q4	18,19	18,10	18,13	18,18	18,20	18,19	18,05
Q5	60,61	59,83	59,28	60,22	60,46	60,59	58,05
Q5/Q1	17,8	15,7	14,7	17,0	17,7	17,8	12,4
Atkinson Coeff.	0,6773	0,5884	0,5767	0,6527	0,6687	0,6773	0,5196
Theil Coeff.	0,6385	0,6151	0,5992	0,6267	0,6344	0,6380	0,5650
Log(P90/P10)	2,4410	2,3210	2,2560	2,3810	2,4330	2,4410	2,1030
Variance Log.	1,0030	0,9021	0,8402	0,9667	0,9870	1,0030	0,7399
Gini	0,5558	0,5436	0,5361	0,5501	0,5540	0,5556	0,5176

Source: Elaborated by the authors based on CASEN survey 1990.

Table N°3
Indicators of the Per-Capita Income Distribution
Chile, 1994

Metropolitan Region

Indicator	Income Net of Social Policies	Income with Health Subs.	Income with Education Subs.	Income with Monetary Subs.	Income with Housing Subs.	Income with Credito Fiscal	Income with Social Policies
Q1	3,27	3,64	3,81	3,38	3,31	3,28	4,30
Q2	6,65	6,88	7,03	6,73	6,69	6,65	7,35
Q3	10,46	10,52	10,62	10,47	10,46	10,43	10,78
Q4	17,43	17,39	17,43	17,45	17,49	17,53	17,35
Q5	62,19	61,57	61,12	61,97	62,06	62,11	60,22
Q5/Q1	19,0	16,9	16,0	18,3	18,7	18,9	14,0
Atkinson Coeff.	0,6676	0,6442	0,6208	0,6787	0,6624	0,6676	0,5787
Theil Coeff.	0,8371	0,8196	0,8020	0,8299	0,8329	0,8355	0,7760
Log(P90/P10)	2,4200	2,3240	2,2700	2,3880	2,3970	2,4190	2,1230
Variance Log.	0,9432	0,8968	0,8530	0,9467	0,9335	0,9432	0,7655
Gini	0,5740	0,5644	0,5582	0,5707	0,5724	0,5735	0,5445

Rest of the Country

Indicator	Income Net of Social Policies	Income with Health Subs.	Income with Education Subs.	Income with Monetary Subs.	Income with Housing Subs.	Income with Credito Fiscal	Income with Social Policies
Q1	3,67	4,38	4,68	3,92	3,72	3,67	5,61
Q2	7,36	7,87	8,16	7,54	7,60	7,37	8,81
Q3	11,53	11,81	11,94	11,67	11,39	11,57	12,31
Q4	18,98	18,90	18,87	18,90	19,01	18,96	18,77
Q5	58,45	57,03	56,35	57,97	58,29	58,43	54,50
Q5/Q1	15,9	13,0	12,0	14,8	15,7	15,9	9,7
Atkinson Coeff.	0,6192	0,5403	0,5114	0,5949	0,6103	0,6197	0,4352
Theil Coeff.	0,5974	0,5578	0,5391	0,5834	0,5932	0,5693	0,4914
Log(P90/P10)	2,3270	2,1510	2,3200	2,2680	2,3090	2,3300	1,8740
Variance Log.	0,9082	0,7815	0,7230	0,8610	0,8913	0,9101	0,6039
Gini	0,5343	0,5133	0,5034	0,5271	0,5324	0,5341	0,4760

Total Country

Indicator	Income Net of Social Policies	Income with Health Subs.	Income with Education Subs.	Income with Monetary Subs.	Income with Housing Subs.	Income with Credito Fiscal	Income with Social Policies
Q1	3,29	3,84	4,09	3,47	3,33	3,29	4,81
Q2	6,77	7,10	7,32	6,85	6,76	6,73	7,81
Q3	10,72	10,95	11,08	10,83	10,81	10,77	11,35
Q4	17,96	17,87	17,89	17,94	17,99	18,00	17,81
Q5	61,26	60,23	59,63	60,90	61,11	61,20	58,21
Q5/Q1	18,6	15,7	14,6	17,6	18,4	18,6	12,1
Atkinson Coeff.	0,6505	0,5845	0,5570	0,6331	0,6426	0,6508	0,4891
Theil Coeff.	0,7581	0,7278	0,7071	0,7466	0,7537	0,7565	0,6675
Log(P90/P10)	2,4170	2,2740	2,2040	2,3740	2,4190	2,4180	2,0330
Variance Log.	0,9688	0,8660	0,8096	0,9382	0,9545	0,9700	0,6971
Gini	0,5651	0,5495	0,5411	0,5598	0,5634	0,5647	0,5200

Source: Elaboration by the authors based on CASEN Survey 1994.

Table Nº4
Indicators of the Per-Capita Income Distribution
Chile, 1996

Metropolitan Region

Indicator	Income Net of Social Policies	Income with Health Subs.	Income with Education Subs.	Income with Monetary Subs.	Income with Housing Subs.	Income with Credito Fiscal	Income with Social Policies
Q1	3,62	4,07	4,30	3,77	3,70	3,67	4,95
Q2	7	7,26	7,57	7,09	7,05	7,08	7,98
Q3	10,94	11,12	11,36	11,01	11,07	11,10	11,62
Q4	18,62	18,49	18,71	18,59	18,56	18,99	18,51
Q5	59,82	59,06	58,05	59,54	59,63	59,16	56,93
Q5/Q1	16,5	14,5	13,5	15,8	16,1	16,1	11,5
Atkinson Coeff.	0,6663	0,5828	0,6162	0,6319	0,6205	0,6635	0,5099
Theil Coeff.	0,6008	0,5785	0,5523	0,5928	0,5953	0,5846	0,5204
Log(P90/P10)	2,3660	2,2600	2,1900	2,3400	2,3410	2,3500	2,0400
Variance Log.	0,9417	0,8460	0,8136	0,9247	0,9176	0,9322	0,7012
Gini	0,5467	0,5348	0,5231	0,5425	0,5440	0,5414	0,5051

Rest of the Country

Indicator	Ingreso Inicial	Ingreso con Sub. Salud	Ingreso con Sub. Educación	Ingreso con Sub. Monetarios	Ingreso con Sub. Vivienda	Ingreso con Crédito Fiscal	Ingreso con Políticas Sociales
Q1	3,51	4,46	4,68	3,81	3,56	3,51	5,87
Q2	7,19	7,88	8,12	7,43	7,26	7,21	8,99
Q3	11,39	11,75	11,90	11,56	11,44	11,45	12,39
Q4	18,97	18,91	18,91	18,99	19,00	19,07	18,85
Q5	58,93	57,01	56,38	58,21	58,74	58,76	53,91
Q5/Q1	16,8	12,8	12,0	15,3	16,5	16,7	9,2
Atkinson Coeff.	0,6684	0,5630	0,5423	0,6333	0,6492	0,6684	0,4462
Theil Coeff.	0,5839	0,5319	0,5157	0,5649	0,5788	0,5806	0,4548
Log(P90/P10)	2,3840	2,1300	2,0700	2,2900	2,3600	2,3700	1,8200
Variance Log.	0,9756	0,7607	0,7417	0,9014	0,9483	0,9744	0,5749
Gini	0,5404	0,5123	0,5037	0,5306	0,5380	0,5391	0,4679

Total Country

Indicator	Ingreso Inicial	Ingreso con Sub. Salud	Ingreso con Sub. Educación	Ingreso con Sub. Monetarios	Ingreso con Sub. Vivienda	Ingreso con Crédito Fiscal	Ingreso con Políticas Sociales
Q1	3,3	4,02	4,26	3,53	3,35	3,32	5,21
Q2	6,85	7,29	7,56	6,98	6,86	6,86	8,22
Q3	10,86	11,15	11,38	11,01	10,97	11,01	11,76
Q4	18,48	18,39	18,52	18,46	18,51	18,70	18,44
Q5	60,52	59,15	58,28	60,02	60,31	60,11	56,38
Q5/Q1	18,3	14,7	13,7	17,0	18,0	18,1	10,8
Atkinson Coeff.	0,6869	0,5883	0,5756	0,6530	0,6653	0,6858	0,4789
Theil Coeff.	0,6264	0,5872	0,5626	0,6121	0,6209	0,6145	0,5131
Log(P90/P10)	2,4600	2,2800	2,1900	2,4200	2,4600	2,4700	1,9800
Variance Log.	1,0258	0,8436	0,8163	0,9683	0,9996	1,0199	0,6602
Gini	0,5565	0,5360	0,5252	0,5493	0,5540	0,5529	0,4974

Source: Elaboration by the authors based on CASEN Survey 1996.

Table Nº5
Indicators of the Per-Capita Income Distribution
Chile, 1998

Metropolitan Region

Indicator	Income Net of Social Policies	Income with Health Subs.	Income with Education Subs.	Income with Monetary Subs.	Income with Housing Subs.	Income with Credito Fiscal	Income with Social Policies
Q1	3,25	3,72	4,09	3,41	3,34	3,25	4,76
Q2	6,74	7,00	7,39	6,85	6,82	6,74	7,81
Q3	10,74	10,80	11,06	10,78	10,82	10,74	11,22
Q4	18,02	17,82	17,95	17,98	18,03	18,05	17,70
Q5	61,25	60,66	59,52	60,98	60,99	61,22	58,50
Q5/Q1	18,8	16,3	14,6	17,9	18,3	18,8	12,3
Atkinson Coeff.	0,6875	0,6123	0,5699	0,6668	0,6571	0,6878	0,5083
Theil Coeff.	0,6502	0,6312	0,6002	0,6417	0,6432	0,6492	0,5709
Log(P90/P10)	2,4900	2,3800	2,2400	2,4600	2,4600	2,4900	2,0800
Variance Log.	1,0371	0,9172	0,8380	1,0004	0,9988	1,0380	0,7239
Gini	0,5626	0,5518	0,5374	0,5582	0,5593	0,5624	0,5200

Rest of the Country

Indicator	Ingreso Inicial	Ingreso con Sub. Salud	Ingreso con Sub. Educación	Ingreso con Sub. Monetarios	Ingreso con Sub. Vivienda	Ingreso con Crédito Fiscal	Ingreso con Políticas Sociales
Q1	3,25	4,15	4,61	3,67	3,32	3,25	5,86
Q2	7,05	7,69	8,16	7,34	7,11	7,05	9,00
Q3	11,35	11,64	11,96	11,46	11,39	11,36	12,36
Q4	18,87	18,70	18,81	18,78	18,90	18,90	18,60
Q5	59,48	57,82	56,46	58,75	59,28	59,44	54,18
Q5/Q1	18,3	13,9	12,2	16,0	17,9	18,3	9,2
Atkinson Coeff.	0,6710	0,5335	0,5284	0,5999	0,6472	0,6715	0,4095
Theil Coeff.	0,6015	0,5546	0,5197	0,5792	0,5957	0,5999	0,4625
Log(P90/P10)	2,4900	2,2500	2,1000	2,3800	2,4700	2,4900	1,8500
Variance Log.	1,0668	0,8208	0,7543	0,9310	1,0235	1,0687	0,5781
Gini	0,5466	0,5212	0,5035	0,5351	0,5440	0,5463	0,4687

Total Country

Indicator	Ingreso Inicial	Ingreso con Sub. Salud	Ingreso con Sub. Educación	Ingreso con Sub. Monetarios	Ingreso con Sub. Vivienda	Ingreso con Crédito Fiscal	Ingreso con Políticas Sociales
Q1	3,06	3,76	4,18	3,36	3,13	3,06	5,16
Q2	6,68	7,14	7,55	6,88	6,75	6,69	8,20
Q3	10,81	10,99	11,31	10,89	10,87	10,81	11,60
Q4	18,31	18,12	18,24	18,25	18,35	18,36	18,02
Q5	61,14	59,99	58,71	60,62	60,90	61,08	57,02
Q5/Q1	20,0	16,0	14,0	18,0	19,5	20,0	11,1
Atkinson Coeff.	0,6890	0,5701	0,5551	0,6316	0,6649	0,6894	0,4518
Theil Coeff.	0,6551	0,6209	0,5857	0,6388	0,6486	0,6537	0,5400
Log(P90/P10)	2,5500	2,3400	2,2100	2,4600	2,5200	2,5500	1,9900
Variance Log.	1,1044	0,8978	0,8228	1,0012	1,0632	1,1057	0,6631
Gini	0,5644	0,5460	0,5295	0,5563	0,5616	0,5641	0,5028

Source: Elaborated by the authors based on CASEN Survey 1998.

Furthermore, it is worth emphasizing that the significant fall in inequality at a country level as a result of the subsidies received by households is robust to changes in the indicator utilized. However, in regional analysis the statistical significance of this reduction, estimated by means of the bootstrapping technique, is sensitive to the measurement of distribution chosen (See Tables N° 6 and 7).

When the Gini coefficient is considered, the social expenditure always has a significant impact on the distribution at a country level; however, in 1990, its significance does not remain guaranteed in the regions I, III and XII, while in 1996 and 1998 the exceptions are the II and XII regions.

In contrast, the behavior of the variance of log-income indicates that in both periods social policy significantly reduces inequality in every region of the country. These differences in estimated impact of social policy can be explained by the relative larger sensibility of this indicator (with respect to the Gini coefficient) to changes in the lower part of the income distribution.[80]

It is appropriate to ask which indicator is best utilized given the objective of this paper: Which social programs favor to a greater extent a reduction in inequality? What explains the differing impacts of social policy at a regional level? And lastly, what are the policy implications that arise from the evidence collected?

Indicators and Targeting of Programs

First, it should be noted that even when among the social programs considered there are some which are typically universal, these are of health and education, they also maintain a certain degree of absolute targeting (at least by self-selection) and also relative targeting (even when the per capita subsidies are of an equal amount for individuals of differing per capita income quintiles, certain relative targeting would exist, since a greater per capita income of a smaller household gives greater relative importance to the subsidies). Such relative and absolute targeting would explain why indicators such as Log Variance of Income better capture the extent of social impact of policy on inequality, since social policies contribute more significantly to a reduction of inequality depending on how important the subsidies are for households having lower per capita net income.

---

[80] The cumulative frequency distribution of income is called the Lorenz Curve; the Gini coefficient measures the distance the Lorenz curve is from the 45 degree line of perfect inequality. A Gini of 0.0 indicates perfect inequality; a Gini of 1.0 equals perfect inequality. The variance of the log of income measures the distance from mean income of each person or household.

Table N°6
Impact of Monetary, Education, Health and Housing Subsidies
on the Distribution of Per-capita Income
(Gini Coefficients)

Zone or Region	Net Income of Social Policies 1990	Income with Social Policies 1990	Significance of the change	Net Income of Social Policies 1996	Income with Social Policies 1996	Significance of the change	Net Income of Social Policies 1998	Income with Social Policies 1998	s
Metropolitan Region	0,5426 (0.5358, 0.5490)	0,5146 (0.5077, 0.5211)	*	0,5467 (0.5370, 0.5561)	0,5051 (0.4936, 0.5142)		0,5626 (0.5550, 0.5716)	0,5200 (0.5120, 0.5294)	
Rest of Country	0,5556 (0.5488, 0.5610)	0,5097 (0.5026, 0.5153)	*	0,5404 (0.5336, 0.5480)	0,4679 (0.4612, 0.4760)		0,5466 (0.5409, 0.5525)	0,4687 (0.4628, 0.4749)	
Total Country	0,5558 (0.5515, 0.5602)	0,5176 (0.5129, 0.5221)	*	0,5565 (0.5495, 0.5626)	0,4974 (0.4906, 0.5045)	*	0,5644 (0.5590, 0.5701)	0,5028 (0.4968, 0.5089)	
I	0,5393 (0.5160, 0.5646)	0,5059 (0.4824, 0.5317)		0,4966 (0.4644, 0.5270)	0,4377 (0.4064, 0.4691)		0,4806 (0.4577, 0.4999)	0,4212 (0.3989, 0.4411)	
II	0,5237 (0.5102, 0.5365)	0,4916 (0.4777, 0.5045)	*	0,4834 (0.4629, 0.5050)	0,4425 (0.4217, 0.4639)		0,5164 (0.4846, 0.5434)	0,4692 (0.4359, 0.4969)	
III	0,5293 (0.5068, 0.5514)	0,4926 (0.4697, 0.5143)		0,5748 (0.5497, 0.5931)	0,5138 (0.4833, 0.5363)	*	0,4964 (0.4819, 0.5102)	0,4173 (0.4017, 0.4312)	*
IV	0,5335 (0.5178, 0.5493)	0,4794 (0.4641, 0.4959)	*	0,5251 (0.5075, 0.5414)	0,4492 (0.4311, 0.4667)	*	0,5420 (0.5167, 0.5635)	0,4590 (0.4317, 0.4824)	*
V	0,5337 (0.5158, 0.5501)	0,4938 (0.4751, 0.5107)	*	0,4957 (0.4840, 0.5067)	0,4422 (0.4306, 0.4541)	*	0,5146 (0.5052, 0.5248)	0,4578 (0.4473, 0.4688)	*
VI	0,5051 (0.4912, 0.5169)	0,4595 (0.4452, 0.4718)	*	0,5126 (0.4927, 0.5324)	0,4423 (0.4216, 0.4630)	*	0,5188 (0.5051, 0.5337)	0,4417 (0.4266, 0.4579)	*
VII	0,5845 (0.5647, 0.6088)	0,5348 (0.5144, 0.5602)	*	0,5470 (0.5237, 0.5751)	0,4628 (0.4380, 0.4926)	*	0,5246 (0.5077, 0.5377)	0,4315 (0.4132, 0.4447)	*
VIII	0,5557 (0.5400, 0.5689)	0,5024 (0.4867, 0.5170)	*	0,5671 (0.5461, 0.5865)	0,4877 (0.4641, 0.5091)	*	0,5730 (0.5599, 0.5840)	0,4865 (0.4715, 0.4987)	
IX	0,5775 (0.5573, 0.5968)	0,5246 (0.5029, 0.5452)	*	0,5513 (0.5392, 0.5631)	0,4505 (0.4372, 0.4621)	*	0,5993 (0.5785, 0.6196)	0,4986 (0.4745, 0.5223)	
X	0,5818 (0.5626, 0.6078)	0,5351 (0.5145, 0.5619)	*	0,5512 (0.5303, 0.5745)	0,4651 (0.4433, 0.4899)	*	0,5331 (0.5200, 0.5435)	0,4387 (0.4257, 0.4496)	
XI	0,5059 (0.4848, 0.5279)	0,4514 (0.4294, 0.4743)	*	0,4974 (0.4804, 0.5180)	0,4275 (0.4101, 0.4475)	*	0,5783 (0.5272, 0.6306)	0,5100 (0.4558, 0.5659)	
XII	0,5220 (0.5034, 0.5502)	0,4796 (0.4595, 0.5080)		0,4812 (0.4477, 0.5208)	0,4334 (0.3988, 0.4735)		0,5386 (0.4833, 0.5886)	0,4868 (0.4313, 0.5391)	

Source: Elaborated by the authors based on CASEN Surveys 1990, 1996 and 1998.

Table N°7

Impact of Monetary, Education, Health and Housing Subsidies
on the Distribution of Per-capita Income
(Variation of Income Logarithm)

Zone or Region	Net Income of Social Policies 1990	Income with Social Policies 1990	Significance of the change	Net Income of Social Policies 1996	Income with Social Policies 1996	Significance of the change
Metropolitan Region	0,9746 (0.9497, 1.0008)	0,7790 (0.7583, 0.7957)	*	0,9416 (0.9114, 0.9730)	0,7012 (0.6753, 0.7234)	*
Rest of Country	0,9745 (0.9576, 0.9877)	0,6837 (0.6733, 0.6946)	*	0,9755 (0.9556, 0.9946)	0,5749 (0.5619, 0.5877)	*
Total Country	1,0031 (0.9909, 1.0167)	0,7399 (0.7306, 0.7498)	*	1,0257 (1.0075, 1.0431)	0,6602 (0.6468, 0.6729)	*
I	0,8736 (0.8210, 0.9253)	0,6898 (0.6485, 0.7280)	*	0,8429 (0.7709, 0.9055)	0,5240 (0.4741, 0.5791)	*
II	0,9348 (0.8951, 0.9812)	0,7193 (0.6880, 0.7524)	*	0,9035 (0.8183, 0.9947)	0,5809 (0.5389, 0.6244)	*
III	0,8505 (0.8028, 0.8902)	0,6495 (0.6085, 0.6893)	*	1,2489 (1.1260, 1.3528)	0,7077 (0.6318, 0.7773)	*
IV	0,8752 (0.8351, 0.9156)	0,5962 (0.5692, 0.6220)	*	0,8729 (0.8267, 0.9303)	0,5248 (0.4940, 0.5640)	*
V	0,9256 (0.8743, 0.9734)	0,6905 (0.6570, 0.7182)	*	0,8207 (0.7845, 0.8553)	0,5512 (0.5265, 0.5784)	*
VI	0,8693 (0.8252, 0.9054)	0,6063 (0.5753, 0.6290)	*	0,7854 (0.7410, 0.8208)	0,4873 (0.4621, 0.5159)	*
VII	0,9970 (0.9517, 1.0420)	0,6922 (0.6583, 0.7296)	*	0,9238 (0.8761, 0.9874)	0,5157 (0.4794, 0.5661)	*
VIII	0,9988 (0.9655, 1.0487)	0,6411 (0.6162, 0.6690)	*	1,0871 (1.0308, 1.1451)	0,6132 (0.5735, 0.6516)	*
IX	1,0928 (1.0462, 1.1491)	0,7148 (0.6827, 0.7508)	*	1,0276 (0.9841, 1.0665)	0,5132 (0.4869, 0.5336)	*
X	0,9184 (0.8851, 0.9582)	0,6730 (0.6470, 0.7046)	*	0,8889 (0.8467, 0.9331)	0,5316 (0.4976, 0.5675)	*
XI	0,7971 (0.7426, 0.8544)	0,5585 (0.5154, 0.6034)	*	0,8243 (0.7681, 0.8850)	0,4991 (0.4688, 0.5367)	*
XII	0,8860 (0.8449, 0.9356)	0,6827 (0.6332, 0.7391)	*	0,7726 (0.6898, 0.8828)	0,5240 (0.4611, 0.6091)	*

Source: Elaboration by the authors based on CASEN Surveys 1990, 1996 and 1998.

The preceding argument is reflected in Tables N°8 and 9. The first of these presents absolute values, while the second shows percentage values. In these Tables, the first column presents information regarding income quintiles for the years 1990, 1994, 1996 and 1998. The second column shows the average value of the per capita income without considering the public sector subsidies. Columns 3-6 present the average amount of monetary, health, education and housing subsidies. The seventh column (in kind) corresponds to the horizontal sum of the subsidies in health, education and housing. Finally, the last column (social policies) corresponds to the sum of the subsidies in kind (health, education and housing) and monetary subsidies.

In the period 1990-1998 an increase in the absolute importance was produced (per capita average value) for the various types of subsidies considered, which benefited various levels of income in the population, since the average value of the per capita subsidies received per person increased in all quintiles; however, upon analyzing the importance of such subsidies as a proportion of per capita income for the quintiles, it can be seen that this grew more strongly in the lower income quintiles and remained practically unaltered for the richest segment of the population. By way of illustration, the average value of all subsidies included in the analysis more than doubled, going from $4,483 pesos to $10,225 per capita (currency value of November of 1998), which meant an increase in its participation upon per capita income from 5.4% to 8.2%; however, an analysis by quintiles reveals that the relative importance of these subsidies grew from 49.0% to 89.1% in the first quintile and only from 0.8% to 0.9% in the fifth quintile, reflecting a greater relative focusing of the subsidies and thus favoring a greater reduction in inequality at a country level.

Table N°8
Average amount of per-capita subsidies
by net per-capita income quintile
(In $ of November 1998)

Year	Net Income of Soc.Pol.	Monetary Subsidies	Health Subsidies	Education Subsidies	Housing Subsidies	Total In-Kind Subsidies	Total p.capita subsidies
1990	**83.665**	**708**	**997**	**2.459**	**320**	**3.775**	**4.483**
Q1	14.141	1.020	2.117	3.545	251	5.914	6.934
Q2	28.854	823	1.604	2.875	310	4.789	5.612
Q3	45.846	662	1.095	2.220	358	3.673	4.335
Q4	76.080	595	526	1.893	350	2.768	3.363
Q5	253.581	438	-366	1.755	329	1.717	2.155
1994	**105.212**	**706**	**2.073**	**3.443**	**393**	**5.909**	**6.615**
Q1	17.318	1.174	3.395	5.433	294	9.121	10.295
Q2	35.406	902	2.718	4.192	342	7.252	8.154
Q3	56.715	676	2.094	3.378	434	5.907	6.583
Q4	94.489	516	1.373	2.603	464	4.440	4.956
Q5	322.272	261	782	1.603	429	2.815	3.075
1996	**115.917**	**1.065**	**2.936**	**4.699**	**576**	**8.212**	**9.277**
Q1	19.097	1.661	4.961	7.000	449	12.410	14.071
Q2	39.499	1.429	3.884	5.716	540	10.139	11.567
Q3	63.268	1.130	3.045	4.658	657	8.360	9.490
Q4	107.134	801	2.058	3.766	704	6.528	7.329
Q5	350.769	303	729	2.313	533	3.575	3.878
1998	**124.335**	**1.135**	**2.299**	**6.125**	**666**	**9.090**	**10.225**
Q1	19.028	2.295	4.910	9.182	568	14.660	16.955
Q2	41.544	1.497	3.782	7.500	629	11.911	13.408
Q3	67.171	1.029	2.469	6.256	803	9.528	10.557
Q4	113.868	613	678	4.870	779	6.327	6.940
Q5	380.107	241	-345	2.814	552	3.021	3.262

Source: Elaboration by the authors based on CASEN Surveys 1990, 1994, 1996 and 1998.

Consequently, the final contribution of any social program, in terms of a reduction of income inequality, doesn't only depend on how quickly subsidies decrease (in absolute amounts) with increases in the income of its beneficiaries, but also on how important such subsidies are for the population, with respect to income.

Table N°9
Relative Amount of Average Per-Capita Subsidies
by Net Per-Capita Income Quintile
(as a % of Net Per-Capita Household Income)

Year	Monetary Subsidies	Health Subsidies	Education Subsidies	Housing Subsidies	Total In-Kind Subsidies	Total Subsidies
1990	0,8	1,2	2,9	0,4	4,5	5,4
Q1	7,2	15,0	25,1	1,8	41,8	49,0
Q2	2,9	5,6	10,0	1,1	16,6	19,4
Q3	1,4	2,4	4,8	0,8	8,0	9,5
Q4	0,8	0,7	2,5	0,5	3,6	4,4
Q5	0,2	-0,1	0,7	0,1	0,7	0,8
1994	0,7	2,0	3,3	0,4	5,6	6,3
Q1	6,8	19,6	31,4	1,7	52,7	59,4
Q2	2,5	7,7	11,8	1,0	20,5	23,0
Q3	1,2	3,7	6,0	0,8	10,4	11,6
Q4	0,5	1,5	2,8	0,5	4,7	5,2
Q5	0,1	0,2	0,5	0,1	0,9	1,0
1996	0,9	2,5	4,1	0,5	7,1	8,0
Q1	8,7	26,0	36,7	2,4	65,0	73,7
Q2	3,6	9,8	14,5	1,4	25,7	29,3
Q3	1,8	4,8	7,4	1,0	13,2	15,0
Q4	0,7	1,9	3,5	0,7	6,1	6,8
Q5	0,1	0,2	0,7	0,2	1,0	1,1
1998	0,9	1,8	4,9	0,5	7,3	8,2
Q1	12,1	25,8	48,3	3,0	77,0	89,1
Q2	3,6	9,1	18,1	1,5	28,7	32,3
Q3	1,5	3,7	9,3	1,2	14,2	15,7
Q4	0,5	0,6	4,3	0,7	5,6	6,1
Q5	0,1	-0,1	0,7	0,1	0,8	0,9

Source: Elaboration by the authors based on CASEN Surveys 1990, 1994, 1996 and 1998.

However, there still remains one question: If the year 1990 is compared with 1998, how much of the reduction in income inequality can be attributed to the increase in social expenditures and how much to a better targeting of programs to the poor?

Between 1990 and 1998 there is no evidence of significant improvement in the absolute targeting of the social programs considered. In 1990 only 56% of the subsidies reached the two lowest income quintiles, while in 1998 this percentage rose to 59%. Although this finding seems to indicate an improvement in focusing programs, the simulation exercises carried out show that this variation did not significantly impact the income distribution. By way of illustration, if the total resources assigned to social programs in 1998 had been targeted just as in 1990 (when social expenditure was substantially smaller) they would not have made a significant change in the contribution of social policy to a reduction of income inequality; this is evident from utilizing measurements such as the ratio of income between the richest 20% and the poorest 20% of the population, which for the year 1998 is 20.0 times, after considering the net income of social policy, this is reduced to 11.1 times; but it would have been of 11.0 times if the resources available in 1998 had been assigned just as they were in 1990.

Therefore, the drop in inequality from 1998 to 1990 as result of social policies, should be attributed exclusively to the growth of social expenditure in the period. This does not mean that targeting was not important, or could not be important. Rather, it shows that there was no improvement in targeting that allows explanation of the greater impact of social programs on income distribution.

Subsidy Areas

Besides, it is worth mentioning that of all the social programs considered, subsidies in education are those that give the greatest impulse to reduction in inequality. This larger contribution can be explained because in all regions the average amount of subsidies in education is greater than that of health, housing and, even monetary subsidies (See Table N°10).

Table N°10
Average Amount of Per-Capita Subsidies
Period 1990-1998

	Average Per-Capita Amount ($ of Nov. 1998)				Relative Per-Capita Amount of Subsidies			
	1990	1994	1996	1998	1990	1994	1996	1998
Net Income	83.665	105.212	115.917	124.335				
Monetary Subsidies	708	706	1.065	1.135	15,8	10,7	11,5	11,1
Health Subsidies	997	2.073	2.936	2.299	22,2	31,3	31,7	22,5
Education Subsidies	2.459	3.443	4.699	6.125	54,8	52,0	50,7	59,9
Housing Subsidies	320	393	576	666	7,1	5,9	6,2	6,5
In-Kind Subsidies	3.775	5.909	8.212	9.090	84,2	89,3	88,5	88,9
Total Subsidies	4.483	6.615	9.277	10.225	100,0	100,0	100,0	100,0

Source: Elaboration by the authors based on CASEN Surveys 1990, 1994, 1996 and 1998.

Regional Impact

The distinct emphasis given to social policy throughout the different zones of Chile must explain the diverse impact of these programs on the inequality of each region. One way of look at this point is to consider that Chilean social policy has as its main objective poverty reduction, and consequently should satisfy the basic needs of the population. As such, the effort of focusing expenditure in the different geographical zones of the country, could be more or less successful in reducing the poverty of each zone, and as consequence, have varying impact on income distribution.

One element to emphasize with respect to the impact of expenditure in terms of distribution, is whether or not the relation of inequality between the various regions is affected by social policies.

In Table Nº11 the regions have been listed by level of inequality (as measured by varying per capita income definitions). It illustrates that while the ranking of inequality varies from year to year, the impact of social policies has heterogeneously affected the ranking for each period of analysis.

With the objective of simplifying the previous results, Table Nº12 classifies the regions into 3 groups: High Inequality (the 4 regions having a greater Gini coefficient for the period), Lower Inequality (the 4 regions having a lower Gini coefficient) and Average Inequality (the remainder of the regions). Then, it is possible to identify cases such as the year 1994, in which the relative position of regions showing greater inequality was not affected as a result of social programs, but did improve in absolute terms. Analogously, cases such as that of Region V whose relative position gets worse in 1998, as a result of government action reducing inequality more in other regions.

Therefore, although a certain direct relation between poverty and the significance of impact of social programs on inequality is detected, it is not clear that these programs contribute to a relative improvement of the "high inequality" regions. As it happens, this depends on the year of analysis and becomes even more uncertain when considering that the differences in regional inequality must be significant to be accepted statistically.

Table Nº11
Ranking of Regions according to Per-Capita Income Inequality
(Gini Coefficients)

Zone or Region	Net Income of Soc.Pol	Rkg	Net Income of Soc.Pol	Rkg	Net Income of Soc.Pol.	Rkg	Net Income of Soc.Pol	Rkg	Income with Soc Policies.	Rkg	Income with Soc Policies.	Rkg	Income with Soc. Policies.	Rkg	Income with Soc. Policies	Rkg
	1990		1994		1996		1998		1990		1994		1996		1998	
Metropolitan Region	0,5426		0,5740		0,5467		0,5626		0,5146		0,5655		0,5051		0,5200	
Rest of the Country	0,5556		0,5343		0,5404		0,5466		0,5097		0,5296		0,4679		0,4687	
Total Country	0,5558		0,5651		0,5565		0,5644		0,5176		0,5588		0,4974		0,5028	
I	0,5393	8	0,5164	6	0,4966	4	0,4806	1	0,5059	9	0,5115	7	0,4377	2	0,4212	2
II	0,5237	4	0,5050	5	0,4834	1	0,5164	4	0,4916	5	0,5031	5	0,4425	5	0,4692	8
III	0,5293	5	0,4745	2	0,5748	13	0,4964	2	0,4926	6	0,4723	2	0,5138	13	0,4173	1
IV	0,5335	6	0,5031	4	0,5251	7	0,5420	9	0,4794	3	0,4976	4	0,4492	6	0,4590	7
V	0,5337	7	0,4948	3	0,4957	3	0,5146	3	0,4938	7	0,4908	3	0,4422	4	0,4578	6
VI	0,5051	1	0,5285	8	0,5126	6	0,5188	5	0,4595	2	0,5245	8	0,4423	8	0,4417	5
VII	0,5845	13	0,5531	10	0,5470	8	0,5246	6	0,5348	12	0,5482	10	0,4628	8	0,4315	3
VIII	0,5557	10	0,5430	9	0,5671	12	0,5730	11	0,5024	8	0,5383	9	0,4877	11	0,4865	9
IX	0,5775	11	0,5750	13	0,5513	11	0,5993	13	0,5246	11	0,5692	13	0,4505	7	0,4986	11
X	0,5818	12	0,5570	11	0,5512	9	0,5331	7	0,5351	13	0,5500	11	0,4651	10	0,4387	4
XI	0,5059	2	0,5166	7	0,4974	5	0,5783	12	0,4514	1	0,5096	6	0,4275	1	0,5100	12
XII	0,5220	3	0,4388	1	0,4812	2	0,5386	8	0,4796	4	0,4359	1	0,4334	3	0,4868	10
R.Metropolitana	0,0000	9	0,0000	12	0,0000	10	0,0000	10	0,0000	10	0,0000	10	0,0000	12	0,0000	13

Source: Elaboration by the authors based on CASEN Surveys 1990, 1994, 1996 and 1998.

Table 12

Classification of Regions of the Country According to Gini Coefficient

Inequality	Year 1990		Year 1994		Year 1998	
	Net Income of Soc. Pol.	Income with Soc. Pol.	Net Income of Soc. Pol.	Income with Soc. Pol.	Net Income of Soc.Pol.	Income with Pol. Social
High	7, 8, 9,10	7, 9, 10, 13	7, 9, 10, 13	7, 9, 10, 13	8, 9, 11, 13	9, 11, 12, 13
Average	1, 3, 4, 5, 13	1, 2, 3, 5, 8	1, 2, 6, 8, 11	1, 2, 6, 8, 11	4, 6, 7, 10, 12	2, 4, 5, 6, 8
Low	2, 6, 11, 12	4, 6, 11, 12	3, 4, 5, 12	3, 4, 5, 12	1, 2, 3, 5	1, 3, 7, 10

Source: Elaborated by the authors, based on CASEN Survey 1990, 1994 and 1996.

Finally, Tables N°13 and 14 present the changes in the distribution of per-capita income between the years 1990 and 1998, at both a national and regional level. For the period, the diagnosis with respect to the evolution of inequality, especially in the regions, is sensitive to the indicator used. The distribution of income net of social policies, as measured by the Gini coefficient, did not vary significantly throughout the country; only regions I, VII and X experienced a significant fall in inequality, while in the Metropolitan Region a significant increase in the indicator is evident. Once the amalgam of subsidies that households receive is incorporated, a change in inequality can be seen, in that it was, in fact, reduced on a country level and, in particular, in the non-metropolitan regions; which at a less aggregate level is ratified in regions I, III, V, VII and X. In contrast, significant increases in inequality are not generated in any zone.

Likewise, upon considering as a measurement the variance of the logarithm of per-capita net incomes it can be seen that, statistically, inequality increased significantly at a country level for the period 1990-1998, while regionally only the increase in inequality in regions VIII, IX and X, and the decrease in regions II and V were significant. Once the subsidies received by household members are included, the diagnosis changes, due to the fact that a significant reduction in inequality is detected at a country level, in the Metropolitan Region, and in the other regions. However, no significant changes in income distribution are registered in regions VIII and XI.

Table N°13
**Impact of Monetary, Education, Health and Housing Subsidies on the Distribution
Of Per-Capita Income, 1990-1998**
(Gini Coefficients)

Zone or Region	Net Income of Soc.Pol. 1990	Net Income of Soc.Pol. 1998	Significance of Change (98/90)	Income with Soc.Policies 1990	Income with Soc.Policies 1998	Significance of Change (98/90)
Metropolitan Region	0,5426 (0.5358, 0.5490)	0,5626 (0.5550, 0.5716)	*	0,5146 (0.5077, 0.5211)	0,5200 (0.5120, 0.5294)	
Rest of the Country	0,5556 (0.5488, 0.5610)	0,5466 (0.5409, 0.5525)		0,5097 (0.5026, 0.5153)	0,4687 (0.4628, 0.4749)	*
Total Country	0,5558 (0.5515, 0.5602)	0,5644 (0.5590, 0.5701)		0,5176 (0.5129, 0.5221)	0,5028 (0.4968, 0.5089)	*
I	0,5393 (0.5160, 0.5646)	0,4806 (0.4577, 0.4999)	*	0,5059 (0.4824, 0.5317)	0,4212 (0.3989, 0.4411)	*
II	0,5237 (0.5102, 0.5365)	0,5164 (0.4846, 0.5434)		0,4916 (0.4777, 0.5045)	0,4692 (0.4359, 0.4969)	
III	0,5293 (0.5068, 0.5514)	0,4964 (0.4819, 0.5102)		0,4926 (0.4697, 0.5143)	0,4173 (0.4017, 0.4312)	*
IV	0,5335 (0.5178, 0.5493)	0,5420 (0.5167, 0.5635)		0,4794 (0.4641, 0.4959)	0,4590 (0.4317, 0.4824)	
V	0,5337 (0.5158, 0.5501)	0,5146 (0.5052, 0.5248)		0,4938 (0.4751, 0.5107)	0,4578 (0.4473, 0.4688)	*
VI	0,5051 (0.4912, 0.5169)	0,5188 (0.5051, 0.5337)		0,4595 (0.4452, 0.4718)	0,4417 (0.4266, 0.4579)	
VII	0,5845 (0.5647, 0.6088)	0,5246 (0.5077, 0.5377)	*	0,5348 (0.5144, 0.5602)	0,4315 (0.4132, 0.4447)	*
VIII	0,5557 (0.5400, 0.5689)	0,5730 (0.5599, 0.5840)		0,5024 (0.4867, 0.5170)	0,4865 (0.4715, 0.4987)	
IX	0,5775 (0.5573, 0.5968)	0,5993 (0.5785, 0.6196)		0,5246 (0.5029, 0.5452)	0,4986 (0.4745, 0.5223)	
X	0,5818 (0.5626, 0.6078)	0,5331 (0.5200, 0.5435)	*	0,5351 (0.5145, 0.5619)	0,4387 (0.4257, 0.4496)	*
XI	0,5059 (0.4848, 0.5279)	0,5783 (0.5272, 0.6306)		0,4514 (0.4294, 0.4743)	0,5100 (0.4558, 0.5659)	
XII	0,5220 (0.5034, 0.5502)	0,5386 (0.4833, 0.5886)		0,4796 (0.4595, 0.5080)	0,4868 (0.4313, 0.5391)	

Table N°14
**Impact of the Monetary, Education, Health and Housing Subsidies
on the Distribution of Per-Capita Income, 1990-1998**
(Variance of Log Income)

Zone or Region	Net Income of Soc.Pol. 1990	Net Income of Soc.Pol. 1998	Significance of Change	Income with Soc.Policies 1990	Income with Soc.Policies 1998	Significance of Change
Metropolitan Region	0,9746 (0.9497, 1.0008)	1,0371 (1.0128, 1.0624)	*	0,7790 (0.7583, 0.7957)	0,7238 (0.7074, 0.7400)	*
Rest of Country	0,9745 (0.9576, 0.9877)	1,0668 (1.0440, 1.0881)	*	0,6837 (0.6733, 0.6946)	0,5781 (0.5667, 0.5887)	*
Total Country	1,0031 (0.9909, 1.0167)	1,1043 (1.0866, 1.1215)	*	0,7399 (0.7306, 0.7498)	0,6632 (0.6701, 0.6962)	*
I	0,8736 (0.8210, 0.9253)	0,8420 (0.7698, 0.9115)		0,6898 (0.6485, 0.7280)	0,5395 (0.4919, 0.5873)	*
II	0,9348 (0.8951, 0.9812)	0,8041 (0.7395, 0.8599)	*	0,7193 (0.6880, 0.7524)	0,5635 (0.5142, 0.6096)	*
III	0,8505 (0.8028, 0.8902)	0,9459 (0.8788, 1.0087)		0,6495 (0.6085, 0.6893)	0,5048 (0.4736, 0.5372)	*
IV	0,8752 (0.8351, 0.9156)	0,9546 (0.9045, 1.0028)		0,5962 (0.5692, 0.6220)	0,5222 (0.4834, 0.5526)	*
V	0,9256 (0.8743, 0.9734)	0,8964 (0.8606, 0.9323)	*	0,6905 (0.6570, 0.7182)	0,5914 (0.5619, 0.6183)	*
VI	0,8693 (0.8252, 0.9054)	0,8803 (0.8317, 0.9219)		0,6063 (0.5753, 0.6290)	0,4997 (0.4712, 0.5263)	*
VII	0,9970 (0.9517, 1.0420)	0,9345 (0.8792, 0.9895)		0,6922 (0.6583, 0.7296)	0,4869 (0.4523, 0.5175)	*
VIII	0,9988 (0.9555, 1.0487)	1,2172 (1.1630, 1.2778)	*	0,6411 (0.6162, 0.6690)	0,6146 (0.5886, 0.6377)	
IX	1,0928 (1.0462, 1.1491)	1,2574 (0.1907, 1.3316)	*	0,7148 (0.6827, 0.7508)	0,6026 (0.5611, 0.6448)	*
X	0,9184 (0.8851, 0.9582)	1,0794 (1.0167, 1.1527)	*	0,6730 (0.6470, 0.7046)	0,5014 (0.4765, 0.5230)	*
XI	0,7971 (0.7426, 0.8544)	0,9138 (0.8428, 1.0060)		0,5585 (0.5154, 0.6034)	0,5562 (0.5005, 0.6268)	
XII	0,8860 (0.8449, 0.9356)	0,8373 (0.7088, 0.9676)		0,6827 (0.6332, 0.7391)	0,5361 (0.4526, 0.6227)	*

Source: Elaborated by the authors based on CASEN Surveys 1990 and 1998.

Sensitivity Analysis of Base Assumption

As indicated earlier, the preceding results rest on the assumption that $1 in subsidies in kind equals $\alpha = \$1$ in available household income. However, the evidence indicates that possibly $\alpha < 1$, because the valuation of social expenditure on the part of its beneficiaries cannot be perfect, furthermore there is a certain potential inefficiency in social expenditure. Alternatively, it could be that $\alpha > 1$, when the difference in quality between the goods provided by the public and private sectors are less than the price differential between them.

Due to the aforementioned considerations, the impact of the various programs considered has been sensitized, thus obtaining Gini coefficients for per capita income corrected for social policy, for the years 1990, 1996 and 1998 at varying levels of $\alpha \leq 1$ (See Table N°15).

Using this sensitivity analysis as a starting point, it can be seen that the reduction in income inequality generated by social programs, would have been significant in 1996 and 1998 (1990) even if the valuation of the individuals and the inefficiencies in social expenditure had led to only 20% (30%) of the expenditure increasing consumption opportunities and household welfare. Such a conclusion is especially interesting in a context in which: 1)Chilean social policy has been designed to fight poverty and not income inequality; 2) The study is based on the immediate impact of social expenditures, without considering the well known medium and long term impact of social policies such as education and child nutrition.

Table N°15
Sensitivity Analysis of the Impact of Monetary, Education, Health and Housing
on the Distribution of Per-Capita Income (total
(Gini Coefficients)

	Gini Coefficients 1990	Confidence Interval	Significance of Change	Gini Coefficients 1996	Confidence Interval	Significance of Change	Gini Coefficients 1998	Confidence Interval	Significance of Change
Net Income of Soc.Pol.	0,5558	(0.5515, 0.5602)		0,5565	(0.5495, 0.5626)		0,5644	(0.5590, 0.5701)	
Income with Soc.Policies									
Alfa									
0	0,5558	(0.5515, 0.5602)		0,5565	(0.5495, 0.5626)		0,5644	(0.5590, 0.5701)	
0,1	0,5517	(0.5473, 0.5560)		0,5469	(0.5403, 0.5535)		0,5576	(0.5521, 0.5633)	
0,2	0,5476	(0.5432, 0.5520)		0,5409	(0.5343, 0.5475)	*	0,5509	(0.5454, 0.5567)	*
0,3	0,5436	(0.5392, 0.5480)	*	0,5350	(0.5283, 0.5417)	*	0,5444	(0.5388, 0.5502)	*
0,4	0,5397	(0.5352, 0.5441)	*	0,5292	(0.5226, 0.5360)	*	0,5380	(0.5323, 0.5439)	*
0,5	0,5359	(0.5314, 0.5403)	*	0,5236	(0.5169, 0.5305)	*	0,5318	(0.5260, 0.5377)	*
0,6	0,5321	(0.5275, 0.5365)	*	0,5181	(0.5114, 0.5250)	*	0,5257	(0.5199, 0.5317)	*
0,7	0,5284	(0.5238, 0.5328)	*	0,5128	(0.5060, 0.5197)	*	0,5198	(0.5139, 0.5258)	*
0,8	0,5247	(0.5201, 0.5292)	*	0,5075	(0.5008, 0.5145)	*	0,5140	(0.5081, 0.5200)	*
0,9	0,5211	(0.5165, 0.5256)	*	0,5024	(0.4956, 0.5095)	*	0,5083	(0.5024, 0.5144)	*
1	0,5176	(0.5129, 0.5221)	*	0,4974	(0.4906, 0.5045)	*	0,5028	(0.4968, 0.5089)	*

Source: Elaborated by the authors based on CASEN Surveys 1990, 1996 and 1998.

Characterization of the Beneficiaries

As mentioned earlier, this methodology assigns a monetary value to each individual for the benefit that he or she has received in the form of education, health, housing or monetary subsidies. One advantage of assigning such subsidies to an individual level, and then aggregating per household, is that it allows us to explore those common characteristics that determine the receipt of the various government subsidies.

With information regarding the subsidies received by each household and the socio-economic characteristics collected by the CASEN survey, a linear model of regression was estimated,[81] in which the dependent variable was defined as the logarithm of the subsidies received. The independent variables included multiple characteristics for each household, such as the logarithm of the per-capita household income (a key variable in the definition of Chilean social policies); the zone (urban/rural) and region in which this household resides; the age and schooling of the head of the household and of the spouse, the number of children and adults of differing genders and ages; the rate of dependence (measured as the relationship between the number of employed and the number of household members); and some housing characteristics such as the number of bedrooms and the availability of electrical, drinking water and sanitation services. It is important to clarify that the purpose of this model is to find multiple correlations among the variables involved, rather than establishing some relationship of causality.

Table N°16 presents the results of the regression for 1998.[82] It shows that for individual social programs and in total (Overall Social Policy), expenditures tend to favor lower income households, those located in rural zones, and those whose heads of household are either women or retired individuals. Likewise, it can be inferred that only a small linear relationship exists between the age of the head of household (and the spouse) and the per-capita subsidies received. The presence of children between the ages of 5 and 15 years elevates the subsidies received, while with a greater number of adults they are reduced.

In comparison, the more people at work there are in a household, relative to total members, the benefits obtained by the household are lower. Likewise, the greater the schooling of the head of household and the spouse, the benefits received are also lower. The housing characteristics reflect, in turn, that the greater the number of bedrooms the less probable it is to benefit from the various social programs. Finally, the region in which the household resides is also important in explaining the subsidies received by its members, especially if the regions considered are I, XI and XII which are the most favored, while the V, VI, VII, VIII, and the Metropolitan regions receive lower per-capita subsidies.

Finally, some findings should be highlighted regarding the various areas subsidized. In health, no significant differences are found between rural and urban zones, while the existence of children less than 4 years old has a direct influence on the subsidies received, and there seems to exist a greater focus on regions IV, VIII and IX. As for the education sector, subsidies increase with the age of the head of household, while at the same time the schooling of the head of household and the spouse do not explain the magnitude of the increase, which is a reflection of the universal character of Chilean educational policy. In the housing area, the greater the income of the household the greater the benefit received (this makes sense when considering that although the percentage of the value of subsidized housing is smaller in those programs accessible to higher income households, the value of the housing rises, thus raising the rent attributed). In addition, the housing subsidy calls attention to the fact that the greater the number of household members the lower the subsidy, perhaps due to the pre-requirement of savings of the housing policy of the last decade. These subsidies seem to be better focused in regions II and XII.

---

[81] A truncated TOBIT model was also estimated. However, given that a large part of the population received some subsidy, the results were similar to those estimated by an OLS (Ordinary Least Squares) model.
[82] The results commented on here are of great interest. All are statistically significant for the usual confidence tests.

Table N°16

OLS Regression:Logarithm of Per-Capita Subsidies

by Housing Characteristics, Year 98

	Health		Education		Monetary		Housing		Total	
	Coefficient	t-	Coefficient	t-	Coefficient	t-	Coefficient	t-	Coefficient	t-
Net Per-Capita	-	-	-	-	-	-	0,11	10,7	-	-
Urban	0,00	0,1	-	-	-	-	0,06	1,9	-	-
Female Head of	-	-	0,18	7,1	-	-	0,13	2,7	0,07	3,4
Retired Head of	0,19	12,2	0,03	1,5	0,37	11,1	-	-	0,18	11,2
Age of	-	-	-	-	-	-	-	-	0,00	3,1
Age of Spouse	0,00	14,1	0,00	-	0,00	16,8	0,00	8,4	0,00	-
Age of Head of	-	-	0,01	6,6	-	-	0,00	1,3	0,00	4,7
Age of Head of Hous.	0,00	9,3	0,00	-	0,00	4,1	0,00	-	0,00	-
Children(boys)<4	0,14	12,9	-	-	-	-	-	-	-	-
Children(girls)<4	0,09	4,3	-	-	-	-	-	-	-	-
Children(boys) between 5-	-	-	0,08	13,6	-	-	-	-	0,23	35,1
Children(girls) between 5-	-	-	0,08	6,4	-	-	-	-	0,21	16,4
Children(boys) between 11-	-	-	0,19	28,8	-	-	-	-	0,30	42,2
Children(girls) between 11-	-	-	0,13	8,3	-	-	-	-	0,28	20,5
Adult	-	-	-	-	-	-	-	-	-	-
Adult	-	-	-	-	-	-	-	-	-	-
Employed(Household	-	-	-	-	0,10	2,7	0,11	2,8	-	-
Schooling Head of	-	-	0,00	0,3	-	-	0,00	0,7	-	-
Schooling of	-	-	-	-	-	-	0,00	1,5	-	-
Availability of Potable	-	-	0,01	1,0	-	-	0,03	0,9	0,02	2,4
Availability of Sewer	-	-	-	-	0,01	0,6	-	-	0,01	1,0
Availability of	0,00	0,3	0,01	1,8	-	-	0,16	4,5	0,07	7,8
Total	-	-	-	-	-	-	0,03	5,7	-	-
II	-	-	-	-	-	-	0,16	2,2	-	-
III	0,02	0,8	-	-	-	-	-	-	-	-
IV	0,10	4,2	-	-	-	-	-	-	-	-
V	0,03	1,4	-	-	-	-	-	-	-	-
VI	-	-	-	-	-	-	-	-	-	-
VII	0,03	1,1	-	-	-	-	-	-	-	-
VIII	0,09	3,8	-	-	-	-	-	-	-	-
IX	0,10	4,3	-	-	-	-	-	-	-	-
X	-	-	-	-	-	-	-	-	-	-
XI	-	-	0,05	1,4	0,09	1,6	0,01	0,2	0,11	3,2
XII	-	-	0,12	3,8	-	-	0,35	4,3	-	-
Metropolitan	-	-	-	-	-	-	0,07	1,3	-	-
Consta	10,06	139,0	9,92	140,4	12,29	114,4	6,76	42,7	12,04	173,9
R2	0,265		0,174		0,318		0,330		0,256	
F-	392,2		164,9		266,1		113,6		350,6	
Number of	35.95		25.64		24.47		8.38		41.25	

Conclusions

Even though Chile has been characterized as an economy of rapid growth and uneven income distribution, this paper shows that social policy constitutes an effective tool in reducing such inequality. This is especially interesting in a context in which social policies have been traditionally designed with the objective of fighting the problem of poverty and not of inequality.

The methodology proposed outlines a new scenario for characterizing inequality in Chile. In contrast to prior studies, this methodology assigns to each household, only the subsidies in kind actually received by its members for each period of analysis, based on self-reporting. Then it determines if the impact of these subsidies on income distribution is significant or not.

Application of this methodology makes it evident that social policy, implemented in the form of monetary, health, housing and, especially, education subsidies are key to improving income distribution, even in a context in which only the immediate impact of this combination of subsidies is considered.

The reduction in inequality at a country level is robust for the various indicators chosen, while the impact of these social policies differs at a regional level, and its significance is sensitive to the indicator of distribution chosen. The disparities in inequality observed throughout the regions of the country remained stable, probably as consequence of the differing emphasis given to social policies in each region. It is not so much the absolute focusing as the relative focusing of social programs that contributes to a decrease in the concentration of income, especially when regions of extensive heterogeneity are analyzed, as well as the initial levels of inequality and income.

Another finding is that social policy reduced inequality in every year of interest, but it showed a relatively greater impact in 1998 than in 1990, which could be explained by a greater assignment of resources to the subsidy programs, a greater efficiency of the Government in targeting resources, and/or self-selection on the part of the beneficiaries of Government subsidies. However, the overall drop in inequality between 1990 and 1998 as a result of social policies is primarily due to the expansion of social programs, not the improvement in their targeting. This does not mean that improvements in targeting could not be important, only that in the period under study it was the expansion of the size of social programs that accounts for the beneficial impact on income distribution.

Finally, it is worth highlighting that based on a sensitivity analysis of the impact of social expenditure, we reach the conclusion that reduction in income inequality would have been significant even if the valuation of the individuals and the inefficiencies in social expenditure had led to only 20% (30%) of the expenditure increasing consumption opportunities and household welfare. This conclusion is especially interesting in a context where, as previously mentioned, social policy has been designed only to fight poverty. Furthermore, this study does not consider the well-known medium and long term impact of policies such as education and child nutrition.

Several natural extensions to this study can be outlined: a more in-depth analysis of the focus and progressivity of the health, education and housing programs here considered; breakdown by rural-urban areas; and consideration of aspects such as regional prices and economies of scale within household, with their corresponding implications in the measurement of inequality and poverty in Chile. Likewise, the methodology developed in this research has a great potential to link the diverse characteristics of households with the benefits received from the Government, which would allow better understanding of the effectiveness of social policy in the reduction of poverty and inequality. This is true because such policies are not only directed to lower income households, but rather, usually tend to satisfy more general needs, taking into account their composition and size.

REFERENCES

Beyer, H. 1997. "Distribución del Ingreso: Antecedentes para la Discusión." *Estudios Públicos* N° 65. Centro de Estudios Públicos, Santiago, Chile.

Bravo, D., and Marinovic, A. 1997. "Desigualdad Salarial en Chile : 40 años de evidencia." *Universidad de Chile, Departamento de Economía.*

Bravo, D., D. Contreras, and T. Rau. 1999. "Wage Inequality and Labor Market in Chile 1990/1996: a Non-Parametric Approach." *Universidad de Chile, Departamento de Economía.*

Contreras, D. 1996. "Pobreza y Desigualdad en Chile: 1987-1992. Discurso, Metodología y Evidencia Empírica." *Estudios Públicos* N° 64, Santiago, Chile.

Contreras, D. and J. Ruiz-Tagle. 1997. "Cómo medir la Distribución de Ingresos en Chile ¿Son distintas nuestras regiones? ¿Son distintas nuestras familias?." *Estudios Públicos* N° 65, Santiago, Chile.

Contreras, D. 1999. "Distribución del Ingreso en Chile: Hechos y Mitos". *Perspectivas.*

Cowan, K. y De Gregorio, J. 1996. "Distribución y Pobreza en Chile: ¿Estamos mal ? ¿Ha habido progresos ? ¿Hemos retrocedido ?." *Estudios Públicos*, N° 64.

Escobar, B. y P. Meller. 1996. "Efecto Regional del Modelo Exportador. Evolución del Diferencial Salarial entre Regiones y Santiago." P. Meller (ed). *El Modelo Exportador Chileno: Crecimiento y Equidad.* CIEPLAN.

Gutiérrez, H. 1989. "Metodología para Identificar Subsidios en el Sector Salud". Doc. Serie Investigación N° 96. Universidad de Chile, Santiago. Departamento de Economía.

Haindl, E.; Budinich, E. e I. Irarrázaval. 1989. "Gasto Social Efectivo: Un Instrumento para la Superación Definitiva de la Pobreza." ODEPLAN. Universidad de Chile, Santiago. Facultad de Ciencias Económicas y Administrativas.

Infante, R. y C. Revoredo. 1993. "Gasto Social y Nivel de Ingreso de las Familias Pobres". En R. Infante (ed), *Deuda Social. Desafío de la Equidad.*, Prealc-OIT, Chile.

Larrañaga, O. 1994. "Gasto Social en Chile. Incidencia Distributiva e Incentivos Laborales." Serie Investigación. I-76. Programa de Postgrado en Economía. ILADES / Georgetown University, Santiago, Chile, Mayo.

Meller, P. y A. Tokman. 1996. "Apertura Comercial y Diferencial Salarial en Chile". P.Meller (ed), *El modelo exportador chileno. Crecimiento y equidad.* Mayo.

MIDEPLAN. 1993. "Programas Sociales: Su Impacto en los Hogares Chilenos. CASEN 1990." Santiago, Chile.

MIDEPLAN. 1994. "Integración al Desarrollo. Balance de la Política Social: 1990-1993." Santiago, Chile. Enero.

MIDEPLAN. 1996a. *Balance de 6 años de las políticas* sociales. Agosto.

MIDEPLAN. 1996b. "Realidad Económico-Social de los Hogares en Chile. Algunos Indicadores Relevantes Encuesta CASEN 1992-1994." 1ª edición. 111-112, Santiago, Chile, Julio.

MIDEPLAN. 1996c. "Pobreza y Distribución del Ingreso en Chile. 1996. Resultados de la Encuesta de Caracterización Socioeconómica Nacional." Santiago, Chile. Julio.

MIDEPLAN. 1999. "Distribución e Impacto Distributivo del Gasto Social en los Hogares 1998". Documentos Sociales. Departamento de Estudios Sociales. Santiago, Chile. Julio.

Ministerio de Salud. 1988. "Manual del Programa Nacional de Alimentación Complementaria". Santiago, Chile.

Parra, J. 1996. "Impacto de las Transferencias Intergubernamentales en la Distribución Interpersonal del Ingreso en Colombia". Archivos de Macroeconomía. Documento 43. Unidad de Análisis Macroeconómico. Departamento Nacional de Planeación. Colombia. Marzo.

Robbins, D. 1994. "Relative Wage Structure in Chile, 1957-1992 : Changes in the Structure of Demand for Schooling." *Estudios de Economía*. Santiago de Chile. Noviembre.

Ruiz-Tagle, J. 1999. "Chile: 40 años de desigualdad de Ingresos". Documento de Trabajo 165. Universidad de Chile. Departamento de Economía.

Schkolnilk, M. 1996. "Estudio de Incidencia Presupuestaria: El Caso de Chile". Serie Regional de Política Fiscal 83. CEPAL-PNUD. Santiago, Chile.

Vélez, C. 1994. "La Magnitud del Gasto Público Social en Colombia". *Coyuntura Social* 11. Fedesarrollo. Bogotá, Colombia. Noviembre.

Vélez, C. 1995. *Gasto Social y Desigualdad. Logros y Extravíos.* Departamento Nacional de Planeación. República de Colombia.

World Bank 1997. "Chile. Poverty and Income Distribution in a High-Growth Economy: 1987-1995". Report 16377-CH.

Younger, S., M. Villafuerte y L. Jara. 1997. "Incidencia distributiva del gasto público y funciones de demanda en el Ecuador: Educación, Salud y Crédito Agrícola del BNF". Borrador. Febrero.

APPENDIX 1

Previous Methodologies for the Valuation of Health and Education Subsidies

In recent years, two efforts to characterize the distributive impact of Chilean social expenditure have been undertaken. In the following, a review will be made of the methodology utilized by the Ministry of Planning and Cooperation (MIDEPLAN) and Larrañaga (1994) to valuate social programs that benefit distinct quintiles of income, and on this basis, to measure their impact in terms of distribution.

Methodology of MIDEPLAN

The basic source of information for MIDEPLAN is the CASEN Survey, which only provides information regarding the distributive incidence of the main social programs launched by the government. The expenditure in social programs in education and health, included in the CASEN Survey, are distributed by quintiles of households, that are then classified on the basis of their autonomous per capita family income.

First, a methodology of valuation of government subsidies is outlined, differentiated by monetary subsidies (pecuniary transfers) and non-monetary (subsidies in kind, in other words- goods or services):
i)   Monetary subsidies: The amount of resources spent in each program is assigned among the quintiles, according to the access that the households declare to have had, in the CASEN Survey.
ii) Non-monetary programs: Valuation schemes of high complexity are outlined, due to the great heterogeneity of the services that the Government subsidizes:

Education.[83] To valuate the subsidies in education, the quantity of resources that the beneficiaries receive monthly is estimated, according to level of income, and thus quantify the contribution of such subsidies to family income.

The Government finances, through a system of subsidies, students that at different grades, are registered in subsidized private schools, municipal schools and private institutions. The transfers received by the first two types of establishments are based on the students' average attendance and the corresponding amount of the subsidy per student (it differs according to grade level, beneficiary population and geographical location). Meanwhile, private institutions receive a special subsidy for technical-professional education.

MIDEPLAN then outlines a formula for calculating the subsidy per student in the various education programs: pre-school, basic, technical-professional high school, and scientific-humanist high school; in addition to the subsidies that are offered through the School Nutrition Program and Financial Credit to University Students. In this way, the direct and indirect expenditures per student are accounted for, according to educational level, and are then distributed among the households.

---

[83] Waiser, Myriam (1993) "Social Expenditure in Education: Distribution and Impact of the Fiscal Contribution", in MIDEPLAN (1993) (op. cit.).

Health.[84] To valuate health subsidies, the benefit is calculated for each type of medical attention reported, minus the cost which the beneficiaries incur.

Towards this end, types of medical attention are defined and total medical treatment received by quintile is determined. The information used was based on data from the National Health Fund (FONASA) and the National System of Health Services (SNSS). The subsidies associated with each type of medical attention delivered were valuated.[85] The total amount of the subsidy is equal to the amount of medical treatment of each type received, multiplied by the subsidy associated with each one. The Calculation of these subsidies was based on the assumption that the benefit of each medical treatment received is at least equal to the cost of providing it.

To determine the costs incurred by the users, the total amount of bills and co-payments are distributed by quintiles, as reported in FONASA and SNSS accounts.

After valuation of the health and education subsidies, MIDEPLAN obtains a profile of income distribution in Chile by quintiles of households, having incorporated, in addition to the monetary income and attributed rent, the expenditures made by the public sector on social programs.

Methodology Utilized by Larrañaga (1994)

In addition to considering the social programs considered in the CASEN Survey, Larrañaga extends the analysis to programs of lesser importance in terms of total social expenditure. To do this, new forms of identifying beneficiaries are outlined.

The CASEN Survey provides information regarding 16 of the 63 programs treated in the classification of the Directorate of Budgets (Dipres), which meant a 73% share of social expenditure budgeted for 1993.

The remainder of the programs, not included in the CASEN Survey, are divided into:
1)   Those nonexistent in 1990, especially in the social investment area - FOSIS, youth training, vulnerable groups;
2)   Programs not identified in the household survey, of low representation in the sample or that favor the population in general;
3)   Expenditure in administration and supervision of social programs.

Larrañaga utilizes different assignment criteria for the various social programs. For example, the expenditure in programs that are mentioned in the CASEN Survey are distributed on the basis of information compiled in the Survey, on a quintile level. While, for the other three groups of programs, new assignment criteria are designed by quintiles: refined distributive weighting of programs; number of beneficiaries by income quintile -before expenditure per beneficiary; population in condition of poverty; average incidence of the amalgam of social expenditure, etc. Given the available information, such criteria were shown to be the best approximation to the true distribution of expenditure for the beneficiaries of each program. The objective was to optimize the use of available information.

---

[84] Araiz, Sonia and Bridges, Germán (1993) Social "Expenditure in Health," in MIDEPLAN (1993) (op. cit).
[85] In this case, speaking of "subsidy" refers to the "rough benefits" of the medical attention provided, that is, without discounting the costs that the users incur.

In this way, the distributive weighting obtained for a base year (1990), is utilized to assign among income quintiles, the expenditure budgeted for each program, for the period 1990-93. Additionally, given the available information, the study worked with data of expenditure budgeted as provided by the Directorate of Budgets rather than the actual expenditure.

HEALTH SUBSIDIES VALUATION

Subsidy	Modalities	Form of Valuation (1)	Average Value 1996 (2)
National program of Complementary Nutrition (Minsal/ Provisions Center)			
PNAC – children	Basic programs of Reinforcement, according to nutritional state and age	Unit cost + IVA = Billing Value / Quantity of food distributed.	3.468
PNAC–pregnancies and wet-nurses	Basic programs and Reinforcement, according to nutritional state and age	Unit cost + IVA = Billing Value / quantity of food Distributed.	2.710
Health Care Services (MINSAL / FONASA)	Differences according to insurance group of FONASA, modality of treatment and type of medical service	Net subsidy of each type of Medical Service(4)=price attributed Minus co-payment Minus billing	
Preventive Health control	Differences according to modality of treatment (depending on the service provider)	FONASA Tariff "Medical treatment", both modalities (FONASA Beneficiaries: 100% of Subsidy in institutional modality and 50% of subsidy in free choice)	4.143/3
Medical consultations because of Illness or Accidents	Differences according to modality of Treatment	FONASA Tariff "Medical Treatment", both modalities	4.143/3
Specialist Consultations	Differences according to modality of Treatment	FONASA Tariff "Medical Treatment ", both modalities	4.143/3
Urgency Consultations	Differences according to modality of treatment	FONASA Tariff "Medical Treatment ", both modalities	4.143/3
Dental Care	Great heterogeneity in care and absence of statistics for patient controlled per year	(Rough value of annual odontological care) / (12* number of Patient in control in Dec. 94)	3.105/3
Laboratory Exams	Great heterogeneity in installations, modalities of attention	Rough monthly average value, for Each year	1.054/3
X - Rays and Ecography Exams (Imaging)	Great heterogeneity in installments, modalities of treatment	Rough monthly average value, for each year	6.409/3

Appendix 2 (continued)

Subsidy	Modalities	Form of Valuation (1)	Value Average 1996 (2)
Surgical Operations	Great heterogeneity of facilities, Modalities of treatment	Rough monthly average value, in Each year (excludes int. obstetrics)	56.060/3
Hospitalization	Institutional modality	FONASA Fee,	3.711/3
	Free choice modality	FONASA Fee, level 1	3.711/3
Normal Pregnancy	Institutional modality	Attention average tariff with Surgeon or with matrona	100.897/12
	Free choice modality	FONASA Fee, level 1, treatment with surgeon	100.897/12
Caesarean Delivery	Institutional modality	FONASA Fee, treatment with surgeon	154.572/12
	Free choice modality	FONASA Fee, level, treatment with surgeon	.572/12
Maternal Rest Subsidy and of Enf. Seriously ill Child Less than 1 yr.		Value of Med. Leave = (4.5/12) times the Taxable Monthly Income of a Beneficiary with a child less than 1 year old and that is occupied or absent temporarily	
(Superintendency of Social Security)			
Additional 2% Billing Subsidy		Additional Billing= 2% of the taxable Monthly Income of the Beneficiary	
(Superintendency of ISAPRE)		(Limit 7 or more charges: 2%*4,2 UF)	

Note:
(1) : In all cases, the monthly value of the subsidy received has been obtained from each member of the household. Elaborated by Author.
(2) : In November 1998 pesos.
(3) : Information regarding food distribution regulation for pregnant women and wet-nurses is not available.
(4) : The concept of Net subsidy of each Installment is utilized only to measure the distributive impact of social expenditure on health, through valuation of the medical care actually received by each member of a household. However, in this study the methodology additionally followed the measurement of the subsidy as the value based on public health insurance (valued according to the frequency of use medical services by individuals of various age ranges and gender, to relative prices of 1996) minus the monthly payments of people for insurance (provisional health billings) and services provided (co-payments).

Source: Elaborate by the authors, based on information provided by the Ministry of Health, FONASA, Provisions Center. Superintendency of Social Security and Superintendency of ISAPRE.

APPENDIX 3

VALUATION OF EDUCATION SUBSIDIES

Subsidy	Modalities	Form of Valuation (1)	Average Value 1990 (2)	Average Value 1994 (2)	Average Value 1996 (2)
School Nutrition program					
Program of School Nutrition in Basic Schools (JUNAEB and MINEDUC)	Assignment of breakfast, snack and/or lunch, differentiated by its Energy content (calorie).	Unit cost of each type of ration, differentiated by region, for 21 work days per month.			
	- Breakfast or snack		1.890	1.939	2.123
	- Lunch		4.720	4.156	4.452
	- Breakfast (or snack) and lunch		6.610	6.096	6.575
	- Breakfast, lunch and snack		8.500	8.034	8.699
Nutrition Program School in Average Education (JUNAEB / MINEDUC)	Assignment of breakfast, snack and/or lunch, differentiated by its Energy content (calorie).	Unit cost of each type of ration, differentiated by region, for 21 work days per month			
	- Breakfast or snack		Only Basic Education	3.193	2.569
	- Lunch			5.646	6.900
	- Breakfast (or snack) and lunch			8.840	9.470
	- Breakfast, lunch and snack			12.033	12.040
JUNJI Pre-school education — INTEGRA					
JUNJI		Monthly average expenditure per Child registered in the program.	20.340	24.264	24.153
INTEGRA		Monthly average expenditure per Child registered in the program.	16.141	26.394	31.156
Establishments Dependent on Mineduc					
Mineduc Contributions to Private corporations (Delegated administration, MINEDUC)	Different contribution according to Corporation.	Monthly Contribution by Mineduc, Per student registered in Nov. of 1994	21.686	25.976	28.892

Appendix 3 (continued)

Subsidy	Modalities	Form of Valuation (1)	Average Value 1990 (2)	Average Value 1994 (2)	Average Value 1996 (2)
System of Subsidies for Municipal establishments and Private Subsidized: (MINEDUC)	Differences according to type and grade, geographical zone and Rural area.	Regular Subsidy per student Assistant = Subsidy Base (3) * Zone Factor (4) + + Ruralness Increment (5) - Disct. Shared Financ. (6)			
Pre-school Education		Base 1990: 0,9090 USE	7.827*z		
		Base 1994: 0,9090 USE		7.833*z+r	
		Base 1996: 1,2778 USE			10.733*z+r
Basic education - 1° to 6°	Half-day, Less than 18 Years old.	Base 1990: 1,0000 USE	8.611*z		
		Base 1994: 1,0000 USE		8.618*z+r	
		Base 1996: 1,2808 USE			10.759*z+r+fc
Basic education - 7° and 8°	Half-day, Less than 18 Years old.	Base 1990: 1,1070 USE	9.532*z		
		Base 1994: 1,1070 USE		9.539*z+r	
		Base 1996: 1,3928 USE			11.699*z+r+fc
High School Scientific - Humanist	Half-day, Less than 18 Years old.	Base 1990: 1,2450 USE	10.720*z		
		Base 1994: 1,2450 USE		10.729*z+r	
		Base 1996: 1,5578 USE			13.085*z+r+fc
High School Technical Professional (T. P.)	- Agricultural and Maritime	Base 1990: 2,2450 USE	19.331*z		
		Base 1994: 1,9700 USE		16.976*z+r	
		Base 1996: 2,3268 USE			19.545*z+r+fc
	- Industrial	Base 1990: 1,8450 USE	15.887*z		
		Base 1994: 1,4800 USE		12.754*z+r	
		Base 1996: 1,8068 USE			15.177*z+r+fc
	- Commercial and Technical	Base 1990: 1,2450 USE	10.720*z		
		Base 1994: 1,3000 USE		11.203*z+r	
		Base 1996: 2,6168 USE			13.581*z+r+fc
Basic education – Adult	Evening prog, individuals	Base 1990: 0,3160 USE	2.721*z		
	Over 18 Years old.	Base 1994: 0,4740 USE		4.085*z+r	
		Base 1996: 0,9408 USE			7.903*z+r

Appendix 3 (continued)

Subsidy	Modalities	Form of Valuation (1)	Average Value 1990 (2)	Average Value 1994 (2)	Average Value 1996 (2)
Adult Grade School Education (C. H. and T. P.)	Evening Prog, individuals Over 18 Years old. Not Differentiated by type of teaching.	Base 1990: 0,3750 USE Base 1994: 0,5630 USE Base 1996: 1,0718 USE	3.229*z	4.851*z+r	3.797*z+r
Basic Special Education Differential		Base 1990: 2,3000 USE Base 1994: 3,0000 USE Base 1996: 4,2504 USE	19.804*z	25.852*z+r	35.703*z+r-fc
Additional resources per Student (MINEDUC): Educational statute	Differentiated by dependence of the	Monthly assignment of Educational Statute per student.			
(Allocation for undertaking in Difficult conditions)	Establishment: - Municipal - Private Subsidized		Did not exist.	2.443 1.439	909 363
Unit of Professional Improvement (UMP), Contribution to Differential groups and non Educational Allowances	Differentiated by region and dependence of the establishment: - Municipal - Private Subsidized	(UMP + Group Contribution Differential + Subsidy Extraordinary to non-school) per student and month.	Did not exist.	1.069 832	783 126
Contribution of city Councils By Attending student (Compensation of Deficit)	Differentiated by regions (7). Assigned, exclusively, to municipal establishments	Contributions of the Municipalities (Area Education) By student and month.	676	1.641	3.140
School supplies Program (JUNAEB)	2 notebooks of 40 pages, 1 pencil, 1 eraser, 1 box of 12 color pencils. Only basic educ.	Monthly cost of school supplies = Budget spent in 1994 / Total number of sets distributed.	Did not exist.	563/12	630/12
School texts (MINEDUC)	Only for Basic education students, differentiated by course. Municipal establishments and private subsidized	Monthly cost of the texts used in each Grade level	Not asked CASEN 90.	1.052/12	1.311/12
Oral Health Program (JUNAEB) Fluoride Gel Application	Less than 15 Years old, Basic Education (Municipal) Partly Subsidized. Differentiated by rural-urban zone(excluding Regions I and V water fluoridation	Monthly cost of the program per school going child, by zone (8)	Did not exist.	1.257/12	1.257/12

Appendix 3 (continued)

Subsidy	Modalities	Form of Valuation (1)	Average Value 1990 (2)	Average Value 1994 (2)	Average Value 1996 (2)
Oral Health Program (JUNAEB) (continued) Modality Covenants	Differentiated by regions, according to the N° Dental Fillings(PO) in each type of treatment: - High Integral (children of 1° basic) - High Maintenance (2° to 8° basic)	(Average Subsidy per PO * average PO for the highest in the region) + subsidy for other Expenditures the highest in each.	Did not exist.	961	1.073
School Health Program (JUNAEB)	Children of 1° to 3° Basic. Revision of the teacher conducts to attention Primary (free) or secondary.	Cost of the program per child registered (includes treatment, exams and processing)	Did not exist.	480 / 83	388 / 957
Scholarships (CASEN Survey) Application Scholarships	Exclusively for students of Upper Education.	Amount of the scholarship received, in monthly terms	Not asked		
Other Scholarships	All levels of Education.	Amount of scholarship received, in Monthly terms.	CASEN 90. Not asked		
Fiscal Loans (CASEN Survey)	Exclusively for students of Upper Education.	Amount of credit received, in monthly terms	CASEN 90.		

Note:
(1) : In all cases, the value of the subsidy received has been obtained for each household member, in monthly terms.
(2) : In pesos of November of 1998.
(3) : Expressed in USE = Unit of Subsidy Educational, a unit of accounting of the Ministry of Education, variable over time in terms of pesos.
(4) : Factor that varies according to region and province in which the council or private-subsidized establishment is located.
(5) : Allocation that depends on the degree of physical isolation of the educational establishment. In 1990 it was impossible to attribute the allocation by Ruralness, in 1994 this approached through the monthly expenditures in increments of ruralness by student, according to region and dependence of the establishment. In 1996 it was possible to attribute to each establishment a corresponding assignment of ruralness: rural standard or incremental ruralness
(6) : The modality of shared financing was established in 1993, as such it is not considered in 1990. Likewise, due to the scarce available information in that respect, this was only analyzed for the year 1996. The bias on 1994 figures due to this could be discarded due to the small significance of the system at that year and that the average charge of the establishments was small and implied no per-pupil subsidy discounts.
(7) : No available Information for the IX Region, in the year 1994.
(8) : Elaborated by the authors based on Díaz et al. (1996) "Social Valuation of Fluoridation Alternatives for the Prevention of Cavities in Rural Zones", MIDEPLAN / Catholic University of Chile, Santiago, Chile, November.

Source: Elaborated by Author, based on information provided by Ministry of Education, National Organization of Aid and Scholarships, National Organization of Pre-Schools, National foundation for the Integral Development of the Smaller one and CASEN Survey 1990, 1994 and 1996.

APPENDIX 4 VALUATION OF HOUSING SUBSIDIES

Subsidy	Objective segment	Form of Valuation (1)	Average Percentage 1990 (2)	Average Percentage 1994 (2)	Average Percentage 1996 (2)
PROGRAMS OF CHILEAN HOUSING POLICY (MINVU)					
Basic housing	Low income Families in marginal housing. Urban and Rural zones.	Percentage of housing value Subsidized by average of each year.	1990: 75,4	1990: 75,4 1991: 75,5 1992: 75,2 1993: 74,4 1994: 65,9	1990: 75,4 1991: 75,5 1992: 75,2 1993: 74,4 1994: 65,9 1995: 61,8 1996: 61,0
Progressive housing	Extremely Marginal Families. Rural and urban zones. Program prompted in November of 1990 (reason it was not considered for this year).	Percentage of housing value subsidized by average of each year	1990: Did not exist	1990: Did not exist. 1991: 85,9 1992: 81,3 1993: 87,6 1994: 90,3	1990: Did not exist. 1991: 85,9 1992: 81,3 1993: 87,6 1994: 90,3 1995: 92,7 1996: 89,0
Special Industry Program (PET)	Families with income that allows compliance with requirements of savings and payment of dividends. Collective application.	Percentage of housing value Subsidized each year, approximated as the fraction of maximum housing value that was required as prior savings.	1990: 20,0	1990: 20,0 1991: 20,0 1992: 20,0 1993: 20,0 1994: 22,5	1990: 20,0 1991: 20,0 1992: 20,0 1993: 20,0 1994: 22,5 1995: 22,5 1996: 22,5
Unified subsidy (ITS)	Medium income families. Urban and distinct types and values of - rural zones. Programs consider - housing, differentiated with respect to proportion of subsidy And prior savings required.	Percentage of housing value subsidized of average each year, approximated by average housing subsidy value of the different types of housing.	1990: 29,7	1990: 29,7 1991: 29,7 1992: 28,0 1993: 26,9 1994: 25,5	1990: 29,7 1991: 29,7 1992: 28,0 1993: 26,9 1994: 25,5 1995: 22,5 1996: 20,8

Appendix 4 (continued)

Subsidy	Objective segment	Form of Valuation (1)	Average Percentage 1990 (2)	Average Percentage 1994 (2)	Average Percentage 1996 (2)
Rural subsidy	Families of modest resources, Rural sector.	Percentage of housing value Subsidized by average of each year.	1990: 56,5	1990: 56,5 1991: 56,1 1992: 60,1 1993: 60,7 1994: 62,4	1990: 56,5 1991: 56,1 1992: 60,1 1993: 60,7 1994: 62,4 1995: 62,1 1996: 62,4
Neighborhood Improvement Program (Neighborhood Clean-up) Lots with Services	Marginal Sectors. Sanitary Improvement, pest eradication and fumigation of neighborhoods.	Percentage of housing value subsidized, in accordance with the legislation in force since 1982.	1990: 75,0	1990: 75,0 1991: 75,0 1992: 75,0 1993: 75,0 1994: 75,0	1990: 75,0 1991: 75,0 1992: 75,0 1993: 75,0 1994: 75,0 1995: 75,0

Note:
(1) : In every case, the value of the subsidy received has been calculated for each household from the rent that the owner estimates that he would pay, if the house in which he lives were not his property (attributed rent). The housing subsidy has been considered as a flow of services that are paid monthly, valuated as that part of the rent attributed (alternative cost) that is attributable to the subsidy received to acquire the housing.
(2) : In November 1998 pesos.

Source: Elaborated by the authors, based on information from the Ministry of Housing and Urbanization, and the Sub-secretary of Regional Development, Interior Ministry.

Background Paper 3

INCORPORATING SOCIAL SERVICES IN THE MEASUREMENT OF POVERTY

Osvaldo Larrañaga
Department of Economics
Universidad de Chile

Introduction

This chapter provides an integrated analysis of poverty in Chile during the 90´s, adding the dimension of social services to the traditional income component. As is well known, social services are typically distributed on a subsidized basis to the middle and low income sections of the population. On the other hand, the traditional measurement of poverty is based on income (or expenditure) shortfalls relative to the poverty line or amount of income (expenditure) which is required to attain a set minimum standard of living. Income poverty refers only to those needs which are addressed with market commodities. However, access to education, health care and housing is also an essential determinant of the standard of living of the population. As the provision of social services varies across countries and periods, the exclusive dimension of income poverty renders an incomplete picture of the welfare of the respective populations.

The chapter is organized into three sections. The first section presents some analytical considerations regarding the inclusion of social services in the measurement of poverty. The second section discusses a set of possible indicators to measure the lack of access to social services, illustrating the results with data for the year 1998. Section three develops a comparative analysis for the years 1990 and 1998, which makes it possible to evaluate the evolution of income poverty vis-à-vis the developments in the access to social services.

Some Analytical Considerations

The traditional measures of poverty are based on income (expenditure) shortfalls. The most common methodology defines a household as poor if household income (expenditure) per equivalent adult (y) is below the poverty line (z): $Yi < Z$

The poverty line is the cost of the basket of commodities that each equivalent adult in the household requires to attain a given minimum standard of living. There are countries where the poverty line is determined as a fraction of the median income, emphasizing the relative or "social" content of the standard of living. On the other hand, most countries have chosen a less relative concept for the poverty line. In these cases, the typical methodology consists in the valuation of a standard food basket, which is based on actual expenditure patterns and the recommended calorie intake level. Expenditure in non-food requirements is calculated from the Engel coefficient (food share) for the "representative" household.

This procedure does not consider social services which are provided by the government on a subsidized basis, as is typically the case with education, health care and housing. These services are not accounted for in the monetary income (y) which forms the basis of the measurement of poverty. Neither are they considered in the calculation of the poverty line, which is based on the pattern of actual or effective expenditure.

It follows that the measurement of poverty renders an incomplete picture of the standard of living of a household. It excludes social services like education, health care and housing, which are no less important than market commodities for the standard of living of the population.

The previous argument refers to the classical view which sees poverty as insufficiency of economic means to attain a given minimum standard of living. As authors such as Sen have argued, social services allow people to fulfill their basic capabilities and functionings: the "doings and beings" which are the constituents of living. In this chapter we focus on the former view.

It is well known that the measurement of poverty is characterized by several methodological shortcomings and empirical problems. The identification of the poor depends on what definition is utilized for variables like income, household, equivalence scale and others. The poverty line depends on what "representative" household is chosen to derive the normative standards of food and non-food expenditure. There is also the question of what adjustment the poverty line should have as per capita income increases over time. Aggregating the individual poor as a single parametric measure raises another set of conceptual and operational issues; different poverty measures differ in the weights each poor individual gets in the final parameter.

A sensible position at this point is to follow Ravallion (1994) and to focus on poverty comparisons rather than poverty levels. What most matters is evaluating the evolution of poverty over time or to compare poverty levels across regions or countries. Poverty comparisons can deal with the previous kinds of issues when the relevant factor remains constant across time or location (fixed effects). The analysis of stochastic dominance applied in Atkinson (1987) makes it possible to generalize poverty comparisons across poverty measures and poverty lines by analyzing changes in the income distribution functions.

However, the exclusion of social services in the measurement of poverty is not solved by means of poverty comparisons. The provision of these services has experienced important changes over time and across countries. By way of example, real spending in education and health care increased by more than double in the Chilean economy in the 1990-98 period, whereas per capita income increased by 57% in the same period. It follows that a comprehensive measure of poverty, which includes access to social services, is likely to show a higher reduction in poverty than traditional income based measures.

On the other hand, Chile presents one of the highest rates of life expectancy and years of schooling in Latin America, which are the result of economic development and decades of previous investment in human capital. Therefore, a comprehensive measure of poverty should rank Chile in a better position than traditional income poverty indicators.

How to include social services in the measurement of poverty?   The problem therefore is how to incorporate access to social services in the measurement of poverty. One possibility is to apply the methodology of full income presented in chapter two. As we may recall, full household income consists of two components: (i) total monetary income, including an imputed rent in the case of own housing; (ii) an estimate of the monetary value of social services which are accessed on a subsidized basis.

Let Y be full income, X a vector of subsidized social services and V a vector of associated values or "prices" for these services. Assuming the case of free provision (100% subsidy) full income is given by the expression:

(1) $$Y = y + VX$$

There are two fundamental approaches to estimate V (Cornes, 1994). First, V can be valued at the production cost of social services. Second, the tabulation of V can be based on the demand price or marginal benefit that social services provide to consumers. In spite of the analytical convenience of the latter procedure, the production cost methodology is far easier to implement and as such is followed in chapter three of this study.

Regardless of its advantages in the measurement of the income distribution, the full income methodology presents one crucial shortcoming that prevents its utilization in the analysis of poverty. This refers to the non fungible nature of in-kind subsidies like social services.

To observe this point consider that applying the methodology of full income to the measurement of poverty would require a "*full poverty line*". This corresponds to the income poverty line *plus* the cost of some standard social services basket. Let Ωj represent the threshold for social service j and let Ω be the associated vector.

Then, the full poverty line Z is defined as:

(2) $$Z = z + V?$$

According to this methodology, a household is now poor whenever:

(3) $$Y_i < Z$$

However, the following situation can arise:

(4a) $$y_i < Z$$

(4b) $$Y_i > Z$$

This is, that full income can exceed the full poverty line but monetary income can be lower than the monetary poverty line. This can happen if the household has low monetary income but enjoys generous access to subsidized social services. Here, according to the full income methodology, the household is not poor. However, household members could be experiencing severe deprivation in essential needs, as they lack money income to buy adequate access to market commodities such as food, clothing, heat and others. The problem arises from the impossibility to sell the "excess" of social services and acquire the market commodities in deficit.

The full income method can therefore lead to serious inconsistencies in the measurement of poverty. The problem is serious enough to advise not using the full income methodology in the evaluation of poverty. Notice that the problem can be particularly severe in countries like Chile, where the low income population has ample access to social services. Notice also that the problem would be less serious if social services were valued according to their marginal valuation by consumers. In this case an "excess" of social services relative to market commodities would render a low marginal valuation of those services and the full income methodology would be less likely to identify as non poor a household with severe deprivation in money income.

From the previous discussion it follows that the inclusion of social services in the measurement of poverty has to consider the non fungible nature of in-kind subsidies.

In this respect, consider that household i attains some minimum standard of living according to:

(5a) X_{ij} $= ?_j$ $j = 1,\dots\dots J$

(5b) y_i $= z$

The above expression establishes that a non poor household must address two conditions. First, money income must suffice to attend needs which are satisfied with market commodities. Second, the household must have access to a basket of social services which is adequate to satisfy the corresponding needs.

Two methodological issues arise in this context. First, the analysis should be extended to consider the case where social services can be purchased in the market (at a higher cost and quality than the subsidized alternatives). Second, social services address specific needs which depend on the demographic characteristics of the household. Not every household requires the same basket of social services.

The first point can be addressed straightforwardly by considering that a household is not poor whenever:

(6) y_i $= z \ P ?$

Where P is the vector of market prices for social services. Expression (6) is a sufficient condition to not be poor. It establishes that money income in the not poor household is enough to buy all required commodities in the market, including the standard basket of social services.[86] Notice that a household cannot satisfy (6) but qualifies as non-poor if it satisfies both (5a) and (5b).

The second issue relates to the specific needs addressed by social services at the household level. The demand for education services is a function of the number of young members of the household; the demand for health care services depends on the demographic (gender and age)

---

[86] Expression (6) assumes that the "amount" Ω is provided by the market. This could not be the case if the provision of free social services by the government causes the market to specialize in high quality services (Xp), where Xo > Ω

composition of the household, etc. Let d be a vector of the demographic characteristic of the household. Then , conditions (5a) and (6) have to be rewritten as:

(5') $X_{ij}(d_i) = ?_j(d_i)$ $j = 1, \ldots \ldots J$

(6') $y_i \quad = x \; P \; ? \; (d_i)$

Evaluation Space

The measurement of income poverty is a rather standardized procedure. In this way, the methodology to compute the poverty line on the basis of food and non-food requirements can be readily replicated, provided the necessary information is available.

Instead, incorporating social services in the poverty measure is far less documented and admits a more discretionary approach.

A first issue is to identify the evaluation space to be utilized. We are interested in poverty as human deprivation originating in the *lack of economic means*. This is a more restricted but more precise definition than human deprivation as such, which can relate to different kinds of conditions. To see this point consider the case of an economically affluent person, who suffers some physical disability originating from a genetic condition. This person can be classified as disabled or physically ill, but certainly not as poor. On the other hand, a healthy person whose access to routine medical treatment is prevented because of financial constraints classifies as someone who lacks the means to achieve health care coverage.

A second issue is the choice between outcome versus resource variables for the measurement of poverty. Our position favors the latter alternative. Consider once again the health dimension, where life expectancy and DALY´s (Disability Adjusted Living Years) are examples of outcome variables.[87] On the other hand, access to health care services is a resource variable. As such, it constitutes one of the many determinants of the health status of a person in addition to genetic, environmental and socioeconomic factors.

According to the 1993 World Development Report, two of the most important inputs in the "health production function" at the household level are income and education (World Bank, 1993). In this way a final outcome like a short life expectancy can be the consequence of income poverty or lack of education rather than lack of access to health care.

It follows that the measurement of poverty based on resource variables lends itself to a more operational and policy oriented analysis than to focus on outcome variables. At this point it must be noted that income poverty also emphasizes a resource variable: money income is one of the several determinants of welfare.

A related difficulty is whether the lack of access to some social service (say, education) originates from demand or supply factors. Take for example a 12 year old child who is not attending school. Is this due to a family decision or to the lack of school infrastructure? In the first case the decision

---

[87] Or closely related to final outcome variables such as welfare, well-being, quality of life, etc

probably reflects a condition of income poverty and it would be mistaken to classify this household as lacking both income *and* access to social services.

Another important factor is related to the quality of social services. A child who attends primary school is expected to obtain some educational achievements: literacy, arithmetic knowledge, a basic reasoning structure. Failure to achieve these objectives renders useless the access to school. It follows that the definition of thresholds regarding the access to social services must include substantive contents, besides the quantitative dimension.

However, this takes us back to the outcome vs. resources issue as contents like educational achievement can be defined as a type of outcome. However, the difference between learning to read and, say, life expectancy relies on the relative weight between endogenous factors (social policy) and exogenous factors (natural and socioeconomic factors). Clearly, learning to read is mostly a responsibility of the school, *including* the compensating extra effort that should take place in the case of disadvantaged children. Instead, life expectancy is strongly influenced by factors exogenous to the health policy.

Identifying Indicators and Thresholds

The Data.   The data comes from the 1990 and 1998 CASEN household surveys. Micro data provided by household surveys are unique in allowing the analysis of the distribution of welfare and its determinants among households. The description of the CASEN surveys can be found in chapter two. The 1990-98 period is characterized in Chile by the return to democracy. One of the most important policies undertaken by the governments in this period has been the surge in public social spending as a means to achieve "growth with equity". As a result, total public social spending increased by 86.4% in real terms during this eight-year period. The largest expansion is to be found in the education and health care sectors (125.8% and 110.8%, respectively). The expansion in social spending was financed through economic growth and a tax reform introduced at the outset of this period.

The data provided by CASEN surveys allows a detailed analysis of income poverty. The balance regarding social services is mixed. Access to housing and related infrastructure is well documented. The Casen survey contains information about the type and quality of the building materials of the dwelling; number of household members per room; access to electricity, drinking water and sewage facilities. On the other hand, access to education is considered by the following variables: adult illiteracy, school attendance and grade level for age. Access to health care is proxied by getting medical treatment when necessary and by how timely this access is. [88]

All tabulations regarding income poverty follow the chapter two definitions. A person is classified as poor if the household income per adult equivalent is below $ 37.889 in 1998 pesos. Live-in servants are treated as separate households. Keeping in mind that official poverty statistics are different to the extent that they are based on per capita income and live-in servants are not considered.

---

[88] Because the data base used here is the CASEN survey, the emphasis is education, health and housing. Other dimensions of poverty which might also be important in a concept of welfare, such as security and violence, are not considered. Similarly, the CASEN survey is strong on housing indicators, but does not measure very well health indicators, such as mortality and morbidity, availability of health services, etc.

Education.   The CASEN household survey provides some information about the educational achievements of the adult population. Table 1 reports literacy rates in 1998, reaching 95.4% of the population older than 14. The literacy rate increases with per capita household income. 88.4% of the very poor report they are literate as compared to 90.5% of the poor (not indigent) and 96.3% of the non poor population. Literacy rates do not vary according to gender.

Table 1: Literacy Rates by Income Poverty in 1998
(population older than 14)

	Very poor	poor	Non-poor	Total
Literate	88.4	90.5	96.3	95.4
Illiterate	11.6	9.5	3.7	4.6
Total	100.0	100.0	100.0	100.0

Source: Calculations based on 1988 CASEN survey.

Table 2 presents average years of schooling of the population older than 23, classified by age and gender. This indicator is more informative regarding the educational attainment of the adult population than the literacy rate, in a middle-developed economy. The youngest cohorts, in their late 20's, are close to achieving an average of 12 years of schooling, equivalent to complete secondary education. The profile of years of schooling and age reflects the expansion in the coverage of education during the last few decades. There is no gender gap in the total years of schooling for the most recent cohorts; on the other hand, the oldest cohorts show a slight advantage for males.

Table 3 presents mean years of schooling across income groups. On average, the very poor exhibit 6.2years of schooling while the poor but non-indigent reach 6.7 years. The gap is substantial in relation to the non-poor population, who reach on average 9.8 years of schooling. But it is worth noting that the Chilean poor are more educated than the average Latin-American (poor *and* non-poor).

Table 2: Mean Years of Schooling by Age and Gender in 1998

Age	All	Male	Female
24-27	11.5	11.5	11.6
28-31	11.2	11.2	11.2
32-35	10.7	10.7	10.7
36-39	10.3	10.5	10.1
40-43	10.1	10.2	9.9
44-47	9.7	10.0	9.5
48-51	8.8	9.0	8.5
52-55	8.2	8.5	7.8
56-59	7.4	7.7	7.1
60-64	6.9	7.3	6.6

Source: Calculations based on 1988 CASEN survey.

Table 3: Mean Years of Schooling by Income Poverty in 1998
(24 or older)

	All	Male	female
Very poor	6.2	6.3	6.1
Poor	6.7	6.4	6.7
Non-poor	9.8	10.1	9.6

Source: Calculations based on 1988 CASEN survey.

The educational level of the adult population is a crucial determinant of key social and economic outcomes: GDP growth, social integration, democratic rule and so on. However, for the objective of incorporating social services in the measurement of poverty the educational achievements *of the young* is the most interesting variable. Assessing the current means households have to achieve some given standard of living relates more naturally to the access to schooling of the young rather than the older population. The main exception is the condition of adult illiteracy, which nowadays prevents integration to social and economic life.

We utilize two indicators for evaluating the access of the young to education: for drop-outs we compute "lost" years of schooling relative to some standard or reference level; for those attending school a measure of grade fallbehind is developed to assess educational achievement. Scores in national standardized educational tests are not available at the individual level, preventing their utilization in this study.

Our first indicator -educational deficit for the drop-out population- is defined as the number of lost years of schooling with regard to a reference period of 8 years. The latter is equivalent to complete primary education, which represents a formal (compulsory) minimum level of schooling in Chile. The variable is calculated for the population between 8 and 24 years old. We also report this indicator for a reference period of 12 years of schooling or complete secondary education, which by most accounts constitutes the minimum schooling level required by the job market and other dimensions of social integration.

Table 4 reports the results in the former case. In 1998, 5.7% of the 8-24 population had dropped out from school before reaching 8 years of schooling, while the remaining 94.3% were either in school or had already completed primary education. Breaking these results down by income poverty shows that the ratio of non-attendance is 13.0% for the very poor population, 9.9% for the poor non-indigent and 4.4% for the non-poor.

Table 5 reports the results when a standard of 12 years of schooling is utilized. In this case, 16.7% of the 8-24 population had dropped out from school before reaching 12 years of schooling, while 83.3% was attending school or had completed secondary education. Among the former the mode is 4 (lost) years. Although differences in secondary school attendance are significant between the poor and non-poor populations, this gap is far lower than inequality evaluated in the income dimension.

The next question is about the reasons for non-attendance of the drop-out population. In particular, we are interested in knowing the relative importance of supply vs. demand factors. It turns out that the latter are by far the most important reason behind non attendance to school. About 85% of those who dropped-out before completing secondary school report a demand related factor as the main reason for non attendance; 42% are at work or looking for a job; 13% help in household activities; 9.5% are pregnant or already have a child; 8,5% are "not interested" in school, etc. On the other hand, 15% report a supply-related factor as the main reason for not attending school: "absence of a school nearby", "no vacancies at the school" or "difficulties in access or transportation".

Table 4: Lost Years of Schooling I
(Difference between 8 and the actual years of schooling for drop-outs between 8-24)

Lost years	Very poor	Poor	Non-poor	Total
0	86.9	90.1	95.5	94.3
1	3.1	2.2	1.37	1.5
2	3.6	2.7	1.3	1.7
3	2.1	1.8	0.8	1.1
4	1.6	0.9	0.4	0.6
5	1.1	0.9	0.2	0.4
6	0.7	0.3	0.2	0.2
7	0.6	0.2	0.1	0.2
8	0.1	0.0	0.0	0.0
Total	100.0	100.0	100.0	100.0

Source: Calculations based on 1998 CASEN survey.

Table 5: Lost Years of Schooling II
(Difference between 12 and the actual years of schooling for drop-outs between 8-24)

Lost years	Very poor	poor	Non-poor	Total
0	76.1	78.7	84.9	83.3
1	1.2	1.4	2.1	1.9
2	1.9	2.4	2.5	2.4
3	3.5	2.8	2.4	2.5
4	5.3	5.4	3.7	4.1
5	3.1	2.2	1.3	1.5
6	3.6	2.7	1.4	1.7
7	2.1	1.8	0.8	1.1
8	1.6	0.9	0.5	0.6
9	1.1	0.9	0.2	0.4
10	0.7	0.3	0.2	0.2
11	0.6	0.2	0.1	0.2
12	0.1	0.0	0.0	0.0
Total	100.0	100.0	100.0	100.0

Source: Calculations based on 1998 CASEN survey.

Our second indicator of school achievement is grade delay, or the actual grade level compared to the expected grade level for age. . The variable is defined as a lag of two or more years with regard to expected schooling grade. For example, a child is expected to attend first grade at six years of age. Thus, a 9 year-old student who has just passed the first grade is one year behind the expected norm; a student aged 16 attending 8th grade is 3 years behind, etc. Grade delay is a function of two factors: repetition and late entry into school.

This variable was calculated for every primary and secondary student between 7 and 24 years of age. The results are presented in Table 6 and report that 19.5% of the student population is behind the norm, although most cases present only one year of grade delay. The divergence of the grade delay variable across income subgroups shows that grade delay increases with income poverty. About 30% of very poor students exhibit some grade delay. The ratio decreases to 24.4% in the case of the poor non-indigent students and 16.9% for the non poor.

Table 6: Grade Delay by Income Poverty
(% of the non tertiary level student population)

	Very poor	Poor	Non-poor	Total
None	70.0	75.7	83.1	80.5
1 year	16.6	14.6	10.7	11.9
2 years	7.3	6.1	3.6	4.4
3 years	3.2	2.3	1.2	1.6
4 or more	2.9	1.3	1.3	1.5
Total	100.0	100.0	100.0	100.0

Source: Calculations based on 1998 CASEN survey.

We now attempt to integrate the individual indicators of educational deficit in a single measure at the *household level*. A first example of these measures is an indicator variable which takes a value of one (deficit) if any of the following situations occurs: some member of the household older than 15 is illiterate; some member of the household aged 8-23 is not attending school and has not completed primary education; some member of the household is attending school but is two or more years behind the expected grade. Results are presented in Table 7, which shows that 26.9% of households fall into the category of educational deficit, varying from 48.5% for the very poor to 16.3% for the non poor households.

Table 7: Educational Deficit at the Household Level I
(% of households)

% of households	Very poor	Poor	Non-poor	Total
Without deficit	51.5	54.7	76.4	73.1
With deficit	48.5	45.3	23.6	26.9
Total	100.0	100.0	100.0	100.0

Source: Calculations based on 1998 CASEN survey.

An alternative measure is shown in table 8. This time the variable represents the number of times a deficit occurs at the household level. For example, the variable takes a value of 2 if there are two members of the household below the educational standards: a child who has dropped out of primary school and another who is three years behind the expected grade for his age. This measure provides more information about the educational deficit than the previous alternative. Notice that the total (rather than per capita) deficit is the appropriate variable under our framework of analysis.

**Table 8: Educational Deficit at the
Household Level II (% of households)**

	Very poor	Poor	Non-poor	Total
0	51.5	54.6	76.4	73.1
1	26.1	25.8	17.7	18.9
2	11.6	11.4	4.4	5.5
3	6.1	4.9	1.1	1.6
4	2.7	2.4	0.3	0.6
5	0.8	0.5	0.1	0.2
6	0.9	0.3	0.0	0.1
7	0.1	0.1	0.0	0.0
8	0.1	0.0	0.0	0.0
Total	100.0	100.0	100.0	100.0

Source: Calculations based on 1998 CASEN survey.

Housing. The current housing situation in Chile is characterized by a high proportion of home-ownership: almost 70% of households own the dwelling where they live. On the other hand; 16.5% of households rent their dwellings; 9.9% correspond to cases in which the dwelling is lent to them by relatives and in 3.3% the dwelling is a part of their employment benefits (Table 9).

Regarding the conditions under which the dwelling was acquired, 77.7% of owners have already paid for the property while the remaining 22.3% is still servicing the debt incurred in the purchase. More interestingly, for the present study, 34.5% of owners purchased their dwellings accessing some public subsidy (Table 10). In Chile, most housing subsidies are of a demand nature. Potential beneficiaries apply for a subsidy on the basis of a set of socioeconomic variables. The subsidy typically consists of a portion of the price of the dwelling, which is directly acquired by the beneficiary in the housing market.

Table 9: Housing - Property Structure in 1998

Own house	69.6
Rented	16.5
Lent	9.9
Employment Fringe benefits	3.3
Other	0.7
Total	100.0

Source: Calculations based on 1998 CASEN survey.

Table 10: Housing - Distribution of Owners

Already paid	77.7
Servicing debt	22.3
Of which:	
Purchased with public subsidy	34.5
No subsidy	65.2
Total	100.0

Source: Calculations based on 1998 CASEN survey.

The Casen survey obtains a number of characteristics of the dwelling. Among others, the number of habitable rooms; the type and condition of the floor, ceiling and walls, the access to electricity, drinking water and sewage facilities. In every case some minimum standard can be defined and then we can evaluate whether the standard is actually met by each household. An index of housing deficit can be calculated as the number of variables below standard.

The box below presents the set of proposed standards. These are adapted from the minimum housing standards as defined by the Ministry of Planning (Mideplan) in Chile.

Box 1:

Standards for Housing	
Below Standard	
Material conditions of dwelling	
Floor	Dirt floor or floor in bad condition regardless of the material
Ceiling	fonolite, scrap or ceiling in bad condition regardless of the material
Walls	Mud, Scrap-materials, unlined panels or walls in bad condition regardless of the material
Number of habitable rooms	Less than one bedroom for every three people
Access to infrastructure	
Electric power	No access or illegal connection
Drinking water	When the source is a river, spring or underground well (without internal piping system)
Sanitation facilities	No system, or box over ditch, canal or other system.

Source: Based on Mideplan housing standards.

Table 11 presents the results in terms of the percentage of the households that experience deficits in every housing dimension. The ratio fluctuates in the range of 3.6% to 15.9% according to the chosen indicator, which implies a much lower incidence than income poverty. Moreover, only a minor fraction of the very poor and poor population experiences deprivation in the housing variable. This could be interpreted as proof of the impact of social policies on the welfare of the population, although any conclusions have to be qualified because of the arbitrary nature of the chosen thresholds.

Table 11: Housing – Percentage of Households below Standards, 1998

	Very poor	Poor	Non-poor	Total
Dwelling materials:				
Ceiling	21.2	15.7	5.4	7.2
Floor	19.9	16.0	4.8	6.6
Walls	33.7	27.1	9.1	11.9
Crowding:				
Persons/room	18.7	16.2	4.2	6.1
Infrastructure:				
Electricity	12.9	10.4	2.6	3.8
Drinking water	20.6	17.8	4.6	6.7
Sewage facilities	43.2	38.4	11.7	15.8

Source: Calculations based on 1998 CASEN survey.

The next step is to derive an index which aggregates the different types of housing deficits. Here, it seems natural to posit that a household which only lacks access to, say, drinking water is less deprived than one which lacks access to drinking water *and* electricity. However, we lack information about the weights that every dimension should have in this aggregate measure. More precisely, we do not know the welfare loss associated with the lack of drinking water versus the one related with the lack of electricity. At this point it makes more sense to utilize a system of equal weights and to interpret the results *as the number of unmet housing standards* (without a precise welfare meaning).[89]

Table 12 presents this index at the household level. The index takes values between zero (no housing deficit) to a maximum of seven (all dimensions are below standard). According to this indicator, 72.7% of households have no deficit in housing, 11.9% experiences one type of deficit; 6.5% two types, etc. The index of housing deficit is closely related to income poverty: 62.3% of the very poor experience at least one type of deficit as compared to 57.1% of the poor but non indigent population and 21.3% of the non-poor.

Table 12: Housing Deficit Index (households)

	Very poor	Poor	Non-poor	Total
0	37.7	42.9	78.7	72.7
1	17.7	21.0	10.3	11.9
2	14.2	13.3	5.2	6.5
3	14.7	11.2	3.4	4.8
4	8.2	6.2	1.4	2.2
5	4.5	3.2	0.6	1.1
6	2.2	1.4	0.4	0.6
7	0.7	0.5	0.0	0.1
Total	100.0	100.0	100.0	100.0

Source: Calculations based on 1998 CASEN survey.

As expected, there are significant differences in the housing deficit index between urban and rural areas (Table 13). Only 20.6% of rural households meet all housing standards as compared to 81.2% of urban households. National aggregates are strongly influenced by urban statistics, consistent with the low proportion of rural population (14% of total households).

It is interesting to analyze the deficit situation of dwellings that were acquired with public subsidies. A high incidence of the deficit index would reveal failures in the public housing policy. Table 14 shows the housing deficit index for dwellings that were acquired with and without subsidies. The comparison favors the former group: dwellings acquired with public subsidies are more likely to meet the standards in terms of materials, access to infrastructure and lack of crowding. The data is non-conditional and must be interpreted with caution. Additional information is provided by examining the deficit index in the subset of dwellings acquired with public subsidies after the year 1990. Somehow surprisingly, the deficit index for this subgroup does not improve as compared to the aggregate. More than a fifth of the newer dwellings present at least one dimension below standard, which points to problems of the housing policy in terms of quality standards.

---

[89] This procedure is also contains a bias, since the more indicators that are used, the more likely one is to find a deficiency. In a sense, we give equal weight to the chosen indicators, and a zero weight to all other indicators which are not being used.

Table 13: Housing Deficit Index
(households): urban vs. rural

	Urban	Rural	Total
0	81.2	20.6	72.7
1	10.4	21.2	11.9
2	4.1	21.7	6.5
3	2.7	17.3	4.8
4	1.1	9.6	2.2
5	0.4	5.4	1.1
6	0.1	3.4	0.6
7	0.0	0.7	0.1
Total	100.0	100.0	100.0

Source: Calculations based on 1998 CASEN survey.

Table 14: Housing Deficit Index (owners)

	All public subsidies	Subsidy after 1990	No subsidy	Total
0	81.3	78.2	72.7	75.6
1	10.7	11.5	10.8	10.8
2	3.7	4.7	7.1	5.9
3	3.1	3.9	5.1	4.4
4	0.8	1.0	2.3	1.8
5	0.3	0.4	1.2	0.9
6	0.1	0.2	0.6	0.5
7	0.0	0.0	0.1	0.1
Total	100.0	100.0	100.0	100.0

Source: Calculations based on 1998 CASEN survey.

Health Care. The health condition of a person is a key determinant of his welfare (or well-being). As already discussed, access to health care is only one determinant of the health status of the person. This is also influenced by a plethora of other variables at the micro and macro levels. Our interest is to evaluate whether a person gets adequate access to health care when in need. Accomplishing this objective can be particularly demanding in terms of the information which is required for rendering operational concepts like "adequate" and "in need".

The Casen survey asks whether the person is affiliated to some health insurance system, which in the Chilean case can be private or public. In each case a contribution of 7% of labor income has to be paid. Private insurance offers coverage according to contributions paid and demographic related risk factors. Public insurance is of a social nature: coverage is provided regardless of contributions paid. Besides, a person with low income can access the public sector under the condition of "indigence", which does not require a monetary contribution.

Table 15 presents a classification of the population according to health system affiliation. About 90% of the population is covered by one or other scheme; the public social insurance being the largest with a coverage of 61.7% of the total population. A sizable number of those affiliated to the public system (about 40%) classify as "indigent" and do not pay contributions.

Should we use this variable to ascertain the condition of "access to health care when in need"? There are two main considerations for this question. Firstly, we need to know whether the "non affiliated" condition is equivalent to lack of access to health care. Secondly, we need to evaluate if belonging to a formal health insurance implies that a person gets adequate access to heath care when in need.

Table 15: Affiliation to Health Insurance System
(% of population)

	Very poor	Poor	Non-poor	Total
Public/indigent	67.9	44.6	17.3	24.5
Public/contributor	19.6	39.8	38.0	37.2
Private	2.6	5.3	28.3	23.1
Others	0.5	0.9	4.0	3.3
Non- affiliated	9.2	8.8	11.5	10.9
Doesn't know	0.3	0.7	1.0	0.9
Total	100.00	100.00	100.00	100.00

Source: Calculations based on 1998 CASEN survey.

The former consideration arises because two contrasting situations can be related to the "non affiliation" condition. On the one hand, it can relate to a supply factor: the person is not covered by some public or private health insurance scheme because he/she faces some binding constraint that prevents such affiliation. On the other hand, it can reflect a demand factor: the person voluntarily chooses not to have health insurance because he/she favors self-insurance.

The former seems unlikely in the Chilean case. This is because participating in a formal health insurance is compulsory for every active or retired worker and his/her dependents. Furthermore, the public health system acts as a last resort insurance, supplying health care services to everyone who demands it, regardless of affiliation to a health insurance scheme. Thus, every Chilean has in principle access to health care when in need.

But this is clearly not good enough. We would like to know if access to health care is actually provided, aside from formal coverage by insurance. If possible, we would be interested to know about the quality and efficacy of the health care services which are provided to the population. Getting access to very low quality health services is not equivalent to getting "adequate" access to health care when in need.

Data limitations are a binding factor at this stage. The Casen surveys contain very few questions about these kinds of issues. Besides, the information is provided by self-reporting, which can reflect patient satisfaction but not necessarily objective health outcomes.

One source of information provided by the Casen survey is whether a person who experiences some kind of illness, injury or related condition, receives medical attention. "Attention" is defined as getting access to medical services if necessary. On the other hand, we classified as "no attention" the following reasons for not attending a health facility after illness, injury or a related condition: "utilization of home medication or alternative medicine", "difficulties to access health care" or "other reasons".

According to the results reported in table 16, 16.8% of the population did not look for medical attention after experiencing some illness, injury or related condition. However, most of these cases (88%) correspond to the reason: "did not attend a health care facility; utilized home medication or alternative medicine". This predefined answer is ambiguous enough to include cases where attending a health facility was not necessary or was not worth the effort. The latter alternative would reflect supply constraints while the former is more demand (preference) oriented.

The incidence of the "no attention" answer shows little variation across income populations. 21.8% of the very poor did not get medical treatment as compared to 18.5% of the non-indigent poor and 16.2% of the non-poor. This evidence suggests that the "no attention" condition reflects a demand rather than a supply factor. [90]

Table 16: Access to Health Care after Illness, Injury or Related Condition

	Very poor	Poor	Non-poor	Total
Attention	21.8	18.5	16.2	16.8
No attention	78.2	81.5	83.8	83.2
Total	100.00	100.00	100.00	100.00

Source: Calculations based on 1998 CASEN survey.

A more dramatic case arises in the case of dental attention. 38.5% of the population who required some kind of treatment did not get access to a proper facility ("requested attention without success" or "didn't ask but in need"). The reason behind this large number is that dental treatment is not usually covered by public or private health insurance.[91] However, it can be argued that access to dental treatment classifies as a basic need in a mid-developed economy like Chile.

Table 17: Access to Dental Treatment When in Need

	Very poor	Poor	Non-poor	Total
Treatment	46.5	46.4	64.9	61.5
No Treatment	53.5	53.6	35.1	38.5
Total	100.00	100.00	100.00	100.00

Source: Calculations based on 1998 CASEN survey.

How timely has the access to health care for the population who looked for medical treatment after experiencing illness, injury or a related condition been? This question provides some hints about the quality of health care services. The predefined answers in the Casen questionnaire are: "timely", "rather late", "late" and "don't know". Table 18 presents the results by income poverty subgroups. It turns out that 85.5% of the population who looked for health care reported timely access. Income makes some difference in getting timely access: 77.9% of the very poor report a timely access as compared to 86.7% of the non-poor.

---

[90] Assuming that the non-poor are not supply constrained.

[91] The public sector provides dental care in the case of "emergencies", which, in effect, means extractions.

Table 18: How Timely Was the Access to Health Care?

	Very poor	Poor	Non-poor	Total
Timely	77.9	80.3	86.7	85.5
rather late	14.2	11.8	7.5	8.3
Late	4.9	5.5	3.1	3.5
doesn't know	2.9	2.4	2.7	2.7
Total	100.0	100.0	100.00	100.00

Source: Calculations based on 1998 CASEN survey.

The previous indicators relate to the access of the population to the health care system when in need (disease, accident, etc). This is undoubtedly a central aspect of the health care sector. However, the main objective of health systems should be to keep the population healthy. This function is related to the development of lifestyles that are consistent with this objective, including preventive activities that are supplied by the health sector itself, such as controls and early detection examinations.

Some information about preventive health activities is provided by the Casen survey (see Table 19). Thus, 11.3% of the population has attended at least one preventive control during the last year; 63.0% of women older than 14 have taken the Papanicolau test at least once in their lives, 48.3% during the last three years; 30.8% of the population older than 14 had smoked at least one cigarette during the past three months, 6.3% smoked at least 10 cigarettes a day. The incidence of these factors between the poor and non-poor population is quite similar. The situation in the high income strata (not shown in the table) is somewhat better with the Papanicolau - 67.3% of women in deciles 8-10 have taken the exam at least once in their lives and 53.5% during the past three years - but rather similar in the incidence of preventive controls and smoking habit.

In conclusion, for those preventive health activities reported in the Casen survey there is no strong evidence that the low income population is below standard, when the reference is provided by the access of the higher income strata population. This does not imply that these records are in line with normative standards.

Table 19: Preventive Health Activities

	Very poor	Poor non-indigent	Non-poor	Total
Preventive control (% who attended during last year)	13.3	12.4	11.0	11.3
Papanicolau (% of women older than 14)				
at least once in lifetime	57.3	58.4	64.0	63.0
at least once in past 3 years	44.4	45.5	48.9	48.3
Smokers (% older than 14)				
10 cigarettes or more a day	5.1	5.3	6.4	6.3

Source: Calculations based on 1998 CASEN survey.

In contrast to education and housing, health care deficits show up only in the subset of household whose members experience some health condition which requires medical attention. How to deal with the rest of the households? Clearly, it would be mistaken to assume that they are free of health care deficits. Most health related events are of a random nature, which explains why health insurance plays a central role in the organization of the health sector. Therefore, the relevant issue in our discussion is to ascertain the probability of lacking adequate attention when this may be needed.

One way to proceed is regressing the probability of lacking adequate health care against a set of observable variables in the subgroup of cases who experienced need, and then using this model to impute the predicted values to the rest of the population. However, the statistical adjustment of these regressions turned out to be very low, eroding the validity of this procedure.

We therefore followed a less demanding methodology, consisting of a random imputation of the probability of lacking adequate healthcare attention. This procedure was applied for the variables: not getting medical attention when in need or not getting a timely access after looking for medical attention. The imputation was based on the actual frequencies shown by these variables across deciles of the distribution of household income per equivalent adult (see table 20).

Table 20: Access to Health Care Services by Deciles of Income Distribution

	% in need	% who did not get attention when in need	% who got late attention	% in Dental need	% who got dental attention when in need
1	0.239	0.246	0.153	0.197	0.691
2	0.237	0.175	0.165	0.184	0.669
3	0.239	0.195	0.136	0.198	0.631
4	0.255	0.150	0.161	0.204	0.574
5	0.253	0.173	0.168	0.209	0.522
6	0.230	0.144	0.134	0.223	0.485
7	0.227	0.181	0.093	0.246	0.412
8	0.214	0.172	0.080	0.228	0.299
9	0.215	0.112	0.081	0.271	0.274
10	0.198	0.129	0.082	0.325	0.096

Need: population who needed attention over total population.
No attention: population who did not get attention when in need.
Late attention: received treatment but with delay.

Source: CASEN survey, 1998

Putting it All Together

What relationship exists between income poverty and deficits in social services? Throughout the previous sections we have already presented two-way tabulations for the relation between income poverty and each social service deficit. Income poverty correlates with social service deficits, although there are many cases that exhibit only one type of deprivation. In this section we present the general case by considering the interactions between the four dimensions under study: income, education, housing and health care.

The general results are presented in table 21. This shows the percentage of households for which deprivation occurs along every possible combination of the four variables. In this way, the first set of results refers to the incidence of poverty along a single dimension. It is important to interpret these figures as *marginal* frequencies for each variable. For example, 16.1% percent of households are income poor, which may or may not be accompanied by other types of deprivation. This applies to every entry in table 21.

It is also important to keep in mind that the various measures of poverty are not strictly comparable. One reason for this is that we lack a theoretical framework to identify comparable poverty thresholds across the different dimensions. This renders a comparative analysis of poverty across these dimensions meaningless. Thus, it would be wrong to establish that the incidence of housing poverty is, say, higher than income poverty, because it might be the case that the threshold for housing is more demanding than the threshold for income.

Having said that, table 21 shows that the percentage of households which show deprivation in at least one variable varies between 16% for income to 25% for housing; overall, 48.9% fail to pass at least one threshold. However, only 1.5% of households presents deprivation in all four dimensions. These numbers suggest a rather heterogeneous profile of households. On the positive side it can be said that poverty is not an overwhelming condition, in which poor households are deprived in every possible dimension. On the negative side, only 51.1% of households are above the poverty thresholds in all four dimensions.

Table 21: Percentage Households with Deficits (marginal frequencies)

One dimension	
Income	16.1
Housing	25.4
Education	22.6
Health Care	19.3
Two dimensions	
Income-housing	9.4
Income-education	7.3
Income-healthcare	4.9
Housing-education	10.9
Housing-healthcare	7.1
Education-healthcare	6.3
Three dimensions	
Income-housing-education	4.9
Income-housing-healthcare	2.9
Income-education-healthcare	2.1
Housing-education-healthcare	3.1
Four dimensions	
Income-housing-education-healthcare	1.5

Source: Calculations based on 1998 CASEN survey.

The previous exercise is not aimed at producing a single measure of poverty. If this were the case, we could define a household as poor if it fails to achieve at least one threshold. In this case we would have an upper limit for the incidence of poverty at 48.9% of households. On the other hand, a lower limit would be provided by defining as poor a household that fails to achieve all thresholds, setting the incidence of poverty at 1.5% of households. In between these two limits we have a wide array of alternatives to generate "a number" to represent the incidence of poverty in the country.

The reason against producing such a single "number" has already been stated. We lack a single measure to represent deprivation across these different dimensions. As a result, different poverty dimensions are not cardinally comparable. That being the case, it is more advisable to have several measures of poverty deprivation rather than to integrate them all into a single but ultimately meaningless measure.

Poverty Comparisons between 1990 and 1998

The following discussion focuses on the comparison of the several dimensions of poverty between the years 1990 and 1998. The period is long enough to identify trends in the evolution of these indicators. Moreover, the 1990-98 period is characterized by strong growth in both per capita income and public social expenditure, which renders it particularly interesting for the analysis of the evolution of income poverty and the other dimensions of the standard of living.

Table 22 summarizes in the first place the evidence about the reduction in income poverty. Utilizing the official poverty line the percentage of households whose income per equivalent adult is below this threshold, fell from 28.8% in 1990 to 14.5% in 1998 (32.1% to 17.0% of population). The reduction in poverty generalized to other measures, such us the poverty gap and the FGT-2 (shown in the table), and other measures of income, such us per capita household income (not shown).

As established in chapter two, the reduction in income poverty has a strong correlation with the process of rapid economic growth that has taken place in Chile since 1987.

What has happened with the evolution of other poverty dimensions? Table 23 presents the case of education, where social public expenditure increased by 125.8% in real terms during the 1990-98 period. Our indicators of educational deficit - adult illiteracy, grade fallbehind and lost years of schooling - show some improvement through the course of these years. The percentage of households with (at least one) deficit in education declined from 30.6% to 26.9% during the period. The gains are greater if we look at the severity of the deficit: the percentage of households where two or more members suffer an educational deficit decreased from 12.8% in 1990 to 7.8% in 1998.

Table 22: Income Poverty in 1990 and 1998
(household income per adult equivalent)

	1990	1998
Population		
Headcount	32.1	17.0
Poverty gap	11.3	5.7
FGT-2	5.8	2.9
Households		
Headcount	28.8	14.5
Poverty gap	10.1	4.9
FGT-2	5.2	2.5

Source: Calculations based on 1990 and 1998 CASEN surveys.

Table 23: Educational Deficit at the Household Level, 1990 vs. 1998

	1990	1998
Incidence		
% of households with deficit	30.6	26.9
Severity: % of households with deficit		
categorized by number of members with deficit		
One	17.8	18.9
Two	7.6	5.5
Three	3.0	1.7
Four or more	2.2	0.8
Total	100.0	100.0

Source: Calculations based on 1990 and 1998 CASEN surveys.

The set of indicators behind the variable "deficit in education" is presented in table 24. All these variables show some improvement during the 1990-98 period, with the exception of the illiteracy rate which increased slightly between both years (which can be attributed to statistical interference). The percentage of the population between 9 and 23 that abandoned school before completing primary education declined by 12 percentage points during this period. Those who dropped out of school before graduating from secondary education fell by 7.7 percentage points. In both cases there are significant gains in the severity of the indicator: the percentage of the youth population who dropped out of primary school four or more years before graduation declined from 5.1% to 1.4%; those who dropped out four or more years prior to graduating from secondary school declined from 15.1% to 9.9%. On the other hand, the grade fallbehind indicator shows a smaller reduction - only three percentage points - during the period. Thus, 22.5% of the student population was lagging behind at school in 1990; eight years later the percentage had declined to 19.5%.

Table 24: Educational Deficit by Categories, 1990 vs. 1998

	1990	1998
Illiteracy (%, older than 15)	3.7	4.6
Lost years of schooling - I (reference 8 years, population 9-23)		
None	82.3	94.3
One	4.0	1.5
Two	5.7	1.7
Three	2.9	1.1
Four or more	5.1	1.4
Lost years of schooling- II (reference 12 years, population 9-23)		
None	75.6	83.3
One	2.6	1.9
Two	3.3	2.4
Three	3.4	2.5
Four or more	15.1	9.9
Grade fallbehind (% non tertiary students, ages 7-23)		
None	77.5	80.5
One	13.8	12.0
Two	5.2	4.4
Three	2.0	1.6
Four or more	1.5	1.5

Source: Calculations based on 1990 and 1998 CASEN surveys.

All things considered, the reduction in the educational deficit looks rather small when compared with the reduction in income poverty and the increases in public social spending which characterize the 1990-98 period. It can be argued that the indicators utilized to measure (lack of) achievements in education are of a partial nature. Or that the extra spending in education requires a longer time horizon to materialize into improved educational outcomes. These and other related arguments can be put forward to argue in favor of a brighter picture in the levels of education. On the other hand, it can be argued that quantitative indicators like the ones provided by the Casen survey overstate the educational level. To illustrate this point consider that the rate of illiteracy reported by this survey is almost nil, whereas a recent evaluation of effective adult literacy showed that most of the adult Chilean population is below the minimum standard.[92]

Gains in deficit reduction in the housing dimension are much larger than in education. Table 25 presents the evolution of the housing deficit between 1990 and 1998. It shows that the percentage of households, which exhibit at least one dimension below standard, decreased from 42.8% in 1990 to 27.3% in 1998; those exhibiting four or more dimensions below standard declined from 10.5% to 4.4%. These figures are in line with the reduction in income poverty or the increases in public social spending.

Table 25: Housing Deficit Index
(households), 1990 vs. 1998

	1990	1998
No deficit	57.2	72.7
One	14.7	11.9
Two	9.5	6.5
Three	8.1	4.8
Four or more	10.5	4.0
Total	100.0	100.0

Source: Calculations based on 1990 and 1998 CASEN surveys.

A look at the specific indicators identifies the period 1990-98 as one of large gains across all housing dimensions (Table 26). In effect the incidence of most housing deficiencies decreases by about half during these years. The largest gain occurs in access to electricity, where households in deficit were only 3.8% in 1998 (down from 11.8% in 1990). In contrast, 15.8% of households were still experiencing deficit in sewage facilities in 1998, down from 24.6% in 1990.

Table 26 Housing: Percentage of Households below Standards. 1990 vs. 1998

	1990	1998
Dwelling materials		
Ceiling	14.4	7.2
Floor	14.0	6.6
Walls	21.8	11.9
Crowding		
Persons/room	10.1	6.1
Infrastructure		
Electricity	11.4	3.8
Drinking water	11.9	6.7
Sewage facilities	24.6	15.8

Source: Calculations based on 1990 and 1998 CASEN surveys.

---

[92] Second International Adult Literacy Test,.

Turning to the case of health care, the results are less conclusive. The reason for this lies in the data reported by the Casen survey, which is not very helpful for evaluating the access of the population to health care services (Table 27). This feature already turned up in the previous section, where the measurement of healthcare deficits was an exercise of a more hypothetical nature than in the cases of education and housing. Matters get worse when a time comparison of the indicator is attempted. As shown in table 27, the percentage of the population self-reporting lack of access to proper health care more than doubled in the 1990-98 period, a result that goes against all predictions and should be attributed to methodological flaws in the health module of the Casen questionnaire. Moreover, the second indicator for identifying a deficit, the "timely" dimension of healthcare access, was not reported in the 1990 Casen.

It seems rather awkward that a household survey whose aim is to measure the incidence of social spending fails to inform us about some very basic questions related to deficits in healthcare access.

This raises the need to revise the Casen questionnaire. As we have already said, household surveys are a unique instrument to evaluate the distribution of welfare across the population. Accordingly, they have to be skillfully designed and administered.

Table 27: Health care Percentage of Households below Standards, 1990 vs. 1998

	1990	1998
Medical attention		
% did not get attention when in need	8.2	16.8
% untimely access	N/A.	11.8
(% who experienced need in last 3 months)	(24.9)	(22.0)
Dental attention		
% did not get attention when in need	39.8	38.5
(% who experienced need in the last 6 months)	(30.1)	(23.3)

Source: Calculations based on 1990 and 1998 CASEN surveys.

Conclusions

The objective of the chapter is to incorporate social services in the measurement of poverty in the light of the Chilean experience of the 90′s. The rationale for this is clear: access to education, health care and housing is an essential determinant of the standards of living of the population. However, the typical assessment of poverty based on income shortfall excludes these services to the extent that they are provided on a subsidized basis to the middle and low income strata of the population.

The measurement of income poverty is a rather standardized procedure. Instead, incorporating social services in the poverty measure is far less documented and consequently more difficult in both the analytical and applied dimensions.

Our approach is based on the notion of poverty as human deprivation originating in the lack of economic means to render the analysis consistent with the methodology to measure income poverty. It follows that we are more interested in resources rather than outcomes when choosing the evaluation space; and in supply rather than demand factors when assessing the lack of access to some social service.

One particular problem arises from the non-fungible nature of in-kind subsidies. It follows that the full income method utilized in chapter three can lead to serious inconsistencies in the measurement of poverty. The problem is serious enough to advise not using this methodology in the evaluation of poverty. Moreover, different poverty dimensions (income, education, housing and health care) are not cardinally comparable. That being the case, it is more advisable to have several measures of poverty deprivation rather than to integrate them into a single but essentially meaningless measure.

In spite of these difficulties it must be emphasized that measuring and evaluating the access of the population to subsidized social services is a must for two reasons. First, social services address essential dimensions of the standard of living of the population; focusing only on income poverty renders only a partial assessment of this variable. Second, it does not make sense that the government evaluates its social policies by concentrating on the evolution of income poverty, a variable far beyond its control, without monitoring what is going on in those dimensions where most of the social spending is actually channeled: education, health care and housing.

Our operational measure to assess lack of access to education comprises three types of variables at the household level: whether some member of the household older than 15 is illiterate; whether some member of the household aged 8-23 is not attending school while not having finished primary education; and whether some member of the household is attending school but is two or more years behind expected grade. The results for the year 1998 show that 26.9% of households fall into the category of educational deficit, varying from 48.5% for the very poor to 16.3% for non-poor households.

Turning to the housing dimension, the Casen survey asks for a number of characteristics of the dwelling. Among others, the number of habitable rooms; the type and condition of the floor, ceiling and walls, access to electricity, drinking water and sanitary facilities. In every case some minimum standard is defined and then we evaluate whether the standard is actually met by each household. An index of housing deficit is then calculated as the number of dimensions below standard.

The results for the year 1998 show that 75.6% of households have no deficit in housing, 12.3% experience one type of deficit; 5.8% two types and 6.3% three or more types. The index of housing deficit relates closely to income poverty: 59.5% of the very poor experiences at least one type of deficit as compared to 52.7% of the non-indigent poor and 19.2% of the non-poor.

Somehow, surprisingly, the deficit index shows that more than a fifth of the dwellings acquired with public subsidies after the year 1990 present at least one dimension below standard, which points to problems of housing policy in terms of quality standards.

We would like to know if access to health care is actually provided, asides from the formal coverage by insurance. If possible, we would be interested to know about the quality and efficacy of the health care services which are provided to the population. Getting access to very low quality health services is not equivalent to getting "adequate" access to health care when in need.

The assessment of access to healthcare turns out to be more difficult because of data limitations. In this way, 16.8% of the population did not look for medical attention in 1998 after experiencing some illness, injury or related condition. However, it is not clear whether the lack of attention responds to a supply or demand factor. This question provides some hints about the quality of health care services. On the other hand, 85.5% of the population who looked for health care reported a timely access whereas the remaining 14.5% experienced delays in access to healthcare services.

When looking at the intersection of deficits in the dimensions of income, education, housing and health care, it turns out that the percentage of households which shows deprivation in (at least) one variable varies between 16% and 25%; those which show deprivation in two dimensions represents 5% to 11% of total households; the incidence falls to 2%-5% in the case of simultaneous deprivation in three variables. Finally, only 1.5% of households present deprivation in all four dimensions.

These numbers suggest a rather heterogeneous profile of households. On the positive side it can be said that poverty is not an overwhelming condition, where poor households are deprived in every possible dimension. On the negative side, only 51.1% of households are above poverty thresholds in all four dimensions (48.9% fail to achieve at least one threshold).

Finally, we assess the evolution of these measures of deficit in the 1990 and 1998 period. These years are characterized by strong growth in both per capita income and public social expenditure, which renders them particularly interesting for the analysis of the evolution between income poverty and the other dimensions of the standard of living.

As established in chapter two, the percentage of households whose income per equivalent adult is below this threshold fell from 28.8% in 1990 to 14.5% in 1998 (32.1% to 17.0% of population).

In the case of education, public social expenditure increased by 125.8% in real terms during the 1990-98 period. Our indicators of educational deficit - adult illiteracy, grade fallbehind and lost years of schooling - show some improvement along these years. The percentage of households with (at least one) deficit in education declined from 30.6% to 26.9% during the period. The gains are larger if we look at the severity of the deficit: the percentage of households where two or more members experience educational deficit decreased from 12.8% in 1990 to 7.8% in 1998.

However, all things considered, the reduction in the education deficit looks rather small when compared with the reduction in income poverty and the increases in public social spending.

Gains in deficit reduction in the housing dimension are more encouraging as the percentage of households which exhibit at least one dimension below standard decreased from 42.8% in 1990 to 27.3% in 1998; those exhibiting four or more dimensions below standard declined from 10.5% to 4.4%. These figures are in line with the reduction in income poverty or the increases in public social spending.

A comparative analysis in the case of health care is prevented by the methodological shortfalls in the Casen questionnaire, which raises the need to review this instrument. Household surveys are a unique instrument to evaluate the distribution of welfare across the population. They have to be designed and administered accordingly.

REFERENCES

World Bank (1993). *World Development Report 1993: Investing in Health.* Oxford University Press: Oxford, New York.

MIDEPLAN (1998). CASEN – Caracterización Socioeconómica Nacional. Santiago, Chile. www.mideplan.cl

Background Paper 4

THE TARGETING OF GOVERNMENT PROGRAMS IN CHILE:
A QUANTITATIVE AND QUALITATIVE ASSESSMENT
Carine Clert and Quentin Wodon[93]

Introduction

The government of Chile has been using for many years a system for the targeting of many of its income transfers and other social programs. The system is based on the *ficha* CAS, a two page form that households must fill if they wish to apply for benefits. Each household is attributed a score on the basis of the *ficha* CAS, and this score is used to determine eligibility not only for income transfers (e.g., pension assistance and family allowances), but also for water subsidies, access to social housing, and childcare centers. At the local level, municipalities also use the form for the targeting of their own programs and safety nets. Almost a third of all Chilean households have been filling the form. Taken as whole, the programs which are targeted using the *ficha* CAS play a major role not only in the alleviation of poverty, but also in its prevention by enabling vulnerable households to receive or not state and municipal support.

This papers provides an assessment of the *ficha* CAS system using both quantitative and qualitative methods of investigation. After describing the *ficha* CAS system and the main income transfers and other programs which are targeted using the system, the paper uses data from the nationally representative 1998 CASEN survey to provide quantitative measures of performance for each program. Following Wodon and Yitzhaki (2000), the quantitative performance measures are based on a decomposition of the Gini income elasticity of the various programs into a targeting component which is based on who benefits from the programs and who does not, and an allocation component which captures the impact of the variability in program benefits among participants. Overall, the programs appear to be well targeted.

The good quantitative performance of the program does not mean that the *ficha* CAS is without any limitations. In order to look in some detail at these limitations, the paper relies on a study of the experience, perceptions and recommendations of poor citizens on the one hand and practitioners using the *ficha* CAS at the local level on the other hand (Clert, 2000a, 2000b). Evidence derives from a stratified survey of 88 randomly sampled households in the municipality of Huechuraba, a comparatively poor area in the Greater Santiago area and from qualitative interviews with a sub-sample of households. Evidence also derives from focus-group discussions and semi-structured interviews with professionals located in that municipality and from interviews with central government officials. The fieldwork was carried out between December 1997 and June 1998. The triangulation of household-level interviews and focus group discussions with municipal staff in Huechuraba revealed that poor households often lack information about the government programs and how to apply for their benefits. The qualitative work also revealed

[93] Both authors are with the World Bank. Comments can be sent to cclert@worldbank.org and qwodon@worldbank.org. The paper was funded by the World Bank under the Chile Poverty Assessment (Norman Hicks) and the Regional Study on Extreme Poverty and Social Exclusion in Latin America (Estanislao Gacitúa-Marió and Quentin Wodon). Assistance from Rodrigo Castro-Fernandez and Corinne Siaens is gratefully acknowledged. The authors are grateful for the Chilean government's comments which greatly improved this paper. The views expressed in the paper are those of the authors and need not represent the views of the World Bank, its Executive Directors, or the countries they represent.

potential deficiencies and biases in the eligibility criteria and associated targeting methods based on the *ficha* CAS. While the targeting system as a whole is sound, recommendations can be made for improving its effectiveness and its fairness.

The paper is divided in four sections. Section One introduces the paper by presenting some background information on the *ficha* CAS and the targeted safety nets and other social programs reviewed in this paper. Section Two provides evidence for a quantitative assessment of the targeting of some of these social entitlements using the CASEN household survey data while Sections Three sheds light on the a more qualitative assessment of targeting methods, based on the experience and views of the poor themselves and of social practitioners. Conclusions and policy implications are provided in the last section.

Background

This section first sheds light on the official means-testing instrument used by the Chilean government, the *ficha* CAS or CAS form. It then puts the forthcoming findings of the paper in context by presenting the key safety nets and programs reviewed in this paper and their importance in the social protection of the poor.

The *Ficha* CAS

Introduced during the military regime (1973-1989) and modified by the post-1990 democratic governments, the *ficha* CAS[94] is a two page form which is used for determining the eligibility of households to a number of Government programs including not only monetary transfers (*Subsidios Monetarios*), but also access to low income housing and childcare centres.[95]   A reproduction of the form is provided in Appendix Two. The form provides detailed information on housing conditions of the dwelling unit (e.g., material used for the construction of the housing unit, number and type of rooms, access to water, latrine and sanitary services, access to electricity, etc.); on members of the dwelling unit (their occupation, educational level, date of birth, and income. Additional information is provided on material assets held by the household (housing status, television, heating equipment, and refrigerator). Points are allocated to households on the basis of the information provided, with the number of points fluctuating between 380 and 770 points. Households with a total of inferior to 500 points are considered as extremely poor and those with a total number of between 500 and 540 points are considered as poor. The Ministry of Planning MIDEPLAN is responsible for the design of the *ficha* CAS. The recruitment of the employees administrating the form is done at the discretion of the municipality, but training must be provided by the Ministry. Municipalities usually separate the activities of data collection and data entry from those of needs assessment. Data collection and entry tend to be done by a department of social information within the municipality, while the control of the needs assessment is usually done by social workers and *técnico*-sociales (welfare assistants).

The national income transfer programs which are targeted using the CAS scoring system apply the formula in a strict manner in order for determining eligibility. The score obtained by a household automatically and exclusively prevails, so that eligibility depends only on the number of points obtained. The *ficha* is also used for targeting locally financed safety nets, but in this

---

[94] Ficha de Estratificación Social.
[95] At present the official name of the form is the *ficha* CAS-II.

case social workers and other professionals can often give some weight to other eligibility criteria such as the presence of a chronic illness, the civil status of household members, and their actual financial resources at the time of request (the *ficha* is completed every three years, and there may be differences between the status of households when they apply for benefits, as compared to their status when they filled the form). For housing programs as well, differences can be observed in the use of the *ficha* at various levels of government. Professionals dealing with central government programs (*viviendas básicas* and *vivienda progresiva*) must follow the method of calculation defined by the Ministry of Housing (SERVIU), while professionals involved in municipal initiatives have some discretionary power.

One of the advantages of using the *ficha* for many different programs is that this reduces the cost of means-testing. The cost of a CAS interview is about US$8.65 per household. The Ministry of Planning estimates that 30 percent of Chilean households undergo interviews, which seems reasonable given that the target group for the subsidy programs is the poorest 20 percent. The CAS system is used as a targeting instrument for utility subsidies, income transfers, social housing subsidy, and pension subsidies among other programs. Because the fixed administrative costs of targeting are spread across several programs, the CAS is very cost-effective. In 1996, administrative costs represented a mere 1.2 percent of the benefits distributed using the CAS system. If the administrative costs of the CAS system were to be borne by the water subsidies alone, for example, they would represent 17.8 percent of the value of the subsidies.

The Targeted Programs: Their Role in Fostering Security and Alleviating Poverty

Many national and local Government programs rely on the CAS system for their targeting. Locally, *Comunas* generate from their own budgets other safety net programs which vary in their amount and eligibility criteria, but these cannot be evaluated with the CASEN. The national programs implemented with the *ficha* CAS and reviewed in this paper include means-tested pensions, family allowances, water subsidies, social housing, and child care. As developed below, most of these social entitlements play a major potential role in decreasing vulnerability and alleviating poverty, which makes the issue of targeting a crucial one. Full descriptions of the programs is provided in Appendix One.

- *Pensions PASIS (Pensión de Asistencia)*: Means-tested state pensions are provided to elderly and/or disabled individuals through PASIS. To be eligible, an elderly individual needed to have a total income below half of the minimum pension allowance, which was CP$ 23,415 per month in 1998.[96] The eligibility threshold for the disabled is the amount of the minimum pension allowance. While the income transfers provided through PASIS are low in comparison with the minimum wage, household interviews in the *Comuna* of Huechuraba suggest that the transfers can be significant in the eyes of those who do not have any other source of income or family support to rely upon. In addition, those who receive PASIS pensions are automatically eligible for free access to public health services through the health gratuity card. By securing an entitlement to health, PASIS thus provides low income elderly and invalid or disabled people with a key mechanism of long term social protection.

- *Family allowances SUF (Subsidio Unico Familiar)*: Family allowances are important because they help in coping with the extra expenses due to the birth of children, as well as with the possibility of a reduction in earnings due to the fact that pregnant women and women who

---

[96] In 2001, the PASIS is now worth 35104 Chilean pesos.

have delivered may have to stop working for a while. The loss in earnings is particularly likely for women involved in precarious jobs which do not provide them with maternal and other family benefits. The amount per child above three years of age was CP$2,500 per month in 1998, at the time the CASEN was implemented. The amount per child below three years of age was CP$2,800. Maternal benefits were also $2,800 per month for a period of ten months, with eligibility as of the fifth month of pregnancy.[97]

- *Water subsidies SAP (Subsidio Agua Potable)*: The water subsidy provides an allowance for the cost of consumption of up to 15 cubic meters per month. As noted by Gomez-Lobo and Contreras (2000; see also Estache, Foster, and Wodon, forthcoming, for a review), the subsidy was introduced in 1990 to reduce the impact of rising prices after the reform of the water sector. The initial take-up of the program (i.e., the percentage of eligible households participating in the program) was low in the first year, at 5 percent only, because the eligibility threshold and the value of the subsidy were too low to make it worthwhile for households to participate. To increase take-up, water companies were given the opportunity to propose customers as potential subsidy recipients, which was in their interest in order to increase payment rates. The subsidy covers from 20 percent to 85 percent of the bill for the first 15 cubic meters of monthly consumption. MIDEPLAN uses regional data on water consumption and tariffs, as well as socioeconomic conditions, to determine the funds made available to each region. Within each region, subsidies are allocated to municipalities who then determine household eligibility using the *ficha* CAS. As for other programs targeted with the *ficha* CAS, household eligibility is re-assessed every three years, and the subsidy can be withdrawn by utilities if the household has more than three months of arrears in paying its share of the bill.

- *Social housing*: The programs of *vivienda básica* and *vivienda progresiva (etapas I –II)* provide subsidies for the construction of new housing units, or the improvement of existing units. The amount of the subsidy is determined in UFs, which are monetary units.[98] Apart from eligibility criteria according to the *ficha* CAS, the households must contribute to the construction costs and thereby provide evidence of savings when applying. The program is important not only to satisfy basic needs, but also because the lack of safe and secure shelter has been shown to reduce the ability of women to work because of their reluctance to leave their children at home (risks of accidents in sub-standard housing, such as electrical shocks). Good housing conditions are also essential for individuals involved in home-based wage employment or micro-enterprise, and for reducing crowding and the associated social risks of domestic violence.

- *Child care*: The childcare programs of the JUNJI and *Fundación* INTEGRA are also targeted using the *ficha* CAS. The programs provide care for children whose mothers are working. Since vulnerable low-income women are more likely to be affected than men by exclusion from the labor market and by poor quality of employment, this type of program for affordable or even free childcare is important from a gender point of view and for building work experience and incentives among poor women.

---

[97] These figures refer to the period during which the micro-study in Huechuraba (See Section III) was implemented. These amounts have changed since. For instance, in July 2001, the SUF is now worth 3452.
[98] In 1998, one UF was worth approximately CP$460.

A Quantitative Evaluation

This section provides a quantitative assessment of the targeting performance of the social programs which are implemented nationally and for which we have information in the nationally representative 1998 CASEN survey (*Caracterización Socioeconómica Nacional*) implemented by the Ministry of Planning MIDEPLAN.

There are various ways to evaluate quantitatively the targeting performance of the programs whose eligibility is based on the *ficha* CAS. The most common measures of targeting performance used in the literature are based on the so-called errors of inclusion and exclusion. An error of inclusion is observed when a household which is not part of the program's target population receives the program's benefits. An error of exclusion is observed when a household which is part of the program's target population does not receive the program's benefits. This approach for measuring targeting performance has been used among others by Gomez-Lobo and Contreras (2000) for Chile's water subsidies. In this paper however, we use an alternative (and arguably better) indicator of performance which takes into account not only who benefits from social programs and who does not, but also to what extent various households benefits (the program benefits may vary from one household to another). The method is explained in Box 5.1, and it relies on three key parameters for understanding the impact of various programs on social welfare:

- *Gini income elasticity (GIE)*: The overall impact on social welfare of changing at the margin the budget allocated by the government to a given program is a function of the program's Gini income elasticity (GIE hereafter). If the GIE is equal to one, a marginal increase in the benefits will not affect the Gini coefficient in after-tax after-benefit per capita income, and thereby the effect on social welfare can be considered as neutral (no change). If the GIE is less (greater) than one, then an increase in program benefits will decrease (increase) the Gini of income, and thereby increase (decrease) social welfare. The smaller the GIE, the larger the redistributive impact of the program and the gains in social welfare. Importantly, since the GIE is estimated for a dollar spent on the program, we can compare programs which are of different scale in terms of outlays.

The GIE can be decomposed into the product of a targeting elasticity and an allocation elasticity.

- *Targeting elasticity*: The targeting elasticity measures what would be the impact of a program on social welfare if all those who benefit from the program were receiving exactly the same benefit. In other words, the targeting elasticity provides the impact of pure targeting (who gets the program and who does not) on social welfare. Lower and upper bounds can be provided for the targeting elasticity, and these bounds depend on the share of the population which participates in the program. The higher the share of participants in the population, the closer the bounds. The intuition beyond this result is that it is easier to target a program to the very poor when the share of the participants among the population is low. The practical relevance of the bounds is that they enable an analyst to compare the targeting performance of programs of different sizes.

- *Allocation elasticity:* The allocation elasticity measures the impact of social welfare of the differences in the benefits received by various program participants. Lower and upper bounds can also be provided for the allocation elasticity. The combination of the information provided by the targeting and allocation elasticities enables the analyst to assess whether the good (bad) performance of a given program is due to good (bad) targeting or to a good (bad) allocation of benefits among participants.

In the 1998 CASEN, it is feasible to estimate both the targeting and allocation elasticities for the income transfers provided by PASIS, SUF, and the water subsidies. Additionally and for comparison purposes, we also compute the targeting and allocation elasticities for another type of means-tested family allowances which is different from SUF and does not rely on the *ficha* CAS (according to the CASEN questionnaire, these allowances provide CP$3,025 for households with gross income below CP$91,800, CP$2,943 for households with gross income between CP$91,800 and CP$186,747, and CP$1,000 for households with gross income between CP$186,747 and CP$365,399). For the housing and child care programs, the information available in the CASEN enables us to compute the targeting elasticity only because we do not have the amounts allocated (or the cash value of the in-kind benefits), but the targeting elasticity should be fairly close to the overall GIE because there are relatively few differences in benefits allocation between households in these programs (the amounts for the housing allocations are fixed, and the child care benefits only depend on the number of young children that a working mother may have).

The results of the estimation are provided in Table 1. To understand how Table 1 works, let's consider the case of the pension assistance provided under PASIS. The table indicates that the GIE for PASIS is –0.58, which is fairly low and hence highly redistributive (any elasticity below one indicates that the corresponding program is redistributive; a negative elasticity implies a large redistributive impact). The GIE for PASIS is equal to the product of the targeting elasticity (-0.56) and the allocation elasticity (1.05). The fact that the allocation elasticity is close to one suggests that there are few differences in pension benefits among PASIS participants. In other words, the redistributive impact of the program comes from its good targeting based on the *ficha* CAS. As for the participation rate in the program of 6.1 percent, it determines (together with the value of the overall Gini for per capita income of about 0.57) the lower and upper bounds for the targeting and allocation elasticities. For comparison purposes, other sources of pension income have been included in Table 1 even though these are not targeted through the ficha CAS and are provided in many cases by private operators. Clearly, and as expected, the pension assistance provided through PASIS is much more redistributive than other pensions.

More generally, two main conclusions can be drawn from Table 1:

- *High overall redistributive impact, but differences between the various programs:* All the programs targeted according to the *ficha* CAS have a large redistributive impact per peso spent. This is evidenced by the low values of the GIE elasticities for the income transfers and water subsidies, and by the low values of the targeting elasticities for the housing and child care programs (for these programs, we cannot compute an allocation elasticity, so that the GIE remains unknown). Yet, some programs are better targeted than others. Among income and other transfers, the SUF family allowances have the best performance, while water subsidies have a somewhat lower performance. Among the other social programs, the child care programs tend to be slightly better targeted than the housing programs, perhaps because of the savings requirements required for participation in the later.
- *Good targeting, with few differences in allocation:* The redistributive impact of the programs is due to their good targeting, which is based on the ficha CAS. The fact that the GIE tends to be close to the targeting elasticity (because the allocation elasticities are close to one) suggests few differences in the amount of benefits received from the various programs by different

households. Only in the case of water do we have an allocation elasticity well below one, probably because those who consume more water and thereby receive more subsidies tend to be higher up in the distribution of income.

Table 1: Gini Income Elasticity of Social Programs Targeted According to the *Ficha* CAS

	Income transfer programs and water subsidies			
	Non-PASIS pensions (not targeted)	Pension assistance PASIS	Family allowances SUF	Water subsidies
Gini income elasticity (GIE)	0.91	-0.58	-1.03	-0.35
Program participation rate p	15.7%	6.1%	11.5%	6.4%
Mean allocation received	7634.04	503.16	155.68	47.61
Overall Gini for per capita income G_y	0.57	0.57	0.57	0.57
Targeting elasticity				
Lower bound	-1.49	-1.66	-1.56	-1.65
Actual value	0.47	-0.56	-0.95	-0.43
Upper bound	1.49	1.66	1.56	1.65
Allocation elasticity				
Lower bound	-1.19	-1.06	-1.13	-1.07
Actual value	1.91	1.05	1.09	0.80
Upper bound	1.19	1.06	1.13	1.07
	Other targeted programs				
	Housing Viv. Basica	Housing Viv. Prog I	Housing Viv. Prog II	Child care JUNJI	Child care INTEGRA
Gini income elasticity	NA	NA	NA	NA	NA
Program participation rate p	5.8%	1.1%	0.2%	1.7%	1.3%
Overall Gini for per capita income G_y	0.57	0.57	0.57	0.57	0.57
Targeting elasticity					
Lower bound	-1.66	-1.74	-1.76	-1.73	-1.74
Actual value at individual (per capita) level	-0.41	-0.68	-0.59	-0.50	-0.71
Actual value at household level	-0.32	-0.54	-0.48	-0.44	-0.65
Upper bound	1.66	1.74	1.76	1.73	1.74

Source: Authors' estimation using 1998 CASEN survey.

BOX 1: METHODOLOGY FOR THE QUANTITATIVE EVALUATION

To assess the impact on welfare of government programs per dollar spent in each program, we Wodon and Yitzhaki (2000). Denote by $\bar{y}$ the mean income in the population and by G the Gini index of income inequality. A common welfare function used in the literature is $W = \bar{y}(1-G)$. The higher the mean income, the higher the level of social welfare, but the higher the inequality, the lower the aggregate level of welfare. This welfare function takes into account not only absolute, but also relative deprivation (people assess their own level of welfare in part by comparing themselves with others). Using the implicit distributional weights embodied in this welfare function, we can derive the marginal gains from additional investments in government programs. If $\bar{x}$ denotes the mean benefit of a social program x across the whole population, and if η is the Gini income elasticity of that program (defined below), increasing at the margin the funds allocated to the program by multiplying the outlays by $1 + \Delta$ for all program participants, with Δ small, will result in a marginal social welfare gain equal to:

$$dW = (\bar{x}\,\Delta)(1 - \eta\,G) \tag{1}$$

Equation (1) makes it clear that considerations related to both growth (as represented by the mean marginal benefit $\bar{x}\,\Delta$) and distribution (as represented by the Gini income elasticity η times the Gini index G) must be taken into account in program evaluations. The Gini income elasticity η (hereafter GIE) measures the impact of an increase of one dollar, distributed as a constant percentage change in the benefits of the program, on income or consumption inequality. Denoting by x the household (per capita) benefit from the program, by y income, by $F(y)$ the cumulative distribution of income, and by $\bar{x}$ the mean benefits of the program over the entire population, the GIE is:

$$\eta = \frac{\text{cov}(x, F(y))}{\text{cov}(y, F(y))} \frac{\bar{y}}{\bar{x}} \tag{2}$$

If the elasticity equals one, a marginal increase in benefits will not affect the Gini coefficient in after-tax after-benefit income. If the elasticity is less (greater) than one, then an increase in benefits will decrease (increase) the Gini of income. The smaller the elasticity, the larger the redistributive impact of the program and the gains in welfare. Since the GIE is estimated for a dollar spent on the program, we can compare programs which are of different scale in terms of outlays. A decomposition of the GIE can be used to differentiate between two properties of a program that can affect its impact on welfare: targeting and the allocation mechanism among participants (internal progressivity). The decomposition enables the analyst to assess whether the (lack of) performance of social programs and policies is due to either the selection mechanism for participants or the allocation of benefits among program participants. To differentiate between targeting and internal progressivity, define z as the targeting instrument:

$$z = \begin{pmatrix} \bar{x}_P & if & h \in P \\ 0 & if & h \notin P \end{pmatrix} \tag{3}$$

That is, z is equal to the mean benefit among participants for households who participate in the program and it is zero for households who do not participate (one could substitute the average benefit by an indicator which is equal to one without affecting the results.) The variable z is an indicator of targeting because it is only concerned with whom is affected by the program, rather than with the actual benefit received. Using this definition of z, we can rewrite the GIE as a product of two elasticities as follows:

$$\eta = \left(\frac{\text{cov}(z, F(y))}{\text{cov}(y, F(y))} \frac{\bar{y}}{\bar{z}} \right)\left(\frac{\text{cov}(x, F(y))}{\text{cov}(z, F(y))} \frac{\bar{z}}{\bar{x}} \right) = \eta_T \eta_A \tag{4}$$

Box 1 (continued)

The first term is related to the targeting of the program (targeting effect). The second term is the progressivity among participants (allocation effect)The distributional impact of a program depends on the product of its targeting and allocation elasticities. Good targeting, for example, can be offset by a bad allocation mechanism among program beneficiaries. Equation (6) is useful to assess whether the (lack of) performance of a program is due to its targeting or to the allocation of benefits among beneficiaries. But one can go further by establishing bounds for the values of the targeting and allocation elasticities. Specifically, the minimum and maximum values of the targeting elasticity depend on the share the population participating in the program and the overall Gini. Denoting by p the share of the population participating in the program, and by G_y the overall Gini, it can be shown that :

$$-\frac{(1-p)}{G_y} \leq \eta_T \leq \frac{(1-p)}{G_y} . \qquad (5)$$

The lower bound increases with the proportion of the population reached by the program and the level of income inequality. The relationship between the lower bound and the share of program participants is straightforward. The more households the program reaches, the less effective targeting can be because each additional participating household makes it more difficult to focus resources on the poorest. If all households participate, *p=1* and the lower bound is zero. The fact that the targeting capacity declines with the overall level of inequality is perhaps more surprising, because one might expect that the higher the inequality, the higher the potential for redistribution through targeting. The intuitive explanation is that the higher the inequality, the further apart households are from each other, so that adding a small amount of resources to the program participants does not reduce inequality by a lot (remember that the elasticities capture the impact on inequality and social welfare on e per dollar basis). A similar reasoning applies for the intuition regarding the upper bound, and the two bounds are symmetric around zero.

Lower and upper bounds can also be provided for the allocation elasticity. As shown in the appendix, the minimum and maximum values of the allocation elasticity depend on the share the population participating in the program, but not on the overall Gini:

$$-\frac{1}{(1-p)} \leq \eta_A \leq \frac{1}{(1-p)} , \qquad (6)$$

As the share of the population participating in the program increases, the interval for the allocation elasticity increases as well, because a higher participation rates provides more opportunities for differentiation in the allocation of the benefits among participants of the program. It is important to note that the interpretation of what a good elasticity need not be the same for the targeting and allocation elasticities. In the case of the targeting elasticity, one would hope to obtain an elasticity below zero, which would indicate a good targeting performance. But if the targeting elasticity is below zero, one would hope to have an allocation elasticity above zero in order to keep the overall elasticity negative. At In reverse, if the targeting elasticity is positive, suggesting bad targeting, one would hope to have a negative allocation elasticity. It should also be emphasized that the interpretation of the upper and lower bounds for both elasticities changes depending on whether we are dealing with taxes or transfers. In the case of targeting for example, when comparing transfers, the lower bound is typically the best that can be achieved, while when dealing with taxes, it is the upper bound that one would like to reach. Note finally that equations (5) and (6) enable us in principle to compare the targeting and allocation effectiveness of programs with different participation rate, since the bounds depend on that participation rate. (The role played by the overall per capita income Gini in the bounds for the targeting elasticity is less important since the Gini is identical for all programs at any given point in time.)

Qualitative Evaluation: An Actor-Oriented Approach

The quantitative evaluation provided in the previous suggests that the programs targeted according to the *ficha* CAS have a good redistributive impact. This does not mean, however, that there are no problems or challenges with the *ficha* CAS targeting or with the outreach of the various programs. In this section, in order to go beyond our quantitative results, we present findings from an exploratory study on poverty, access to government programs, and social exclusion in Chile conducted in 1998 by Clert (2000a, 2000b). Using an actor-oriented approach, the research used both quantitative and qualitative methods (see Box 2) to explore the priorities, experience and perceptions of three sets of actors concerned with poverty reduction: a) the government leadership; b) the residents of Huechuraba, a socially disadvantaged *Comuna* of Greater Santiago, and c) public agents involved at different levels of policy formulation and implementation. For the purposes of this paper, we focus on the views from households and social workers.

BOX 2: METHODOLOGY FOR THE QUALITATIVE EVALUATION

Much of the research on social exclusion is done without consultation with those who experience social disadvantage and those who formulate and implement social policies. The qualitative evaluation of the *ficha* CAS presented here is part of a broader study on poverty and social policy in Chile carried out by Clert (2000b) using an actor-oriented methodology. The research was carried within a social exclusion framework which recognizes the multidimensionality of poverty (e.g., the connection between distributional and relational dimensions), the role of institutional factors in the generation of social disadvantage, and its time and spatial aspects. More specifically, the research explored the priorities, experience and perceptions of three sets of actors concerned with poverty reduction; a) the residents of Huechuraba, a socially disadvantaged district of Santiago through a micro study; b) local and central government staff concerned with poverty reduction at different levels of the state apparatus, through interviews and focus groups, and c) the government leadership, through a study of official policy documents and discourse. This methodology allowed to confront central government priorities with the reality of poverty and social exclusion, as experienced and perceived by both Huechuraba's residents and the social practitioners implementing the policies. The fieldwork was carried out between December 1997 and June 1998.

The Micro-Study of the Residents of Huechuraba

. The study of the residents of Huechuraba took place between December 1997 and May 1998. The research included an area survey, a small household survey, and qualitative interviews.

Area survey. The micro-study started with a *comuna* survey. Like traditional 'community surveys', it aimed at identifying the characteristics of the area. Given the complex and multidimensional questions raised by a social exclusion perspective, this entailed going beyond the usual area profile used in poverty assessments. It also required a review of secondary resources and an extensive use of key informant interviews: 25 key informant interviews were conducted in December 1997 (13 municipal agents including managers of programs, departments and one administrator; five agents involved in service provision; five social leaders of community-based organizations; two NGO representatives; and one resident who had lived in a poor sector of the *comuna* for the last thirty years).

The household survey. The survey was based on a stratified random sample of 88 households living in Huechuraba. Given the spatial heterogeneity of the *comuna*, the stratified sample was used to ensure the adequate representation of all neighborhood units and *campamentos* (informal settlements). However, given the focus of the study on social disadvantage, the most well-off area of the *comuna* was excluded from the survey. Regarding respondents, the female head of household or the female partner of the male

Box 2 (continued)

identified as the head of household was chosen for the interviews. If the head of household was a male living by himself or with children, then he was the respondent. Despite the preference for female respondents for practical and methodological reasons, the research also saw the importance of including male respondents in order to elicit differences in the experience of social disadvantage between men and women. In the end, there were 18 men out of a total of 88 respondents. In terms of content, the questionnaire aimed at getting information on labor market participation and access to social entitlements (social programs, benefits, social services), as well as organizational and relational issues relevant for the social exclusion perspective adopted (e.g., participation in organizations, level of information on social entitlements, reliance on social networks for the provision of care). The questionnaire was divided between questions on the respondent herself, and questions regarding other household members, which aimed at capturing intra-household differences. After completion of the survey, the data was entered and analyzed using the Statistical Package for the Social Sciences (SPSS). Basic frequencies and cross-tabulations helped in selecting interviewees for the sub-sample qualitative interviews.

Qualitative interviews. The household survey was followed by a sub-sample of 24 semi-structured interviews. A 25 percent non-random sub-sample of the original questionnaires was selected, ensuring that the sub-sample was as representative as possible of the overall profile found in the household survey. In order to better capture intra-household differences and a wide range of experiences of exclusion, the household head was not always chosen as the interviewee. In order to elicit gender-based differences, a little more than a third of the interviews were conducted with men, and on three occasions the choice was made to interview separately both the male and the female partners within the same household. The semi-structured interviews aimed at exploring subtle visible mechanisms of exclusion such as perceptions of exclusion and/or discrimination on the basis of specific elements of identity (e.g., age, gender, place of residence) and causal relationships suggested by the preliminary results from the quantitative data analysis of the larger household survey. The interviews focused on capturing the personal experience and the perceptions of exclusion/inclusion of the interviewees in areas identified in the survey questionnaire, including, for instance, the job interview process when searching for employment and the perceptions of the quality and accessibility of various social entitlements. Each interview ended with a participatory exercise in the form of a Venn Diagram, which was used to highlight perceptions of social and institutional relationships. Derived from Participatory Rural Appraisal (P.R.A.) methods and based on the drawing of circles, this exercise asks whether there exist different actors or institutions that are relevant to participants in terms of their capacity to help and/or care for them in times of trouble. It also allows inquiring into the perceived caring and helping capacity of these actors and institutions.

Focus groups and interviews with public agents

The key criterion for the selection of public agents was to obtain the insights of agents located at different stages of the policy process, from the level of local implementation and practice to the level of central policy formulation and agenda setting. On this basis, the choice was made to select professionals within the municipality of Huechuraba as well as central government officials. The research used different qualitative techniques for the two types of agents. The interviews were conducted in June 1998.

Local government staff. The Huechuraba municipality was similar to other local government structures in that the unit for 'community Development' DIDECO (*Dirección para el Desarrollo Communitario*) was responsible for social development and poverty reduction. Therefore, most of the agents interviewed were located there. Since the micro-study had already provided an opportunity to interview middle managers and social planners, only three local officials were selected and the focus was

Box 2 (continued)

placed on agents located at lower hierarchical echelons of the municipality, i.e., social workers and welfare assistants (*técnico-sociales)* for the welfare (*Atención Social)* and housing sub-units. This choice was made mainly for two reasons: a) the positions of the agents placed them in direct contact with disadvantaged residents; and b) the agents occupy a key place in the minds of disadvantaged residents, as identified by the micro-study. In terms of techniques, focus groups (four in total) were used for social workers, welfare assistants and CAS surveyors since they were sufficiently numerous and homogeneous in their educational level and the tasks they performed. Additionally, four semi-structured interviews were used for local managers located at a higher hierarchical level.

Central government staff. There were two key criteria for the selection of these agents. First, senior civil servants had to be closely involved in the process of policy formulation and agenda-setting, and also directly involved with the government's anti-poverty strategy. Second, the position of the civil servants needed to allow them to discuss different aspects of the government's anti-poverty strategy, from overall orientations and priorities to social policy methods and planning. Nine policy advisors and planners located at the Ministries of Finance, Planning, Labor (Institute of Vocational training SENCE), Women and the Secretariat of the Presidency were selected. Semi-structured interviews were used.

The View from the Households

Clert's micro-study showed that exclusion from safety nets and other social entitlements strongly relates to lack of access to information. Three key findings emerged from the household quantitative survey as to the degree of information on social entitlements among household heads or spouses living in the *comuna* of Huechuraba. First, on average, the proportion of respondents who declared not having heard at all of the social entitlement under review was relatively high, at 51 percent of the sample. Second, this proportion varied depending on the kind of social entitlements. It reached 74 percent for benefits such as municipal programs in health and education which provide safety nets (e.g., free provision of medicine or material help for the buying of the school uniform). It was also high for the main national program against poverty among women-headed households, since 70 percent of the female respondents had not heard of the program at all. The awareness rates were better for social funds (which tend to be promoted through radio and TV), and vocational training classes which have been for long a priority of both central and local governments. However, even when the respondents had heard of the social entitlements, a large share did not know how to apply to these benefits. For instance, among the respondents who knew about the existence of vocational training courses, half did not know how to apply for these courses. Given the fact that the survey was carried in a poor neighborhood whose inhabitants are primary targets for the government's programs, this lack of information is probably detrimental to the success of the programs.

One way to analyze the causes of the poor transmission of information to the programs' potential beneficiaries is to look at the ways 'informed' respondents gained their knowledge. Taking the example of the government's income transfers (*subsidios monetarios)*, Figure 1 points to four ways in which information was obtained by households on these programs. The most frequent sources of information were close contacts such as friends, family and neighbors (43 percent of the total number of informed respondents). More official actors such as municipal social workers or health centers rank second, contributing to 37 percent of the informed respondents. Among these more official sources of information, the impact of direct visits to the home of respondent by a social workers was large. Social organizations such as neighborhood associations were at the source of information on government programs in only 6 percent of the cases. Finally, more distant modes of information such as posters or radio announcements accounted for only 5 percent of the informed respondents.

Figure 1: Sources of Information on Income Transfers Among Poor Households

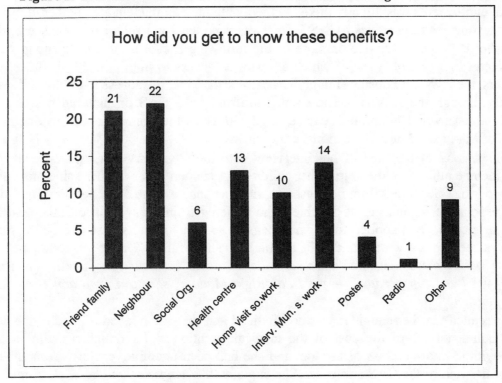

Note: The state income transfers consist of SUF, SUM, SRN, SAP, and PASIS

Source: Households Survey in Clert (2000a, 2000b). Share of respondents

These findings suggests that three main causes may be at the source of the lack of information about social entitlements among the poor. First, the isolation of some among the poor from social networks (e.g., family and neighbors) may reduce access to information. Second, the lack or irregularity of visits to the municipal centers of information by the poor may also reduce their exposure to information.   Third, the fact that only a minority of households benefit from spontaneous home visits by social worker also reduces the likelihood of being informed (many of these visits are organized during *barridos* which are general 'sweeps' of an area). Although statistics such as those provided in Figure 1 cannot claim conclusive causal links, they do raised concerns about the mobility of public actors such as social workers who need to be in close contact with those among the poor who experience social isolation and disadvantage the most. Focus group discussions with practitioners from Huechuraba confirmed the concern regarding the lack of mobility and outreach among social workers. The social workers and *técnico-sociales* called themselves for more mobile initiatives (such as the *barridos*) in order to better identify existing needs rather than solely responding to demands from applicants coming to the municipality. As a social worker summed it up: "*We need more people on the ground, accompanying processes. Before the integration of people into social programs, you need to make an assessment of who might need these programs. This is the opposite of what we're doing now in most cases, which is to wait for the demand to come and help people benefit from the program."*

Another important finding of the study was that the rejection of the respondents' applications for different social entitlements was directly linked to them obtaining an inadequate number of points on the means-testing instrument *ficha* CAS. This was reported by a majority of unsuccessful respondents who had applied for one or more of the following social entitlements: the gratuity card (also named *tarjeta de indigencia*) which allows free access to public health facilities, the income transfers, the low-cost housing (mainly *vivienda básica*) and the access to public childcare centers (mainly through the JUNJI).[99] The emphasis of the *ficha* CAS on material possessions may overlook the risks which households can be faced with and which can make them vulnerable. The examples of Maria and Margarita can make this clear.

- Maria, who was 52 at the time of her interview with the CAS surveyor, was without any source of income other than the help of her children. A sudden illness in her spine prevented her from working. Separated from her husband, she was unable to obtain a pension from him. She was responsible for her eldest daughter who suffered from a psychiatric illness and for her daughter's child. She applied for a small pension, but the points she scored on the *ficha* CAS at the screening test were found to be too high, as she recalls: *"They came to see me, she asked me if I had a washing machine –yes I do I said to her, 'do you have a centrifuge machine' - yes I do, 'refrigerator', – yes I do, 'Right Madam', she said, 'you don't have any right to a pension'."*

- Margarita recalled that her daughter was hospitalized and that she needed the indigence card since she could not afford the cost of the medical attention. Her daughter's illness had coincided with Margarita's loss of her job, and she had been unemployed for two months at the time of the visit of the CAS surveyor. She explains: *"When she came here, she found me better than I am now.... In those years and because I had been working, I had my floor impeccable. Inclusively I wasn't polishing the floor with wax but with brown shoe product. So it looked really shiny.... She was looking everywhere and so she told me, just like that: how could I buy floor wax if I didn't have money to cook and to meet my expenses. I told her it was illogical, since it was two months that I was out of work, but when I was working, I had bought the wax. And my little plants, my little things... With time, I had been buying them and so now that I was in need, without a job, I wasn't going to take out a piece of the table, or a bit of the armchair. This, she didn't understand.... I told her: 'You mix up poverty with cleanliness. I'm poor I said, maybe I don't have a lot to put into the casserole. Yet I have a rag, I said, and I still have something to clean."*

These examples show that both applicants were unable to generate any income, so that they were becoming highly vulnerable, one through her illness and the other through the loss of her job. While their life events justified external support to prevent them from falling further into poverty, the rules of targeting excluded them from such support because a presumption of well-being was

---

[99] From a gender perspective, exclusion from public childcare centers constitutes a contradiction between the priority assigned to female labor-market insertion and the use of exclusionary rules of selection by the Public Institution for Childcare in Chile (JUNJI). At the national level, SERNAM has managed to remove the exclusionary rule for women heads of households, but the new rules have not yet filtered to the local level. Furthermore, it seems that the rule still applies to women who were not household heads.

based on their possession of a number of assets. Margarita's reasoning suggests a logic for the granting of government support which contrasts with the more rigid criteria of the *ficha* CAS instrument.

The View From Social Workers and Welfare Assistants

Drawing on interviews and focus-group discussions with local staff, Clert (2000a, 2000b) also analyzed the experiences and perceptions of municipal professionals in direct contact with disadvantaged citizens. The social workers and welfare assistants (*técnico-sociales*[100]) who use the means-testing instrument provided by the *ficha* CAS in their daily work mention their frustration with the rigidity of the eligibility criteria associated with the *ficha* CAS. Following on site visits and in-depth interviews with residents, they would at times conclude that assistance was needed without being able to offer it because of the results of the CAS point system. As one social worker put it: *"social reality is much more dynamic, changing and complex than the criteria."* Or as a *técnico-social* reflected: *"Criteria are designed for extreme situations, but in practice most situations are not as extreme... The CAS surveyor might tell us the lady earns 100,000 pesos. Right, but she must pay for rent, water, electricity and food. This will never be enough for four people!"*

Local level staff stressed in focus groups the need for less focus on material possessions such as a color TV, the type of roof materials and the like. Questions relating to possessions were seen as outdated, given *'the overall development of the country' and 'people's easy access to goods such as a refrigerator... through credit facilities'*. Another argument was that possessions deflected attention from the central issue of the applicant's means of livelihood. A *'more relevant way to assess poverty'*, would be *'to ask if and how people manage to make ends meet'*. *Técnico-sociales* also mentioned that low-income sectors often improve the quality of their house and equipment by low-cost, self-help means. Therefore, such improvements do not necessarily reflect an increase in income or security. Rather, they reflect people's desire to *'have a better life'* and to gain greater dignity. *Técnico-sociales* also noted that rigid criteria could end up making people more vulnerable to destitution and long-term insecurity. By denying state financial support, the emphasis on enumerating possessions in targeting indirectly left people with no other option than to sell their assets *'in order to survive'*. Finally, local staff made a number of suggestions for improving the targeting system of the *ficha* CAS:

- *Indicators of vulnerability:* Professionals suggested to pay greater attention to vulnerability indicators so as not to exclude people who are in need of assistance even though they may appear to be non-poor on a assets basis. As one professional put it: *'surveyors ask how much do you make a month? They don't ask what kind of job people do, what kind of contract they have, if they have one'*. The recommendation from social workers would be to pay more attention to labor market exclusion.

- *Private transfers:* Local staff pointed to the dangers associated with the way the CAS form takes into account private transfers (e.g., from relatives and friends) registered under the category *'ayuda de terceros'*. CAS surveyors must translated private transfers, whether in kind or in cash, into an average monthly income. Imposed by MIDEPLAN rules and long before by the former military regime, this obligation originates in the assumption that benefit claimants tend to lie about their actual sources of livelihood. While local staff

---

[100] The 'social technicians' are welfare assistants who, unlike social workers, do not have a university degree.

recognized that this could be true for a certain proportion of claimants, they also warned against hasty generalizations. They suggested that such rules ended up distorting the reality and reliability of people's survival strategies and needs. As one worker put it:

"Why can't they believe that some people don't have any money to live? You often find an older woman who tells you "señorita, ...I don't do any pololitos[101], I've got nothing". So, the surveyor asks "but what do you live on then señora"? So she says "my son brings me a kilo of rice..., my neighbor offers me a kilo of sugar and pieces of bread". The surveyor transforms all this into money and her points increase. But then, the señora explains "because I'm on my own, if the neighbor gives me three pieces of bread, I eat half of it at lunch time because sometimes I get nothing else to eat. Then I eat the other half, I still keep some for the day after and sometimes I eat bread that is two days old". It's real, people have told me this and I've been able to observe it so often in my site visits.... But sometimes the surveyor only heard "look, the neighbor offers me two pieces of bread a day"!"

Such experiences lead some *técnico-sociales* to push for reflecting as faithfully as possible the applicants' own words in this area and for avoiding mechanical assumptions for the valuation of private transfers.

- *Intra-household allocations:* A third area of reform suggested by professionals was the need for CAS means-testing methods to recognize intra-household allocations. This is particularly important from a gender perspective, and it can be illustrated with a reference to pregnant teenagers. Classified as dependants, they end up being excluded from maternity benefits. Unable to afford a place of their own, these future single mothers are assumed to benefit from their parents' support but as a *técnico-social* put it:

"We're talking about a pregnant kid who needs a bit of support here...! Fair enough, her parents might help her a bit, somehow, sometimes. But sometimes parents also reject them, tell them off... So the girls come to the municipality for help but there's no support there either..."

The assumption of the parents' support is all the more worrying in the Chilean context as many studies have pointed to the strong stigmatization attached to teenage pregnancy (Latorre et al, 1996).

- *Training of surveyors:* Fourth and lastly, the professionals raised the need for better training of the surveyors themselves and for a better sensitization to the issues outlined above.

The Changes Introduced in September 1999: Achievements and Persisting Challenges

In 1999, there was an official recognition of some of the limitations of the targeting system of CAS, with particular emphasis on the outdated character of variables such as the presence of a television and the like. The MIDEPLAN (1999) report on the modernization of the CAS system clearly stated that "in the last 13 years, the current (CAS) Model had lost most of its ability to identify eligible population among the poor across the socio-economic spectrum". Based on mathematic simulation models, the Government introduced three key changes to the CAS system. First, the revised CAS system dropped the questions of electricity access (under the housing

---

[101] *Pololito* is a colloquial name for casual work or temporary job.

factor) and of TV access (under material assets or *patrimonio)*, which are no longer considered to reflect poverty since an increasing number of households have access to those goods. Second, different systems for rural and urban areas were eliminated and merged into a single, national assessment. Third, it introduced a revised system of weights and scaling of the various factors. In the new model and as illustrated in Table 2 below, the weights for housing increased despite the elimination of electricity access. In the newly created factor Income-Assets (*Ingreso familiar/Patrimonio)*, the weight Income sub-factor lowers while the overall equipment/material assets increases. The weights for the factors education (years of schooling) and occupation of the head of dwelling unit remain overall the same.

Table 2. Relative Weights of Each Variable in the revised CAS SYSTEM

Factor	Variables	Orginal Model		Revised Model
		Urban	Rural	National
Housing	Wall	3.92%	4.01%	3.64%
	Floor	1.96%	2.00%	3.64%
	Roof	3.92%	4.01%	3.12%
	Crowding	2.44%	2.50%	5.72%
	Water	3.67%	3.76%	3.46%
	Sanitation	4.89%	5.01%	2.96%
	Tub-shower	1.22%	1.25%	3.46%
	Electricity	2.44%	2.50%	-
	Total, housing	24.46	25.04	26.00
Education	Education, HH head	8.96%	20.33%	25.00%
Occupation	Highest Job Status of Couple	22.12%	24.94%	22.00%
Income	Per capita family income	24.58%	25.04%	11.61%
Assets	House and Lot (owned)	15.87%	3.70%	3.51%
	TV	1.35%	0.31%	-
	Refrigerator	1.31%	0.30%	5.94%
	Water Heater	1.31%	0.30%	5.94%
	Total	100.00	100.00	100.00

Source: MIDEPLAN (1999:39).

The elimination of TV access and electricity access certainly are achievements towards a better targeting performance. Trials of the new system indicate that the revised system it is more effective in identifying the poor, and the non-poor, and therefore preventing errors of inclusion of the non-poor in social programs. For instance, MIDEPLAN (1999: 36) reported that in the revised system, 53.1 % of families would see their level of points lowered i.e. become classified as "poorer" while 46.9% would see theirs increase. In terms of implications for access to benefits, the proportion of families with a total number of points lower than 550, that is those families entitled to the benefits described in section I above, increases from 22% (908,223) in the old model to 26.6% (1,096,973) in the revised model.

Nevertheless, concerns can also be raised. While errors of inclusion may be diminished, errors of exclusion of poor and vulnerable households could still occur. On the revised quantitative model in particular, it is noteworthy that key indicators of need and vulnerability are still not incorporated into the CAS system, such as issues of intra-household allocations;[102] precariousness

---

[102] The occupation factor remains the occupation of the head of the dwelling unit.

of the type of occupation;[103] degree of indebtedness; and illness. Private transfers, whether in cash or in kind, even if minimal, are still registered under the category 'ayuda de terceros' and translated into an average monthly income. Finally, findings from the Huechuraba study and interviewees with practitioners suggested that possible errors of exclusion should be measured not only quantitatively but also qualitatively. However, the methods used have been exclusively quantitative mathematic simulation models.

The Impact of Additional Eligibility Criteria: Housing and Child Care

Despite significant achievements, some additional rules used for determining eligibility to social services also have exclusionary effects. In the eligibility rules used by the Ministry of Housing SERVIU for its own programs, the information provided by the *ficha* CAS is only one element among others. Specifically, applicants with an adequate number of CAS points cannot be eligible if they do not meet required level of savings (Table 1). Affordability, therefore, is a key obstacle. As one worker put it for the program of basic housing (*vivienda básica*): *'This programme is frustrating...It's supposed to be targeted at the poorest yet people with no saving capacity can't have access to it.'*

The difficulties encountered by households for benefiting from public housing programs can also be illustrated with the examples of the so-called *allegados*. These are self-help organizations in which people collectively advocate for public housing and pool their savings towards this end.[104] Group-based housing applications have been encouraged by the post-1990 Chilean democratic governments. But *allegados* are more likely to succeed in getting low-cost houses for their members if they all have the same savings capacity, and apart from being unable to be successful in their own application for the government's housing programs, many tenants can't even save enough to be part of *allegados* committees. In a household interview, the secretary of one *allegados* committee suggested that some *directivas* (rules from the association's board) put pressure to keep out those with precarious or insufficient saving capacities. The selection process of membership deserves to be quoted in detail:

> *The secretary:* There is a minimum to get into the scheme. We were around 50, but this was still useless. Either people didn't have the money or they couldn't be reached …. So we started to eliminate people.
> The interviewer: *How did you select your people then?*
> *The secretary:* We started to ask for money, they had to give us a certain amount of money by a certain deadline. We went to every address we had, explained what we were doing …. In the end, we only kept 15 out of the 50. They were those who really had the money and all their papers in order.
> The interviewer: *How much did they need to be selected?*
> *The secretary*: We put a minimum of $300,000 (i.e., more than four times the minimum wage.)

---

[103] MIDEPLAN had initially proposed another alternative model for the calculation of CAS, incorporating new variables such as access to health insurance and pensions -as part of the job contract -under the occupation factor. However, incorporating new variables would have required to apply the CAS survey again and these administrative and financial costs were considered too high at the time (MIDEPLAN, 1999).

[104] The term refers to a housing status in which the *allegado* is allowed by the person who officially owns or rents the house to live under the same roof without paying a rent, although they sometimes share bills and other costs.

The inability to save is particularly widespread among the low-income elderly because they are no longer able to generate new income. This makes it difficult for them to receive help for the improvement of the quality of their homes, which in turn makes them more vulnerable to health risks (e.g. exposure to the cold and deficient sanitary services) and social risks (exposure to theft and aggression). To some extent, the rules used for access to housing programs also exclude women. Although women heads of households are usually given an additional 10 points in their application for social housing, the women who were previously married and whose ex-husbands own a house are not entitled to apply for social housing because the government benefit is only given once and to the family rather than to the individual.

Another example of exclusionary rules can be observed with regards to childcare. Apart from having the adequate number of points in the CAS index, the mother of the child must show proof of employment and associated working hours. This criteria tends to exclude three categories of women: teenage mothers who wished they could complete their schooling instead of entering the labor market; women involved in precarious employment with irregular working hours such as cleaners or domestic workers; and most of all, female job-seekers whose mobility ends up being considerably restricted.[105]

Conclusion and Policy Implications

The quantitative evaluation of the targeting performance of the government programs whose eligibility rules are based on the scoring system of the *ficha* CAS suggests that the scoring system is effective in identifying the poor and in helping to maximize the redistributive impact of state-funded pension assistance, family allowances, water subsidies, housing subsidies, and childcare programs. While some programs are better targeted than others, all programs are rather successful at channeling resources to the poor and very poor. This does not mean, however, that the *ficha* CAS system does not have some weaknesses. Several of these weaknesses have been revealed by the qualitative evaluation. In this conclusion, we would like to highlight a few recommendations for improving Chile's targeting system.

In order to improve the impact of the government's income transfers and social programs, it may be necessary for government agents to get closer to the poor. Two suggestions can be provided. First, it may be useful to implement a more effective communication strategy since it appears that the poor still lack access to the relevant information about the various programs. Many poor households do not know about the existence of the programs, and among the households who are aware of the programs, many do not know how to apply for benefits. Second, it may be useful to encourage more contacts between the poor and social workers. Beyond the reception of applications at the municipal welfare office, initiatives such as the "sweeping" of areas could be encouraged, so a to reach those among the poor who have weak connections to municipal institutions. Better contacts between social workers and the poor may also help if social workers are given some latitude to depart from the strict scoring system of the *ficha* CAS in order to respond to situations of vulnerability which are not well measured by the simple possession of assets.

---

[105] Women involved in illegal activities –mainly prostitution- are also systematically excluded and therefore miss any chances of reinsertion opportunities through the possibility for instance, to attend training courses.

Related to this last point about vulnerability, more emphasis could be placed in the *ficha* CAS system on the prevention as opposed to the alleviation of poverty. Targeting rules for centrally financed income transfers and other social programs could be revised so as to prevent the fall of vulnerable people into a vicious circle of loss. This is especially important in a context of high unemployment rates which tends to provoke brutal changes in the lives of the poor. The means-testing approach of the *ficha* CAS may lead to the exclusion of households in need of assistance when the CAS criteria fail to adequately measure the dynamic and complex reality of deprivation. The emphasis on material possessions could be reduced in the CAS in order to make place for indicators such as the loss of a job or a sudden illness.

Another finding from the qualitative research refers to the need to adapt eligibility rules in order to better take into account intra-household allocation patterns. Paying attention to individual needs in the household also cuts across the variable of age. This was illustrated by the difficulty for pregnant teenagers to gain access to maternal benefits when they live in larger households. The potential for gender discrimination also exists in the access rules to means-tested housing and child care. Another group which may not be covered well enough is the low income elderly, especially when informal private transfers are taken into account by CAS surveyors in order to determine eligibility for pension assistance.

Finally, from a methodological point of view, this paper has illustrated the benefits of going beyond quantitative assessments for the evaluation of targeting instruments. On the basis of quantitative simulation models,[106] the Chilean government recently introduced some modifications to the *ficha* CAS, including a lesser emphasis on possessions. But the system still has limits which tend to be overlooked by government officials. One more recommendation emerging from this paper would be to collect in a systematic and periodic way the views and opinions not only of the local staff who actually implement means-testing on the basis of the CAS form, but also of poor and/or vulnerable households themselves.

---

[106] MIDEPLAN (1999).

REFERENCES

Clert, C. 1996. "Género, Pobreza y Exclusión Social en Chile," SERNAM Working Paper 54. Santiago de Chile.

Clert, C. 2000a. *"Policy Implications of a Social Exclusion Perspective in Chile: Priorities, Discourse and Methods in Question."* Ph.D. thesis. London School of Economics.

Clert, C. 2000b. "Social Exclusion, Gender and the Chilean Government's Anti-Poverty Strategy: Priorities and Methods in Question." In E. Gacitua Mario and C. Sojo, Editors, *Social Exclusion and Poverty Reduction in Latin America.* Washington, DC.: World Bank and FLACSO

Estache, A., V. Foster, and Q. Wodon. Forthcoming. *Infrastructure Reform and the Poor.* Washington, DC.: World Bank.

Gomez-Lobo, A., and D. Contreras. 2000. "Subsidy Policies for the Utility Industries: A Comparison of the Chilean and Colombian Water Subsidy Schemes." University of Chile, Department of Economics, Santiago de Chile.

MIDEPLAN, 1999. *Estudio del factor discriminatorio de la ficha CAS. Propuesta del mejoramiento del cálculo de puntaje,* Santiago

MIDEPLAN, 1998. *Programas y Subsidios Sociales de Gobierno Priorizados Mediante Ficha CAS-2,* Santiago de Chile.

UNDP, 1998, *Informe Sobre la Seguridad Humana en Chile,* Santiago de Chile.

World   Wodon, Q., and S. Yitzhaki, 2000, Evaluating the Impact of Government Programs on Social Welfare: The Role of Targeting and the Allocation Rules Among Program.Beneficiaries.   Washington   DC.:   World   Bank.

APPENDIX 1: DESCRIPTION OF SOME OF THE MAIN PROGRAMS TARGETED ACCORDING TO THE FICHA CAS

BENEFIT	Nature (amounts in Chilean pesos relate to the year 1998 and are monthly amounts)	Who can apply?	Eligibility criteria
FOR ALL BENEFITS AND PROGRAMS BELOW		-	- The common eligibility criteria is to show evidence of lack financial resources, according to the evaluation made through the means-testing survey with the *ficha CAS* - be a resident of the *comuna* (borough) responsible for the selection of beneficiaries
PASIS Pensión Asistencial Pensions for the elderly and for the disabled			
- Pensión de Ancianidad (pension for the elderly)	- minimal amount: $23,415 - automatically entitles the elderly with a card allowing free access to public health services (*tarjeta de gratuidad médica*) - the pension can no longer be provided if the beneficiary situation stops meeting the criteria. This is usually evaluated following the visit by a *ficha CAS* surveyor.	Low-income elderly people over 65 years of age	- be older than 65 years at the time of the survey with the *ficha CAS* - lack of access to any other social insurance including pensions - total income inferior to 50% of the minimal pension amount (aprox. 23,415)
- Pensión de Invalidez (Invalidity)	- the benefit has a duration of 3 years and can be renovated, provided that the requisites are still met (mainly number of points with the *ficha CAS*) - automatically entitles the elderly with a card allowing free access to public health services	Physically disabled people (*personas inválidas*), older than 18 years of age - No access to other pensions or other forms of social protection mechanisms (*sin previsión social*)	- the total income of the applicant *and* of his family group (comprising all other members of the dwelling unit) cannot be superior to the minimal pension
- Pensión de Invalidez para Deficientes Mentales	Same as above	Same as above, except the following characteristics: - mentally disabled people - no age requirement	Same as above
SUF Subsidio Unico Familiar (family allowances)			
- al Menor (child benefit)	- child benefit - amount: $2500 - duration: 3 years- can be renewed	All dependent children, under 15 years of age or studying children under 18	- for children under 6, health control must be up to date - for children older than 6, must be enrolled in primary education (Educación Básica) - the child cannot perceive an income equal or superior to the amount of the benefit
a la Madre (maternal benefit)		Mothers of the children selected for the *subsidio al menor*	- the father of the child cannot receive family allowances from other sources (e.g. through his employer)
- Maternal	- maternal benefit - amount: 2800 received ten times.	Pregnant women. To be allowed from their fifth month of pregnancy	- the father of the child cannot receive family allowances from other sources (e.g. through his employer)
- Recién Nacido	- child monthly benefit of 2800 pesos – lasts for three	Mothers who benefit from the *subsidio*	

	maternal and who do not have access to other forms of social protection (*sin previsión social*)	years from the birth of the child	
Subsidio de agua potable	Low income families facing difficulties to pay for water services	- state contribution to the consumption/use of drinkable water and water sewerage (*alcantarillado*) - *This contribution finances half of the consumption of water up to a maximum of 15 m3*	- be up to date with the payment of water and sewerage services
Housing programs[107]			
Vivienda Progresiva I Etapa	-families facing emergency situation in terms of their housing or simply lacking adequate housing of housing -\- particularly (but not necessarily) applies to families living under free-rent arrangements (*allegados*) - elderly people who are not owners of or assigned with a *vivienda*, and who did not previously receive a housing subsidy	Subsidy of 132 UF for the construction of housing. The program *vivienda progresiva* has two stages. Stage I (etapa I) comprises, as a minimum, of an urbanized site and a sanitary unit (bath/kitchen) total value: 140UF). The applicant's contribution will be 8 UF, of which 3 UF are necessary as a requisite for the application.	- All those who are registered and who meet the criteria will enter the selection process according to the strict order of 'points' obtained in the specific survey conducted with *ficha CAS* - The applicant must have saved the equivalent of 3 UF. - group-based applications are encouraged
Vivienda Progresiva II Etapa		- 2d stage of the program above improvement of the housing unit	- specific and complex criteria – see MIDELAN (1998:21)
Vivienda Básica (basic housing)	Low-income households willing to have access to housing in a definite manner (*en forma definitiva*)	- construction of solid housing unit (can include i) one-floor house; ii) two-floor houses; and iii) apartment in a three-floor building block. - Total value is 240 UF and the financement is arranged as follows: - applicant's savings (10 UF- see eligibility criteria) - 140 UF state subsidy (in monthly dividends throughout 12 years) - and the remaining through the applicant's own contribution (monthly dividends)	- All those who are registered and who meet the criteria will enter the selection process according to the strict order of 'points' obtained in the specific survey conducted with *ficha CAS* - the applicant must have saved the equivalent of at least 5 UF in order to be able to enter the process of selection. By the time the housing is available for delivery, the applicant must show evidence of the same amount of savings.
Childcare programs			
Programs JUNJI, INTEGRA	- for children between 84 days and a years and 11 months (children under five)	Integral care of the child in childcare centers (includes health, food provision, social welfare –*atención social*- and dental-medical attention)	- in addition to *ficha CAS*, there is a 'social report' evidencing lack of resources. - mother must be working , with certificate certifying the mother's working situation, her income, working hours and type of activity.

---

[107] Other centrally financed housing programs include the rural housing subsidy (*Subsidio Habitacional Rural*).

APPENDIX 2. CAS FORM AT THE TIME OF THE QUALITATIVE FIELDWORK (DECEMBER 1997)- ENCUESTA CAS

SISTEMA DE INFORMACIÓN SOCIAL
SECCION 0: DATOS GENERALES

Región Metropolitana	1	1	3		Comuna Huecharaba

	Folio No	
Provincia	2	1		Unidad Vecinal		Fecha de Encuesta	dia/mes/ano

			3	0	4
					4
		2	1		5
					1 Urbana
					2 Rural

Nombre del Campamento, Poblacion o Villa		Código	Manzana	Cod. Calle	Nombre de la Calle o Camino	Numero	Block/Casa	Depto/Sitio
Sector				Cod. Calle	Nombre de la Calle, Camino o Carretera	Numero	Aceratona	

Encuesta: _____
Revisor: _____
Supervisor: _____

SECCION 1: PROTECCIÓN AMBIENTAL

MATERIALES USADOS EN MUROS EXTERIOES DE LA VIVIENDA

1. Ladrillo, concreto o bloque
2. Albañería de Piedra
3. Tabique forrado
4. Adobe
5. Mixto aceptable (combinación de material pero alguno de tipo 1 a 4)
6. Barro, quinona, pirca
7. Tabique en forro interior
8. Desecho (cartón, latas, sacos, etc)
9. Mixto deficiente (combinación de materiales pero ninguno de tipo 1 a 4)

MATERIAL UTILIZADO EN EL PISO DE LA VIVIENDA

1. Radier revisto (radier cubierto con parque, tabla, linóleo, flexit, baldosa, alfombra, etc)
2. Radier no revisto (radier a la vista)
3. Mixto aceptable (combinación de materiales, pero alguno de tipo 1 a 4)
4. Madera colocada sobre solera o vigas
5. Madera, plástico o posteriores colocados directamente sobre la tierra
6. Piso de tierra
7. Mixto deficiente (combinación de materiales, pero ninguno de tipo 1 o 2)

MATERIAL UTILIZADO EN EL TECHO DE LA VIVIENDA

1. Teja, tejuela, losa, piedra
2. Zinc o pizarreño con cielo interior
3. Mixto aceptable (combinación de materiales, pero alguno de tipo 1 o 2)
4. Zinc o pizarreño, sin cielo interior
5. Fonolita
6. Paja, coirón, totora, caña
7. Desecho (cartón, latas, sacos)
8. Mixto deficiente (combinación de materiales, pero ninguno de tipo 1 o 2)

SECCION 2: HACIMIENTO

22 PIEZAS OCUPADAS DE LA VIVIENDA

Dormitorios _____
Estar (living) _____
Comedor _____
Estar – Comedor _____
Cocina (sólo si es utilizada como estar o comedor _____
Total de Piezas _____

SECCION 3: SANEAMIENTO Y CONFORT

TIPO DE ABASTECIMIENTO DE AGUAS DE LA VIVIENDA

El agua proviene de red pública de agua potable
1. Con llave dentro de la vivienda
2. Con llave dentro del sitio fuera de la vivienda
3. De llave de pilón o grifo ubicado fuera del sitio

El agua no proviene de red pública de agua potable
4. Con llave dentro de la vivienda
5. Con llave dentro del sitio, pero fuera de la vivienda
6. Por acarreo

SISTEMA DE ELIMINACIÓN DE EXCRETAS DE LA VIVIENDA

De uso exclusivo (No comparte con otras viviendas)
1. W.C. conectado a alcantarillado
2. W.C. conectado a fosa séptica
3. Letrina sanitaria
4. Pozo negro

De uso compartido (con otras viviendas)
5. W.C. conectado a alcanterilla
6. W.C. conectado a losa séptica
7. Letrina sanitaria
8. Pozo negro
9. No tiene (eliminación a campo libre)

DISPONIBILIDAD DE TINA O DUCHA

De uso exclusivo (no comparte con otras viviendas)
1. Tina o ducha, con agua caliente
2. Tina o ducha, sin agua caliente

De uso compartido (con otras viviendas)
3. Tina o ducha, con agua caliente
4. Tina o ducha, sin agua caliente
5. No tiene

SUMINISTRO ELECTRICO DE LA VIVIENDA

La vivienda dispone de electricidad
1. Con medidor particular
2. Con medidor compartido (con otras viviendas
3. Sin medidor
4. La vivienda no dispone de electricidad

DECLARACIÓN: Declaro que los datos proporcionados son
Legítimos y asumo la responsabilidad por ello.

FAM 1 _____
FAM 2 _____
FAM 3 _____
FAM 4 _____

SECCION 4: IDENTIFICACION DE LOS RESIDENTES (Todos)

												SEC. 5: OCUP. ING. *Todos los de 14 años y mas*					SEC 6 SUB	SEC 7 EDU
No de orden	Jefes de Familia	Apellido Paterno	Apellido Materno	Primer Nombre	RUT – RUN o Cedula de Identidad con digito verificador	Fecha de Nacimiento Día/Mes/Año	Sexo	Relación de Parentesco	Familias	Hogares	Parejas	Categoría Ocupacional	Monto de Ingresos (en pesos)	Periocidad Ingreso	Permanencia trabajo	Ingresos secundarios	Subsidios monetarios (Todos)	Años de estudio aprobados
1																		
2																		
3																		
4																		
5																		

SECCION 8: PATRIMONIO   JEFE DE FAMILIA Y/O SU PAREJA

FAMILIA No.

Registre en esta columna los números que usó para identificar a las familias que habitan en vivienda. Si en la vivienda viven mas de cuatro familias use una segunda ficha de encuesta.

Para cada familia que habita en la vivienda indique la situación bajo la cual ocupa el sitio.
1. Sitio propio, sin deudas.
2. Sitio propio, sin deudas atrasadas.
3. Sitio propio, con deudas atrasadas.
4. Arrienda el propietario del sitio sin pagos atrasados.
5. Usan el sitio, pero no creen que pueden ser desalojados en los próximos meses.
6. Usan el sitio, pero si creen que pueden ser desalojados en los próximos 6 meses.

¿La familia tiene algún televisor que funciones?
1. Tiene TV en colores
2. Tiene TV en blanco y negro
3. No tiene TV.

¿La familia tiene calefón o termo para calentar el agua?
1. Si tiene calefón o termo
2. No tiene calefón o termo

¿La familia tiene refrigerador que funcione?
1. Si tiene refrigerador
2. No tiene refrigerador

Background Paper 5

GOVERNMENT PROGRAMS FOR THE INSERTION OF YOUTH AND WOMEN IN CHILE'S LABOR MARKET: A DISCUSSION

Rodrigo Castro-Fernandez, Carine Clert, and Quentin Wodon[108]
July 28, 2001

Introduction

Poverty can be conceptualized as the inability to generate a sufficient and stable income, as well as the inability to have access to quality basic services in order to meet basic needs. A key determinant of poverty is the lack of insertion into the labor market, with access to jobs understood both quantitatively and qualitatively. Certain low-income groups face specific disadvantages on the basis of age, gender or ethnic origin, and these disadvantages may lead to multiple and reinforcing exclusion mechanisms.

In Chile, labor-based inclusion policies and training programs have been targeted at social groups seen as especially vulnerable. Using results from the 1990 CASEN household survey, the democratic governments identified youths and women heads of households as target groups in need of training. This lead to the creation of two training programs: one for women (*Capacitacion para Mujeres Jefes de Hogar*), and one for youths (*Chile Jóven*). Do young workers and women need these special training programs? If yes, do programs such as PMJH and *Chile Joven*, as they stand, succeed in promoting the labor market insertion of their beneficiaries and in addressing the obstacles faced by low-income youth and female heads of households in finding and keeping good jobs? Are there other segments of the population which also require special attention from policy makers? Although this paper cannot address all these questions in a comprehensive manner, it does provide an introductory discussion of the issues.

The paper has three main sections. Section II first provides evidence based on the nationally representative 1998 CASEN survey about the level of unemployment, the quality of employment among those employed, the extent of training, and the reasons for opting out of the labor force among various segments of the population, including young workers, women, and the poor. It is shown that youths and women tend to more often unemployed or out of the labor force than other groups of workers. They also tend to receive less training, and to have a lower quality of employment when employed. These results suggest that there is indeed a need for training programs targeted at young workers and women in Chile.

The next two sections provide a discussion of the performance of the two government programs. After briefly describing the two programs, section III summarizes existing quantitative results from recent evaluations (Santiago Consultores, 1998; CIDE, 1997). Although the methodologies used for the quantitative evaluations carry the risk of bias in the findings, the results are nevertheless informative. Section IV then presents findings from a qualitative study by Clert (2000a, 2000b) to assess to what extent the two programs tackle the many obstacles to labor

---

[108] The authors are with the Latin America Region of the World Bank. The paper was funded by the World Bank under the Chile Poverty Assessment and the Regional Studies Program for Latin America. The authors benefited from comments from the Government of Chile. The views expressed in the paper are those of the authors and need not represent the views of the World Bank, its Executive Directors, or the countries they represent.

market insertion faced by youths and women.   The section also reviews some of the challenges that remain for helping these groups to fully participate in labor markets, and it mentions the possibility that other groups may need support as well. The paper does not, however, take into account recent changes in the programs for youth and women heads of households.

Employment, Age, Gender, and Poverty

The first question that can be asked regarding government training programs for young workers and women is whether the intended beneficiaries need these programs. Tentative answers to this question can be provided by looking at simple cross-tabulations comparing the employment status and the training received by young workers and women to the employment status and training of other groups. This is done in this section. Alternatively, to go beyond simple cross-tabulations, one could use regression analysis to look at the determinants of per capita income, and thereby poverty, and to assess the role of employment. While this is not done in this paper, such regressions are provided in another paper by Castro-Fernandez and Wodon (2000) also prepared for the poverty assessment of Chile conducted at The World Bank. It is worth mentioning that the regressions show, among other findings, that households whose heads are female face a higher probability of being poor, and that unemployment and a lack of labor force participation among women also lead to a higher probability of being poor in their household.

Here, we focus on comparative results regarding the labor market insertion of youths and women versus other groups. In the statistical appendix to this paper, detailed cross-tabulations are provided to give an idea of the employment and training characteristics of young workers and women, as compared to the same characteristics for other groups of workers. All tables are based on the nationally representative 1998 CASEN survey, and they all have the same format. The tables give the share of the population in a given age group and a given income group (defined by income quintiles nationally, within urban areas, and within rural areas) which has a given characteristic. The following comments can be made:

- Higher *unemployment among young workers:* Younger workers tend to have a higher probability of being unemployed and searching for work. Nationally, among male workers (appendix table 1), 11.7 percent of workers aged 18 to 24 years were searching for work in 1998, as compared to 8.2 percent in the 25-34 year group, 5.9 percent in the 35-54 year group, and 5.5 percent in the 55-64 year age group. Unemployment is also higher nationally for younger female workers (appendix table 2), at 9.2 percent in the 18-24 year age group, 6.0 percent in the 25-34 year group, 3.7 percent in the 35-54 year group, and 1.4 percent in the 55-64 year age group. While unemployment rates are higher in urban than in rural areas, the same type of patterns emerges by age groups for both genders.

- *Higher unemployment and inactivity among workers living in poorer households:* Unemployment rates are higher in the poorer segments of the population. For example, among the male and female workers aged 18 to 24, the national unemployment rates are 27.9 percent and 16.0 percent in the first and poorest quintile, as opposed to 3.6 percent and 3.5 percent in the fifth and richest quintile. Of course, the observation that unemployment is higher among the poor is a bit of a tautology to the extent that unemployment implies lower labor earnings, and thereby a higher probability of being poor. The marginal impact on unemployment on per capita income controlling for other household and individual characteristics is estimated in the section on regression analysis. It is also worth noting that inactivity rates among young workers living in poor households tend to be higher since few are enrolled in higher levels of schooling. This is true especially in urban areas.

- *Lower labor force participation among women, especially among the poor:* In appendix tables 1 and 2, those who are not in the labor force (and not in an educational institution for the 18-24 age group) are considered as inactive. While it is hardly surprising that inactivity rates are much higher for women than for men, it is striking to note the very high inactivity rates among women belonging to poor households. This suggests (and will be confirmed by regressions) that having women being out of the labor force may be a major determinants of poverty in Chile, in both urban and rural areas.

- Among those working, few differences in the number of hours worked and the number of jobs held by age group and by income bracket, but large differences by gender: The differences by age groups and income brackets among male workers in terms of the number of hours worked per week and the number of jobs held (one or more) tend to be smaller than the differences in unemployment and inactivity, even though a larger share of the better off tend to have two or more occupations. Not surprisingly, women are much more likely than men to be employed only part time, and it would be less likely to have two or more occupations. Still, from the patterns across quintiles observed in the tabulations, it is not obvious that underemployment is a major determinant of poverty in Chile.

- *Somewhat lower quality of employment for young workers and women, especially among the poor:* Appendix tables 3 and 4 provide statistics on whether workers have a contract or not, and when they have one, whether they have a fixed term appointment or an open-ended appointment. The table also indicates whether workers have a permanent, fixed term, or "by the task" job, and whether their job is during day-time or night-time (or shift). The information provided suggests a somewhat greater exposure of young workers and women to precarious employment. But the differences are not extremely large. For example, nationally, 13.3 percent of male workers aged 18 to 24 year have no contract, versus only 10.0 percent among older workers. For female workers of the same age, the comparison is 8.75 percent versus 7.69 percent. The differences are larger by income groups, with workers living in poor households being more likely to have lower quality or less reliable jobs.

- *Differences in the reasons for not working by age, gender, and income group:* Appendix table 5 provides the reasons for not being in the labor force. Disabilities and diseases are cited more often by the poor for not working, while among the lower age group, being a student is cited more by the rich. There is no surprise there. As expected as well, the rate of discouragement is higher among the poor than the rich. Domestic duties and child care are much more prevalent as reasons for not working among women in poor households than in rich households. This may be due to the fact that poorer households do not have the means to pay for outside help. It may also be due in part to the fact that poorer households tend to have more children. Still, the sheer magnitude of domestic work and child care as a reason for not working among poor women suggests that training programs should pay attention to the issue (as we will see, *Mujeres Jefes de Hogar* and *Chile Jóven* do pay attention.)

- *Lower access to training for young workers, women, and the poor:* Appendix table 6 provides statistics on the training received by various groups. Most of the training is provided by firms or paid for by the individual themselves, and this naturally tends to exclude poorer individuals. The poor are slightly more likely than the non poor to participate in government programs, but this does not compensate for their disadvantage. Importantly, the poor tend to be almost as interested in receiving training than the non-poor, so that if opportunities were available, they would participate more. The differences in attitudes towards training do not differ widely by age groups or gender. Finally, the lack of knowledge about government programs appears to be a key reason for not receiving training.

Program Description and Quantitative evaluation

Program Description. To improve the employment prospects of young workers and women from disadvantaged social backgrounds, the government has created two training programs: *Chile Jóven* and PMJH (*Capacitacion para Mujeres Jefas de Hogar*). Table 1 provides an overview of the two programs. The objective of both programs is to facilitate the labor market insertion of their target groups through vocational training and other forms of support. A central premise of both programs is that since program participants face multiple difficulties in finding good employment, the programs should take these difficulties into account.

Table 1: Chile Jóven and PMJH (Programa Jefas de Hogar): Overview of the two Programs

	Chile Jóven	PMJH (Programa Jefas de Hogar) *Now called "Mujeres de Escasos Recursos, Preferentemente Jefas de Hogar"*
Target Group	Low-income youths Between the ages of 15 and 24	Low-income women who are heads of households. Since 1998, women in male-headed households can also participate.
Coverage	First phase: Reached 120,000 Second phase: Objective was 70,000	First phase: 18,000 women reached by 1997 Second phase: Objective for 2000 was 50,000
Main components in first phase	First phase 1991-1995 - vocational training – coordination by SENCE and competitive selection of private training centers - childcare facilities during training period - access to information - reinforcement of municipal job centers	First phase: 199?-1997 - vocational training through the National Institution for Vocational Training (SENCE) - childcare facilities during training period - housing (e.g., additional points for housing application of female heads of households) - access to dental health - judicial aspects/legal advice
Key changes with second phase	Second phase 1996-1999 - stronger emphasis on the labor market insertion, including stronger incentives for private training centers to offer formal employment at the end of training course - end of specific components such as access to childcare for female participants	Second phase 1998-present - stronger emphasis on labor market insertion - institutionalization of the program within sectoral ministries under the coordination of SERNAM and increased contribution of municipalities
Financing	First phase: IDB and Chilean Government, including *comunas* (municipal funds) Second Phase: End of IDB funds	First phase: Chilean Government, mainly SERNAM and *comunas* (municipal funds) Second phase: Institutionalization of the program, mainstreaming of gender issues involved, and greater responsibilities of sectoral ministries, Central Government and municipal funds

Source: Own elaboration.

Quantitative evaluation of Chile Joven   This section summarizes the results of a quantitative evaluation of *Chile Joven (Fase II)* prepared by Santiago Consultores (1998). The evaluation was done by comparing treatment and control groups. The treatment group consists of a sample of young individuals who participated in the program. The control group consists of individuals who did not participate in the program, but were neighbors of a sub-sample of program participants. To be included in the control group, for the period corresponding to the training program, the individuals needed to a) be unemployed, inactive or underemployed; b) not attend a day-time schooling program; c) be between 16 and 27 years of age and d) not be enrolled in a training program for young people. The treatment and control groups were broadly comparable in terms of gender, age, schooling, job experience, and socioeconomic background. However, it is likely that the treatment and control groups differed in a number of unobserved variables, so that the results obtained in the evaluation may be biased. This will be discussed below. Note that the evaluation differentiates the treatment group in three sub-groups, according to whether the youths who enrolled in the Chile Joven and graduated in 1997 participated in each of the three following program modalities: CEL, AA and FJT.

- CEL (*Capacitacion y Experiencia Laboral en Empresas*): The modality focuses on developing semi-qualified skills among program participants. The modality provides 250 hours of courses ("theory") together with internship of 3 months in a firm. The participants receive a stipend for their transportation and food costs, and a health insurance against accidents.

- AA (*Aprendizaje Alternado*): The modality alternates training within the training institution and within a firm under the guidance of a teacher. The teacher helps in defining the skills to be acquired through the training, and the training lasts from 6 months to one year. The participant receives a fixed-term-contract and the minimum wage. Participants must be between 15 and 24 years of age, and they must be literate. To be eligible, participants must be unemployed, underemployed or inactive and being listed as searching for employment in the municipal labor office of their residence.

- FJT (*Formacion de Jovenes para el Trabajo*): The modality is designed to prepare participants for the creation and the management of a small independent business. The participants receive 250 hours of theory as well as practical skills. As with the CEL modality, the participants receive a stipend for their transportation and food costs, and a health insurance against accidents.

The evaluation of *Chile Joven* provides information on the job status of individuals before and after training (or before and after the period corresponding to training for the control group). The difference in status is computed for both the treatment (column [3] in table 2) and control groups (column [6] in table 2). If in column [7] in table 2, the differences are more (less) favorable for the treatment group than for the control group, one may *conjecture* that controlling for other factors (such as changes in the labor market which affect both groups similarly), the training provided by the modality is having a positive (negative) impact. The outcomes variables selected for comparing the performance of the three modalities are the employment status of the youths (with the various categories summing to 100 percent), as well as their employment rate (number of employed youths divided by number of active youths) and their labor force participation rate (number of active youths divided by total number of youths).

Apparently, all three programs seem to be highly successful in that the unemployment rate among participants is much lower after training than before, while there are few differences in unemployment rates for the control group (in both groups, the impact in terms of labor force participation is negligible). Although these results are encouraging, their magnitude is a bit surprising, and it may be that the evaluation suffers from a bias. Specifically, if the participants in *Chile Joven* are among the more dynamic individuals who are willing to make sacrifices in order to be trained and to find employment, we would expect that they would register some progress after the training, even though this progress may not be due to the training itself. In other words, the evaluation method used here may not adequately take into account the selection of the individuals who participate in the program (i.e., the fact that the participants choose to participate in the program for reasons that may not be observed by the researchers). To take into account the sample selection problem, one would need to use so-called randomization or instrumental variable techniques in the evaluation, but this was apparently not done. As shown in the case of Mexico's Probecat program for example, the methods used for the evaluation of training program can have a large impact on the evaluation results (Wodon and Minowa, 2000), and it is unclear whether the results for *Chile Joven* would be robust to the use of different evaluation techniques. As a matter of fact, most training and re-training programs in countries belonging to the Organization for Economic Co-operation and Development have been found to have limited impacts, and when the programs have been found to have some impact, this impact tends to vanish after a few years (Dar and Gill, 1998). The fact that *Chile Joven* may have a large impact is unusual, so that the results must be taken with caution.

Table 2: Employment by Modality within Chile Joven (entries are percentages)

	Treatment Group			Control Group			Performance
	Before (1)	After (2)	Difference (3 = 2 − 1)	Before (4)	After (5)	Difference (6 = 5 − 4)	Difference (7 = 6 − 3)
CEL							
Employed	31.5	55.0	23.5	42.0	40.3	-1.7	25.2
Unemployed	42.8	22.1	-20.7	27.9	27.1	-0.8	-19.9
Inactive (no student)	21.0	16.4	-4.6	21.2	20.8	-0.4	-4.2
Inactive (student)	4.7	6.5	1.8	8.9	11.8	2.9	-1.1
Total	100.0	100.0		100.0	100.0		
Employment rate	42.4	71.3	28.9	60.1	59.8	-0.3	29.9
Participation rate	74.3	77.1	2.8	69.9	67.4	-2.5	5.3
AA							
Employed	30.3	64.9	34.6	41.2	39.9	-1.3	35.9
Unemployed	51.5	15.6	-35.9	28.2	27.5	-0.7	-35.2
Inactive (no student)	13.3	12.2	-1.1	21.2	20.0	-1.2	0.1
Inactive (student)	5.0	7.3	2.3	9.5	12.6	-3.1	5.4
Total	100.0	100.0		100.0	100.0		
Employment rate	37.0	81.0	44.0	59.0	59.0	0	43.0
Participation rate	81.8	80.5	-1.3	69.4	67.4	-2.0	0.7
FT							
Employed	31.6	56.0	24.4	42.2	36.6	-5.6	30.0
Unemployed	37.5	16.4	-21.1	26.8	29.3	2.5	-23.6
Inactive (no student)	23.0	21.8	-1.2	26.7	29.2	2.5	-3.7
Inactive (student)	7.9	5.8	-2.1	4.2	4.9	0.7	-2.8
Total	100.0	100.0		100.0	100.0		
Employment rate	46.0	77.0	32.0	61.0	56.0	-6.0	38.0
Participation rate	69.1	72.4	3.3	69.0	65.9	-3.1	6.4

Source: Santiago Consultores (1998).

Without discussing in detail all the other results of the evaluation, it is worth mentioning a few findings according to the gender, age bracket, and level of education of program participants. As indicated in table 3, there is no universal performance rank for the three modalities in terms of the impact of the training on employment by gender and age bracket. While for one modality, the men may gain more than women, for another modality the women may gain more than men. The same is observed for the various age groups. By contrast, it seems that the employment gains are systematically larger for those with a better education in all three modalities. If this is the case, it would mean that Chile *Joven* still has difficulties in helping those with the lowest education level,[109] i.e. those who are more likely to be among the poorest of the poor. This concern also appears in the qualitative evaluation (see section IV).

Table 3: Performance by Modality within Chile Joven by Gender, Age Bracket, and Education Level

	CEL	AA	FT
Gender			
Males	2	1	2
Females	1	2	1
Age			
15 - 19	3	1	2
20 –24	1	3	3
25 +	2	2	1
Education			
Primary and lower	3	3	3
Secondary incomplete	2	2	2
Secondary complete or more	1	1	1

Source: Constructed from Santiago Consultores (1998). The gender, age bracket or education level in which the modality has the largest impact gets a ranking of "1", while the other groups get rankings of "2" or "3".

Quantitative Evaluation of PMJH. This section summarizes the results of a quantitative evaluation of the *Programa de Capacitacion para Mujeres Jefas de Hogar* (PMJH) prepared by the Centro de Investigacion y Desarrollo de la Educacion or CIDE (1997). The evaluation is based on a sample of women who participated in the program from 1995 to 1997. The evaluation was done on the basis of a survey and interviews, but the analysts did not use a treatment and control group methodology, so that once again, as was the case for *Chile Joven*, it is not clear whether the good results obtained for PMJH are due to the self-selection of the participants into the program. Despite these methodological limits, it remains worthwhile to give the main results, which can be summarized according to the impact of the program on both employment and its quality.

- *Employment:* When asked whether PMJH improved their conditions for a job search, 61 percent of the women interviewed answered yes, while 39 percent answered that they had

---

[109] As Tohá (2000) argues in her study on youth and social exclusion, education shapes inequalities at an early age. While the average number of years of schooling among Chilean youths has increased in the 1990s and coverage is almost universal in primary education, 47 percent of the young interrupt their schooling at a later stage because of socio-economic problems. In the age group 14-17, boys tend to drop out of school due to the household need for additional income, while girls tend to do so because of their involvement in domestic or reproductive tasks, such as raising brothers and sisters or their own children (Silva, 1996; Letelier,1996). The latter is also commonly reported in a context where teenage pregnancy is still high (Tohá, 2000). Since 1990, schools are no longer allowed to exclude teenage or pregnant teenagers. This decision was made by R. Lagos when he was Minister for Education.

remained in the same job search readiness after the training. As indicated in table 3, the unemployment rate is lower by 15 percentage points among participants after training in the program, from 58 percent to 43 percent.

- *Quality of employment:* The quality of employment also appears to have been improved by the training, with a larger share of the women employed as salaried workers with open-ended contracts after program participation. The salary level and the numbers of hours worked also tend to improve.

Table 4: Job Situation, Participation Mechanisms, Job Stability of the PMJH Beneficiaries

	Before	After			
Employment			**Salary level (Pesos)**		
Employed	42.0	57.0	< $60,000	21.0	15.5
Unemployed	58.0	43.0	$60,001-$90,000	38.5	17.5
Type of employment			$90,001-$120,000	27.7	36.5
Self-employed	11.4	13.4	$120,001-$150,000	8.8	17.0
House work	44.3	25.7	$150,001-$180,000	2.0	8.0
Salaried worker	24.9	42.5	$180,001-210,000	1.3	0.5
Temporary worker	4.7	1.0	> $210,001	0.7	2.0
Others	14.7	17.4	**Hours worked**		
Stability			< 11 hours	8.2	7.9
Open-ended contract	25.3	51.2	11-12 hours	11.6	9.9
Fixed term	12.7	14.7	22-35 hours	27.2	15.8
Deal-based	43.0	19.4	36-48 hours	27.2	38.6
Fees-based	12.7	12.7	49-60 hours	14.3	21.8
Task-based	1.2	7.8	> 61 hours	11.5	5.9
Replacement	3.8	3.9			
Test	1.2	2.3			

Source: CIDE (1997).

Qualitative Evaluation

In this section, to complement the results of the quantitative evaluations reported so far, we use material from a qualitative study by Clert (2000a, 2000b) which gives evidence as to whether the two programs succeed in addressing the many types of disadvantages and constraints faced by participants. We first review some of the strengths of both programs before pointing to some remaining weaknesses.

Strengths of the Two Programs

- *Lack of work-related networks (informal and formal):* Unemployed workers applying for jobs feel that rejections are in large part due to certain pre-requisites asked for by prospective employers, such as the need for the applicant to present references and recommendations.[110] The problem is that young unemployed workers often lack informal contact networks which

---

[110] Another request often made by employers is a certificate of clear antecedents with respect to the justice system. This type of request may affect adversely men who report a precarious relationship with the police. Although arbitrary arrests of citizens due to their "suspicious" behavior (*detención por sospecha*) were officially forbidden by the Frei administration, Clert's (2000a) study suggests that some violence may still be inflicted on men by *carabineros* (the police) and the *Policía de Investigaciones* of *comunas*. When this happens, the rights violation often begins with an *arbitrary arrest*, either in the street or at home, involving the use of physical force, usually during special operations.

can serve not only as referees for potential employers, but also as sources of information on job availability. This lack of social assets contributes to youth unemployment, which in turn restricts access to work-related networks. Women also lack access to informal employment networks. While men tend to have many friends who are work colleagues or were former colleagues, the networks of unemployed women tend to belong to other circles, for example related to the neighborhood where they live. Apart from lacking informal networks, young workers and women are not always able to rely on formal support network. Specifically, while the relationships between job-seekers and municipal job centers (the *Oficina Municipal de Información Laboral* in Chile) can be determinant for finding employment, the job centers' working arrangements and practices do not always respond adequately to the needs of specific groups of job-seekers such as individuals with literacy or mobility problems and the physically disabled. Additionally, while municipal job-centers may help, potential employers may prefer calling on professional employment agencies rather than value municipal job centers. To deal with these issues, the government's training programs help program participants to build their social and relational assets. In the case of Chile Jóven, internships in firms (*práctica laboral)* are key, and the program improves the process of job-searching by looking at institutional dimensions (e.g., capacity-building in municipal job centers). The approach has been to move away from bureaucratic to dynamic and inclusive management. As for the *Programs Jefas de Hogar*, it is noteworthy that the second phase gave serious consideration to these issues by the reinforcement of the component of *intermediación laboral*, building up bridges between low-income women and municipal job centers.

- *Lack of income for job search costs:* Searching for a job can be costly, and the lack of income of unemployed workers may represent a barrier to their employment. One example is the cost of transportation in urban areas. Clert's study among residents of the peripheral *comuna* of Huechuraba in Santiago reveals that many job seekers who could not afford to spend money on transportation saw their mobility and their chances to find jobs restricted. In 1983, bus fares were freed from pricing restriction and their cost has increased subsequently. While governments have been able to limit somewhat the pace of these increases, recent fares have been affected by the rise of oil prices. Moreover, in Santiago, many low-income *comunas* still do not have access to the metro system. This is especially problematic for workers who must change location, for to go to construction sites. Both training programs address the problem of affordability by providing free vocational training courses and a financial allowance in order to compensate for costs of both transportation and maintenance.

- *Lack of child care:* The access to extra-household networks helps for women who lack access to affordable childcare. In rural areas, Valdés (1996) has shown that female temporary workers involved in fruit-picking (*temporeras de la fruta*) rely on family networks for the care of their children. In urban areas however, access to this kind of support is more difficult. In Clert's study in Huechuraba, 37 percent of the respondents with children under eight said that they could not rely on anybody to leave the children with (Figure 1). The trade-offs between work and child care faced by women often leads them to leave a full-time job, accept part-time employment or employment with inferior working conditions, or simply opt out of the labor force when they get children (SERNAM, 1996). The lack of access to free or low-cost childcare thus remains a major obstacle to the labor market insertion of women. Both training programs have made efforts to include a childcare component, even though the latter is only guaranteed for the training period. The program *Mujeres Jefas de*

Hogar also included the expansion of access to other key areas, such as social housing and access to the justice system. The link with law centers has been instrumental in addressing issues arising within the private environment of women heads of households. For example, women have been able to receive help and orientation in terms of pension allowances from their former partners or in terms of domestic help. Improving access to housing has also been important, since program participants have expressed concern about leaving their children in unsafe homes when going to work.

Figure 1. Reliance on Social Networks for Childcare

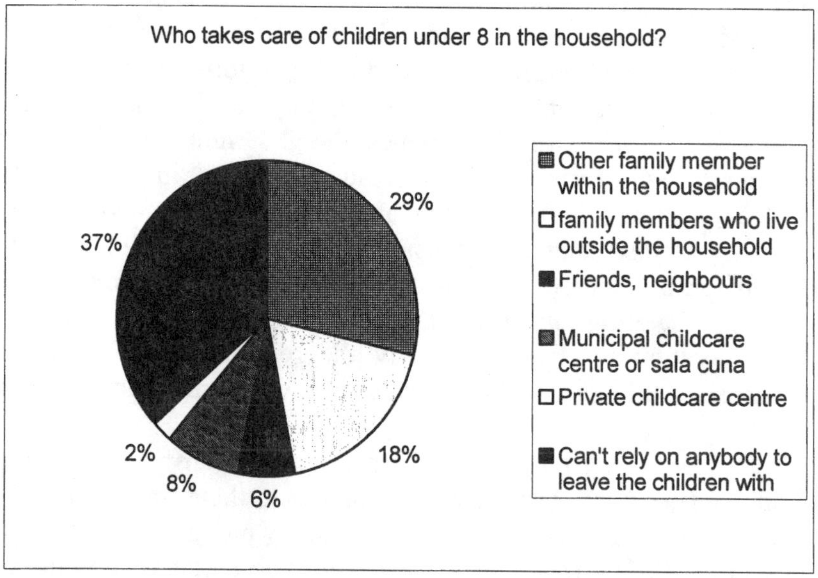

Source: Clert (2000b), based on a household survey for January-February 1998

- *Difficulties of finding a job due to age and/or physical appearance:* In Clert's study, some of the more subtle perceptions of exclusion from labor markets relate to elements of the respondents' identity such as age, physical appearance, place of residence and disability. Margarita, a women aged 52, had worked as a domestic worker all her life but was fired by her employer two years before the time of the Huechuraba survey and has remained unemployed since then. She explains: "*One goes to a place and the offer says 'Needs domestic worker more than 25 until, let's say, 40'. So what's the matter? Those of us who are over 50, we don't have the right to work?* The social construction of physical appearance also affects women and young men. A key informant from the municipal job bureau explained that qualifications were not the only factor at a job interview: "*The employer weighs certain criteria: good appearance (buena presencia), experience, knowledge. [A good appearance relates to] the look, there are things about details. For instance, you have people who come here with their pony tail, their earring... Presentation counts for 25 percent. But it is true that they will tell them 'I already hired someone else'. They won't say I don't take you because you look ugly.*" The training programs show an awareness of the subtle mechanisms of discrimination which tend to be used by employers in their hiring practices. Non-written rules of selection have been addressed in the contents of vocational training courses. Program participants value the acquisition of presentation skills, writing skills for resumes, and communication skills. Interestingly, the program *Mujeres Jefas de Hogar* gives participants free access to dental health, in part because early consultations with participants for the program design showed that women faced discrimination due to the importance given to physical appearance and personal presentation by firms.

- *Difficulties of finding a job due to the area of residence or other factors:* The residents of the *Pincoya* Sector of the *comuna* of Huechuraba have felt discriminated against because of the reputation of the area as a rough and dangerous area peopled by dishonest inhabitants. For example, Jose who lived in the Pincoya sector, reported the following: *"They ask me from which comuna I come from. I say 'Huechuraba'. And where is that? Nothing more but they look at me in a certain way with a gesture as if it meant... ah, there you have to come in with your back turned to make people believe that you are getting out."* This and similar type of discrimination are especially difficult to fight, but the government has promoted awareness and sensitization campaigns to combat the stigma attached to low-income youth, which often tends to be associated with delinquency, violence and threat (Tohá, 2000). Similarly, the program *Mujeres Jefas de Hogar* has promoted a recognition of social diversity within Chilean society by disseminating a positive image of various types of families. Within the government, the program contributed to a better recognition of the heterogeneity of poverty by public policy. As a senior official put it: *"Women heads of households used to suffer from a triple discrimination: being poor , being a woman and being a single mother... With regard to women heads of household for instance, there's now greater cultural acceptance of the diversity of family types ... Years ago they appeared in statistics but there wasn't a social recognition that they existed."*

Limits of the Two Programs. Low-income youth and women tend to be more exposed to labor market exclusion than other groups of workers. They face a higher probability of being unemployed, a lower probability of receiving privately funded training, and a lower probability of having a good, long-term contract when employed. The specific difficulties faced by young workers and women justify the existence of targeted public programs for these groups. In this paper, we have discussed two of these programs: Chile Joven and the PMJH. These programs share an integrated approach to fighting the exclusion from labor markets. While they have a number of strengths discussed in the previous section, they also have several limits.

- *Education and literacy requirements*: A lack of a good education leads to difficulties in finding a job, but it also makes it more difficult to participate in some of the training programs since the completion of secondary education is increasingly required by training centers, including those involved in *Chile Joven*. One may be led to believe that literacy is not a major issue since according to the CASEN, the illiteracy rate among (urban) adults is relatively low. Yet while the survey only asks for a yes/no answer to the question *"Can you read and write?"*, it is well-known that an appropriate assessment of literacy should also take into account those people who can read and write, but with considerable difficulty. Since the program for *Mujeres Jefas de Hogar* explicitly includes literacy among its eligibility criteria, it may not be able to reach very poor women with low levels of education.

- *Emphasis on prompt labor market insertion and cream-skimming*: In the second trienum of the Frei administration, a stronger emphasis has been placed on the productive impact of both training programs, and especially *Chile Jóven*. While the program *Mujeres Jefas de Hogar* has maintained its concern for an integrated approach, *Chile Jóven* – now under the sole coordination of the National Institute for Training SENCE – has restricted its objective to the creation of jobs through the provision of vocational training, with less emphasis on gender aspects (at least by mid-1998.) and at-risk youth, who used to attend special courses through a sub-component executed by the social fund FOSIS. The program has also increasingly been relying on private training centers. In theory, the focus of the program is on young people from low-income households, as assessed by the *ficha de caracterización socio-económica* that applicants in municipal job centers. But in practice, certain training centers are applying their own selection criteria in order to ensure a prompt labor market insertion of their trainees. As a government official explained: *'Training centers tend to organize their own process of selection We are really concerned about those issues. Some training centers strictly apply SENCE criteria, others don't. Some prefer to select young participants who completed their secondary education (media completa). They think that these young people will "fit" better, that they are more "socially included". They think "these young people won't drop out, they won't fail us".* This suggests that the selection practices of private training centers tend to exclude the most disadvantaged among young participants ("cream-skimming"). In other words, by generating financial incentives for training centers to ensure prompt labor market insertion, the program could potentially create perverse effects with regard to the quality of its targeting.

- *Lack of programs for middle-age men:* The respondents of the age group 45-64 in Clert's study mention age-based discrimination in hiring and dismissal practices. Manuel, aged 53, was a semi-killed worker, a welder. He had been working for many years in the same building company. At the conclusion of one construction job, the firm suddenly stopped sending him to further construction sites. Similar exclusionary practices occurred in the hiring process, as Manuel further described his search for work: *"I went to different firms... I kept knocking at doors. I managed to work in two or three places but it occurred again, the same thing. They told me 'so hasta luego, 'you're useless'. And simply, in many parts, they didn't even give me the job. They looked at me up and down. The job ad was there but they said 'no, we already hired someone'. Also, I used the phone, I phoned them from outside the site and they still said that they needed people and I had just talked to them. So, this is how you realize that you're discriminated against."* Individuals of the age group 45-64, who are already excluded from the labor market, are paradoxically also excluded from vocational training programs restricted to the young. The policies which have been centered on women and the young so far should be extended to men in their late forties and beyond. As an official from the Ministry of Planning put it: *"If you think about it, those who are considered vulnerable are children, women, old people, ethnic groups... and the only ones who aren't considered vulnerable, who are they? The men who don't belong to any ethnic minority or who are not elderly, nor young, nor children."*

- *Institutional issues:* In the second phase of PMJH, the decision was made to mainstream the program by making it part of the interventions of sectoral ministries and municipalities. At the central government level, Clert's (2000b) study reveals that this lead to a questioning of the priorities of the ministries which had been influenced by traditional perceptions keeping women in their reproductive roles. While such questioning is good news, a government official explained *"there is still a conception of women household heads that impedes the reformulation of programs. For instance we want women to have access to primary health care. Within that, an important line and aspiration on the part of working women has been odontological attention. But primary health care in this country is still centered on what is related to women's reproductive role, maternal and infant programs, etc.".* The risk highlighted by this official in the mainstreaming of PMJH was for the program to lose what made it different, i.e. its attempt at tackling social discrimination. Serious challenges are also faced for the implementation at the municipal level. Despite improvements, gender awareness has not reached municipal staff equally, and social planners expressed concern with the institutional and programmatic segmentation which had been associated with the target group approach of programs such as PMJH. As one manager put it: *"Gender is a theme that crosses everything. However, ... there are people who deal with poverty and gender issues separately"*. Despite programs such as PMJH, gender issues remain synonym of women's issues with a realm of intervention distinct from the anti-poverty and employment generation initiatives.

- *Structural issues in the labor market and the education system:* Evaluations have shown that access to jobs improves for all the different sub-components of the training courses (Santiago Consultores, 1998). However, on closer scrutiny, labor market insertion differs according to gender and age. The proportion of female beneficiaries who find a formal employment is 10 percent lower than for males. Similarly older participants are more likely to find jobs than younger participants (those between the ages of 15 and 19). This tends to be due to structural features of the labor market which cannot be solved by the training programs alone. Senior government officials interviewed in Clert's (2000a, 2000b) point to the insufficiencies of the programs. After referring to the crucial importance of issues such as labor rights, the level of wages and seasonal work in the generation of female poverty, one manager argued: *"There are areas where discrimination is very strong and where social policies have not any impact.... We prepare women's entry into the labor market, we generate conditions, we provide tools, networks, institutional contacts but at the end of the day the one who hires is the empresario [entrepreneur], and the one who fixes the level of wages is the empresario in a framework of labor laws that leaves working women very unprotected ... However good our program will look, it will be useless it will fail you if there aren't broader conditions."* Social inclusion policies cannot foster change if they only rely on special programs that have no impact on the exclusionary environment of the groups at which they are targeted. This applies also to *Chile Jóven*. In its initial phase, the program was willing to stimulate the combination of studies with employment on the part of beneficiaries and to contribute to their reinsertion into school. However, according to Tohá (2000), such reinsertion has rarely occurred, and some beneficiaries have interrupted their schooling as a result of their participation into the program. Clearly, the target group approach of the implementation of special programs will not be enough for fighting poverty and social exclusion. Broader efforts will also be needed for the education system and the functioning of labor markets.

Conclusion

The evidence presented in this paper relates to the training programs as they stood in 1998-1999. Our conclusions and policy orientations should therefore taken with the necessary caution. Nevertheless, the paper sheds light on the key questions raised in the introduction. Five findings are worth emphasizing.

First, the identification of serious cumulative disadvantages among low-income youths and women, and particularly among women heads of households, suggests that these population groups need special multi-faceted training programs such as those provided by Chile Joven and PMJH.

Second, some of the innovative features of these programs may have been threatened recently. With the higher emphasis placed on the productive components of both programs, there is a risk that the other social barriers to employment experienced by program beneficiaries might be overlooked. While there may be a rationale to improve the productive components of the programs, their integrated approach should also be maintained and their innovative features should be mainstreamed into other policy interventions both at the central and local government levels.

Third, the analysis stresses the limitations of labor based inclusion programs. The programs tend to have a limited impact on the social exclusion of their beneficiaries. Structural problems related to low wages, widespread casual employment, and exclusionary hiring practices simply cannot be dealt with the programs alone. As argued in more details in Clert (200a), wider policy reforms are needed.

Fourth, the evidence suggests that other segments of the population may also require special attention. The qualitative study points to the limits of the target group approach. For example, individuals in their forties, who are excluded from the labor market due to age stigmatization, cannot participate in state vocational training programmes restricted to the young.

Lastly, subtle processes of exclusion which relate to the social construction of identity based on physical appearance, place of residence and age suggest the need for public information campaigns and incentives for firms in order to counteract stigmatization in hiring practices. Some of the policies which have been centered on women and the young so far could be extended to other groups suffering from stigmatization.

REFERENCES

CIDE (Centro de Investigación y Desarrollo de la Educación). 1997. *Evaluación Ex Post del Programa de Capacitación par Mujeres jefas de Hogar.* Santiago, Chile.

Clert, C., 2000a, *"Policy Implications of a Social Exclusion Perspective in Chile: Priorities, Discourse and Methods in Question"*, Ph.D. thesis, London School of Economics.

Clert, C., 2000b, Social Exclusion, Gender and the Chilean Government's Anti-Poverty Strategy: Priorities and Methods in Question, in E. Gacitua Mario and C. Sojo, Editors, *Social Exclusion and Poverty Reduction in Latin America.* Washington, DC.: World Bank and FLACSO.

Dar, A., and I. S. Gill. 1998. On Evaluating Retraining Programs in OECD Countries. *World Bank Research Observer* 13:79–101.

Letelier, M.E. 1996. *Alfabetismo Femenino en Chile de los 90.* Santiago: UNESCO-UNICEF.

Santiago Consultores. 1998. *Principales Aspectos del Estudio "Evaluación Ex Post Programa Chile Joven Fase II".* Santiago.

SERNAM. 1996. *Igualdad de Oportunidades para la Mujer en el Trabajo.* Santiago: SERNAM..

Silva, M.L. 1996. Mujer y Educación. MINEDUC.

Tohá. C. 2000. Jóvenes y Exclusión Social en Chile. E. Gacitua Mario and C. Sojo, Editors. *Social Exclusion and Poverty Reduction in Latin America.* Washington, DC: World Bank and FLACSO.

Valdes, X. 1996. *Lo Material y lo Simbólico en la Problematización de la Pobreza: Mecanismos y Dispositivos de Integración Asalariada en la Agricultura de Exportación.* Santiago: SERNAM.

Wodon Q., and M. Minowa. 2001. Training for the Urban Unemployed: A Reevaluation of Mexico's Probecat, in S. Devaradjan, F. Hasley, and L. Squire, editors. *World Bank Economists' Forum.* Washington DC.: World Bank,.

APPENDIX 1: EMPLOYMENT, MALE POPULATION BY AGE GROUP, CHILE 1998 (all entries are percentages)

	Urban Quintiles					Urban	Rural Quintiles					Rural	National Quintiles					Nat'l
	1	2	3	4	5	Total	1	2	3	4	5	Total	1	2	3	4	5	Total
18-24 year old																		
Working last week	27.5	50.8	54.2	58.8	40.4	47.1	37.4	69.0	71.7	74.5	61.7	61.1	28.0	52.5	57.8	59.5	43.9	49.2
Searching last week	27.7	13.6	9.9	6.1	3.4	11.7	25.7	6.6	7.1	2.6	4.5	11.5	27.9	13.6	10.0	5.9	3.6	11.7
Inactive	14.7	12.2	8.0	7.5	4.3	9.2	18.9	10.8	7.5	10.2	9.7	12.2	16.0	12.1	8.1	8.2	4.8	9.6
Student	34.3	26.4	33.3	35.5	63.5	38.5	19.1	14.2	16.4	16.9	26.1	17.1	31.9	24.2	29.0	33.7	58.0	35.4
25-34 year old																		
Working last week	58.9	85.2	85.7	88.6	87.1	82.7	73.8	87.4	91.0	94.8	94.5	85.8	60.3	84.4	86.4	89.2	87.6	83.1
Searching last week	26.7	8.0	7.4	4.4	2.9	8.6	12.8	3.9	1.8	0.7	1.6	5.3	25.2	7.7	6.8	4.3	2.8	8.2
Inactive	11.8	6.0	4.8	3.6	3.1	5.4	13.1	8.6	6.7	4.4	2.1	8.5	12.2	7.2	5.4	3.7	3.2	5.8
Working <20 hours/week	5.4	2.5	1.7	2.0	2.9	2.6	5.5	2.2	1.2	1.0	6.0	2.8	5.7	2.2	2.2	1.9	2.9	2.7
Working 20-39 h/week	7.7	5.1	5.4	6.7	8.2	6.6	8.2	5.5	7.5	6.8	8.2	7.0	7.9	4.9	5.8	6.8	8.1	6.6
Working 40-49 h/week	54.3	52.3	58.6	57.6	52.5	55.2	56.6	62.0	70.9	55.3	53.8	61.2	54.7	54.9	59.6	56.8	53.6	56.0
Working 50+ h/week	32.5	40.1	34.3	33.7	36.4	35.6	29.7	30.3	20.4	37.0	32.1	29.0	31.7	38.0	32.4	34.6	35.4	34.7
1 job last week	96.9	95.8	94.7	93.6	89.7	93.7	95.5	96.4	93.6	94.3	88.7	94.7	96.3	96.3	95.1	92.8	90.6	93.8
2+ jobs last week	3.1	4.1	5.2	6.4	9.9	6.2	4.5	3.6	6.4	5.7	11.2	5.3	3.7	3.7	4.8	7.1	9.1	6.1
35-54 year old																		
Working last week	62.1	86.2	92.1	93.1	97.6	87.9	74.3	89.1	92.2	94.9	95.6	86.2	62.9	86.1	91.9	93.0	97.1	87.6
Searching last week	25.0	6.0	2.4	1.9	0.3	6.0	13.6	2.4	1.1	1.4	0.1	5.4	23.6	5.8	2.6	2.0	0.4	5.9
Inactive	12.8	7.7	5.5	4.8	2.0	6.0	12.1	8.5	6.6	3.7	4.4	8.4	13.4	8.0	5.6	4.9	2.4	6.4
Working <20 hours/week	6.4	3.3	3.2	1.8	1.9	2.9	2.4	3.6	2.5	1.5	2.6	2.7	5.4	3.4	3.1	2.1	1.9	2.9
Working 20-39 h/week	7.1	5.8	8.1	7.6	8.3	7.5	12.6	7.2	10.1	9.7	7.9	9.7	8.7	6.6	7.4	8.2	8.4	7.8
Working 40-49 h/week	49.8	54.8	52.0	53.1	49.5	51.8	49.5	59.1	56.7	55.9	44.3	54.4	49.9	55.4	53.8	51.9	50.1	52.2
Working 50+ h/week	36.7	36.1	36.7	37.5	40.2	37.7	35.6	30.1	30.7	32.8	45.2	33.2	36.0	34.6	35.8	37.7	39.7	37.1
1 job last week	96.2	94.6	95.1	94.1	90.4	93.7	94.8	93.6	90.5	91.8	81.9	92.2	95.6	94.6	94.4	94.1	90.4	93.4
2+ jobs last week	3.8	5.4	4.9	5.8	9.5	6.3	5.2	6.3	9.4	8.2	18.1	7.8	4.4	5.4	5.6	5.8	9.6	6.5
55-64 year old																		
Working last week	33.0	62.2	70.4	75.9	81.4	68.8	53.5	80.4	80.5	91.7	95.3	77.1	39.0	63.7	71.5	78.1	82.5	70.4
Searching last week	24.0	8.5	4.2	2.6	0.7	6.1	9.6	1.7	1.1	0.3	0.0	3.2	20.4	7.4	3.8	2.4	0.7	5.5
Inactive	43.0	29.3	25.5	21.5	18.0	25.1	36.9	17.9	18.4	8.0	4.7	19.7	40.6	28.9	24.7	19.6	16.8	24.1
Working <20 hours/week	10.9	7.2	4.8	5.1	2.3	4.7	5.6	2.1	2.7	3.8	3.0	3.4	8.5	6.1	4.3	5.1	2.3	4.4
Working 20-39 h/week	10.1	9.2	10.6	9.9	9.4	9.8	12.4	9.3	13.8	10.2	9.6	11.1	12.0	7.9	11.6	10.1	9.7	10.1
Working 40-49 h/week	45.0	47.0	48.9	48.7	49.4	48.5	44.5	54.8	47.7	48.9	50.5	49.5	42.5	53.1	47.5	48.1	49.6	48.8
Working 50+ h/week	34.0	36.6	35.6	36.3	38.9	37.0	37.4	33.8	35.7	37.0	37.0	36.0	37.0	32.9	36.6	36.8	38.4	36.8
1 job last week	95.4	97.0	93.7	96.1	91.8	94.1	99.2	98.3	91.4	88.6	87.9	93.3	96.9	97.2	94.5	94.6	91.4	94.0
2+ jobs last week	4.6	3.0	6.3	3.9	8.2	5.9	0.8	1.7	8.6	11.4	12.1	6.6	3.1	2.8	5.5	5.4	8.6	6.0

Source: Authors' estimation using 1998 CASEN survey.

APPENDIX 2: EMPLOYMENT, FEMALE POPULATION BY AGE GROUP, CHILE 1998 (all entries are percentages)

	Urban Quintiles						Rural Quintiles						National Quintiles					Nat'l
	1	2	3	4	5	Total	1	2	3	4	5	Total	1	2	3	4	5	Total
18-24 year old																		
Working last week	12.2	26.0	34.3	41.6	37.2	30.6	9.6	19.3	44.8	39.4	27.4	24.0	11.1	22.2	35.2	40.2	37.4	29.8
Searching last week	17.3	10.5	9.0	7.0	3.7	9.4	9.4	9.4	6.9	2.1	0.7	7.8	16.0	10.7	8.8	7.6	3.5	9.2
Inactive	41.7	44.5	32.1	19.1	10.9	29.2	63.2	49.3	35.9	34.6	48.7	49.4	45.3	47.9	34.7	21.4	12.3	31.8
Student	31.4	22.0	29.5	39.6	56.0	36.0	17.9	23.3	14.3	28.0	24.7	20.2	29.5	21.3	25.4	38.3	53.9	33.9
25-34 year old																		
Working last week	21.9	35.6	44.9	63.2	75.1	49.0	10.0	22.4	43.6	54.2	64.1	26.4	17.6	30.9	44.5	58.8	74.4	46.1
Searching last week	11.3	7.4	6.6	3.8	2.7	6.2	6.7	4.0	2.5	1.7	0.7	4.4	10.7	6.8	6.1	4.2	2.6	6.0
Inactive	64.5	55.7	47.3	29.5	19.4	42.6	82.9	72.6	53.4	42.4	34.1	68.4	69.7	61.2	48.0	34.4	19.8	45.9
Working <20 hours/week	17.8	10.1	7.6	5.1	3.3	6.7	19.1	10.0	11.4	1.0	6.0	9.5	20.1	8.7	8.9	5.8	3.2	6.9
Working 20-39 h/week	20.3	16.9	15.0	14.8	14.7	15.6	20.8	15.8	13.6	13.3	14.9	15.3	20.5	18.1	16.0	13.9	14.6	15.6
Working 40-49 h/week	40.3	50.8	58.0	57.8	60.8	56.3	37.7	57.0	54.7	59.0	48.1	53.0	35.4	52.7	55.1	57.7	61.0	56.1
Working 50+ h/week	21.6	22.2	19.4	22.4	21.2	21.4	22.5	17.2	20.3	26.7	31.0	22.2	23.9	20.5	19.9	22.6	21.2	21.4
1 job last week	95.6	97.4	97.5	97.3	91.6	95.4	98.8	99.2	99.8	99.7	90.8	98.5	95.2	97.9	97.6	97.5	92.3	95.6
2+ jobs last week	4.4	2.5	2.4	2.5	8.3	4.5	1.2	0.8	0.2	0.2	8.9	1.5	4.8	2.1	2.2	2.4	7.7	4.3
35-54 year old																		
Working last week	20.8	36.2	45.6	55.5	67.8	46.7	9.2	19.7	32.1	40.4	52.2	23.2	17.1	31.0	43.2	52.5	66.6	43.8
Searching last week	10.9	3.7	3.1	2.1	1.5	4.0	2.6	1.2	0.7	0.7	0.2	1.4	9.5	3.3	3.1	2.2	1.4	3.7
Inactive	67.7	59.7	51.0	42.0	30.4	48.8	88.0	79.1	67.2	58.9	47.4	75.3	72.8	65.4	53.4	45.0	31.7	52.1
Working <20 hours/week	22.5	10.2	10.7	4.8	5.1	8.2	19.0	14.7	7.6	6.5	4.4	10.2	22.9	11.1	10.9	6.2	4.7	8.3
Working 20-39 h/week	19.9	19.8	18.2	18.8	15.6	17.9	33.3	17.3	14.2	18.2	22.6	19.6	22.5	18.5	18.9	18.5	16.1	18.0
Working 40-49 h/week	31.2	44.8	46.2	49.6	49.9	46.9	31.3	45.8	56.1	47.8	40.8	46.3	30.4	43.7	47.0	47.9	50.4	46.9
Working 50+ h/week	26.4	25.3	24.9	26.7	29.3	27.0	16.4	22.2	22.1	27.5	32.2	24.0	24.2	26.7	23.2	27.5	28.8	26.8
1 job last week	94.1	95.8	97.0	95.4	93.9	95.1	96.6	97.8	98.0	92.8	91.9	95.8	93.4	96.2	96.8	96.0	93.7	95.2
2+ jobs last week	5.9	4.2	3.0	4.5	6.0	4.8	3.4	2.2	1.9	7.2	8.0	4.2	6.6	3.8	3.1	3.9	6.2	4.7
55-64 year old																		
Working last week	10.1	18.8	27.8	29.0	45.3	28.1	6.7	9.7	9.8	16.8	39.1	12.4	8.6	16.4	23.5	26.9	43.9	25.7
Searching last week	4.0	1.7	1.9	0.5	0.8	1.6	0.5	0.8	0.0	0.0	0.0	0.3	3.1	1.9	1.1	0.8	0.7	1.4
Inactive	85.9	79.1	70.3	70.5	53.9	70.2	92.9	89.5	90.2	83.2	60.9	87.3	88.4	81.3	75.4	72.2	55.4	72.8
Working <20 hours/week	39.7	19.2	12.9	10.3	7.0	12.2	32.6	13.1	0.1	9.5	2.4	10.1	37.4	23.8	10.9	10.3	7.4	12.1
Working 20-39 h/week	13.8	21.4	23.5	24.1	18.0	20.5	41.0	34.9	34.6	19.4	5.8	24.9	21.0	18.5	26.6	24.6	17.1	20.9
Working 40-49 h/week	23.7	33.6	41.1	38.5	44.9	40.2	19.7	38.0	32.1	37.8	54.0	38.3	23.7	31.6	38.9	40.4	44.6	40.1
Working 50+ h/week	22.8	25.7	22.4	27.1	30.1	27.0	6.6	14.0	33.2	33.3	37.9	26.7	18.0	26.1	23.6	24.7	31.0	27.0
1 job last week	99.3	96.6	95.7	97.0	98.1	97.3	99.8	99.6	97.4	93.0	94.2	96.4	99.2	96.7	96.4	97.3	97.5	97.3
2+ jobs last week	0.7	3.4	4.3	3.0	1.9	2.7	0.2	0.4	2.6	7.0	5.8	3.6	0.8	3.3	3.6	2.7	2.5	2.7

Source: Authors' estimation using 1998 CASEN survey.

APPENDIX 3: QUALITY OF EMPLOYMENT, MALE POPULATION BY AGE GROUP, CHILE 1998 (all entries are percentages)

	Urban Quintiles					Urban Total	Rural Quintiles					Rural Total	National Quintiles					Nat'l Total
	1	2	3	4	5	Total	1	2	3	4	5	Total	1	2	3	4	5	Total
18-34 year old																		
Contract signed	31.37	47.76	49.25	47.46	41.82	44.03	16.82	36.19	40.30	35.97	25.82	31.08	16.12	42.31	48.52	51.76	45.40	42.20
No contract signed	18.09	13.44	12.29	9.68	6.73	11.72	21.01	27.51	23.24	22.29	13.01	23.17	16.89	18.66	14.09	10.94	7.81	13.33
Permanent contract	23.17	36.58	39.03	40.27	37.27	35.84	9.71	25.10	27.20	23.82	18.01	20.68	10.31	30.64	38.20	42.40	40.30	33.70
Fixed term contract	7.44	10.08	8.84	6.08	3.83	7.17	6.03	10.42	12.30	11.67	7.62	9.64	5.19	10.61	8.98	8.14	4.48	7.52
35-64 year old																		
Contract signed	37.67	52.84	55.33	50.24	44.83	48.39	22.84	38.73	35.16	31.83	20.24	30.68	24.89	49.91	51.92	50.65	46.35	45.59
No contract signed	15.92	12.51	9.14	5.11	3.09	8.62	22.10	20.66	15.98	8.43	9.88	17.55	16.75	15.68	11.11	6.77	3.81	10.03
Open (long term) contract	28.83	43.61	47.88	44.23	41.75	41.70	16.57	30.84	28.68	27.01	18.60	24.51	18.26	39.37	43.95	44.73	42.99	38.99
Fixed term contract	7.99	8.01	6.84	5.29	2.72	5.96	5.35	6.83	5.89	4.52	1.53	5.43	5.98	9.22	7.20	5.18	3.05	5.88
18-34 year old																		
Permanent, day-time job	27.28	38.83	43.68	45.12	48.17	41.33	30.81	38.89	43.16	49.60	54.58	39.96	20.33	36.90	41.94	48.39	51.92	41.13
Permanent, night or shift	5.61	10.43	9.84	9.51	8.04	8.79	1.15	3.05	4.86	4.15	3.14	3.09	3.55	7.59	9.93	9.87	7.78	7.99
Fixed term, day-time job	15.15	13.87	10.87	10.11	4.60	10.64	21.59	33.13	30.16	24.49	16.92	27.10	14.82	19.56	15.42	10.68	5.82	12.96
Fixed term, night or shift	1.60	2.01	2.15	1.14	0.57	1.47	0.51	0.82	1.04	1.10	0.40	0.80	1.24	1.84	1.67	1.34	0.84	1.38
By the task, day-time	3.87	5.27	4.34	4.43	3.34	4.24	3.83	3.11	2.85	5.51	4.57	3.67	3.89	4.23	4.14	4.55	3.93	4.16
By the task, night or shift	0.90	0.28	0.53	0.17	0.13	0.38	0.07	0.33	0.30	0.16	0.18	0.22	0.38	0.52	0.50	0.23	0.21	0.36
35-64 year old																		
Permanent, day-time job	32.47	50.09	57.05	62.71	75.41	57.15	42.07	54.69	59.84	67.70	76.75	55.51	30.43	48.26	56.57	63.01	74.58	56.89
Permanent, night or shift	6.67	11.33	12.29	12.62	8.48	10.37	1.53	2.55	2.80	3.94	2.26	2.46	6.62	9.35	10.44	10.19	8.59	9.12
Fixed term, day-time job	15.13	13.54	11.36	7.74	4.87	10.10	22.82	25.48	20.77	17.23	12.67	21.51	15.41	17.17	13.79	10.29	5.95	11.90
Fixed term, night or shift	1.76	1.46	1.04	1.08	0.58	1.14	0.34	0.31	0.34	0.41	0.36	0.34	1.10	1.58	1.21	0.82	0.59	1.02
By the task, day-time	5.99	6.42	3.97	4.96	3.34	4.84	2.91	4.15	5.38	3.76	3.29	3.90	4.26	5.62	5.61	4.91	3.41	4.69
By the task, night or shift	0.64	0.32	0.42	0.34	0.27	0.39	0.31	0.27	0.31	0.01	0.49	0.27	0.50	0.47	0.40	0.34	0.21	0.37

Source: Authors' estimation using 1998 CASEN survey.

APPENDIX 4: QUALITY OF EMPLOYMENT, FEMALE POPULATION BY AGE GROUP, CHILE 1998 (all entries are percentages)

	Urban Quintiles						Rural Quintiles						National Quintiles					Nat'l
	1	2	3	4	5	Total	1	2	3	4	5	Total	1	2	3	4	5	Total
18-34 year old																		
Contract signed	8.32	19.93	32.49	37.54	41.64	28.57	3.31	9.38	21.14	25.06	31.24	11.96	5.21	15.82	26.22	36.48	45.59	26.44
No contract signed	8.70	10.62	9.45	8.40	6.92	8.77	4.62	8.18	17.32	9.95	2.93	8.64	7.27	9.29	10.61	9.40	7.12	8.75
Permanent contract	5.98	14.63	25.93	31.59	37.42	23.67	1.68	4.73	15.42	18.12	23.67	7.83	3.51	10.74	20.19	30.26	40.88	21.64
Fixed term contract	2.22	4.72	5.73	5.26	3.82	4.37	1.59	3.95	5.47	5.82	7.19	3.73	1.65	4.52	5.47	5.26	4.32	4.29
35-64 year old																		
Contract signed	9.70	18.24	23.52	26.77	34.88	23.24	2.17	6.20	10.06	12.31	16.31	7.19	4.33	13.34	19.60	26.78	35.54	21.16
No contract signed	10.67	9.97	9.40	6.87	4.42	8.09	3.17	5.23	7.98	4.44	4.94	5.01	7.75	8.91	10.13	7.42	5.04	7.69
Open (long term) contract	8.11	15.02	20.85	24.36	32.76	20.85	0.53	2.91	5.30	9.60	15.02	4.34	3.02	10.23	16.35	24.07	33.58	18.70
Fixed term contract	1.53	2.99	2.31	2.05	1.83	2.13	1.36	2.78	4.68	2.63	1.29	2.58	1.15	2.84	2.97	2.35	1.71	2.19
18-34 year old																		
Permanent, day-time job	11.79	21.81	34.39	39.31	46.32	31.34	4.85	8.33	24.05	29.35	42.28	13.63	8.04	16.18	28.43	39.20	50.45	29.07
Permanent, night or shift	0.49	1.71	2.71	3.45	2.99	2.31	0.11	0.48	2.10	1.92	0.63	0.81	0.71	1.01	2.31	3.31	3.07	2.12
Fixed term, day-time job	5.04	7.74	6.74	5.96	3.33	5.72	4.31	10.36	15.93	12.68	5.32	9.31	4.51	8.16	7.67	6.57	3.97	6.18
Fixed term, night or shift	0.61	0.58	0.48	0.83	0.34	0.56	0.11	0.31	0.33	0.22	1.10	0.27	0.40	0.55	0.57	0.63	0.47	0.53
By the task, day-time	1.00	2.19	2.17	1.65	1.92	1.80	0.51	1.45	1.00	2.61	0.47	1.11	1.04	1.59	1.83	1.96	2.06	1.71
By the task, night or shift	0.20	0.11	0.26	0.10	0.12	0.16	0.00	-	0.76	0.07	0.10	0.16	0.20	0.16	0.26	0.07	0.11	0.16
35-64 year old																		
Permanent, day-time job	14.53	24.47	31.78	38.07	54.33	33.64	3.36	9.99	16.42	25.40	44.31	13.56	7.98	17.19	28.58	36.74	55.07	31.03
Permanent, night or shift	1.71	1.93	2.78	2.97	2.72	2.46	0.16	0.52	0.27	1.76	1.15	0.55	0.69	2.09	1.73	3.19	2.93	2.21
Fixed term, day-time job	6.59	6.63	5.34	4.53	2.13	4.92	4.70	5.76	7.45	5.38	3.15	5.53	5.43	6.38	6.35	5.02	2.56	5.00
Fixed term, night or shift	0.36	0.76	0.37	0.33	0.32	0.42	0.13	0.01	0.01	0.11	0.12	0.07	0.27	0.64	0.41	0.27	0.32	0.37
By the task, day-time	1.90	2.01	2.23	1.68	1.69	1.89	0.46	0.94	1.77	0.82	0.17	0.89	1.33	1.78	2.03	1.89	1.73	1.76
By the task, night or shift	0.19	0.21	0.13	0.07	0.14	0.15	-	0.05	0.03	-	0.17	0.02	0.09	0.14	0.20	0.05	0.16	0.13

Source: Authors' estimation using 1998 CASEN survey.

APPENDIX 5: REASON FOR NOT WORKING, MALE AND FEMALE POPULATIONS BY AGE GROUP, CHILE 1998 (all entries are percentages)

	Urban Quintiles						Rural Quintiles						National Quintiles					Nat'l
	1	2	3	4	5	Total	1	2	3	4	5	Total	1	2	3	4	5	Total
Men 18-34 year old																		
Housework or child care	-	-	-	-	-	-	-	-	-	-	-	-	-	-	-	-	-	-
Disabilities or disease	2.28	1.63	1.14	0.84	0.38	1.19	3.55	4.79	2.32	2.32	0.88	3.31	2.47	2.65	1.50	1.00	0.27	1.49
Student	11.03	9.41	13.90	16.02	27.26	15.90	8.45	5.95	6.49	5.71	12.87	7.12	15.02	9.55	11.61	13.59	22.88	14.66
Retired with pension	-	-	-	-	-	0.01	0.08	-	-	-	0.06	0.03	0.02	0.06	-	-	0.00	0.00
Other income sources	0.02	-	0.05	-	-	0.01	-	0.02	-	-	-	0.00	-	-	-	-	-	0.01
Intermittent worker	1.74	0.37	0.53	0.34	0.39	0.63	3.49	1.45	0.42	0.21	0.85	1.58	2.60	0.75	0.50	0.20	0.24	0.76
Discouraged/other	2.76	1.76	1.32	1.30	0.48	1.46	3.96	0.66	1.50	1.16	0.14	1.82	4.03	1.67	0.97	1.28	0.27	1.51
Men 35-64 year old																		
Housework or child care	-	-	-	-	-	-	-	-	-	-	-	-	-	-	-	-	-	-
Disabilities or disease	5.63	2.85	1.88	1.28	0.30	2.19	6.54	4.54	5.28	1.28	0.51	4.51	6.61	3.48	2.75	1.35	0.24	2.55
Student	0.11	0.01	0.03	0.20	0.04	0.08	0.03	0.01	-	0.01	-	0.01	0.11	0.07	-	0.09	0.08	0.07
Retired with pension	3.07	4.02	4.43	4.17	3.60	3.88	0.73	2.23	2.26	1.69	1.45	1.64	2.54	3.22	3.18	4.16	4.06	3.52
Other income sources	0.11	0.00	0.09	0.03	0.04	0.05	0.19	0.01	-	-	0.13	0.07	0.30	0.02	0.02	0.00	0.01	0.06
Intermittent worker	1.13	0.78	0.42	0.28	0.22	0.53	3.99	1.08	0.10	0.47	-	1.60	2.53	0.90	0.43	0.19	0.05	0.70
Discouraged/other	1.21	0.84	0.69	0.35	0.23	0.62	1.58	0.82	0.39	0.06	1.13	0.88	1.73	1.15	0.31	0.30	0.24	0.67
Women 18-34 year old																		
Housework or child care	51.95	39.99	27.05	21.58	11.01	29.60	67.83	55.43	38.96	30.90	33.32	53.29	49.89	47.84	35.09	22.35	10.82	32.63
Disabilities or disease	2.12	1.46	1.30	0.49	0.30	1.10	2.50	2.59	1.91	1.43	0.46	2.22	2.22	2.10	1.19	0.63	0.24	1.24
Student	8.74	9.92	12.56	15.65	24.85	14.64	7.24	10.15	5.92	12.71	9.91	8.55	13.18	8.86	10.35	14.92	21.50	13.86
Retired with pension	-	0.02	0.04	-	0.06	0.03	0.01	-	-	-	-	0.00	0.02	0.04	-	-	0.06	0.02
Other income sources	-	-	0.02	0.03	0.05	0.02	0.00	-	-	-	-	0.00	0.03	0.02	0.00	0.01	0.05	0.02
Intermittent worker	0.69	0.27	0.24	0.29	0.51	0.40	0.69	0.45	1.22	0.30	-	0.65	0.75	0.34	0.37	0.27	0.45	0.43
Discouraged/other	2.23	1.83	2.03	1.37	1.35	1.75	2.51	1.71	1.73	2.81	1.51	2.10	2.87	1.79	1.62	1.52	1.28	1.79
Women 35-64 year old																		
Housework or child care	52.12	50.00	45.88	41.53	29.92	43.30	79.55	73.89	66.44	58.44	46.79	70.31	61.86	59.53	48.97	41.57	29.33	46.80
Disabilities or disease	5.49	3.59	2.36	1.49	0.74	2.61	4.58	3.59	4.06	4.55	0.42	3.90	4.90	3.68	3.35	2.20	0.62	2.78
Student	0.32	0.33	0.30	0.31	0.21	0.29	0.37	0.36	0.06	0.47	-	0.29	0.28	0.30	0.36	0.36	0.18	0.29
Retired with pension	4.20	3.03	3.40	3.82	3.11	3.50	2.09	1.32	1.37	1.15	1.69	1.58	4.76	2.24	2.98	3.58	2.81	3.26
Other income sources	0.06	0.05	0.05	0.06	0.01	0.05	0.05	-	-	-	0.16	0.03	0.19	-	0.02	0.01	0.02	0.04
Intermittent worker	0.54	0.36	0.11	0.13	0.27	0.27	0.96	0.52	0.11	-	0.31	0.50	0.73	0.35	0.08	0.28	0.15	0.30
Discouraged/other	1.59	0.94	1.50	1.47	1.42	1.39	0.46	0.46	0.19	0.68	0.98	0.47	1.52	1.00	0.82	1.33	1.59	1.27

Source: Authors' estimation using 1998 CASEN survey.

APPENDIX 6: TRAINING, MALE POPULATION BY AGE GROUP, CHILE 1998 (all entries are percentages)

	Urban Quintiles						Rural Quintiles						National Quintiles					Nat'l
	1	2	3	4	5	Total	1	2	3	4	5	Total	1	2	3	4	5	Total
18-34 year old																		
Training received																		
Training by the firm	5.56	10.29	12.83	14.44	17.81	12.56	0.66	2.71	3.68	7.45	11.44	3.50	3.97	7.04	9.18	14.42	19.19	11.28
Training by Government programs	2.80	2.46	1.92	2.41	1.52	2.19	3.28	2.61	2.80	2.77	4.38	2.96	2.63	2.96	1.96	2.41	1.69	2.30
Training by own resources	0.87	1.42	1.74	3.46	4.27	2.45	0.05	0.11	1.01	0.23	1.87	0.41	0.88	0.81	1.48	1.91	5.21	2.16
Training by other means	0.31	0.56	0.54	0.19	0.32	0.38	0.14	0.21	0.04	0.33	0.39	0.18	0.45	0.34	0.19	0.32	0.49	0.35
No training and interest in training																		
No expected impact of training	2.59	1.99	2.28	1.79	1.05	1.91	2.93	2.50	1.22	2.00	0.91	2.17	2.74	2.55	1.72	2.02	0.96	1.94
Bad experience in previous training	0.19	0.06	0.06	0.01	-	0.06	0.35	0.09	0.11	-	-	0.15	0.18	0.06	0.05	0.09	-	0.07
No special reason mentioned	14.60	13.97	11.29	11.33	8.71	11.80	13.19	11.00	15.91	9.47	6.71	12.29	14.58	13.40	12.44	11.30	8.55	11.87
No training and interest in training																		
Lack of financial resources	12.72	11.09	9.40	8.89	4.03	9.01	11.77	7.05	7.27	6.94	1.57	8.12	12.46	10.53	9.99	8.43	4.21	8.89
No possibility provided by employer	0.88	1.71	2.55	1.98	0.72	1.61	0.71	1.20	0.44	1.25	0.38	0.85	0.65	1.25	1.95	2.47	0.90	1.50
Lack of knowledge of Gvt. programs	15.44	9.81	8.77	6.45	3.02	8.34	26.42	26.70	21.42	20.06	16.67	23.93	18.23	15.03	10.35	8.08	3.68	10.54
Lack of preparation for training	1.06	0.49	0.47	0.60	0.03	0.51	1.62	1.72	1.11	1.68	0.71	1.49	1.15	0.90	0.67	0.57	0.12	0.65
No possibility because studying	10.26	9.25	13.52	15.72	26.46	15.42	6.88	5.54	6.40	6.02	13.58	6.62	12.73	8.84	11.73	13.98	22.45	14.18
No need, no time, or other reason	32.37	36.16	33.70	31.80	31.37	33.02	31.87	38.07	38.25	41.25	41.09	36.98	28.60	35.57	37.46	33.51	31.83	33.58
35-64 year old																		
Training received																		
Training by the firm	5.09	10.08	14.63	18.72	22.18	14.83	1.76	2.71	2.85	3.47	7.53	2.95	4.21	8.39	11.22	15.47	20.83	12.96
Training by Government programs	1.52	1.05	1.42	1.88	1.22	1.42	2.63	2.23	2.12	2.50	3.04	2.43	1.84	1.45	1.38	1.77	1.50	1.58
Training by own resources	0.54	0.39	0.89	2.35	5.59	2.14	0.03	0.16	0.42	1.00	2.31	0.47	0.29	0.45	0.64	1.73	4.97	1.88
Training by other means	0.12	0.29	0.23	0.15	0.35	0.23	0.08	0.41	0.15	0.10	0.47	0.22	0.14	0.20	0.27	0.18	0.33	0.23
No training and interest in training																		
No expected impact of training	4.19	2.82	3.22	2.45	2.10	2.88	4.52	3.64	2.57	1.89	2.68	3.36	4.85	3.55	2.46	2.43	2.18	2.96
Bad experience in previous training	0.21	0.21	0.08	0.03	0.06	0.11	0.04	0.03	0.26	0.47	-	0.14	0.18	0.20	0.07	0.08	0.08	0.11
No special reason mentioned	17.08	16.66	14.73	15.64	12.01	15.05	13.67	15.98	14.85	13.18	12.63	14.38	16.24	16.21	16.02	14.54	12.77	14.95
No training and interest in training																		
Lack of financial resources	11.28	8.73	7.55	7.09	3.10	7.26	6.53	4.84	7.34	4.86	2.05	5.64	10.09	7.80	8.65	6.52	3.65	7.00
No possibility provided by employer	1.46	2.03	2.25	1.29	0.94	1.56	1.39	0.57	1.40	0.62	0.60	1.00	1.31	1.72	2.04	1.54	0.91	1.47
Lack of knowledge of Gvt. programs	12.95	9.91	7.95	5.65	2.43	7.37	22.37	19.42	13.81	16.81	11.37	18.16	15.93	12.62	9.07	7.99	3.20	9.07
Lack of preparation for training	1.78	0.61	0.76	0.34	0.12	0.66	2.81	1.68	1.50	1.36	2.30	1.99	1.80	1.13	0.84	0.66	0.31	0.87
No possibility because studying	0.19	0.05	0.06	0.48	0.39	0.25	0.30	-	-	0.05	-	0.10	0.25	0.07	0.08	0.13	0.50	0.22
No need, no time, or other reason	36.61	40.90	39.56	37.98	41.95	39.53	36.08	41.18	43.71	41.89	39.85	40.13	36.12	40.23	41.35	39.49	40.20	39.63

Source: Authors' estimation using 1998 CASEN survey.

APPENDIX 7: TRAINING, FEMALE POPULATION BY AGE GROUP, CHILE 1998 (all entries are percentages)

	Urban Quintiles						Rural Quintiles						National Quintiles					Nat'l Total
	1	2	3	4	5	Total	1	2	3	4	5	Total	1	2	3	4	5	Total
18-34 year old																		
Training received	1.89	3.92	6.46	10.30	15.69	7.90	0.49	0.80	1.78	5.38	9.48	1.69	1.07	2.32	5.37	8.74	17.07	7.11
Training by the firm	4.77	3.62	3.04	3.56	1.85	3.32	4.25	5.13	4.05	5.02	2.88	4.51	4.41	4.23	3.27	3.39	2.21	3.47
Training by Government programs	0.52	1.81	2.38	3.40	4.17	2.52	0.66	0.18	0.72	0.82	4.13	0.68	0.71	1.26	1.62	2.48	5.09	2.28
Training by own resources	0.52	0.38	0.48	0.19	0.79	0.48	0.03	0.49	0.17	0.17	0.21	0.22	0.40	0.41	0.40	0.29	0.71	0.44
Training by other means																		
No training and interest in training																		
No expected impact of training	0.90	1.04	1.76	0.95	0.82	1.09	1.72	1.28	1.98	2.10	0.33	1.61	1.40	1.23	1.52	0.94	0.74	1.16
Bad experience in previous training	0.28	0.12	0.08	0.15	0.02	0.13	0.08	0.02	0.06	0.84	0.34	0.14	0.17	0.13	0.14	0.18	0.02	0.13
No special reason mentioned	13.81	12.83	12.32	10.87	8.42	11.55	11.48	11.46	12.55	11.25	9.58	11.58	13.41	12.60	13.12	10.44	8.52	11.56
No training and interest in training																		
Lack of financial resources	11.14	10.44	11.44	8.20	4.07	8.93	9.86	6.14	11.02	4.96	4.77	8.22	10.71	9.72	10.89	8.72	4.45	8.84
No possibility provided by employer	0.21	0.59	0.56	1.14	0.63	0.63	0.06	0.02	0.74	2.24	–	0.40	0.10	0.36	0.68	1.21	0.60	0.60
Lack of knowledge of Gvt. programs	19.49	15.29	9.91	7.58	2.83	10.72	29.86	27.04	21.08	18.03	13.28	25.42	19.81	19.20	12.90	9.15	3.16	12.61
Lack of preparation for training	0.91	0.60	0.32	0.29	0.02	0.41	2.07	1.74	1.77	0.93	0.14	1.72	1.11	0.73	0.69	0.37	0.06	0.58
No possibility because studying	7.39	8.88	10.68	15.84	23.73	13.60	5.80	7.75	6.18	11.29	9.83	7.20	11.71	7.17	9.14	14.85	20.47	12.78
No need, no time, or other reason	37.69	39.62	39.50	36.36	36.01	37.79	33.12	37.71	37.60	36.08	44.19	36.16	34.36	39.87	39.35	38.54	35.66	37.58
35-64 year old																		
Training received	1.79	3.18	5.49	10.14	14.40	7.36	0.38	0.83	1.57	4.28	4.19	1.51	1.60	2.16	3.89	7.78	14.69	6.61
Training by the firm	3.46	3.29	2.97	2.97	2.58	3.03	3.66	2.97	3.07	3.24	6.91	3.52	3.35	3.39	2.80	3.13	2.90	3.09
Training by Government programs	0.49	1.37	1.66	2.16	5.28	2.31	0.29	0.33	0.58	1.07	2.34	0.60	0.87	0.78	1.25	1.84	4.83	2.09
Training by own resources	0.20	0.46	0.30	0.38	0.33	0.34	0.11	0.05	0.11	0.18	0.25	0.11	0.22	0.35	0.28	0.26	0.41	0.31
Training by other means																		
No training and interest in training																		
No expected impact of training	1.56	1.49	1.50	1.40	1.44	1.47	0.69	1.12	0.78	0.27	0.16	0.74	1.59	1.32	1.15	1.38	1.44	1.38
Bad experience in previous training	0.08	0.10	0.00	0.12	0.02	0.06	0.05	0.09	0.24	0.17	0.02	0.11	0.05	0.12	0.05	0.08	0.05	0.07
No special reason mentioned	18.19	17.68	18.41	19.84	16.72	18.17	17.59	18.75	18.61	16.01	18.53	17.98	17.70	19.42	18.17	18.39	17.28	18.14
No training and interest in training																		
Lack of financial resources	9.74	8.48	7.62	6.00	3.50	6.90	4.92	4.63	5.37	3.87	1.44	4.55	8.57	7.82	8.07	6.39	3.25	6.60
No possibility provided by employer	0.30	0.61	0.49	0.62	0.49	0.50	–	0.00	0.26	0.05	0.02	0.06	0.09	0.29	0.43	0.79	0.54	0.45
Lack of knowledge of Gvt. programs	15.12	12.73	10.53	6.21	3.43	9.27	25.87	19.51	13.32	15.30	12.29	19.25	17.66	14.87	11.12	8.76	3.35	10.57
Lack of preparation for training	2.12	0.96	0.80	0.49	0.37	0.91	3.81	2.29	3.41	1.98	0.58	2.85	2.40	1.11	1.26	0.91	0.41	1.16
No possibility because studying	0.28	0.12	0.45	0.55	0.44	0.38	0.04	0.04	0.04	0.06	0.08	0.05	0.30	0.22	0.38	0.30	0.44	0.33
No need, no time, or other reason.	36.66	42.25	42.12	40.52	43.78	41.17	34.49	41.12	43.70	42.99	43.64	39.93	36.74	40.45	42.90	42.25	41.95	41.01

Source: Authors' estimation using 1998 CASEN survey.

Background Paper 6

PROTECTING THE UNEMPLOYED IN CHILE: FROM STATE ASSISTANCE TO INDIVIDUAL INSURANCE?

Rodrigo Castro-Fernandez and Quentin Wodon[111]
July 28, 2001

Introduction

Many workers are at risk of loosing their job due to involuntary separations from firms. Traditionally, countries have dealt with those risks through a combination of state-funded unemployment assistance (or insurance) and firm-funded severance payments. Chile has both types of programs. The problem with these types of programs is that they have a number of weaknesses. Unemployment assistance is supposed to help workers who loose their job to smooth their consumption spending during an unemployment spell. Yet when the unemployment benefits are large, there may create incentives for the workers to remain unemployed longer than necessary. This "moral hazard" problem may have been at work in the rise of unemployment rates and the length of unemployment in European economies.[112] As for severance payments programs, they also have the potential of creating distortions in the labor market, not only in the relationships between firms and workers, but also between younger and older workers.

The weaknesses of traditional policies for dealing with unemployment shocks has placed the reform of social insurance programs at the center of the public policy debate. Unemployment insurance saving accounts (UISAs) have been proposed as an instrument to protect workers from the loss in earnings associated with unemployment (e.g., Feldstein and Altman, 1998; Orszag and Snower, 1997). The idea is to have all workers (and possibly their employers as well) deposit a share of their monthly incomes into their UISA, with the balance in the account accruing market interest rates. During an unemployment spell, the workers who would be eligible to do so could withdraw funds from their individual account. It is only when there would be no or few funds left in the account that complementary unemployment assistance allowances would be provided. The fact that the accounts are individualized helps to solve the moral hazard problem. Moreover, the fact that the contribution system is mandatory also helps to solve another problem, namely the adverse selection mechanisms through which only some workers might choose to self-insure, or through which the private insurance firms insuring workers would try to hand-pick those workers with the lowest risk of being unemployed. Overall, the objective of UISAs is to set incentives right. Recent proposals for replacing standard forms of unemployment assistance by UISAs are being implemented in several Latin American countries (e.g., Brazil and Colombia).

---

[111] Both authors are with the Latin America region at the World Bank. The paper was funded by the World Bank under the Chile Poverty Assessment and the Regional Study on Public Spending and the Poor in Latin America. Assistance from Corinne Siaens is gratefully acknowledged. The views expressed in the paper are those of the authors and need not represent the views of the World Bank, its Executive Directors, or the countries they represent.
[112] Beyer (2000) shows that the unemployment duration in Chile is lower than that observed in the OECD, and especially in Europe. In Chile, the average unemployment spell was 3 months over 1995-97, while in OECD countries, more than half of unemployed workers have been unemployed for more than a year (OECD, 1999).

In Chile, the need to rethink the unemployment protection system is reinforced by the fact that the current mix of unemployment assistance and severance payments does not work properly. The unemployment assistance benefit provided by the government is of such a small amount (compared with the minimum wage) that it is insufficient for ensuring adequate protection. Probably in part because the benefits are so low, only 8 percent of the unemployed get benefits (another reason for the low take-up is the fact that only formal sector workers with a certain length of job tenure are eligible). Under the severance payments system, unemployed workers receive one month of pay for each working year with the firm, up to a limit of eleven months of pay. The problem is that many of the workers who need support the most when unemployed because they have few savings are also excluded from the severance payments system because they lack adequate tenure (this is the case for youths and women).[113]

This paper explores some of the implications of replacing in Chile the current job security system with UISAs. To motivate the paper, we start in section 2 by presenting evidence as to the role played by unemployment as a determinant of poverty. Section 3 then discusses the weaknesses of the current system of unemployment protection in Chile (severance payments by firms and unemployment assistance by the government). Section 4 outlines the theoretical rationale for UISAs and discusses the main proposal for UISAs made in Chile so far, in July 1999. The section also analyzes the potential impact on the distribution of income of a shift from the current system to the new one. Section 5 concludes.

Impact of Unemployment on Per Capita Income and Thereby Poverty

Unemployment is a key determinant of poverty in Chile. To motivate the rest of the paper, the objective of this section is to support this assertion by measuring the marginal impact of unemployment and other labor market variables on the per capita income of households and thereby on their probability of being poor. To do so, we use data from the nationally representative 1998 CASEN survey and linear regressions as indicated in Box 1. The dependant variable is the logarithm of per capita nominal monetary income (without imputations). Separate regressions are provided for the urban and rural sectors. Apart from a constant, the regressors include: (a) the geographic location of the household according to Chile's regions; (b) household size variables and their square (number of infants, children, and adults), whether the household head is a woman, the age of the head and its square, and whether the head has a spouse or not; (c) characteristics of the household head, including his/her level of education; whether he/she is employed, unemployed and searching for work, or not working; his/her sector of activity; his/her position; whether he/she works in the public sector; the size of the firm in which he/she works; and whether he/she is underemployed; and (d) the same characteristics for the spouse of the household head when there is one.

While the regressions can be used for poverty simulation (the regression results are robust to the choice of the poverty line), we focus below on the percentage increase in per capita income associated with household characteristics rather than on the impact on poverty per se. Although we present below the regression results in separate tables by topic, only one set of regressions

---

[113] Another weakness of Chile's current system is that severance payments can be cumulated with unemployment assistance. Coloma (2000) has proposed to use the severance payments system as a deductible, in such a way that the worker who has lost his/her job would not become eligible to receive unemployment benefits during the period covered by the severance payments.

with all the relevant exogenous variables were estimated in urban and in rural areas separately. We discuss subsequently (a) the impact on per capita income of demographic and household structure variables; (b) the impact of education; and (c) the impact of employment variables, including the fact of being unemployed.

As indicated in Table 1, per capita income decreases, and thereby poverty increases with the number of infants and children in the household (negative coefficient estimates, with the estimates representing the percentage decrease in per capita income associated with the corresponding variable). While these results make sense, it must be mentioned that they may be sensitive to the methodological choices made for poverty measurement.[114] It is also worth noting that after controlling for other household characteristics, female headed households have a level of per capita income 10 percent below that of male headed households (this type of finding can be used to justify the implementation of special programs and provisions for women heads of households; when a women head of household is unemployed, the combination of the loss of earnings due to the absence of a partner and the woman's own loss is large).

Table 1: Marginal Percentage Increase in Per Capita Income Due to Demographic Variables

	Urban	Rural		Urban	Rural
Number of infants	-0.105	-0.143	Number of adult squared	0.005	0.009
Number of infants squared	-0.002	0.036	Female head	-0.108	-0.112
Number of children	-0.186	-0.204	Age of the head	0.005	0.034
Number of child squared	0.018	0.017	Age of the head squared	-0.001	-0.001
Number of adults	-0.047	-0.038	No spouse for the head	0.018	0.004

Note: The excluded reference categories are a household with a male head and a spouse.

Source: World Bank staff using : CASEN 1998. NS means not statistically different from zero at the 10% level. Coefficients underlined are significant at the 10% level. Coefficients not underlined are significant at the 5% level.

The gains from education are substantial. A household with a head having gone to the university (superior level in table 2) has almost twice the expected level of income of an otherwise similar household whose head has no education at all. Completing secondary schooling brings in an 70 percent gain versus no schooling. Completing primary school brings in a 30 to 40 percent gain. There are some differences in the gains for the head in urban and rural areas, probably because that there are more opportunities for qualified workers in urban. The gains from a well educated spouse are also large and similar in urban and rural areas, but they are slightly smaller than for those observed for the head. This is not surprising given that the employment rate for women is

---

[114] By using per capita income as our indicator of well being, we do not allow for economies of scale in the household, nor for differences in needs between household members. By ruling out economies of scale, we consider that the needs of a family of eight are exactly twice the needs of a family of four. With economies of scale, a family of eight having twice the income of a family of four would be judged better off than the family of four. Thus, not allowing for economies of scale over-estimates the negative impact of the number of infants and children on poverty. Moreover, by ruling out differences in needs between household members, we do not consider the fact that larger households with many children may not have the same needs per capita than smaller households because the needs of infants and children tend to be lower than those of adults. In other words, our poverty line measures the cost of basic needs for an "average" individual, but very large families do not consist of average individuals because infants and children are over-represented in them. Not considering differences in needs also leads to an overestimation of the impact of the number of infants and children on poverty. Nevertheless, even if corrections were made to take into account both differences in needs and economies of scale within the household, a larger number of infants and children would still lead to a higher probability of being poor.

smaller than for men for all levels of education, so that women use their education endowment less than men. Another explanation could be that there is gender discrimination in pay, but this would require further analysis to be established.

Table 2: Marginal Percentage Increase in Per Capita Income Due to Education

	Urban	Rural		Urban	Rural
Household head			Household spouse		
Primary partial	0.398	0.256	Primary partial	0.205	0.325
Primary total	0.365	0.302	Primary total	0.198	0.187
Secondary partial	0.701	0.513	Secondary partial	0.351	0.523
Secondary total	0.651	0.612	Secondary total	0.413	0.506
Superior (university)	0.901	0.814	Superior (university)	0.687	0.789

Note: The excluded reference categories are a household head and a spouse with no education at all.

Source: World Bank staff using CASEN 1998. NS means not statistically different from zero at the 10% level. Coefficients underlined are significant at the 10% level. Coefficients not underlined are significant at the 5% level.

Employment patterns for the head and the spouse also have a large impact on per capita income and thereby on poverty. The regression specification enables us to look at various issues (table 3):

- *Unemployment:* Not surprisingly, having a head or a spouse available for work or searching for employment has a large negative impact on per capita income in both urban and rural areas. In most cases, the household suffers from a drop in income of 20 percent as compared to the case when the head or the spouse is fully employed (these are the excluded reference categories in the regression). While these results probably overstate the impact of unemployment on consumption poverty (households may use smoothing strategies in order to cope with unemployment, and the volatility of consumption expenditures is lower than the variability of income because households save and borrow), the fact that unemployment can lead to serious consequences for per capita income is clear. Moreover, households with a head or spouse not working also tend to have lower levels of income.

- *Underemployment:* Having a head or spouse working less than 20 hours per week is not associated with a low level of per capita income, which suggests that many of those who work few hours can afford to. By contrast, underemployment at the level of 21 to 39 hours per week is associated with lower per capita income and higher poverty in the case of households heads, but not for spouses.

- *Sector of activity and position held:* Having a head or a spouse belonging to the construction, commerce, service, mining/manufacturing/electricity, or transport sector brings in additional per capita income as compared to working in agriculture (the excluded reference category). There is a surprisingly large premium for heads working in the public sector (which is worth investigating further; note however that the data may not be representative of the public sector), and a gain in working for a firm with more than 10 employees. Self-employment is associated with a lower income, and being an employer generates a gain in per capita income, while unpaid family work is associated with poverty.

Table 3: Marginal Percentage Increase in Per Capita Income Due to Employment Variables

	Urban	Rural		Urban	Rural
Household head			Household Spouse		
Employment of head			Employment of spouse		
Available (unemployed)	-0.198	-0.029	Available (unemployed)	-0.171	-0.187
Searching (unemployed)	-0.225	-0.725	Searching (unemployed)	-0.154	-0.058
Not working	0.058	-0.517	Not working	-0.210	-0.598
Sector of activity of head			Sector of activity of spouse		
Mining/Manuf./Electricity	0.302	0.388	Mining/Manuf./Electricity	0.042	0.057
Construction	0.528	0.043	Construction	0.617	1.007
Commerce	0.402	0.501	Commerce	0.278	0.175
Transport	0.491	0.684	Transport	0.458	0.256
Services	0.405	0.204	Services	0.391	0.144
Type of employment of head			Type of employment of spouse		
Self-employed	-0.105	-0.540	Self-employed	-0.215	-0.290
Employer	0.515	-0.054	Employer	0.304	-0.145
Unpaid family work	-0.403	-0.274	Unpaid family work	NS	-0.574
Public sector	1.105	2.154	Public sector	NS	NS
Size of firm > 10 people	0.104	0.054	Size of firm > 10 people	0.187	0.214
Underemployment of head			Underemployment of spouse		
Hours of work per week < 20	0.125	0.154	Hours of work per week < 20	-0.028	0.196
20≤ hours per week ≤39	-0.155	-0.256	20≤ hours per week ≤39	0.187	0.485

Note: The excluded reference categories are a household head and a spouse fully employed (at work and not underemployed), and working as wage earners (as opposed to self-employment) in the agriculture sector.

Source: World Bank staff using CASEN 1998. NS means not statistically different from zero at the 10% level. Coefficients underlined are significant at the 10% level. Coefficients not underlined are significant at the 5% level.

Box 1: Determinants of Poverty: Categorical or Linear Regressions?

It has become a standard practice to analyze the determinants of poverty through categorical regressions such as probits and logits. When using such categorical regressions, it is assumed that the actual (per capita) income of households divided by the poverty line, which is denoted by the latent variable y^*_i, is not observed. We act as if we only know whether a household is poor or not, which is denoted by the categorical variable y_i, which takes the value one if the household is poor, and zero if the household is not poor. If we denote by X_i the vector of independent variables (including a constant), the model is :

$$y^*_i = \beta'X_i + \varepsilon_i \text{ with } y_i = 1 \text{ if } y^*_i > 0 \text{ and } y_i = 0 \text{ if } y^*_i \le 0$$

Under the hypothesis of a normal standard distribution for the error term ε_i, this model can be estimated as a probit. The probability for a household with characteristics X_i of being poor is given by $\text{Prob}[y_i^* > 0] = \text{Prob}[\beta'X_i + \varepsilon_i > 0] = \text{Prob}[\varepsilon_i > -\beta'X_i] = F(\beta'X_i)$ where F denotes the cumulated density of the standard normal distribution. The marginal impact of a change in a continuous variable X_A on the probability for household i of being poor, all other variables being held constant, is $f(\beta'X_i)\beta_A$, where f is the standard normal density. A coefficient β_A positive (negative) implies a positive (negative) effect of an increase in the corresponding variable on the probability of being poor. The marginal probability variations can be measured for any particular value of the X_i vector since $f(\beta'X_i)\beta_A$ depends upon X_i. The convention is to compute the marginal effects at the sample mean. If X_A is discrete, its impact on the probability of being poor can be obtained by comparing the cumulated normal densities at various values.

The main problem with such categorical regressions is that the estimates are sensitive to specification errors. With probits, the parameters will be biased if the underlying distribution is not normal. The alternative is to use the full information available for the dependant variable (indicator of well-being), and to run a regression of the log on the indicator (if its distribution is log normal.) Assume that k^*_i is the normalized indicator divided by the poverty line, so that $k^*_i = y^*_i/z$, where z is the poverty line. A unitary value for w^*_i signifies that the household has (per capita) income exactly at the level of the poverty line. Then, we can run the following regression:

$$\text{Log } k^*_i = \gamma'X_i + \varepsilon_i$$

From this regression, the probability of being poor can then be estimated as follows:

$$\text{Prob}[\log k^*_i < 0 \mid X_i] = F[-(\gamma'X_i)/\sigma]$$

where σ is the standard deviation of the error terms and, as before, F is the cumulative density of the standard normal. This does not mean that probit/logit regressions should never be used. Categorical regressions will typically have better predictive power for classifying households as poor or non-poor. However, to conduct inference on the impact of variables on poverty, it is better to use linear regression. Another advantage of linear regressions is that probabilities of being poor can be computed for any poverty line the analyst whishes to use without having to rerun a new regression for every poverty line. This is with region-specific poverty lines valid for urban or rural areas as a whole, or for specific departments within the urban and rural sectors, only the constant and/or the coefficients of the regional dummy variables in the regression will change, and this happens in a straightforward way.

Weaknesses of Chile's Current Protection System for the Unemployed

A key finding from the previous section is that unemployment for a household head or his spouse generates a loss of up to 20 percent in the household's per capita income. The unemployment assistance and severance payments systems that have been in existence for many years in Chile (see Box 2 for an outline of the history of the two types of programs) are supposed to offset such losses, but the systems as they function today do not succeed in protecting the unemployed. In this section, after briefly mentioning some of the limitations of both types of programs in theory, we discuss their main observed weaknesses.

Unemployment assistance. At the theoretical level, the main critique of unemployment assistance programs (and more generally, of traditional social insurance programs which are funded through tax revenues) is that the programs generate moral hazard. As suggested by Gruber (1997), social assistance and insurance programs can have distorting effects on individual and firm decision-making. The workers who are laid off may take longer to find new employment if they benefit from generous allowances which are funded by others. The employers who are laying off workers regularly may do so because they do not bear the cost of their decisions. Empirical studies show that these distortions exist, and that they can be sizeable.

There are at least three ways of reducing the likelihood of moral hazard. One possibility is to make sure that unemployed workers loose part of their earnings when becoming unemployment (i.e., the unemployment allowances are typically set below the wage previously earned by the workers). Another possibility is to have the unemployment benefit depending on the past contributions to the system by the worker. For example, workers who have contributed more to the system may be entitled to better benefits, and employers who have avoided laying off staff may see their contributions to the system reduced. A third possibility is to require the unemployed workers receiving benefits to be actively seeking work and to accept a suitable job when such a job is offered to them. While the first two methods for reducing the likelihood of moral hazard can be implemented either publicly or privately, the third method is easier to implement when a public agency is in charge of monitoring the unemployed.

In Chile, one could argue that the first possibility for reducing the likelihood of moral hazard by limiting benefits has been taken to such an extreme that today, the problem is not moral hazard *per se*, but rather the inadequacy of the benefits and the lack of coverage of the unemployed population. The deterioration over time in coverage and benefits is shown in table 4, which provides for the period 1980-1999 the unemployment rate in percentage of the labor force, the number of workers receiving unemployment assistance, the total outlays for assistance, and the share of GDP that the outlays represent.

- *Low benefits:* As shown in table 4, each unemployed worker received US$300 on average in 1998 for the full length of the unemployment spell. By comparison, in June 1998, the minimum wage was worth US$178 per month, at which time five percent of the labor force was earning the minimum wage.[115] Given that only one in five unemployed workers was

---

[115] According to the Economy and Labor Program (PET), in April 1996, the gap between the legal minimum wage and the minimum monthly wage required to meet basic needs, defined in the government's minimum basket for the satisfaction of basic needs, was 34.2 percent. That is, the legal minimum wage was CH$58,900 while the salary required by a worker to satisfy his or her basic needs was $89,538.

without a job for less than 2 months in the last quarter of 1998 (table 5), it is clear that the unemployment assistance benefits were low. This can be made more apparent by noting that in the 1998 CASEN survey, unemployment assistance benefits represent only 0.3 percent of total income. At the time of the survey, the unemployment assistance benefits were (Chilean Pesos) CH$17,300 for the first three months of unemployment, CH$11,600 for the next three months, and CH$8,700 for the next six months, versus a minimum wage of about CH$80,500. Table 4 clearly shows that there has been over time an erosion in the unemployment assistance benefits per unemployed worker, with the total outlays for unemployment assistance representing only 0.01 percent of GDP in 1998, versus 0.23 percent in 1980.

- *Low coverage:* Figure 1 shows that only 8 percent of all unemployed workers were receiving benefits in 1998. While this is a higher share of unemployed workers than in 1994, it is well below the levels of coverage of the 1980s. The low coverage is due in part to the fact that only formal workers are eligible, and the decrease in coverage may be accounted for in part by the strength of the Chilean economy during most of the late 1980s and the 1990s. Still, it is also possible that the decrease in coverage is due in part to the erosion of the benefits, with some eligible unemployed workers deciding not to apply for benefits because they do not believe that the benefits are worth the effort.

Table 4: Unemployment Rate and Unemployment Assistance Outlays in Chile, 1980-1999

	Unemp. rate (%)	Number receiving assistance	Assistance outlays (US$M)	Outlays as share of GDP (%)		Unemp. rate (%)	Number receiving assistance	Assistance outlays (US$M)	Outlays as share of GDP (%)
1980	10.40	74,000	56,000	0.23	1990	5.70	33,845	6,000	0.02
1981	11.30	75,000	65,000	0.25	1991	5.30	30,246	6,000	0.02
1982	19.60	131,000	103,000	0.46	1992	4.40	23,432	6,000	0.01
1983	14.60	142,000	95,000	0.43	1993	4.50	19,147	4,000	0.01
1984	13.90	98,000	52,000	0.22	1994	5.90	20,572	6,000	0.01
1985	12.10	97,000	47,000	0.19	1995	4.70	21,282	6,756	0.01
1986	8.80	85,000	31,000	0.12	1996	5.40	21,343	7,234	0.01
1987	7.90	66,051	18,000	0.07	1997	5.30	22,586	7,610	0.01
1988	6.30	51,750	14,000	0.06	1998	6.15	27,290	8,014	0.01
1989	5.30	39,245	9,000	0.03					

Source: Compendios Estadísticos, INE (Instituto Nacional de Estadísticas) and Boletines Mensuales , SSS (Superintendencia de Seguridad Social).

Table 5: Unemployment Duration in October-December 1998 by Gender (entries are in percentage)

Duration in months	Males	Females	All	Duration in months	Males	Females	All
Total	64.67	35.33	100.00	9-12	4.45	9.21	6.13
< 2	22.38	13.25	19.15	12-24	6.09	13.08	8.56
2-4	36.95	26.05	33.10	24-48	0.79	1.98	1.21
4-7	14.86	15.76	15.18	48+	0.50	0.27	0.42
7-9	4.61	5.68	4.99	Never work	9.39	14.75	11.28

Source: Instituto Nacional de Estadísticas

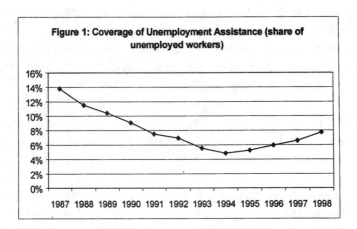

Source: INE

Box 2: Brief Review of the Unemployment Assistance and Severance Payments Systems in Chile

Unemployment assistance (UA). Three periods can be distinguished in the history of the Chilean UA system: until 1974, from 1974 to 1982, and after 1982. The main difference between the system that existed before 1974 and the system in place between 1974 and 1982 consisted in the fact that the pre-1974 system was formed by different programs for different occupational groups (e.g. private employees, workers, bank employees, etc). The reform implemented in 1974 (Law Decree 603) led to some level of harmonization in the eligibility rules and benefits received by workers, and to the extension of the coverage of the system to all formal sector workers, including those from the public sector who were not eligible before. The maximum level of the benefits could not be greater than the 90 percent of four times the minimum wages, nor could it be less than 80 percent of two minimum wages. Differences in funding and benefits persisted between the private and public sectors. Former public employees were entitled to 75 percent of their last wage, while private sector employees were entitled to 75 percent of the average wage earned during the six months before they became unemployed. The assistance granted to former public employees was fully financed by the government, while for former private sector employees, the assistance was financed in through a two percent tax on wages paid by workers (employers also contributed, but to a lower extent). One key requirement for eligibility was to have at least 12 months of tenure/contribution to the system (in continuous or discrete form) in the two years preceding the unemployment spell. After receiving benefits and finding a new job, a worker had to wait for two years before being eligible for assistance again.

The UA system was reformed again in March 1982 (Law Decree 150), in part to tighten the eligibility rules. It was decided that in order to receive assistance, the reason for being unemployed (i.e., fired) was to be beyond the worker's control. The worker also had to be enrolled in the unemployment records of the social security office as well as of the municipality where she or he belonged. It was also decided that a worker would no longer receive assistance if he/she were to refuse a job offer from the Training and Employment National Service, unless the wage offer was less than 50 percent of his/her previous salary. The eligibility conditions regarding the required previous contributions to the system and the length of time necessary before being eligible again for assistance were kept unchanged. The maximum benefits duration was set at 360 days, with decreasing payments over time. The payments were set independently of the pre-unemployment wage. Along with the UA, the workers were made eligible for other benefits such as health and maternal allowances. It was explicitly stated that UA benefits were incompatible with certain other types of incomes (e.g., workfare under the emergency employment schemes used during the 1970s and 1980s). UA benefits were also incompatible with benefits such as allowances received for sick-leave, occupational disease, and work place accidents. One important change brought by the reform relates to the financing of the system. Since 1982, UA benefits are funded by the Unemployment Insurance Fund using general tax revenues, without taxes on private firms and workers.

Severance payments. Since April 1966, the Law No. 16455 deters employers to fire workers without a justified cause. Originally, the system worked as follows. If the layoff was considered unfair by the court, the employee had to be reinstated, or the employer had to provide a severance payment equivalent to one month of pay per year of service, with no maximum threshold. If the layoff was justified, no severance payment had to be provided. In June 1978, the Law Decree No. 2200 reintroduced employee dismissal as a way of putting an end to an employment contract. The employer could layoff a worker without providing a specific reason, provided the worker received a severance payment corresponding to one month of pay for each working year. The rule applied only to workers hired after the Law Decree took effect. The ability of employers to end contracts was confirmed by the Law No. 18018 of August, but the severance payment was reduced to one month per working year with a five-year limit. In December 1990, the Law No. 19010 required again that all layoff be justified, and for all workers hired after August 14, 1981, severance payments were set at one month per working year with a eleven-year limit. The workers hired before that date keep a severance payment with no maximum year limit.

Severance Payments. Severance payment systems have a number of virtues. They strengthen the workers' bargaining position and create an income source for unemployed workers without depressing labor supply. They help older workers who may loose some of their investment in human capital when they are laid off because they had specialized in a given area and they have more difficulty in acquiring new skills. Severance payments also force firms with higher layoff rates to pay a higher part of the cost of protecting the workers who are laid off, thereby reducing the cross subsidies which are implicit in traditional unemployment assistance and insurance mechanisms. In some extreme cases, the firm and the worker may agree to a temporary separation funded by a partial severance payment allowance, with the promise that the worker will be hired again when the firm's situation becomes healthier. This may lower the temporary unemployment that could arise when the firm faces short-term difficult market conditions.

At the same time, despite these interesting features, severance payment systems also have a number of weaknesses. They may discourage firms from investing in their workers' human capital since the programs tend to lead to shorter and less formal contracts (this hypothesis, however, would have to be validated empirically, and other factors may help provide incentives for firms to invest in human capital). Severance payments may also lead firms to reduce wage increases. The employment relationship between the firm and the worker may be distorted because older workers have perverse incentives to induce their layoff and firms have perverse incentives to promote the worker's resignation instead. Severance payments may reduce labor mobility, with older workers not seeking otherwise better jobs out of the fear of losing their accumulated job tenure. The labor market becomes more rigid, so that it cannot adapt well to during the business cycle, since it becomes more difficult for the firms to adjust their payroll when the state of the economy require some flexibility. While some severance payment systems were established in part to provide mandatory savings for retirement, this function is progressively loosing its importance because public and private social security systems are being developed. There is also a risk for workers in that it remains uncertain whether the worker will indeed receive severance payments. The reason leading to a worker's dismissal may also lead to a denial of benefits. Alternatively, if the firm is in a poor economic situation, the worker may have to accept a severance payment of lower value than what is stipulated in the law. The firm's liquidity problem become critical under weak business conditions, which may lead to the dismissal of workers with less tenure even though these workers may be more productive. The workers who have not completed the required number of years in the firm when they are laid off are not eligible for severance payment, so that the system does not provide protection for all.

While Chile's unemployment assistance system has low coverage and low benefits, the problem with severance payments is rather that the coverage and the benefits tend to differ a lot between workers.

- *Uneven coverage:* Mizala et al. (1993) estimated that among formal sector workers, 68 percent of those who might encounter an unemployment spell should be well covered by the severance payments system, in that they would receive an allowance equal to at least three months of pay. The workers who are not well covered tend to be young workers (27 percent are between 15 and 24 year of age, and 41 percent are between 25 and 34 year of age; these two groups represent respectively 16 percent and 35 percent of all formal workers). These groups are not entitled to large severance payments because they lack employment tenure since they are at the beginning their professional life.

- *Uneven benefits:* The disparities which are observed in terms of coverage are also observed in terms of benefits since the benefits are proportional to the tenure of the employee. As shown in table on average a worker that is laid off would have 6.2 months of severance payments. Since the average length of unemployment is about 3 months, the average worker benefits from a small rent and does not necessarily face hardship during an unemployment spell. However, in the case of young workers, the average number of years worked does not provide for a generous severance package. Some of the workers above 35 year of age also lack good severance packages because they have recently changed job or because they found their job after an unemployment spell. Since female workers are over-represented in this last group, they would tend to gain from a reform of the system.

Table 6 : Tenure at the Current Job by Gender and Age Group

Gender	15-24	25-34	35-44	45-54	55-64	65+	Total
Males	1.7	3.8	7.5	11.7	14.5	15.5	6.7
Females	1.7	3.7	5.8	11.1	13.9	9.1	5.0
Total	1.7	3.8	7.0	11.6	14.4	14.9	6.2

Source: Mizala et al. (1993).

The Rationale for Unemployment Insurance Savings Account

Problems with Private Insurance Markets. It was mentioned earlier that a number of mechanisms can be used to reduce the moral hazard problems faced by traditional unemployment insurance systems. If policy makers want to go beyond these mechanisms for reducing moral hazard, a more radical idea is to promote a shift to private insurance markets for the consumption smoothing of unemployed workers. The suggestion is that workers could pay insurance premiums in order to be entitled to unemployment benefits when unemployed. The workers would select their insurer privately, and the insurance market would ensure an appropriate costing of the insurance premiums. There are, however, three problems with this solution: the potential for adverse selection on the part of the worker and the insurer, the inability for private insurers to diversify risk, and the inability for the government to redistribute income with equity objectives in mind.

- *Adverse selection:* There are two types of adverse selection, on the part of workers and insurers.
- *Workers:* First, there is a possibility that only those workers who are likely to loose their job will want to insure. This implies that the premium that these workers will have to pay will be larger than what they would have had to contribute under a mandatory contribution system, so that the mechanisms of solidarity between workers will be reduced. This is why in most state-sponsored insurance programs, the participation of all workers is required. The compulsory participation prevents the opting out of the insurance coverage by the individuals who believe themselves to be low risk. A comparable but not identical outcome could be achieved with private sector provision by requiring that all labor market participants to carry at least some minimum level of insurance.
- *Insurers:* Second, on the part of the insurer, there is an incentive to insure only those workers who are less likely to be unemployed. This may lead to "cream-skimming" and to the rejection from the insurance system of those workers who need insurance the most. Also, given the fact that there is asymmetric information between the worker and the insurer (the worker knows better what his/her probability of becoming unemployed is), some workers who would qualify for participating in the system could be excluded, while others who would

not qualify if the insurer had perfect information could be able to participate. This could lead to a sub-optimal pricing structure for the premiums, and the premiums could be higher because the insurer would face a higher risk due to the imperfect information at its disposal. Finally, in order to reduce their risk exposure on an individual basis, private companies may be unwilling to offer insurance against the risk of unemployment except under very narrowly specified circumstances.

- *Systematic risk:* Due to the business cycle, the risk of unemployment is positively correlated across members of the labor force so that pooling many workers within the same insurance system need not lead to a substantial reduction in the aggregate risk faced by the insurer. To say this differently, unemployment is a largely non-diversifiable risk, except over time. This may lead to a failure of private insurance markets to provide adequate coverage and benefits during recessions. Although fully developed private insurance markets may not exist for the above reasons, it would be a mistake to assume that there are no private market responses at all to respond to the demand for insurance among workers. Firms may be able to insure their employees to some degree, thereby shifting the risk from the labor market to the capital market, where it can be handled more readily via portfolio diversification by shareholders. This is the central insight of implicit contract theory, whereby in exchange for offering relatively stable employment, the firm can afford to pay a lower wage.[116] Yet even successful firms may not be able to fully protect their workers during a recession. Because of their softer budget constraint (and the pressure of public opinion to provide public support when needed), publicly funded insurance mechanisms may be more apt to diversify the risks across time than both insurance companies and employers.

The upshot of the above discussion is that public interventions in markets characterized by moral hazard, adverse selection, and systematic risk can have positive impacts on social welfare. Whether a specific intervention will be beneficial depends on the intervention's design (Green and Riddell, 1993). That is, when policy makers consider the design of social insurance programs, they must weight various factors. For example, while increasing program generosity may lead to increased distortions in behavior, it may also lead to better consumption smoothing, and the gains from consumption smoothing must be weighted carefully against the potential for behavioral distortions in assessing the optimal benefits.

Design of Unemployment Insurance Savings Accounts. In the specific case of a system of unemployment insurance saving accounts (UISA), workers have individualized accounts to which they contribute in periods of employment and from which they draw funds when they are unemployed. Interest payments are credited or debited to their account, depending on its balance (see, for example, the simulations done by Feldstein and Altman, 1998, for the US economy.) A typical design for UISAs should specify the rate of contribution to the system, the limits and rules for drawing funds, the limits on total liability, and the interest rate applied to balances. The main advantage of UISA's is that by internalizing the cost of remaining unemployed (or becoming unemployed), employment incentives are improved. This is particularly true for workers with lower unemployment risk, who are more likely to retire with positive balances in

---

[116] If employees are more risk averse that the owners of firms, which is likely given that human capital risks are difficult to diversify, both the employee and the firm can benefit from such an arrangement. In effect, the employment contract, whether explicit or implicit, involves two transactions: a transaction for the labor services provided by the employee, and an employment insurance provided by the employer. In general, the employer will be better able to deal with the adverse selection and moral hazard problems than a private insurance company.

their UISAs if they manage to avoid unemployment spells. The more likely it is that the system will result in positive final balances, the better the incentives are for keeping jobs and searching for employment opportunities while unemployed. This is because under the UISA system, the incentive to find a new job and to shorten the unemployment spell as much as possible is the fact that any withdrawal decreases the individual's net worth (assets and income), something which does not happen with the more traditional unemployment insurance schemes.[117]

Feldstein and Altman (1998) and Orszag and Snower (1997) have discussed whether UISAs would be appropriate for the US economy. In the proposal made by Feldstein and Altman (1998), workers would contribute roughly 4 percent of their wages to their UISA (there could be some variation in the contribution rate depending on the wage level of the individual), and they would be allowed to withdraw funds under rules yielding benefits similar to those provided by the system of unemployment insurance currently in place (i.e., the wage replacement ratio would be at about 50 percent, with a time limit of six months). Market-based interest rates would be applied to the balance in the accounts, and negative balances would be allowed (i.e., if the account is exhausted, the government lends money to the account). Those workers reaching retirement with a negative balances would be forgiven. Positive UISA balances could be converted into retirement income or bequeathed if the individual dies before retirement age.

The key empirical question is whether UISA accounts based on a moderate savings rate can finance a significant share of unemployment payments, or whether the concentration of unemployment among a relatively small number of individuals would force these workers to rely on government benefits with the same adverse effects that characterize the more traditional unemployment insurance. Feldstein and Altman (1998) used the Panel Study of Income Dynamics (PSID) surveys to simulate a UISA system over a 25 year historic period (1967-1992). Their analysis indicates that even among the individuals who experience unemployment, most would have positive account balances at the end of their unemployment spell. Although about half of the benefit dollars would go to individuals whose account balance is negative at the end of their working life, less than one third of the benefits would go to individuals who also have negative account balances when unemployed. The cost to taxpayers of forgiving the negative balances was estimated to be less than half the cost of the current system. Since the simulations took as given the behavior of workers under the current system, the magnitude of the negative balances may be overestimated, so that the savings could be even larger for tax payers.

Unemployment Insurance Savings Accounts in Chile

The Law Adopted by Congress in April 2001. This section reviews the characteristics of the "PROYECTO DE LEY QUE ESTABLECE UN SEGURO DE DESEMPLEO - LEY NUM. 19.728", (hereafter denoted as the law), an unemployed-worker-job-security-program which is similar to an unemployment insurance savings account. The law was approved by the Chilean Congress in April 2001.

- *Funding:* The UISAs are financed with contributions from workers (0.6 percent of the gross wage) and employers (2.4 percent of the gross wage). This is specified in Article 5. For collection and tax purposes, the contributions are treated as social security payments, and

---

[117] At the extreme, when the rate of contribution to the individual account nears zero, we have the traditional unemployment insurance system. As the rate of contribution to the individual account increases, and the likelihood of negative balances due to unemployment falls, the system becomes closer to self-insurance for retirement.

they are applied to the gross wage up to a maximum of 90 UF[118] (about CH\$1,400,000 or US\$2,500) per month. Workers with more than one job pay the tax for each wage they earn and the various employers pay as well for each contract that a worker may have with them. The maximum period for making payments into the system is 11 years. Out of the 2.4 percent of the gross wage contributed by the employer, 1.6 percent goes to the UISA and 0.8 percent is pooled into a unemployment assistance fund which intervenes when the worker fulfills various requirements (this is explained below). The unemployment assistance fund is complemented by government transfer of about US\$ 10.5 million per year (at the current exchange rate of CP\$600/US\$). The government transfer is funded from general tax revenues.

- *Coverage:* To be eligible for benefits when unemployed, the workers must have lost their job due to one of the reasons specified in the law, with reference to the labor code.[119] Essentially, the worker may not have been at fault in order to receive the benefits. Each worker cannot receive benefits more than twice within a period of 5 years. Workers must also have made a minimum of twelve monthly contributions to the system in order to be eligible for benefits (these contributions do not need to have been made continuously).

- *Withdrawals from the UISA when unemployed:* When unemployed, the workers may withdraw funds from their UISA. If the worker loses his job due to one of the reasons specified in the law, he/she is entitled to a number of withdrawals from his/her account corresponding to the number of years of contribution, with a maximum of five withdrawals. For workers entitled to more that one withdrawal, the amount of the first withdrawal is obtained by dividing the balance available in the UISA by a factor that varies depending on the number of withdrawals the worker is entitled to (the factor is equal to 1.9 for two withdrawals, 2.7 for three, 3.4 for four and 4.0 for five). The amounts for the remaining withdrawals are computed in proportion to the amount of the first withdrawal (90% for the second withdrawal, 80% for the third, and 70% for the fourth). The fifth and last withdrawal corresponds to whatever is left in the account. Depending on the reason for the lay-off, the worker may or may not receive severance pay, and this will affect the withdrawals allowed from the account. Once the worker gets a new job, he/she is entitled to one last withdrawal, but he/she may also decide to keep the corresponding amount in his/her account.[120]

- *Other withdrawals, retirement and death:* If the account holder dies, the balance of the account passes to whomever the worker has designated for this purpose under his contract with the entity managing his/her account. If no one has been designated by the worker, the balance is allocated according to Article 60, N° 2 of the Labor Code. If the holder retires, he can freely dispose of the funds.

- *Withdrawals from the public fund:.* The employer and Government contributions, as specified in Article 5, are pooled in a fund which can be used by those 1) who have made at least 12 monthly contributions to their account, 2) who have been laid off due to one of the reasons mentioned in Article 159, N° 6 or Article 161 of the Labor Code, and 3) whose

---

[118] *Unidad de Fomento,* a standard measure of real living costs.

[119] Workers must have lost their job due to one of the reasons mentioned in the Labor Code in Articles 159, 160, 161 171 (N°1), with the exception of the reasons specified in Article 159, N°4 and N°5.

[120] Under a previous version of the law (known as PROTRAC), a potentially serious problem was the fact that if a worker changed job, he had the possibility of withdrawing the full balance of the funds from the UISA corresponding to his previous job. Of course, the worker could in principle keep the fund in his UISA, but he has no incentive to do so. This is not feasible anymore under the new law, since the worker may only retrieve an amount corresponding to one more month of benefits once he/she finds a new job.

account balance is not sufficient to obtain a predetermined monthly payment stipulated by the law. The predetermined monthly payment is a function the wage earned during the last 12 months of work and is described in Article 25. There are ceilings and floors to the assistance provided, so that the better off do not receive large sums of the money, and those who had low wages do not fall below a subsistence level.

- *Administration:* The collection and payment business is awarded by a public auction to one entity that can be national or international, but must be incorporated in Chile. This entity will run both the unemployment individual accounts and the public assistance fund. The entity is supervised by the Superintendence of Pension Funds (SAFP). The contract is awarded taking into account the proposed fee structure, adjustments, and technical conditions.

Limits of the New System. The law has a number of interesting features in terms of providing adequate incentives for workers. At the same time, it has weaknesses as well, which may not be easy to avoid.

- *Forced savings and lack of flexibility to account for the heterogeneity among workers:* Some workers have stronger short term liquidity constraints and/or higher inter-temporal discount rates than other workers. In a private insurance market, the workers would be free to save as they wish in order to smooth their consumption over time. Those workers who would not save would do so either because: they do not value the implicit insurance that the savings provide, or because they face liquidity constraints and high discount rates. When the same savings rate is imposed on all workers, the system is in theory (an in the absence of externalities) inferior to a private unemployment insurance scheme whereby all workers optimize their consumption pattern over time. However, one of the main reasons to justify a compulsory saving scheme is to avoid externalities such as the fact that workers without savings impose a tax on their relatives and society as a whole. Still, poor workers tend to typically have larger liquidity constraints and higher inter-temporal discount rates, so that there remains a question as to whether the same savings pattern for all is optimal or not.

- *Long-tern unemployment for comparatively poorer workers:* The compulsory saving and unemployment assistance system specified by *the* law does not guarantee the financing of a specific unemployment spell. While it is implicitly recognized that it could be necessary to finance unemployment spells of 5 months or more, the only way to do this is to combine large balances in the UISAs and possibly severance payments. Yet the workers who tend to be poorer and who need assistance the most also tend to have shorter job tenures, so that they will not be well protected under the revised system. Comparatively poorer worker with longer unemployment spells may also lack human capital, in which case the balances accumulated in their UISAs will be even lower simply because their expected wage will also be lower. There may be a need to reinforce the unemployment assistance benefits for these workers, but this may not be feasible if they lack a voice in the debate.[121]

- *Bargaining power and severance payments:* It is not clear what the effect of UISAs could be on the workers' bargaining power. On one hand, the workers would have available funds to protect them from unemployment, and this could improve their bargaining power. On the other hand, if the contribution of firms to the UISA was funded through a reduction in severance payments, the marginal cost of firing workers for the firms would be reduced.

---

[121] Orszag and Snower (1997) explore the possibility by the government to implement balanced-budget redistribution among the unemployment saving accounts by taxing the contributions of the rich and subsidizing those of the poor.

- *Political economy:* Because the unemployment insurance savings account would be compulsory, the cost of the new system(at 2 to 3 percent of GDP) would appear to be much higher than the cost of the current unemployment assistance system (at 0.01 percent of GDP). Although the balances in the UISAs belong to the workers, the system may be perceived as an additional tax, and this may generate opposition. At the administrative level, the logistics involved in a UISA system would be more complex, and therefore more costly, than those involved in the current assistance system.

Distributional Impact. In this last sub-section, our objective is to assess the distributional impact of shifting from Chile's current system of unemployment assistance to a system of UISAs. To do so, we use the method described in Box 3. For each program, the method will yield two key parameters: the GIE (Gini income elasticity) for the benefits of the program, and the GIE for the taxes through which the program is funded. The interpretation of the GIE in terms of the redistributive impact of a policy differs for benefits and taxes.

- *Interpretation of a GIE for a program benefit:* If the GIE of a program (unemployment assistance or UISAs) is equal to one, a marginal increase in the benefits will not affect the Gini coefficient in after-tax after-benefit per capita income, and thereby the effect on inequality can be considered as neutral (no change). If the GIE is less (greater) than one, then an increase in program benefits will decrease (increase) the Gini of income, and thereby increase (decrease) inequality. The smaller the GIE, the larger the redistributive impact of the program and the gains in inequality.

- *Interpretation of a GIE for a tax:* The rules for taxes are reversed as compared to the rules for programs. If the GIE is less (greater) than one, then an increase in tax revenues will increase (decrease) the Gini of income, and thereby decrease (increase) inequality. The larger the GIE, the larger the redistributive impact of the tax and the gains in inequality. If the GIE of a tax is equal to one, a marginal increase in the tax will not affect the Gini coefficient in after-tax after-benefit per capita income, and thereby the effect on inequality can be considered as neutral (no change).

- *Combining the two GIEs:* Since the GIE is estimated for a dollar spent on the program, or a dollar raised in taxes, we can compare programs and taxes which are of different scale in terms of outlays or revenues. This means that we can compare the GIEs of unemployment assistance and of UISAs, as well as the GIEs of the taxes raised to fund the two programs, in order to find the overall impact on social welfare of shifting at the margin from one type of protection of the unemployed to the other.

Two parameters must be estimated to assess the redistributive impact of the current system: the GIE for unemployment assistance, and the GIE for the general tax revenues used to fund the benefits.

- *GIE for the current system of unemployment assistance:* This elasticity was estimated using data from the 1998 nationally representative CASEN survey. It is equal to –0.84, which is highly redistributive. This is not surprising since the take-up of the program is higher among those who have few other resources to cope with the loss of earnings generated by unemployment.

- *GIE for the general tax revenues used to fund the current system:* Using information from Engel et al. (1998), we estimated that the GIE for general tax revenues was 0.90 in 1996 (the current tax system is regressive since the elasticity is smaller than one). Although the income tax is progressive (i.e., the rich pay a higher share of their income in tax, with a GIE of 1.73), the VAT is regressive, with an elasticity of 0.79, and other taxes are also regressive, with a GIE of 0.90. The weighted combination of the elasticities for the three types of taxes yields an overall GIE for tax revenues of 0.90.

- _Combining both estimates:_ As explained in Box 3, all what one has to do to assess the impact of the current system per dollar spent on benefits (and raised in taxes) is to sum the impacts from the benefits and the taxes, which each impact being to the relevant elasticity minus one. For the current system, this yields a marginal impact on inequality proportional to (-0.84-1)-(0.90-1) = -1.74.

Box 3: Analyzing the Impact of the Reform of Unemployment Benefits on Inequality

To analyze the distributional impact of the transition from unemployment assistance to unemployment insurance savings accounts in Chile, we use a source decomposition of the Gini index of inequality proposed by Lerman and Yitzhaki (1985, 1994). Denote total pre-tax per capita income by y, the cumulative distribution function for total per capita income by F(y), and the mean total per capita income across all households by μ_y. The Gini index of inequality can be decomposed as follows:

$$G_y = 2 \, cov \, [y, \, F(y)]/\mu_y \;\; = \;\; \Sigma_i \, S_i R_i G_i$$

where G_y is the Gini index for total income, G_i is the Gini index for income y_i from source i, $S_i = \mu_i/\mu_y$ is the share of total income obtained from source i, and R_i is the Gini correlation between income from source i and total income. The Gini correlation is defined as $R_i = cov \, [y_i, \, F(y)] \, / \, cov[(y_i, \, F(y_i)]$, where $F(y_i)$ is the cumulative distribution function of per capita income from source i. The Gini correlation R_i can take values between -1 and 1. Income from sources such as income from capital which tend to be strongly and positively correlated with total income will have large positive Gini correlations. Income from sources such as unemployment benefits tend to have smaller, and possibly negative Gini correlations. The overall (absolute) contribution of a source of income i to the inequality in total per capita income is thus $S_i R_i G_i$. The above source decomposition provides a simple way to assess the impact on the inequality in total income of a marginal percentage change equal for all households in the income from a particular source. As proven by Stark et al. (1986), the impact of increasing for all households the income from source i in such a way that y_i is multiplied by $(1 + e_i)$ where e_i tends to zero, is:

$$\frac{\partial G_y}{\partial e_i} = S_i (R_i G_i - G_y)$$

This equation can be rewritten to show that the percentage change in inequality due to a marginal percentage change in the income from source i is equal to that source's contribution to the Gini minus its contribution to total income. In other words, at the marginal level, what matters for evaluating the redistributive impact of income sources is not their Gini, but rather the product $R_i G_i$ which is called the pseudo Gini. Alternatively, denoting by $\eta_i = R_i G_i/G_y$ the so-called Gini elasticity of income for source i, the marginal impact of a percentage change in income from source i identical for all households on the Gini for total income in percentage terms can be expressed as:

$$\frac{\partial G_y \, / \, \partial e_i}{G_y} = \frac{S_i R_i G_i}{G_y} - S_i = S_i (\eta_i - 1)$$

Thus a percentage increase in the income from a source with a Gini elasticity η_i smaller (larger) than one will decrease (increase) the inequality in per capita income. The lower the Gini elasticity, the larger the redistributive impact. When conducting policy simulations for the marginal impact on inequality of changes in various income sources, it is easiest to consider the impact on the Gini per dollar or peso spent (or taxed), because that marginal impact is directly proportional to (η_i-1). All what one has to do is to sum the impacts from the various sources one by one, with each impact being equal to the relevant elasticity minus one. For example, in the case study analyzed in the main text, we have two elasticities for the current system: (a) the GIE for the current system of unemployment assistance is –0.84; and (b) the GIE for the general tax revenues used to fund the current system: 0.90 As a result, the marginal impact on inequality of the current system is (-0.84-1)-(0.90-1)=-1.74. Under the new system, the GIE for the UISA-based assistance is –0.46 and the GIE for tax revenues on formal sector wages is 1.00, so that the total impact at the margin is –1.46. Under the assumptions made for the estimates, the new system would be less redistributive than the current system, but it would still be highly redistributive.

There are also two parameters which must be estimated empirically to assess the redistributive impact of the new system: the GIE for the publicly funded unemployment allowance received by workers once they have depleted or exhausted their UISA, and the GIE for the tax on formal sector wages used to fund not only the UISA, but also the unemployment assistance benefits once the UISA has been used.

- *GIE for the UISA-based system of unemployment assistance:* To estimate this parameter adequately, we would need to forecast the probability of being unemployed for formal sector workers, their expected balance in the USIA when becoming unemployed, and their expected public unemployment assistance once the unemployed workers are eligible. This is a difficult task. As a proxy, we can use a GIE representing the position in the income distribution of those unemployed workers whom belonged to the formal sector before becoming unemployed. While the previous sector of employment of the unemployed is not given in the 1998 CASEN, it is part of the information provided in the 1997 "Encuesta Nacional de Empleo". Using this survey, we found a GIE of –0.46. Note that the simplification used to compute the GIE assumes that all the workers who are unemployed and who belonged to the formal sector have the same expected benefit from unemployment assistance after they deplete or exhaust the funds available in their UISA. While the unemployment assistance provided under the USIA system would still be redistributive (the elasticity is less than one), it would be less redistributive than the current system per dollar spent, essentially because in the new system, we implicitly assume that the take-up would not be limited to the poorest.

- *GIE for the current system of unemployment assistance:* Since the taxes that would fund the UISA system are proportional to the wages of formal sector workers, the elasticity for the taxes is equal to the elasticity for the source of income represented by these wages. It turns out that the elasticity is equal to one, so that on the taxation side, the taxes for the USIA have no impact on inequality.

- *Combining both estimates:* Given that under the new system, the GIE for the UISA-based assistance would be –0.46 and the GIE for tax revenues on formal sector wages would be 1.00, the total impact at the margin is proportional to –1.46. Under the simple assumptions made for the estimates, the new system would be less redistributive than the current system, but it would still be highly redistributive.

Conclusion

Unemployment is one of the key determinants of poverty in Chile. When a household the head or its spouse is unemployed, the per capita income of the household is reduced by up to 20 percent (up to 40 percent when both the head and the spouse are unemployed). The policy makers involved in the design of unemployment protection systems must deal with a number of trade-offs. At one extreme, when no unemployment assistance or insurance is provided, the unemployed workers must rely on self-insurance through precautionary savings or informal lending channels, such as loans or gifts from relative or friends, in order to smooth their consumption. At the other extreme, one can fund generous government-sponsored unemployment assistance systems, where a worker's contribution is independent of the benefits received. While the proposals for reform discussed in the literature fall somewhere in between, depending on the specific parameters chosen, moving from a traditional unemployment assistance and severance payments system to UISAs does change substantially the incentives faced by workers.

In Chile, under the current system, the workers receive (rather small) unemployment benefits upon losing their jobs, and potentially larger severance payments. They lose the unemployment benefits when they find a new job, but they keep the severance payments. The unemployment benefits are financed through general tax revenues, while the severance payments are financed by firms. The main problem with the unemployment assistance system is less related to the potential moral hazard that the system might create than to the low value of the unemployment benefits and the low coverage of the program among the unemployed. The main problem with the severance payments system is the fact that the coverage and benefits are uneven, to the detriment of poorer and younger worker as well as women.

Under the UISA system, the workers would receive no "reward" upon losing their jobs, and they would suffer no "penalty" for finding jobs quickly. Each employed worker would make a fixed mandatory minimum contribution to his/her UISA each month, and additional voluntary contributions above the mandatory minimum levels would be permitted. Upon becoming unemployed, an individual worker would be entitled to withdraw a fixed maximum amount per month from his or her UISA (smaller withdrawals would also be permitted). When the individual's UISA balance falls to zero, or is seriously depleted, he/she would be entitled to unemployment assistance. The unemployment assistance would be financed through a tax levied on all wage earners. When workers would retire with a positive balance in their UISA, they would be able to use the balances to top their pensions. Overall, the workers themselves would play a much larger role in the financing their own support during periods of unemployment (Guasch, 2000).

The main advantage of UISAs is that they tend to set the incentives right, without creating distortions in the behavior of employers and firms. That is, the funds taken by an unemployed individual from his/her UISA directly reduces the individual's personal wealth by an equal amount, so that individuals fully internalize the cost of unemployment compensation. UISA systems are not without risks, and special interventions are likely to be needed to protect those workers who tend to be younger, poorer, and less well educated. Although the redistributive impact of a UISA-based system would probably be smaller than the redistributive impact of Chile's current unemployment assistance system, the complementary unemployment assistance component of system would still be highly redistributive.

REFERENCES

Andolfatto, D., and P. Gomme. 1996. "Unemployment Insurance and Labor Market Activity in Canada." *Carnegie-Rochester Conference Series on Public Policy*. 44.

Alvarez, F., and M. Veracierto. 1998. "Search, Self-Insurance and Job-Security Provisions." Department of Economics, University of Chicago.

Anderson, P.M. and B.D. Meyer. 1993. "Unemployment Insurance in the United States: Layoff Incentives and Cross-Subsidies". *Journal of Labor Economics*. 11.

Beyer, H. 2000. "Seguro de Desempleo: Elementos para la Discusión." Puntos de Referencia 222. Centro de Estudios Públicos.

Brown, E., and H. Kaufold. 1988. "Human Capital Accumulation and the Optimal Level of Unemployment Insurance Provision". *Journal of Labor Economics*. 6.

Coloma, F. 1993. "Seguro de Desempleo: Teoria, Evidencia y una Propuesta." Documento de Trabajo, Universidad Católica.

Coloma, F. 2000. "Seguro de Desempleo: Análisis y Propuesta." Puntos de Referencia 221. Centro de Estudios Públicos.

Cortazar, R. , C. Echeverria, and P. Gonzalez. 1995. "Hacia un Nuevo Diseño de Sistemas de Protección de Cesantes." Colección Estudios CIEPLAN No. 40.

Costain, J. S. 1999. "Unemployment Insurance with Endogenous Search Intensity and Precautionary Saving." Working Paper No. 43. Department of Economics, Universitat Pompeu Fabra.

Chiu, W. H., and E. Karni. 1998. "Endogenous Adverse Selection and Unemployment Insurance." *Journal of Political Economy* 106.

Davidson, C., and S. A. Woodbury. 1997. "Optimal Unemployment Insurance." Journal of Public Economics 64.

Feldstein, M., and D. Altman. 1998. "Unemployment Insurance Savings Accounts". *NBER Working Paper* 6860.

Fredriksson, P., and B. Holmlund. 1998. "Optimal Unemployment Insurance in Search Equilibrium." Department of Economics. Uppsala University.

Green, D.A. and W.C. Riddell. 1993. "The Economic Effects of Unemployment Insurance in Canada: An Empirical Analysis of Unemployment Insurance Disentitlement." *Journal of Labor Economics* 11.

Gruber, J. 1997. "The Consumption Smoothing Benefits of Unemployment Insurance." *American Economic Review* 87.

Guasch, J. 2000. "An Alternative to Traditional Unemployment Insurance Programs: A Liquidity-Based Approach Against the Risk of Earning Losses." World Bank.

Hansen, G. D., and A. Imrohoroglu. 1992. "The Role of Unemployment Insurance in an Economy with Liquidity Constraints and Moral Hazard." *Journal of Political Economy.* 100.

Hausmann, R., and H. Reisen. 1996. "Securing Stability and Growth in Latin America: Policy Issues and Prospects for Shock-Prone Economies." OECD.

Hopenhayn, H. A., and J. P. Nicolini. 1997. "Optimal Unemployment Insurance." *Journal of Political Economy* 105.

Hopenhayn, H. A., and J. P. Nicolini. 1999. "Optimal Unemployment Insurance and Employment History." Unpublished manuscript.

Hopenhayn, H. A. 2000. "Unemployment Insurance Savings Accounts: Optimal?" University of Rochester and Universidad Torcuato Di Tella.

Meyer, B. D. 1990. "Unemployment Insurance and Unemployment Spells." *Econometrica* 58.

Mizala, A., and P. Romaguera. 1993. "Seguro de Desempleo y Flexibilidad del Mercado Laboral: Evaluación de la Experiencia Chilena y Análisis de Sistemas Alternativos." Informe Fondecyt.

Mizala, A, P. Romaguera, and Henriquez. 1998 "Oferta Laboral y Seguro de Desempleo: Estimaciones para la Economía Chilena." Serie Economía No. 28. Universidad de Chile: Centro de Economía Aplicada, Departamento de Ingeniería Industrial.

Orszag, J., and D. Snower. 1997. "From Unemployment Benefits to Unemployment Accounts." Birkbech College, London.

Pallage, S., and C. Zimmermann. 1997. "Moral Hazard and Optimal Unemployment Insurance in an Economy with Heterogeneous Skills." Working Paper No. 54. Montreal: CREFE, Universite du Quebec.

Paredes, R. 2000. "Reflexiones en torno al Proyecto de Seguro de Desempleo." Universidad de Chile: Departamento de Economía.

Usami, Y. 1983. "Payroll-Tax Financed Unemployment Insurance with Human Capital." Ph.D. dissertation. MIT.

Valdivia, V. 1996. "Policy Evaluation in Heterogeneous Agent Economies: The Welfare Impact of Unemployment Insurance." PhD Thesis. Northwestern University: Department of Economics.

Wang, C., and S. Williamson. 1996. "Unemployment Insurance with Moral Hazard in a Dynamic Economy." Carnegie-Rochester Conference Series on Public Policy 44.

Zhang, G-J. 1996. "Unemployment Insurance Analysis in a Search Economy." Canada. University of Guelph: Department of Economics.

Background Paper 7

INDIGENOUS PEOPLES IN CHILE: CURRENT SITUATION AND POLICY ISSUES
Estanislao Gacitúa-Marió
August 2000

This report is based on the findings of a Bank mission which visited Chile in December 1999 and January 2000. The mission met with Mr. Rodrigo Gonzalez, National Director CONADI; Luis Henrriquez, Miguel Díaz, Jorge Sanderson, and Domingo Colicoi, CONADI (National); Antonio Mamani, Regional Director, CONADI (I Region); Veronica Silva, Head Social Division, MIDEPLAN; Ana Quintana, Social Division, MIDEPLAN; Carlos Furche, Director ODEPA; Jose Santos Millao and Hilario Huirilaf, Elected Indigenous Board Members, CONADI; Francisco Huenchumilla, Mapuche congresman; Aucan Huilcaman, Victor Naguil, Hector Collasaya, Octavio Viza, Maria Teresa Mamani, Carlos Castillo, Silvia Colque, Crispin Chura, Sergio Plateros, Indigenous leaders; Christian Parker, José Aylwin, Academics; and Domingo Namancura, former National Director, CONADI. The mission was greatly supported by MIDEPLAN and CONADI which provided several background papers prepared by the Chilean Government.

Introduction

Indigenous issues in Chile have become increasingly relevant for policy makers. While there are no current nation-wide estimates, according to the 1992 population census, indigenous peoples in Chile represent 7.5% of the total population, or almost 1 million people, of which about 79% would be urban. Either rural or urban, indigenous peoples experience higher poverty rates (35.6%) than the non-indigenous (22.7%) population and multiple studies indicate that most social indicators for indigenous groups are consistently below national averages.[122] In rural areas, indigenous peoples have little land and tend to be concentrated in extreme fragile, rapidly deteriorating environments. Similarly, water rights of indigenous communities have been severely curtailed. In urban areas, particularly in large urban centers such as Santiago, Concepción and Temuco, indigenous peoples are clustered in the poorest municipalities, with limited access to social services, and a significant proportion of the population is underemployed and/or work in the informal sector. Indigenous peoples struggle with poverty and are subject to racial discrimination, deprived of the means to reproduce its culture.[123]

Starting in 1990, several steps were taken to improve the situation of indigenous peoples. The Aylwin administration (1990-1994) created the Special Commission for Indigenous Peoples (_Comisión Especial de Pueblos Indígenas, CEPI_). CEPI drafted an indigenous bill that was widely discussed by indigenous organizations and the national Congress for over two years. After its approval in October 1993 (_Ley de Desarrollo Indígena 19.253_), a government agency, the National Corporation for Indigenous Development (_Corporación Nacional de Desarrollo Indígena, CONADI_), was established under the Minister of Planning

---

[122] MIDEPLAN, Depto. de Información Social. Encuesta CASEN 1996.Nota: se excluye servicio doméstico puertas adentro y su núcleo familiar.

[123] CERC-Participa. _"La Discriminación a los Mapuches"_. Resultados Encuesta Julio-Agosto 1999. Libertad y Desarrollo, Temas Públicos No 447, 28 de Agosto de 1999. _"Plan Indígena: Solución de Problemas o Solución de Conflictos?"_.

and Cooperation (*Ministerio de Planificación y Cooperación, MIDEPLAN*) with the mandate of ensuring the implementation of the indigenous law. CONADI launched several special programs[124] for indigenous peoples, and begun coordinating with other government programs to facilitate indigenous peoples access to them.

Over the last 3 years, tension between indigenous organizations and the Chilean state have risen and wide-spread mobilizations have taken place. Some of the key issues indigenous organizations have been rallying over are their right to self-determination, restitution of indigenous lands and water rights.[125]

This report is based on the analysis of existing information (census data, CASEN 1996,[126] project documents, MIDEPLAN reports and other papers written by Chilean scholars on the subject of indigenous peoples in Chile), as well as information provided by government officials, indigenous leaders and other qualified informants). The report organizes and summarizes existing information. The objective of this report is to provide a rapid assessment of current indigenous issues and government policies in Chile. Specifically, this note: (a) provides a brief diagnostic of the current situation of indigenous peoples in Chile; (b) identifies key policy issues and challenges; (c) describes what the government is attempting to do in the area of indigenous peoples development (d) analyzes what are the chances of the government's program being successful given the current tensions over such things as land rights between the government and various indigenous groups, especially the Mapuche in the south of the country, and, (e) assesses what role, if any, would there be for the Bank in supporting the government efforts to address indigenous issues.

Diagnostic
Current Situation of Indigenous peoples

Population. According to the 1992 population census, indigenous peoples represent 7.5% of the total population. An estimate based on the CASEN 1996 survey suggest a much lower figure of 4.5% (see Table 1). However, most analysts agree that the population census figures are a better estimate, as even the population census would not reflect the actual number of indigenous population in Chile.[127]

---

[124] Land and Water Fund, Indigenous Development Fund, Indigenous Development Areas, Culture and Education.

[125] Recently, these issues have gained public attention through two specific cases that reflect the different dimensions of the conflict: (i) the approval by CONADI of indigenous land permutations necessary for the construction of a hydroelectric dam at Ralco and; (ii) land takeovers of properties disputed with forestry companies (this includes taking over former communal lands, or lands in dispute, obstruction of public roads, burning of forests and private property, and seizure of buildings and public offices).

[126] At the time of preparing this report, the most updated quantitative information on indigenous peoples in Chile was the CASEN 1996 survey. The results of the CASEN 2000 were not available at that time. Currently, the Bank has asked MIDEPLAN to have access to the CASEN 2000 survey to process and analyze the data pertaining to indigenous peoples in the context of the Regional Study on Extreme Poverty and Social Exclusion.

[127] This sharp difference could be explained by a sampling effect and differences in the questionnaires used by the CASEN survey and the population census. The sample has no representativeness at the municipal level. At the same time, spatial distribution of indigenous population is not uniform across municipalities. Indigenous population is clustered in certain municipalities (rural and urban). Therefore, the sampling strategy of the CASEN survey may result on under-representation of rural areas and urban settings with high concentration of

Almost 80% of the indigenous population lives in urban areas and most of them (40%) in Santiago, followed by Temuco and Concepción. Over the last 15 years there has been a steady trend toward urbanization among indigenous peoples in Chile. This is a key element that needs to be taken into consideration when discussing policy options for the social, economic and cultural integration of indigenous groups in Chile.[128] Regarding spatial distribution in urban areas, indigenous groups are clustered in certain municipalities and, more specifically in neighborhoods which responds to existing social networks of the families or groups that have migrated before. In most cases, indigenous groups are located in poor areas either in the periphery of the city or in the depressed downtown areas.[129]

Table 1: Indigenous Population by Region

	1992 Population Census		1996 CASEN Survey	
	Indigenous Population	Percentage from Total	Indigenous Population	Percentage from Total
Region		%		%
I	25,320	7.5	35,625	9.8
II	16,634	4.0	11,832	2.7
III	8,340	3.6	5,852	2.4
IV	20,961	4.2	2,826	0.5
V	65,270	4.7	21,372	1.5
VI	38,004	5.5	9,635	1.3
VII	34,899	4.2	3,920	0.5
VIII	130,874	7.5	56,509	3.1
IX	145,364	18.6	239,325	29.4
X	71,106	7.5	106,913	10.7
XI	3,473	4.3	5,770	7.0
XII	5,105	3.6	5,605	3.9
RM	433,035	8.2	130,192	2.3
Total	998,385	100	635,376	100
Urban	794,952.	79.6		
Rural	203,433.	20.4		

Source : Population Census, 1992 and 1996 CASEN Survey.

indigenous populations. Regarding the questionnaire, the question of ethnic origin in the CASEN survey is asked in a slightly different way than in the population census questionnaire. For further analysis see MIDEPLAN (1998) *Encuesta CASEN 1996,* Valenzuela (1995) *La Población Indígena en la Región Metropolitana,* CONADI and, CELADE (1994) Estudios Sociodemograficos de Pueblos Indígenas.

[128] Chile is probably the country that has the highest ratio of urban indigenous population from the region, where indigenous peoples are mostly rural. Different studies suggest that a large proportion of the indigenous population from the region is rural, ranging from 80% in the case of Guatemala to 50% in Peru. See Psacharopoulos and Patrinos (1994) *Indigenous Peoples and Poverty in Latin America. An Empirical Analysis,* The World Bank; CELADE (1994) *Estudios Sociodemográficos de Pueblos Indígenas,* CELADE; Jordan (1990) Poblaciones Indígenas de América Latina y el Caribe, FAO/III.

[129] For further information see Rodrigo Valenzuela (1995) *"La Población Indígena en la Región Metropolitana"* and by the same author his study *"Población Urbana en Chile" (1998),* Documento de Trabajo No 8, MIDEPLAN, Departamento de Evaluación Social, Area Indígena. Also, Tabilo et al. (1995) *Las Agrupaciones de Residentes Aymara Urbanos en el Norte de Chile: Adaptacion a La Ciudad y Vinculos con las Comunidades de Origen,* Taller Estudios Aymara.

According to the 1992 population census, the Mapuche is the largest indigenous group in Chile, followed by the Aymaras and Rapanui (see Table 2).[130]   From 1993, Chilean law (No 19.023 D.Of. 05-10-1993) recognizes 8 different indigenous groups (Mapuche, Aymara, Atacameño, Rapanui, Colla, Quecha, Yagan and Kawashkar). In this regard, the 1996 CASEN survey, reports (see Table 2) members for the 8 groups. However, it should be mention that ethnographic and linguistic studies suggest that besides the Mapuche, Aymara and Rapanui, only two other indigenous groups could be found in Chile (the Quechua and the Kawashkar, with only a few individuals).[131]

Table 2: Indigenous Population by Ethnic Group

Ethnic Group	1992 Population Census		1996 CASEN Survey	
	Population	% from total	Population	% from total
Mapuche	928,060	93.0	517,125	81.4
Aymará	48,477	4.8	90,527	14.2
Rapanui	21,848	2.2	7,720	1.2
Atacameño			9,988	1.6
Colla			5,467	0.9
Quechua			3,436	0.5
Yagan			975	0.2
Kawashkar			138	0.0
Total	998,385	100	635,376	100

Socioeconomic Conditions

Indigenous peoples are among the poorest and more vulnerable groups in Chile[132]. The CASEN 1996 survey indicates that incidence of poverty is significantly higher among indigenous (35.6%) than non-indigenous population (22.7%). In average, indigenous families receive almost half the income of non-indigenous families, and 65% of the families are within the lowest two quintiles compared to 44% for non-indigenous. Most economically active indigenous people are in unskilled jobs (31%) and agriculture and fisheries (25%).

Schooling among indigenous peoples is about 2.2 years below the average years of schooling for the non-indigenous population (9.5). In the case of rural Mapuche population, 80% of household heads have less than 4 years of schooling, and only 3% of the rural Mapuche population above 15 years has some type of education beyond high school. Overall educational attainment and performance among indigenous population is very low. Furthermore, according to the ranking of the national system for measuring the quality of

---

[130] The 1992 census only included three groups (Mapuche, Aymara and rapanui), which represent about 95% of the total indigenous population.

[131] However, it should be mention that this proposition has been under severe criticism from academics and indigenous organizations. See Sanchez, *"Estado Actual de las Lenguas Aborigenes en Chile"* in Boletín de la Academia Chilena de la Lengua No 71. The issue that has been questioned is the validity of self-identification (as the only criteria used), vis a vis the command of the language, the identification by other individuals, and the belonging to family or groups that also identify themselves as members of that particular group.

[132] Rapanuis living in Easter Island (*Isla de Pascua*) are the only exception to this rule. According to the CASEN 1996 survey, poverty incidence in the island is only about 3%.

education (SIMCE), from the 44 municipalities with the lowest scores, 26 of them are municipalities with high concentration of indigenous peoples.[133]

Regarding access to health services, about 80% of the indigenous peoples relies on public health services and have no access to private medicine, compared with only 43% of non-indigenous population. Infant mortality among indigenous peoples is higher, particularly in rural areas where it may reach up to 50% in some municipalities. Incidence and prevalence of diseases such as diarrhea (among children), tuberculosis (among adults), and different parasitosis are higher among indigenous peoples than non-indigenous from the same socioeconomic level.[134]

With respect to housing and sanitation, the CASEN survey indicates that only 41% of the indigenous households have sewerage, compared to 76% for non-indigenous. Similarly, only 58% of the indigenous population has access to running water, compared with 90% for non-indigenous. Finally, while 92% of non-indigenous households have electricity, only 65% of the indigenous households have.

Land. From the rural indigenous population, Mapuches represent about 95% of the total. Most rural Mapuche are small scale subsistence farmers that combine on-farm activities (mostly wheat/potato and livestock production and subsistence agriculture) with off-farm activities (seasonal work and petty commerce).[135] Overtime, the survival of rural Mapuches has become increasingly difficult due to the decreasing amount of land available for family farming, the lack of local employment opportunities and the poor quality of the services available to them.

Until the end of the Spanish rule, Mapuche people possessed a territory of almost 10 million hectares which was recognized by the Spanish Crown in the Treaty of Quilin.[136] After independence, the newly created Chilean state begun an aggressive colonization scheme to expand the agricultural frontiers and consolidate its control over the territory. In addition continuous land divisions due to population growth resulted in the average farm size per

---

[133] For further information see Ministerio de Educación de Chile (1997) *Compendio de Información Estadística*.

[134] See Bustos et al. (1997) *Deficit de Crecimiento en Escolares Indigenas y no Indigenas Expuestos a Diferentes Condiciones de Vulnerabilidad Social*. Universidad de Chile. Also Hector Gonzalez (1995), Los Migrantes Aymaras en la Ciudad: Acceso a Educacion Vivienda y Salud.

[135] See Annex O (Volume II)of *"Chile. Strategy for Rural Areas. Enhancing Agricultural Competitiveness and Alleviating Rural Poverty"*. The World Bank (1994). For a detailed analysis of the survival strategies of rural Mapuches see Gacitúa and Bello (1992) *"10 Years Of Land Division A Study Of Three Mapuche Communities In Southern Chile"*, paper presented at the 1992 meeting on the International Rural Sociological Association.

[136] Mapuche leaders have also substantiated this demand based on several other treaties, called *"Parlamentos"*, such as the *Parlamento de Negrete* (1803). Mapuche representatives at the UN working Group made reference to several of these treaties which have not been yet fully reviewed in the UN "Commission of Human Rights Study on Treaties, Agreements and other Constructive Arrangements between States and Indigenous Populations". See also, Aylwin, José. 1990. "Tierra Mapuche: Derecho Consuetudinario y Legislación Chilena". Pp.333-354 en Entre la Ley y la Costumbre.

person decreasing progressively from 6.1 ha/inhabitant in 1884 to 1.9 ha/inhabitant in 1963 to less than 0.8 ha/inhabitant in 1980.[137]

From the initial resettlement in reservations to the current situation, it is possible to differentiate five different periods regarding the legal framework that regulated the indigenous' land tenure system:

- *Reservation and Resettlement*: Between 1880 and 1927 the Chilean government granted <u>Títulos de Merced</u> to indigenous families. This process sought to demarcate the lands occupied by Mapuches' families, confining them to a limited territory. The imposition of the reservation system implied a severe reduction of the lands available and a break down of the material and social conditions of the Mapuche society. About 3,000 Títulos de Merced, covering some 525,000 hectares were granted. However, subsequently Mapuches lost a significant amount of their lands land due to the lack of secure land titles and continuous encroachment in their lands of mostly large agricultural producers.

- *First Division*: By mid 1920s' the lands taken from the Mapuche communities by colonist and large agricultural producers needed to be regularized. Furthermore, the expansion of the agricultural frontier required releasing Mapuches' lands from reservation system under state protection. In 1927, a law was enacted that allowed the voluntary division of the communal lands if all household heads of the community agreed upon the division. From 1927 to 1972 almost 800 communities, about 125,000 hectares, were divided into family units, giving land titles to approximately 13,000 families.

- *Agrarian Reform*: After the enactment of the agrarian reform law in 1966, Mapuche's permanent demand for land gained momentum. In 1972 a new law (17.729) came into effect. A specialized state agency, the *Instituto de Desarrollo Indígena* was created and between 1972 and September 1973, more than 70,000 hectares were transferred to Mapuche communities.

- *Second Division*: This period started with the promulgation of decrees 2568 and 2750 in 1979. This new legislation prompted the division of Mapuche communities. According to the law, the owners would receive individual land titles and their lands no longer would be considered indigenous lands and protected as such. As a result, over 1,600 communities were divided 63,600 individual property titles were granted over 315,000 hectares.

- *Protection*: With the enactment of the Indigenous Law (No 19.253 D.Of. 05-10-93), for the first time in Chilean history, indigenous peoples were officially recognized and their lands protected. A state agency, the National Corporation for Indigenous Development (*Corporación Nacional de Desarrollo Indígena, CONADI*), was created and a land fund was established. As a result, from 1994 to 1999 about 112,000 hectares have been purchased, benefiting some 27,000 families.

---

[137] See Gacitúa (1992) "Fundamentos Socio-Económicos, Culturales y Jurídicos para el Establecimiento de un Banco de Tierras para Pequeños Productores Mapuches en Tres Microregiones de la IX Región" Informe de Consultoría Instituto Nacional de Desarrollo Agropecuario (INDAP).

Sociocultural

Until recently, the so-called "indigenous question" in Chile was equated with the Mapuches. All other indigenous groups were largely overlooked by policymakers (because of their small numbers and geographic isolation) and were only the concern of academics. It has been only with the explicit recognition in the 1993 law of eight distinct indigenous groups[138] that Chilean society has been forced to become aware of its ethnic diversity. However, still Chilean society is a long way from changing the stereotypes regarding indigenous peoples, and developing and mainstreaming more culturally inclusive policy instruments.

In the past, discrimination of indigenous peoples has taken multiple forms, from state policies aimed at the integration of the indigenous population through the educational system, to the use of cultural stereotypes depicting indigenous peoples either as villains or noble-savages or ignorant-lazy people.[139] A recent survey (1999)[140] shows that there is a widespread misinformation and lack of sensibility in Chilean society regarding indigenous peoples and their situation. The study concludes that most non-indigenous respondents do not recognize discrimination as an issue, while at the same time use stereotypes to describe the Mapuche and their problems. At the same time, indigenous respondents indicate they feel discriminated in several dimensions including their physical appearance, the right to use of their own language, perform sacred ceremonies, access resources, benefit from state programs, and participate in the labor market. Urban Mapuches feel they have difficulties to express and carry out their religious beliefs and ceremonies.

The educational system has played a key role as a tool for cultural assimilation as well as a channel for disseminating the Chilean view and stereotypes of indigenous peoples and history. It has been only recently that the Ministry of Education has started to review the national curriculum and to the develop multicultural and bilingual educational programs. However, these have little resources and very limited coverage. Beyond the educational system, government policies have done little to increase the cultural participation of indigenous groups in Chilean society. There is no public policy to stimulate and facilitate the public expression of indigenous culture, particularly in urban areas.

Lack of public policy supporting the development and expression of indigenous culture has been a constraint for increasing indigenous participation in Chilean society. Nevertheless, equally important has been the absence of a pluricultural approach to education. Educating Chilean society to respect and value indigenous culture is essential to change the existing stereotypes. The review of the current curriculum has been a first step. However, the exaltation of positive stereotypes is not enough and does not help to resolve the issue of changing cultures that need to be recognized as such. In this regard, it is important to highlight that the government recently agreed with indigenous groups establishing a special commission on "Truth and History" to look into these issues. To summarize, the absence of dialogue between Chilean society, the state and indigenous groups, and the lack of

---

[138] Mapuche, Aymara, Atacameño, Rapanui, Colla, Quecha, Yagan and Kawashkar.
[139] A recent newspaper article (El Mercurio, 14 de Mayo 2000), by a well know history professor (Sergio Villalobos) triggered a strong debate on these issues that reflects the prevalent stereotypes regarding Mapuches.
[140] CERC-Participa. *"La Discriminación a los Mapuches"*. Resultados Encuesta Julio-Agosto 1999.

agreements regarding the cultural and political rights of these groups are key problems that undermine the relationship between these actors.

While the new legal framework (19.253) represented a significant progress in the recognition of the indigenous cultures, there are still some issues that need to be resolved. Chile has not yet ratified the 1989 OIT's Agreement 169, and the current legislation does not fully reflect its recommendations. Chile's constitution does not recognizes special minority status to indigenous groups and there are no specific mechanisms for indigenous participation i the legislative power. Further, indigenous participation on policy decision making is limited. Indigenous peoples have little participation on the design or control over the development policies that directly affect them.

Historically, indigenous groups, particularly the Mapuche, generated a "culture of resistance" against the discrimination they experienced. This resistance was expressed through their social structure and organizations. In spite of diverse ideologies among indigenous organizations, where each one represents a specific type of leadership, which leads to different relationships with the national society, the function of group maintenance has been given greater importance, and has became a true resistance against discrimination and cultural domination.

Organizations and Social Mobilizations

There are multiple indigenous organizations among the three largest indigenous groups, representing urban and rural communities and a wide variety of objectives and interests. In the north, the Aymara People National Council (*Consejo Nacional del Pueblo Aymara*) represents more than 200 local and regional Aymara organizations addressing from cultural issues to agricultural production to political rights. The *Consejo* has become the primary interlocutor regarding Aymara issues and is the official voice when negotiating with other groups or the Chilean state. In 1997, the *Consejo Aymara* put out a development strategy summarizing their key demands and policy proposals which include intercultural-bilingual education, institutional development and organizational strengthening, economic development funds for indigenous communities, and regularization and protection of water rights, among others.[141]

In Easter Island, the Elders' Council, a traditionally social structure, officially speaks for the people in the island. Nevertheless, over the last year a group of islanders, linked to small tourist business has challenged the leadership of the council. The issue at stake has been the discussion of control over Government lands that would be transferred to the islanders. The Elder's Council has advocated community management of the lands, while the challenging group is pressing for private property rights. One of the main concerns of the Council has been to keep their identity and culture, including their language. In that framework, the Council prefers to foster the island development through the gradual empowerment of the community, while reinforcing the traditional cultural structure. It is important to highlight that the council has strong ties with other Polynesian indigenous groups, as they look towards the Polynesian basin for much of their cultural exchanges. There are a few other Rapanui organizations based in continental Chile that work on cultural issues as well as political

---

[141] Consejo Nacional del Pueblo Aymara (Mallku-T'Alla). Estrategia de Desarrollo Aymara. Iquique, 1997.

rights. While these groups are very important for the islanders living in continental Chile, mostly students, these groups have little influence on the affairs in the island.

Finally, among the Mapuche there are several hundred rural and urban-based organizations, of which 30 or so claim to have either national or regional representativeness. Recently, some of these organizations, such as the *Consejo de Todas las Tierras*, the *Coordinadora Mapuche Arauco-Malleco*, *Identidad Lafkenche*, and *Ad-Mapu*, have been successful in getting media attention, presenting their views on key issues and mobilizing their supporters in public demonstrations. While there is no single organization that represents the Mapuche people, there is a common platform shared by most of the organizations which was developed during the National Mapuche Congress in November 1997.[142] The congress proposed a policy agenda that included among others, assuring Mapuche access and/or control over ancestral lands and water rights, bicultural and bilingual education, constitutional recognition, political representation and autonomy.

Due in part to the large difference in population between the three main indigenous groups, Mapuche issues and organizations have overshadowed the other indigenous groups. Nevertheless, with the new legislation and the creation of CONADI's council, the different indigenous groups have developed stronger coordination among themselves. Last November indigenous peoples elected their representatives to CONADI's council. While some 83,000 were register to vote, only 20,000 participated in the election.[143] The high absenteeism is explained by the fact that this was the first time indigenous peoples elected their own representatives and CONADI had been under severe criticism from some indigenous organizations (see below).

Overtime, indigenous organizations have used multiple strategies for advancing their agenda. Among these, social mobilization has been used at critical times. Recently, three elements have contributed to the development of conflict and mobilization: a) grievances regarding rights to access and control over resources, specifically land and water; b) the lack of a clear government policy and position regarding indigenous conflicts; which indigenous organizations claim has been biased and; c) the demand for autonomy and development policies that would not threaten indigenous rights.

The relationships between the government, indigenous groups, particularly Mapuches, and Chilean society in general have been strained over three main conflicts: i) the Ralco Dam, ii) forestry industry and; iii) existing legislation and the role of CONADI.

Ralco Dam. The dispute over the construction of the Ralco dam on the Bio Bio river, 500 kms south of Santiago, has been one of the most visible conflicts between indigenous groups, environmentalists, the Chilean government and private sector investors. The dam would create a reservoir with a capacity of 1.2 billion cubic meters of water, which would flood 3,467 hectares of land. That area is now home to 91 Pehuenche (Mapuche) families.

---

[142] Congreso Nacional del Pueblo Mapuche. Documento de Conclusiones, Noviembre 1997.
[143] The council member elected are Carlos Reginio Inquiltupa (Aymaras); Sandra Berna Martínez (Atacameños); Alberto Hotus Chávez (Rapuanui), Ilario Huirilef Parra, José Santos Millao Palacios Francisco Chodiman Arnoldo Nanculef Huaiquinao (Mapuches) José Llancapan Calfucura (Urban/Mapuche).

Tension developed over the issue of land permutations and the required approval of CONADI (under the Indigenous Law) of these swaps. Extensive negotiations took place between the potentially affected families, CONADI, and the Spanish-Chilean company Endesa, owners of the project. As a result, 11 of the affected families refused to abandon their ancestral territory, while 80 agreed to swap their property for land elsewhere offered by Endesa as part of a US$20 million resettlement plan. However, Mapuche organizations accused Endesa of obtaining agreement on the land swaps of the 80 families through deceptive means.

The approval of the land permutations sparked tremendous controversy in CONADI's board, ultimately leading to the resignation of two successive CONADI executive directors (and two government appointed board members) who considered the permutations were incompatible with the indigenous law, which would take precedence in the dispute. The government granted Ralco the required permits and the concession for supplying electricity. After a series of court appeals by Mapuche organizations and environmentalists, the Comptroller-General's office authorized the last two concessions on Ralco exploitation and Mapuche land expropriations. Nearly 30 percent of work on the project has been completed, and Endesa has spend some US$157 million of the planned investment of US$540 million.

Forestry Industry. The conflict between the Mapuche and the forestry industry is complex. Its origin goes back to the establishment of the reservation system and the transfer of Mapuche and state lands to private owners[144]. After 1974, forestry companies bought significant amounts of this land. At the same time, the enactment of DL 701 in 1974 granted a 75% subsidy to the forestry industry for each planted hectare. As a result, there was a rapid growth of pine plantations in a vast territory, including Mapuche's ancestral territories in Arauco Malleco and Cautín provinces. Many Mapuche communities lost some of their lands to forestry companies and their traditional means of survival disappeared progressively as they became surrounded by the fast-growing pine plantations which contributed to the depletion of ground water sources, making agricultural production even more difficult.

According to recent estimates at least 30 Mapuche communities distributed in the VIII, IX and X region are in conflict with forestry companies and private owners over some 60,000 hectares of land[145]. During 1999, almost every week there were land occupations by Mapuche communities in the provinces of Arauco and Malleco. These incidents have resulted in occasional violence and confrontations between the police and the indigenous communities.

The conflict between Mapuche communities and forestry companies has escalated and would be very difficult to resolve for several reasons. First there is neither updated nor valid information regarding indigenous land tenure issues. Secondly, the conflict has been extremely politicized. According to some Mapuche organizations, the lands under conflict would be about 200,000 hectares, considering ancestral territories. It is very difficult to

[144] Jorge Iván Vergara, Andrea Aravena, Martín Correa y Raúl Molina (1999) "Las tierras de la ira. Los sucesos de Traiguén y los conflictos entre comunidades mapuches, empresas forestales y Estado. Praxis. Revista de Psicología y Ciencias Humanas N°1, Universidad Diego Portales, Santiago.
[145] Foester, Rolf y Javier Lavanchy. *La Problemática Mapuche*. Análisis del Año 1999. En Sociedad-Política-Economía. Departamento de Sociología, Universidad de Chile, 1999, pp. 65-102.

judge the legitimacy of the claims as there are no studies assessing how much Mapuche land would have been transferred.

Existing Legislation. The two previous cases highlight some of the legal issues that are been raised by indigenous organizations. These conflicts have demonstrated that there are significant limitations in the existing indigenous legislation and that there is no clear legal framework to resolve the disputes. These can be summarized into four main questions: (i) constitutional recognition and autonomy; (ii) ratification of international treaties (OIT 169); (iii) political representation and participation of indigenous peoples; and (iv) the institutional constraints of CONADI, the government agency with government appointees and indigenous representatives, to act independently, to safeguard the indigenous law and to promote indigenous participation in Chilean society.

Indigenous organizations are calling for a modification in the constitution and the legal framework. One of the proposals is that of Congressman Francisco Heunchumilla, a Mapuche who has become increasingly active in advancing indigenous rights in the Chilean Congress. The proposal calls for a constitutional amendment to grant official status of indigenous "peoples" to the various indigenous groups acknowledged in the 1993 law (19.253). This would entail a political pact -between opposed political forces- recognizing rights to indigenous peoples/nations that would allow indigenous participation in the executive and legislative powers. The proposal seeks to ensure a fair representation and participation of indigenous peoples in all institutions. It proposes the establishment of an indigenous voting register and the election of 3 senators and 10 indigenous deputies for the legislative power, as well as the popular election of additional municipal council members representing indigenous peoples in municipalities with more than 5% of indigenous population. It also proposes specific representation and participation of indigenous peoples in the regional governments. Finally, the proposal considers the creation of an elected Indigenous Congress (*Parlamento Indígena*) which would be in charge of setting policy, administrating national resources for indigenous development and nominating the director of CONADI or its successor. However, under the current situation it is very unlikely that the National Congress would approve the proposal developed by Congressman Huenchumilla, or other less ambitious efforts to get Congress ratification of OIT 169.

Government Programs

Starting in 1990, the Aylwin administration (1990-1994) established a Special Commission for Indigenous Peoples (*Comisión Especial de Pueblos Indígenas, CEPI*), which drafted an indigenous bill that was widely discussed by indigenous organizations and the national Congress for over two years. In October 1993 the new law (*Ley de Desarrollo Indígena 19.253*), was approved by the congress. While the law was approved by the congress with significant modifications that curtailed its initial spirit, the law provided a new framework for developing specific policies and programs targeted to the indigenous peoples as well as mechanisms to channel resources through other regular government programs.

A government agency, the National Corporation for Indigenous Development (*Corporación Nacional de Desarrollo Indígena, CONADI*), was established under the Minister of Planning and Cooperation (*Ministerio de Planificación y Cooperación, MIDEPLAN*). CONADI was given the mandate of implementing the indigenous law through specific programs, and coordinating with other government agencies to ensure that other sectoral (health, education, etc.) resources would be accessible to indigenous peoples.

By law (Article 41, Law 19.253), CONADI's decisions are taken by a council. The council is a policy making body composed of (8) representatives of different government agencies, and a Director appointed by the Government, and (8) indigenous representatives, elected by indigenous peoples registered to vote in the indigenous peoples voting register. This mixed composition of CONADI's council was intended as a mechanism to ensure indigenous participation in the decision making process. However, indigenous leaders, as well as legal experts have criticized this arrangement and its outcomes because it has demonstrated serious limitations as the indigenous council members views/votes could be side stepped by the government appointed members and the director. In this regard, the Ralco case put in evidence that the system did not work as intended.

Between 1994 and 1999, CONADI has implemented four main programs: (i) Land and Water Fund; (ii) Development Fund; (iii) Indigenous Development Areas and; (iv) Culture and Education. CONADI's total budget for 1999 was MCh$ 13,346,022 or approximately US$ 25.5 million.

Land and Water Fund (Fondo de Tierra y Aguas). The land and water fund was established as a mechanism to address land tenure issues, including resolving land tenure conflicts (litigations) between indigenous communities and private owners. The fund has four main components: (i) land acquisition; (ii) acquisition of water rights; (iii) irrigation sub-projects and; (iv) legal support (indigenous lands). The land and water fund represents about 60% of CONADI's annual budget. Between 1994 and 1999 the total budget of the land and water fund grew from approximately US$ 5.5 million in 1994 to US$ 16.2 million in 1999 (see table 3 below).

About 75% of the annual fund's budget has been earmarked for land acquisitions. From 1994 to 1999, some 125,000 hectares were acquired under the fund, benefiting approximately 27,000 families. The remaining monies have been used for irrigation (13%), legal costs (5%) and acquisition of water rights (4%).

Table 3: Annual Budget Land and Water Fund

Land and Water Fund	
Year	US$ (million)
1994	5.5
1995	5.1
1996	8.1
1997	10.9
1998	10.1
1999	16.2
Total	55.8

Development Fund (Fondo de Desarrollo). The fund was established to promote and support the development of economic activities through credit, technical assistance and training, seed money and subsidies to indigenous micro-entrepreneurs. To ensure better coordination between programs, most of the activities financed through the fund, particularly those related to small productive projects and technical assistance have been targeted to beneficiaries of the land and water fund. The annual budget for the development fund has remained almost constant over time, experiencing a significant (25%) increase only during 1999 (see Table 4 below). From 1994 to 1999, approximately 8,500 families benefited from the fund. It is also important to highlight that under the fund were financed until 1999 dissemination activities as well as a specific bicultural-bilingual education program.

Table 4: Annual Budget Development Fund

	Development Fund
Year	US$ (million)
1994	2.8
1995	2.9
1996	2.8
1997	2.6
1998	2.9
1999	3.6
Total	18

Indigenous Development Areas (Areas de Desarrollo Indigena, ADIs). Indigenous development areas (ADI) are defined by law (19.253), as delimited geographical areas inhabited by indigenous peoples. These areas have been conceived as local planning units, used for targeting as well as coordinating different government programs to indigenous peoples. To date there are three established ADIs: (i) *San Pedro de Atacama*, (Aymara communities in Northern Chile); (ii) *Alto Bio-Bio*, (Mapuche-Pehuenche communities in the Ralco dam area); and (iii) *Lago Budi*, (Mapuche communities in the IX region coastal zone). Under study is the creation of at least 6 new ADIs in southern Chile (Lumaco, Puren, Lleu-Lleu, Chonchi, Queilen, Quellon).

In the ADIs, CONADI seeks to collaborate with other government agencies to ensure the coordination of public programs, specifically housing, education, health and public works. The ADIs are based on detailed participatory diagnostics in which the communities prioritize with local government authorities investments and government spending in the area over time.

While the three established ADIs have completed their diagnostics and designated their boards, *Alto Bio-Bio* is the most advanced regarding the developed annual investment plans. In total, the *Alto Bio Bio* ADI has channeled almost US$ 6.8 million from different government to this area (see Table 5 below).

Table 5: Public Investment in ADIs

	Alto Bio Bio US$	Lago Budi US$	San Pedro de Atacama US$
1998	2.18		
1999	3.17		N/A
2000*	1.48		
Total	6.83		

*Planned

Culture and Education (Cultura y Educación Indígena). This program involves two main activities: (i) intercultural and bilingual education program and (ii) the scholarship program. The intercultural and bilingual program was recently created (1998) and has little resources to develop independent activities or to support other ongoing programs addressing intercultural and bilingual issues. In 1998, total budget for this program was about US$ 1 million and in 1999 it went down to US$ 895,000. In this regard it is noteworthy to mention the collaboration between CONADI and the National Board of Childcare Centers *(JUNJI)* in Temuco piloting bicultural childcare centers.

Sectoral Programs. As any other citizen, indigenous peoples are eligible for social benefits and assistance including (i) subsidies for families below the poverty line *(CAS)*; (ii) primary health care; (iii) food subsidies for students (primary and secondary) in low income schools; (iv) housing subsidy; (v) unemployment benefits; (vi) technical and financial assistance for productive projects *(FOSIS)*; and (vii) vocational training. In addition to these benefits and the specific programs described above, some sectoral ministries have programs targeted to indigenous peoples.

Education. The indigenous scholarship program managed by the Ministry of Education started in 1991, providing support only university/technical education. In 1992 basic education and high school scholarships were also included into the program. The program has grown from 5,000 annual scholarships in 1994 to 14,000 in 1999. In 1998, the distribution of the scholarships by educational level indicated that 53% of the scholarships went to basic education, 27% to high school students and 20% to higher education. Although high school and basic education scholarships have increased over time, there still is a great demand for more scholarships, particularly in rural areas. In addition to the scholarship program, the Ministry of Education also runs Indigenous Homes (dorms) for students. These homes provide the students with food and shelter as well as facilities to study. Nevertheless there are only a few and with limited capacity. In Santiago, for example, there is only of these homes, with a capacity for less than 30 students.

Health. Starting in 1996, the Ministry of Public health launched a special program *(Programa Salud y Pueblos Indígenas)*, in seven regions (I, II, III, VIII, IX, X, XIII), aimed at increasing access and quality of services provided to indigenous communities. This program involved the training of health staff working with indigenous peoples on intercultural health issues, appointment of intercultural health facilitators in some rural areas with high concentration of indigenous population and support field research on epidemiological and sociocultural factors relevant for indigenous health.

Agriculture. Although INDAP does not have a specific program for indigenous beneficiaries, it has provided support though its current programs to indigenous small farmers. Nevertheless, due to the program's eligibility criteria the poorest Mapuche farmers are not eligible to participate. At the same since the program operates in a decentralized manner through private sector providers, these have neither incentives nor experience to work with indigenous communities which require special attention.

Regarding other programs, it is important to mention the social fund (FOSIS) special program to support reforestation among indigenous communities. Also, the Ministry of

Housing has special procedures for indigenous applicants to the rural housing subsidy. Similarly, the rural electrification program has targeted indigenous households.

August 1999 Pact. In May 1999, the Government established an Indigenous Development Task Force, comprising key public figures and indigenous leaders. This group had the task of identifying key issues and proposing policy aimed at improving indigenous peoples' quality of life. The task force worked for almost three months meeting with indigenous leaders and communities across the country. As a result the task force produced a diagnostic shared by all its members and proposed a public policy agenda that was translated into a development plan (*Pacto de Respeto Ciudadano*), announced by President Frei on August 5, 1999. The three year investment plan of approximately US$ 270 million, was presented as an answer to the urgent demands of indigenous peoples. The objectives of the plan were to develop a multicultural and inclusive society and to promote indigenous participation and the mainstreaming of their cultures. The plan involved 5 areas: (i) infrastructure; (ii) economic development and productivity; (iii) culture and identity; (iv) health and (v) education. The plan included 23 measures such as constitutional recognition, ratification of article 169 of the International Labor Organization Treaty, debt relief for indigenous peoples in need, new loans, special funding and subsidies for indigenous families, increased scholarships, development of bicultural educational programs, more health coverage, special housing programs, and construction of roads in indigenous communities, among others (see annex 1).

This pact was the culmination of multiple indigenous mobilizations frustrated with the real limitations of CONADI in handling the "indigenous problem" and community meetings held by government representatives with indigenous leaders. The government bypassed CONADI, created the task force and sent high government officials to address indigenous demands. The plan was view by some as a positive sign that the government was finally attempting to address indigenous issues. Others,[146] quickly questioned the political intention of the plan, launched a few months before the presidential election, and argued it had no long term sustainability.

The plan came under fire by Indigenous leaders soon after it was announced. Indigenous leaders claimed that the plan involved little new investments (above those already planned under the sectoral tri-annual budgets), and that the moneys were those regularly assigned to government services in the regions. In any event, the empirical question that remains is whether the US$ 90 million per year assigned by the government would be enough to match the needs and to resolve the structural problems indigenous leaders are pointing out. In this context it is important to indicate that if the 150,000 hectares that the Mapuche are claiming (and the government has promised) were to be bought by the Land and Water Fund at market value, this investment would be approximately US$ 225 million, not considering any additional investment in water rights, productive infrastructure, or training. Also, it is important to mention that the plan is mostly targeted to rural Mapuche. Aymaras, Quechuas, Rapanui have been marginally considered. Further, urban indigenous groups have not been specifically contemplated in the plan.

---

[146] See Instituto Libertad y Desarrollo, Témas Públicos (Agosto 1999). Plán Indígena. Solución de Problemas o Solución de Conflictos.

Policy Issues

At the beginning of the 1990s, the situation of indigenous peoples in Chile was critical. The existing legal framework at that time neither recognized indigenous rights whatsoever nor provided special mechanisms for addressing indigenous peoples' issues. Indigenous peoples had almost no participation in government or policy making. Poverty among indigenous peoples was significantly higher than among non-indigenous population. In the case of Mapuches, as a result of several laws (DL 2.578 and 2.750) there had been a systematic loss and fragmentation of indigenous property. Racial and cultural discrimination against indigenous peoples in every-day life were not even considered an issue.

The Nueva Imperial accord signed between indigenous leaders and the future Aylwin administration on December 1989, the establishment of CEPI, and later on the passing of the indigenous law on October 1993 changed the framework for addressing indigenous issues in Chilean society. As a result, a significant improvement of the conditions of indigenous peoples has taken place over the last decade. Nevertheless, the current situation indicates there is a crisis in the relationship between Chilean society-State and indigenous peoples (both urban and rural). There are five main policy issues that require special attention: (i) Legal/Institutional; (ii) Organizational; (iii) Participation and Autonomy; (iv) Access to Resources; and (v) Culture and identity.

Legal Institutional

The legal framework dealing with indigenous issues and the institutional arrangements resulting from that framework need to be improved. The current legislation has significant limitations that make it difficult to resolve the current crisis. First, law 19.253 does not provide for a constitutional recognition of indigenous peoples as distinct groups with special rights. Similarly, there is no ratification of article 169 of the International Labor Organization treaty. Indigenous leaders have already proposed a new indigenous bill addressing these two issues, as well as the right of indigenous peoples to elect their own representatives to the congress and local governments.[147]

Second, at the operational level, the institutional arrangements have proven inadequate. CONADI's board mix composition (indigenous representatives elected by universal vote and government representatives appointed by the executive) is not working as it was intended. Indigenous participation has been subordinated to "national interests" when conflict has arisen (such as in the case of the Ralco dam and other emblematic development projects). It seems that CONADI has not been able to provide or develop the mechanisms for allowing independent indigenous participation. At the same time CONADI appears with severe constraints to advance a clear an unequivocal government policy towards the indigenous peoples. As a result, decisions over sensitive issues in which there is no agreement among the Board members are delayed or carried out without the support of the indigenous representatives which are a minority (8 to 9) in the board. This situation has

---

[147] See Proyecto de Reforma Constitucional que reconoce la existencia de los pueblos indígenas y les otorga participación política en el estado. Indigenosu bill proposed by Congressman Francisco Huenchumilla, submitted for consideration to the National Congress on June 24, 1999.

generated frustration among indigenous peoples and increasing mistrust on CONADI and the government in general.

From an operational standpoint, CONADI, as the sectoral institution in charge of implementing the indigenous policy, lacks the resources and staff required to carry out its responsibilities. CONADI executive staff has systematically requested more resources for increasing the staff and expanding their activities. However, due to fiscal constraints CONADI has not received the funds to go up to the required level of operations. Despite the budget increases in 1999 (17.7%) and 2000 (22.5%), still CONADI does not have enough funds to respond to the demands coming to the Land and Water Fund or the Development Fund. Particularly critical is the situation of the culture and education program which from 1998 has experienced a decrease of 10% in its budget.

Finally, another important issue that needs to be resolved is the lack of consistency between the current indigenous law and other regulatory frameworks such as the electric and water laws. Again, the Ralco dam has put in evidence discrepancies between these legal frameworks needs to be resolved. Issues such as water rights, requisites for land swaps, and the final precedence of each of these regulatory frameworks have different interpretations that need to be harmonized to ensure proper resolution of the current conflicts. Under the current legislation and institutional arrangements, or if a new indigenous law is passed in the future, it is essential to resolve disputes over competence between different legal frameworks addressing indigenous issues. Legal studies are required to asses which legal framework takes precedence under what circumstances and, if needed suggest modifications to these regulations to ensure the existence of transparent and consistent norms and regulations.

Under the current legislation, it would be advisable to revise CONADI's regulations and operational procedures. Existing institutional mechanisms would need to be adjusted. In this regard, there could be two alternative scenarios. First, if indigenous representatives would not have the power to affect government decisions at CONADI's board, it would be best to have an only-government appointed board. In this case, indigenous participation could be channeled mainly through their organizations and potentially elected representatives to the National Congress in the long term. The second alternative would be to increase the autonomy of CONADI's board to define policy issues, administer resources, programs and projects.

Organizational Development

Most indigenous organizations are weak and lack strong coordination among themselves. Further, the existing organizations (urban or rural) have been unable to generate large grassroots support. Each organization has a small group of supporters (or clientele) and most indigenous peoples (particularly among the Mapuche) do not feel represented by the existing national level organizations. There is a problem of representativeness which poses a serious challenge for indigenous organizations. While the existence of multiple organizations will continue to be a reality, and it could be argued is a strength of the indigenous movement in Chile, the need for coordination and establishing common strategies aimed at increasing representativeness and participation at all levels is crucial.

There is an urgent need for organizational development and institutional strengthening. Indigenous organizations need training to develop a new generation of leaders that will be more responsive to their membership and capable of coordinating among themselves. Strengthening indigenous organizations is a crucial condition to ensure broad representation and participation of the indigenous peoples at all institutional levels, from the National Congress to the local governments. Today, most indigenous organizations and their leaders have not developed the skills and expertise required to take full advantage of the existing institutional mechanisms. Further, by strengthening a wide range of organizations the existing problem of lack of representativeness of some of the current leaders will be minimized as more organizations will be able to participate in the political arena and become valid interlocutors with the state and other civil society organizations.

It would be advisable to develop an organizational development and institutional strengthening program targeted to local and regional indigenous organizations. Special attention would need to be given to urban organizations, trying to facilitate the dialogue and coordination between urban and rural organizations, as well as organizations from the different indigenous groups. In this regard, CONADI could play a key role in implementing this program, as well as other government agencies already involved in similar activities, such as the Ministry of Education, _Instituto Nacional de la Juventud_, and _Secretaria General de Gobierno_. Also, it would be highly desirable to include in its definition and implementation non-governmental organizations and academic centers already working with indigenous peoples along the country.

Access to Resources

The issue of access to resources should be carefully analyzed as it has different dimensions for urban and rural families as well as for the different indigenous groups. Increasingly, the indigenous population in Chile will become more and more urbanized. This fact does not necessarily mean that the absolute number of indigenous families living in rural areas will decrease substantially. Rather, it indicates that a growing proportion of indigenous peoples will live in urban settings.

Urban. In the case of the urban indigenous population the key issues regarding access to resources are related to: (i) human capital; (ii) labor market discrimination; and (iii) access to capital. Regarding human capital, most of the indigenous peoples living on urban centers or migrating to them do not have the technical skills required to have access to better employment opportunities. In fact, most of the urban migrants end up working as unskilled construction workers (males), domestic services (females); food industry/service employees (males and females). In the case of Mapuches living in small towns and secondary cities, there is also a significant proportion (males and females) which combine seasonal agricultural work and informal sector activities.

A further problem (that will be analyzed in detailed below) is that even when a indigenous worker has the required technical skills he or she faces a strong labor market discrimination. There are multiple examples of this blunt discrimination from professionals to middle level technical staff, but more importantly among skilled and non skilled workers that are subject to race-based discrimination in hiring and dismissal practices affecting female categories of occupation such as secretarial work, as well as male-dominated categories, such as construction.

Finally in the case of urban (as well as rural) small/micro entrepreneurs or self employed workers they face significant constraints accessing (seed or operational) capital for starting and/or expanding their activities. First, the issue of discrimination plays a significant role in limiting their access to credit. Secondly, lack of collateral and poor knowledge of the system restrict their access too. In this regard, the Development Fund established by CONADI is filling a gap. Nevertheless, the budgetary constraints of CONADI has imposed a severe cap to the program.

Rural. In the case of the rural indigenous population there are two main issues that are the most conflictive ones and have capture all the media attention: (i) land access/control and (ii) access/control of water rights. The land problem affects primarily the Mapuche rural population, while the water issue is relevant for Aymara and Quechua as well as Mapuche communities.

Land. Since their forced confinement to reservations the Mapuche people has demanded compensation and rehabilitation for what they consider a historic debt that the Chilean State and society have for depriving them of vast areas of their land. Estimates suggest that by the late 1970s, Mapuche communities had lost some 250,000 hectares from the original *Títulos de Merced*[148]. Today, Mapuche leaders demand land compensation. This compensation would range from 150,000 hectares for the more conservative estimates made by some leaders that only seek the restoration of the land granted in the *Títulos de Merced* (for example the Mapuche organization *Ad-Mapu* as well as other Mapuche leaders that are in CONADI's board) to more ambitious demands that indicate as goal the indigenous territories occupied before the settlement in reservations, or about 1 million hectares (as the *Consejo de Todas las Tierras* headed by Aucan Huilcaman has suggested), to others than do not set a specific target but leave it open and related to the establishment of territorial autonomy[149]. In this regard, it is important to note that during the recent presidential campaign promises were made to restore 150,000 hectares, which would represent the restitution of the lands granted under the *Títulos de Merced*. Land (and territory) is a key component of the Mapuche demand in particular and of indigenous peoples in general. For Mapuches land is a central component of their world-view, not only as a mean of subsistence but also as an integral part of their identity and relationship with Chilean society.

Addressing the legal-civil dimension of the land question is a necessary step to resolve the current crisis. Recognizing the land rights indigenous groups have is a necessary step to in part compensate them for material losses as well as to rehabilitate them from the historical and socio-cultural perspectives. However, it is essential to keep in mind that the restoration of land does not guarantee the development of socially and environmentally sustainable

---

[148] See Gacitúa (1992) "*Fundamentos Socio-Económicos, Culturales y Jurídicos para el Establecimiento de un Banco de Tierras para Pequeños Productores Mapuches en Tres Microregiones de la IX Región*" Informe de Consultoría Instituto Nacional de Desarrollo Agropecuario (INDAP).

[149] See Ancan, Jose and Margarita Calfio (1999), "*El retorno al País Mapuche. Preliminares para una utopia por construir*" en Liwen # 5 Pp 43-78.

strategies and does not resolve the long term problem of rural indigenous poverty and increasing land pressure (due to simple demographic growth).

Land access is a difficult bottleneck for Mapuche small farmers. Most rural indigenous families have little land in rapidly deteriorating environments with few productive alternatives. However, even if the land available to these families would be doubled from 5 hectares per family to 10 hectares, or tripled to 15 hectares per family, most of these rural Mapuche families would not be able to get enough income as to move out of poverty solely based on an on-farm-based production strategy (including agricultural production, forestry, livestock, etc.). The development of sustainable natural resources management and agricultural production strategies is necessary to generate a subsistence basis. But these need to be in combination with off-farm productive activities, which are essential to ensure the sustainability of the small family farm units. Further, generating off-farm employment opportunities and providing training to the young rural indigenous population is essential to facilitate their out-migration and insertion in the labor market.

Water. According to the water legislation (*Código de Aguas*) passed in 1981 and the constitution of Chile, individuals or enterprises, can obtain private water rights by receiving a grant from the state for new water sources, by prescription or by purchasing water rights, which are fully tradable and transferable. The law differentiate two types of water rights: (i) consumptive, which entitle the owner to completely consume the water without any obligation to replenish it, or (ii) non-consumptive, in which the holder must restore the water at a stipulated quality and quantity. The law also distinguish different categories of consumptive and non-consumptive rights[150].

In 1975, the government through administrative orders froze the use of water at 1975 levels. After the 1981 water code was passed, water rights of indigenous groups were either transferred directly to the private sector (through prescription) or were acquired through non-contested application or bidding and subsequent registration in the water registry (*Registro de Propiedad de Aguas del Conservador de Bienes Raices*). As a result of the above, water rights of indigenous communities have not been regularized, or are been contested, particularly by non-consumptive users (power-hydroelectric companies).

Several conflicts have occurred among different users of water resources, particularly among consumptive and non-consumptive ones. Indigenous groups have been particularly affected by these conflicts over water rights particularly with power companies, as well as with water and sewerage companies, the mining industry, and the forest industry. In a lesser degree there have been also some conflicts with other private users.

Currently there are no estimates of how many families/communities are part of these conflicts, or how much resources are involved. Nevertheless, and indication of the extent of the problem is that CONADI has assisted over the past 5 years more than 4,500 families claiming their water rights.

---

[150] See Rios, Monica and Jorge Quiroz, 1995, *The Market for Water Rights in Chile*, .World Bank Technical Paper 285.

Developing human capital is essential to facilitate and strengthen the social, cultural and economic inclusion of indigenous peoples in Chile. It would be recommendable to develop a technical/vocational training program specifically targeted to indigenous peoples. At the same time it would be important to strengthen the access of indigenous peoples to existing training alternatives (Ministry of Education, Technical Training Service, National Institute for the Youth) through dissemination, special recruitment programs, financial assistance (scholarships), decentralized programs, and on the job-training programs.

Regarding access to productive resources CONADI's Development Fund has proven to be a powerful tool to facilitate access to capital to small/micro entrepreneurs and independent workers. To increase its current impact, the Fund's financing scheme would need to be expanded to match the demand that it has. In addition to expanding the financial resources available to the fund, it would be important to develop a stronger coordination between the fund, FOSIS and training programs, to ensure that the new trainees have access to resources to put to work their skills.

Land restoration is essential for achieving a solution to the current land conflicts The issue is defining the criteria, procedures and the time frame for completing this compensation/rehabilitation of indigenous peoples (particularly Mapuches). The first step would be to clearly map the current land tenure situation and identify the demand for land. It would be essential to identify to the most accurate level possible the current land tenure situation and the demand for land. That is, in order to develop a viable solution it is necessary to have a detailed cadastre of the indigenous lands. After having established the current land tenure situation it would be essential to assess the costs and financial implications involved and initiate a negotiation process. Thirdly, criteria, procedures and mechanisms for implementing this measure would need to be developed[151]. In this regard it would be highly advisable to revitalize the fora[152] established by the government with the participation of representatives of all stakeholders, including the private sector (forestry industry, power companies).

Regarding water rights, it would be advisable strengthening the efforts of the General Directorate of Waters (DGA) to complete a cadastre of indigenous communities' water rights, as well as to foster collaboration between CONADI and DGA to arrive to a clear account of the existing water rights conflicts. With respect to the water code, it would be advisable to analyze possible modifications to it in order to: (i) make sure that indigenous water rights (consumptive/non-consumptive) are properly recognized; (ii) simplify the procedures for indigenous peoples for constituting water rights (over new waters) and registering those rights; and (iii) recognize in the case of conflicts between non-consumptive users and indigenous communities the right of the latter to participate in the administration (and the benefits) of those rights.

Finally, it would be important to strengthen the Water and Land Fund, both with staff and the resources necessaries to carry out the work above indicated. At the same time, more

---

[151] It would be essential to fully apply the mechanisms provided by the current indigenous law (19.253) to protect and regularize indigenous lands and implement the tax exemption provided in the law (to this end an agreement between CONADI and the Ministry of Finance would be required).

[152] The Lagos administration recently (March 14, 2000) convoked a official "*Mesa de Diálogo Indígena*".

resources would be needed to acquire water rights. This would be of particular importance for communities that have lost their rights and for those that would eventually get more land. It would be unrealistic to think of the expansion of indigenous lands without providing the required water.

Participation and Autonomy

A key issue raised by all indigenous organizations is the lack of participation of indigenous peoples at different levels. It has already been mention that participation within indigenous organizations needs to be strengthened. However, the issue refers more to the lack of participation at the policy decision making level, either in the way in which funds for indigenous programs are allocated, or the administration of those programs, or the direct participation in the implementation of those activities, or the more broader absence of indigenous participation in the political and institutional system.

The demand for constitutional recognition of the status of indigenous peoples is an expression of the indigenous peoples' desire to have full participation and control over decisions affecting them. Currently, with a few exceptions, the existing channels for participation at the local level are not working properly. Indigenous participation in the local governments is rather low. This is consequence first of the electoral/political system that does allow the expression of indigenous demands, unless they are a majority in the circumscription and, secondly, even if there are a majority, the lack of appropriate institutional mechanisms for participation and disadvantaged position of the indigenous peoples hampers their capacity to really participate. In this regard, it should be point out that the institutional mechanisms for citizens participation in the local government (such as the municipal council and the neighborhood associations) are not used by many indigenous people who prefer their traditional organizations and networks to participate.

At the macro-level, indigenous participation in the political system and government administration is quite limited. CONADI is the only institution that has attempted to institutionalize a mechanism for indigenous participation in the management of the agency. However, as it was discussed before, this initial intention needs to be revisited in light of the existing conflicts and apparent lack of power of the indigenous representatives to effectively influence the decision making process.

Regional governments in areas with indigenous populations have no special mechanisms to facilitate or ensure their participation. The Indigenous Development Areas (*Areas de Desarrollo Indígena*, ADIs) could be a significant step in that direction; however, in terms of political representation, there are no direct mechanisms for the expression of indigenous views neither at the local/regional government level nor at the legislative level.

All these demand have been articulated into a much complex issue: autonomy. The demand for territorial and or political autonomy (in different degrees) has been manifested by several Mapuche organizations as well as the *Consejo Aymara*. In the case of the Aymaras, the demand for autonomy refers to the recognition of the Consejo Nacional Aymara (as a legislative body), changes in the electoral law to ensure indigenous representation in the local and regional governments, and changes in the judicial system to transfer the resolution of certain legal conflicts to traditional local authorities. Mapuche organizations have been much more ambitious in their demand for autonomy, which includes a territorial dimension. Even though the territorial dimension has not been clearly defined, it would include the current areas of Mapuche rural settlements in the VIII, IX and X regions[153]. In this regard, the bill proposed by Congressman Huenchumilla represents a clear attempt to force the discussion at the national level regarding indigenous participation in the executive power (regional governments) and the legislative power (through the establishment of an Indigenous Legislative Body, the election of a proportion of indigenous representatives to the National Congress and the election of indigenous council members at the municipal level based on the proportion of indigenous peoples in the circumscription).

There are several areas in which it would be possible to strengthen indigenous peoples participation. First, it would be important to strengthen indigenous civil society organizations. In this regard it would be advisable to develop new and expand the existing programs for training indigenous organizations and leaders. Also, it would be important to develop a communications program to disseminate information to and among indigenous organizations and communities. Along with the above, it would be important to develop second tier organizations empowered to represent indigenous interests and negotiate with the government, the private sector and other civil society organizations. Similarly, the role of traditional organizations should be strengthen by recognizing their authority to resolve conflicts within the communities and manage resources.

Indigenous participation would be greatly enhanced if municipal governments would receive specific support to facilitate indigenous participation in local government decision making processes. Municipalities need institutional and operational strengthening to develop specific mechanisms to work with indigenous peoples, particularly in rural areas, but also in urban municipalities. Extension and communication services specifically targeted to the indigenous population would contribute to promote their participation. In this regard, the ADIs constitute an innovative attempt to provide a channel for indigenous participation in the definition of investment priorities and the management of public funding in geographical areas broader than municipalities. Despite the current limitations of the ADIs which do not provide a framework for participation at the regional government level (in terms of balancing funding priorities between different investments), the procedures for establishing and managing an ADI are highly participatory and provide a real opportunity for increasing indigenous control over resource allocation and fostering political participation. In that context, it would be important to expand the number of ADIs and to provide them with additional resources earmarked for supporting and expanding the role of the coordinating units that are supposed to define the investment priorities.

Culture and Identity

Indigenous peoples in Chile have faced permanent discrimination by their different physical appearance, social behavior, beliefs, and world view; to sum up, because of their culture.

---

[153] For a detailed discussion of this issue see Ancan, Jose and Margarita Calfio (1999), "*El retorno al País Mapuche. Preliminares para una utopia por construir*" en Liwen # 5 Pp 43-78, also Reiman-Huilcaman, Alfonso (1999) "Solo Tenemos porciones de tierra pero no control de un espacio territorial en Liwen # 5 Pp99-118. Finally, Elicura Chihuailaf (1999) in *Recado Confidencial a los Chilenos*, provides a general framework linking the demand for participation political and territorial autonomy.

Indigenous peoples have their own culture and history, which makes them different from Chilean society. Because of that, indigenous peoples have systematically experienced discrimination. Nevertheless, indigenous peoples have resisted and today they are demanding full recognition of their rights as a distinct people.

Indigenous societies have experienced significant social and cultural changes over the last 100 years. These changes have been the result of a complex process of transformation carried out by the indigenous groups to manage their conflictive relationship with Chilean society. In other words, such changes represent the elaboration by the indigenous groups of the problems emerging from their relationships with Chilean society, rather than the adoption of cultural patterns or norms imposed by mainstream Chilean society. The indigenous groups' culture and specific group identity have changed but they have remained distinct to that of the Chilean society. Further, within each group different types of identities might have developed over time and changed according to the status of the relationships with Chilean society, in some cases leading to the denial of their own identity. But, in any case, those changes have never erased ethnic identity as inter/intra group categories. In this context, ethnic identity has recently become a source of conflict and mobilization as indigenous groups seek the status of "peoplehood" and other forms of self-determination and autonomy.

In this regard, the key problems that indigenous groups face today are related to: (i) the lack of public recognition and legitimacy of their cultural specificity; (ii) the public use (by the government, the media, the educational system, etc.) of contradictory stereotypes that distort (and deny) their identity; and (iii) the lack of resources and support to express, to develop and to advance their cultural manifestations and identity in Chilean society.

The existing conflicts and prevalent interpretations suggest that Chilean society needs to modify its perception and attitude towards indigenous peoples. A public education and dissemination campaign could contribute to a better understanding of the issues providing coverage of (i) the current situation of indigenous peoples, (ii) the historic causes of its current situation based on the indigenous point of view, (iii) indigenous peoples' values, norms, and social organization; (iv) indigenous peoples expectations and; (v) the potential and value of having a multicultural society.

Multiple actions could be taken to develop an inclusive socio-cultural environment. As a first step to achieve this objective, the Government and indigenous peoples have agreed on the establishment of an independent multicultural commission for truth and reconciliation that would look into the general issue of systematic discrimination and the specific cases of violations of indigenous rights through history. The creation of this commission could be a good instrument to develop a more permanent dialogue and would provide the basic elements for a negotiation between the Chilean state and indigenous groups.

At the educational level, the government could review the curriculum and texts used to ensure at all educational levels that potentially racists and/or discriminatory contents would be eliminated and a multicultural multiethnical approach would incorporated. Also, the curriculum could include specific sections on indigenous culture, identity and history (from the indigenous point of view), presenting indigenous cosmogony, social order, norms and values.

Regarding bicultural/bilingual education, it would be important to develop bicultural/bilingual educational programs particularly for daycare centers, preschool and primary school indigenous students in (rural and urban) areas with high concentration of indigenous peoples. To this end it would be necessary to form qualified teachers and universities would have to develop new academic programs in bilingual/bicultural education. Bilingual/bicultural educational programs would greatly contribute to establish the required educational basis. However, it would be essential to expand the secondary and higher education opportunities for indigenous students. More scholarships, access to credit, and housing facilities would be required.

The establishment of a Indigenous Cultural Fund could be an instrument to provide financial support to the expression of multiple indigenous cultural manifestations. At the same time, the National Science and Technology Commission (CONICYT) could establish a special funding program for academics working on indigenous issues to increase the knowledge on indigenous issues and to facilitate its dissemination and understanding.

Finally, it would be important to include the indigenous dimension as a criteria for assessing the impact of all pertinent government initiatives. In this regard, it would be advisable to incorporate "indigenous impact assessment variables" in the monitoring and evaluation systems used by the different government programs to assess their outcomes and impacts.